American
Cultural
Pluralism and Law

AMERICAN CULTURAL PLURALISM AND LAW

Second Edition

JILL NORGREN AND
SERENA NANDA

PRAEGER

Westport, Connecticut
London

Library of Congress Cataloging-in-Publication Data

Norgren, Jill.
    American cultural pluralism and law / Jill Norgren and Serena
Nanda.—2nd ed.
        p. cm.
    Includes bibliographical references and index.
    ISBN 0–275–94855–2 (alk. paper).—ISBN 0–275–94858–7 (pbk. :
alk. paper)
        1. Minorities—Legal status, laws, etc.—United States.
    2. Multiculturalism—Law and legislation—United States. I. Nanda,
    Serena. II. Title.
    KF4755.N67   1996
    342.73'085—dc20
    [347.30285]   95–37643

British Library Cataloguing in Publication Data is available.

Library of Congress Catalog Card Number: 95–37643
ISBN: 0–275–94855–2 (hc.)
        0–275–94858–7 (pbk.)

First published in 1996

Praeger Publishers, 88 Post Road West, Westport, CT 06881
An imprint of Greenwood Publishing Group, Inc.

Printed in the United States of America

The paper used in this book complies with the
Permanent Paper Standard issued by the National
Information Standards Organization (Z39.48–1984).

10 9 8 7 6 5 4 3 2

To Our Families

Contents

Part III. Gender

Part IV. Community

Preface

During the 1987 Iran/Contra hearings, Senator George J. Mitchell of Maine spoke eloquently about the importance of the rule of law in a multicultural nation like the United States:

Most nations derive from a single tribe or a single race. They practice a single religion. Common racial, ethnic, and religious heritages are the glue of nationhood for many.

The United States is different. We have all races, all religions, a limited common heritage. The glue of nationhood for us is the American ideal of individual liberty and equal justice.

The rule of law is critical in our society. The law is the great equalizer, because everybody in America is equal before the law.

Senator Mitchell's words surely express a fundamental ideal in American society. How closely these words express the reality experienced by many Americans is a question that interested us as a political scientist and a cultural anthropologist. Initially, we followed this interest by team teaching a course, "American Cultural Pluralism and Law," in Thematic Studies, an interdisciplinary, undergraduate program at our college. We drew upon our separate disciplines and our common interests in multiculturalism and law; out of this course grew the first edition of this book.

The very positive responses to that book, published in 1988, and our own experiences in using the book in both disciplinary and interdisciplinary courses, confirmed for us the relevance of the material and the importance of a legal perspective on multiculturalism in the United

States. The debate over cultural diversity has intensified since 1988; there
have been new and important court decisions and some significant new
trends in the issues we discussed. For these reasons we decided that a
new edition of *American Cultural Pluralism and Law* would be useful.

The identifiable central theme of the book remains the same, that is,
the negotiation between law and the many subcultures that make up our
diverse American society. The organization of the book and most of the
material from the first edition are retained, in full or in part. In order to
allow space for four new chapters, we have, reluctantly, deleted parts of
earlier chapters, as well as the entire Jehovah's Witness chapter. We also
reorganized, expanded, and updated the material in some chapters.

We happily acknowledge the many people who have been helpful to
us in our work. First, we recognize our students, for their insights and
interest and their willingness to share with us their own, culturally diverse, perspectives on the law. We particularly want to thank Raymond
Baierlein, Bonnie Fox, Josephine Lao, and Alicia Washington, students
who conducted research for us. The concept of a course based on the
interaction of culturally diverse groups with the law was originally suggested to us by our colleague Dorothy Bracey. Numerous individuals,
within and outside academe, encouraged us in this project, reviewed
parts of the manuscript, made useful suggestions, and provided us with
needed resources, for which we are very grateful: Andrew Altman, James
Bowen, Joan Gregg, Andrew Gordon, Carol Groneman, Tom Litwack,
Gerald Markowitz, Philip Tajitsu Nash, Daniel Pinello, John Pittman, Edward Shaunessy, Philippa Strum, Ric Turer, Rafael Ventura-Rosa, Michael Winkelman, and Jean Zorn. We also very much appreciate the time
given by individuals whom we interviewed on particular subjects: Milton Ferrell, Frank Lono, Haunani-Kay Trask, Richard Robertson, and Jon
van Dyke.

We are especially grateful to Joel B. Grossman, who directed the Na-
tional Endowment for the Humanities Summer Seminar, "Courts in
American Society," at the University of Wisconsin, Madison, which we
attended, serially, in 1983 and 1985, and to Geoffrey White and Lamont
Lindstrom, who directed the NEH Summer Seminar on "Cultural and
Political Identity: Perspectives from the Pacific," at the East West Center,
University of Hawaii, Honolulu, which Serena Nanda attended in 1991.
We happily acknowledge the support of the NEH for giving us the opportunity to pursue our interests in such congenial surroundings. We
wish to thank John Paul Ryan for inviting us to several conferences sponsored by the American Bar Association Committee for Undergraduate
Nonprofessional Legal Studies. We thank this group also for awarding
us a minigrant in 1990–1991, to develop problem-solving exercises to
accompany this book.

We are very grateful to the many groups and individuals who sent us materials essential to our research and writing: The American Jewish Congress; Craig Dean for his materials on homosexual marriage; The Lambda Legal Defense and Education Fund; the Legal Action Center for the Homeless, The New York Coalition for the Homeless; the New York State Attorney General's Office; Gerald M. Sato and Richard Halberstein, attorneys for Japanese American redress plaintiffs; The Utah Civil Liberties Union; the United States Office of Redress Administration; Jay Worona, legal counsel for the New York State School Boards Association; and the Civil Division of the United States Department of Justice. We particularly wish to acknowledge the help of Mr. Juan Cartagena of the Community Service Society of New York, who not only sent us materials on Spanish language and law issues, but was kind enough to comment extensively on our chapter on "Language, Law, and Latinos."

Many individuals and departments at John Jay College and the City University of New York were essential in our completing this project. Our thanks are particularly offered to the PSC/CUNY Research Foundation for awarding us a grant during the academic year 1990–1991. Antony Simpson and the John Jay Library staff were critical to our ability to find the materials we needed and we thank them profusely. We are grateful to Linda John of the Department of Anthropology, who always went the extra mile to help us in our work in a million different—and essential—ways.

Three of our colleagues who were particularly important in the completion of this work are, very sadly, no longer with us. We offer our deepest thanks, posthumously, to William Lewis for his interest and help on our chapter on religion and drug use; Billie Kotlowitz, whose early encouragement of our teaching in Thematic Studies, and whose personal support was instrumental in getting the project underway; and Petra Shattuck, for many years coresearcher with Jill Norgren on issues of Native American–United States legal relations.

Introduction: E Pluribus Unum?

The United States, since its colonial beginnings, has been an increasingly culturally diverse nation. Like other liberal-democratic nations, it faces a fundamental tension: on one hand there is the need to create national institutions, including law, which unify culturally different groups, and on the other, the need to protect human rights by allowing some degree of religious, personal, cultural and local political autonomy. Law (federal and state constitutions, statutes, administrative rules, judicial opinions) is one of the most important mechanisms for addressing this inevitable tension between the needs of the nation-state for some growing consensus around a dominant set of cultural values and institutions, and the needs of groups to enact and increase their autonomy.

The theme of this book is the interaction of law with cultural pluralism in the United States, specifically, the continual negotiation that has occurred between culturally different groups and the larger society. We pursue this theme by raising the following questions: In a democratic nation-state, what is the extent of cultural difference that can be tolerated, consistent with the integrity of the larger body politic? How, in the face of technological, economic, social and political change, does a nation-state, operating under the rule of law, and specifically in the United States under written constitutions, cope with cultural pluralism?

Unlike the United States, most other Western nations emerged from a centuries-long interaction between culturally and politically autonomous groups—tribes, princely states, fiefdoms, religious divisions and regional cultures. In the United States, however, the first settlers and subsequent founders, having decided early on not to regard Native Americans or African Americans as serious partners in the enterprise of nation building, were more easily able to establish a perception of their nation as one created *de novo*. Even so, ideas about the direction of the new colonies engendered conflict as the early immigrants came from a variety of social classes, religious persuasions, and national backgrounds. When conflict arose, the seeming availability of land, only sparsely settled by Native Americans, permitted these early settlers, and later, migrants from the East Coast, to protect their differences by moving. Religious dissenters, led by Ann Hutchinson and Roger Williams, left the Massachusetts Bay Colony to form the new colony of Rhode Island in 1644; the Mormons, fleeing persecution, trekked across the United States and beyond its borders to the Great Salt Lake Basin to find a haven for their unique culture in the 1840s; and in the period after World War II, no longer valuing the diversity of urban culture, and liberated by the mobility afforded by the automobile, America's growing middle class drove to the suburbs, where in relative isolation from city life they created a suburban culture based on the values of homeowning, highways, and homogeneity.

Simultaneous with this development of local cultures there has also been a development of an "American" culture. The people who first came here were Anglo-Saxon, Christian, and in spite of a few communal groups, predominantly adherents of economic individualism. In coming here, they sought a vision of a "new Eden" which, when married to the emerging concept of the nation-state, encouraged the building of a common national culture.

The clarion call of freedom encouraged the belief that the new nation would be tolerant, and even respectful, of cultural diversity, political dissent, and religious differences. This is most eloquently expressed in the American Constitution, specifically the Bill of Rights, whose function is to limit the ability of governments—the instrument of the dominant culture—to tread upon, or annihilate, the cultural, political and religious differences of weaker groups and individuals. However, those who wrote the Constitution, representatives of the dominant culture, had the power to define the limits of tolerance—and they did so; their constitutional call to freedom ignored the plight of African-American slaves by putting off the legal question of slavery, leaving it ultimately to a military resolution in the Civil War.

Immigration, of course, was the greatest source of our nation's diversity, and a testimony to the positive belief in the possibilities of American pluralism linked to the idea that one could advance economically regardless of ascribed status. Immigrants were regarded ambivalently, however. Between 1820 and 1850, most immigrants were from northwestern Europe—Germany, Scotland, Ireland, England, and Scandinavia. They were therefore similar, both culturally and physically, to previous immigrants, and some spoke English, by this time firmly established unofficially as the national language. But even some of these immigrants were viewed with hostility. The Irish and many of the Germans were Roman Catholic and American Protestants feared interference from the Church in Rome. Many immigrants were paupers whose way to America had been paid by European governments eager to get rid of them, and this raised fears about their impact on social life and the economy. In addition, some of the Germans were dissident refugees from the 1830 and 1848 revolutions and brought with them radical political and economic philosophies unsettling to older Americans.

Despite this animus, these northern European immigrants did not face nearly the degree of prejudice and harassment encountered by later immigrants from Asia and southern and eastern Europe. By this time land was not as freely available as it had been earlier, and many of these later immigrants were not, in any case, farmers. Furthermore, because they were needed in the urban industrial labor force, they tended to congregate in dense urban ethnic ghettos. By degree, also, the later newcomers were physically, culturally, and linguistically more different from northern Europeans, and were perceived as extremely threatening to the emerging American culture, based now on Protestantism, liberal democracy, and free enterprise capitalism.

Pressure had been building since midcentury for a national policy of immigration restriction. While nativist sentiment was not initially successful in achieving a national immigration policy, however, and immigration receded as a national issue during the Civil War, the nativist cry "America for Americans!" was effective in obtaining state statutes imposing penalties on racial minorities. These were particularly directed against the Chinese living on the West Coast. The economic depression of the 1870s intensified anti-alien attitudes, resulting in a series of restrictive national immigration laws beginning with the Chinese Exclusion Act of 1882, and culminating in the 1924 National Origins Act. All of these laws were designed to curb the entry of immigrants from Asia and southern and eastern Europe, who were perceived to be "racially unassimilable."

Yet economic needs dictated a more tolerant policy. Since America's burgeoning industries needed workers, and the newcomers accepted low-paying, unskilled jobs which others shunned, they had to be accepted, if only grudgingly. With regard to white immigrants, at least, this necessity was transformed into a virtue, and indeed the rhetoric of the United States was one of the assimilability of culturally diverse groups. This rhetoric was most romantically expressed in the poem, "The New Colossus" by Emma Lazarus, affixed to the Statue of Liberty:

> Give me your tired, your poor,
> Your huddled masses yearning to breathe free,
> The wretched refuse of your teeming shore.

> Send these, the homeless, tempest-tost to me,
> I lift my lamp beside the golden door![1]

The unique character of America to absorb and assimilate culturally diverse peoples was also expressed dramatically by Israel Zangwill in *The Melting Pot:*

> There she lies, the great melting pot—listen!
> Can't you hear the roaring and the bubbling?

Despite this rhetoric, however, it is clear that the immigrants' experience was not one of people quickly, easily, or voluntarily assimilated into the American melting pot. Writings of immigrants and others—women and gays, for example—express the difficulties of experiencing conflicts in values between their own and the dominant American culture, and of rejecting the stereotypes—in film, in literature, in art, and in history—through which they and their cultures have been portrayed.[2] Most poignant of all are the feelings of invisibility expressed by groups who have been excluded from the mainstream of the dominant culture, and who have, at the same time, experienced a sense of having been robbed of their cultural traditions.[3] Even those for whom the American Dream has largely come true have paid a dear price, as the journey which took them up the ladder of social class required in the process, or seemed to require, the shedding of ethnic identity and abandonment of the intimate ties of family and community.[4] Clearly, the most unequivocal, persistent, and pernicious rejection—including rejection by violence—has been experienced by racial minorities and indigenous peoples: Native Americans, Native Hawaiians, African Americans, and Asian Americans.

If the literature from these diverse groups in the United States testifies to their ambivalence about their participation in American society and the impact of American culture, American institutions have been no less ambivalent in their messages to these groups. Although law, and courts in particular, are seen as the institutions most specifically charged with the protection of cultural pluralism and the rights of individuals belonging to subcultural groups, in fact, a close reading of the evidence (statutes, judicial opinions, empirical data on the use of various legal institutions) indicates a certain caution with respect to the ability of law to protect cultural diversity and autonomy. This caution reflects the tension between, on the one hand, a historical ideal of tolerance, most particularly in the Bill of Rights and other later, constitutional protections such as the Fourteenth Amendment, and on the other hand, the obligation of law to protect the integrity, and indeed the very life, of the nation-state.

As this book demonstrates, American courts, both state and federal, have responded inconsistently to the claims of culturally diverse groups in our society. These claims involve, ironically, both getting in and staying out: The Amish, for example, are outsiders who have been permitted by law to protect their cultural autonomy. Other groups, like the Mormons, the Satmar Hasids, Rastafarians, Latinos, Native Americans, Native Hawaiians, and the homeless, wanted to protect their distinct cultural values and activities, but were only partially permitted to do so. Still other groups, including African Americans, Japanese Americans, women, and homosexuals, were—or are—outsiders by virtue of society's discrimination and have used the courts to "get in." In spite of some separatist movements, and periodic interest in the culture of Black Africa, the overwhelming number of African Americans have concentrated on using the law to obtain equal rights and access to the resources of the larger society. And complicating this picture are the many groups who, for different reasons, reject the use of courts to solve their conflicts.

The legal process by which the rights of cultural minorities are most likely to be recognized in the United States appears to be based on the interaction of a number of factors. One of the most important of these factors is the distance of the cultural activity that the group seeks to protect or promote, from the values of the dominant culture—the Judeo-Christian tradition, individualism, republicanism, and capitalism. All our cases, by definition, confront some aspect of the dominant culture. The litigation involving the Mormons, homosexuals, and tramps shows clearly not only the confrontation but the very firm limits of diversity that the law is willing to allow. Even where courts have accommodated diverse cultural practices which challenge or contradict American values, they have done so, as in the Native American peyote case and with the Amish, by describing the most narrow, culturally specific parameters within which the behavior would be sanctioned.

Yet it would be a mistake to view the values of the dominant culture, as expressed by judicial interpretation, as unchanging. A second factor that helps explain the decisions in these cases is the application of evolving standards over time. The striking treatment of the Mormons in the nineteenth century in which the law was used to limit political participation and to seize church property in an effort to punish them for unacceptable sexual, social, and religious practices, does not find a parallel in the twentieth century treatment, for example, of homosexuals. While the courts have adamantly refused to extend key constitutional guarantees to homosexual relationships, at the same time, fundamental political rights are not denied.

With regard to women and African Americans, the application of evolving standards is most clear. In nineteenth-century America the Supreme Court could and did present African Americans as property to be used and moved at the will of their white owners. Similarly in the nineteenth century, justices repeatedly based legal decisions affecting women's rights upon stereotypes of women as timid, delicate, and innocent and "unfit for many of the occupations of civil life." As we move into the last decade of the twentieth century, these cultural visions of African Americans and women are no longer expressed in legal decisions.

History also helps explain the legal treatment of culturally different groups. In periods of national insecurity such as wartime, for example, culturally different groups whose behaviors appear threatening to national interests may find their rights trampled upon, as with the Japanese Americans. The treatment of Mormons, too, can be partly explained by national security interests—the need of the then young nation of the United States to affirm and extend its hegemony.

Where national security is not at issue, and where the size and strength of the group poses no discernible challenge to the political and social order, court decisions favoring group rights are more likely. The Supreme Court support for Amish parents wishing to withdraw their children from the final two years of compulsory education is explicitly predicated on the court's view that the Amish are not only not a threat to the social order, but to the contrary, a model of virtue.

A number of court decisions in cases involving subcultural autonomy suggest that another principle, that of the "slippery slope," also affects outcomes. This concern over the force of precedent and the possibility of a domino-like effect, has inhibited American courts from deciding in favor of large claims for economic redress. Thus in the Sioux lands claim case, as in a number of other large tribal land claims cases, litigation for the return of the land has not been successful, and at best, money has been substituted. Monetary redress for Japanese Americans raises the spectre for the court that other historically wronged groups will make similar claims; thus while federal courts have acknowledged in principle the wrongs committed, the likelihood of granting the large monetary awards currently being sought is very small.

The initiation and judicial reception of litigation can depend also upon the interest of third parties. This third-party participation and intervention takes many forms. In the conflict between the Amish community and local school boards, the ability to challenge dominant culture laws in institutions of the dominant culture was only possible for the law-averse Amish when sympathetic non-Amish lawyers agreed to litigate the case. For Native Americans, among whom there were virtually no lawyers until the late 1960s, lawyers from outside the group were essential in making it possible for them to defend rights and assert claims against the dominant culture. For the homeless, too, third parties have been critical in litigation, a testimony to the expanding nature of a social problem, while the participation of third parties in the Kiryas Joel case is evidence of intensified debate over religion in public life. This partic- ipation of public interest and civil rights organizations in cases involving subcultures has been an increasingly important feature of the challenges to the dominant culture in the latter half of the twentieth century.

Much of what we have suggested implies that courts are not autono- mous, isolated bodies composed of justices neutral toward dominant cul- tural norms and immune to contemporary politics. While on the one hand, judges are sworn to a rule of law which commits them to proce- dural due process and substantive rights and liberties, on the other hand, justices cannot entirely free themselves from the dominant cultural con- text of which their courts are a part. Thus, subcultural groups, as they use courts, must take into account the reality that they are bringing a conflict with the dominant culture into an institution of that same culture which, while committed to the autonomy of law, rights, and liberties, is also part of a nation-state committed to the integrity and unity of the larger body politic.

The negotiation of differences between subcultures and the dominant culture through courts has important consequences for cultural diversity in the United States. One central question about the impact of courts and law on cultural diversity is the extent to which the process of litigation, including but not limited to the court decision, has strengthened or weakened the cultural integrity and/or communal solidarity of the group. There is no simple answer to this question. Does, for example, the use of courts, even in "defensive" litigation, undermine the cultural integrity of a law-averse group like the Amish? How do money pay- ments, to be divided among individuals, as in the Sioux case, affect the culture of a group based on communal ownership? How does law, as in the bilingual cases of *Lau* and *King,* affect group culture when such de- cisions demand that current and future generations of the ethnic group will not be reinforced in using the language of group solidarity? To the extent that African Americans have won rights that hasten their integra- tion into the larger society, does this undermine unique aspects of Af- rican-American culture and social institutions?

In the same vein, it is not simple to explain why the nation-state, through its courts, entertains challenges to dominant culture values by culturally diverse and autonomous groups. A ready and important ex- planation, of course, lies in our being a government under the rule of law specifically committed to civil liberties and civil rights as expressed in the Bill of Rights. More pragmatically, our liberal-democratic state undoubtedly gains legitimacy to the extent that it adheres to its own rules. It is not only the diverse subcultures which must negotiate with the state to maintain their integrity; the nation-state must also find a balance in negotiating with culturally diverse groups, so that it may at minimum survive, and at best prosper. Courts, as representatives of the nation-state, steer a middle course as they constantly calibrate the interests of culturally diverse groups within a social contract that permits and even encourages diversity, but which also demands national unity.

In negotiating between subcultures and the dominant culture, American courts are dependent on a body of law that does not historically address group cultural interests. Indeed, the law in the United States, with its emphasis on individual rather than group rights, has functioned mainly to further American society's assimilationist goals. Unlike other societies, whose constitutions give legal status, and certain privileges as well as rights, to cultural groups, the U.S. Constitution does not mention culture and does not accord explicit rights to groups, cultural or otherwise. A question arises then, as to what are—and might be—the constitutional or other legal bases to which subcultures in the United States can look for protection? For indigenous groups, such as Native Americans, Native Hawaiians, and Mexican Americans, some protection has been found in the law of treaties and federal legislation, and state constitutions. Even these, however, do not affirm group rights to the extent of international law. Historically, the United States has been reluctant to become a signatory to many United Nations resolutions on self-determination for cultural minorities or to participate in international fora on rights for cultural groups, such as indigenous peoples.[5] While it may be argued that the protections of the First Amendment free exercise of religion clause, and such legal strategies as the class action suit, do speak to group rights, nevertheless, it is clear that United States law, in being predicated on the protection of individual rights, promotes assimilation rather than cultural pluralism.

Since World War II, and the creation of nations out of the colonial empires, the spread of the norm of equality in many nations has made egregious forms of subordination illegitimate, spurring cultural minority groups to press claims for equal treatment against the larger society. At the same time, the level of ethnic conflict and violence requires reassessment of any simple solutions to relationships between cultural minorities and the nation-states of which they are a part. In the United States these issues have always been part of our national dialogue. In this book we examine that dialogue as it has been expressed in law.

NOTES

1. Emma Lazarus was asked to contribute this poem, in 1883, as part of a fund-raising effort for the Statue of Liberty. The poem was published in the *New York World* and engraved on the Statue of Liberty in 1903.

2. Frank Chin, "Confessions of a Number One Son," *Ramparts* (1973); Maxine Hong Kingston, *The Woman Warrior: Memories of a Girlhood among Ghosts* (New York: Knopf, 1975).

3. Michael Novak, *The Rise of the Unmeltable Ethnics* (New York: Macmillan, 1971).

4. Norman Podhoretz, *Making It* (New York: Harper and Row, 1967); Marianna De Marco Torgovnick, *Crossing Ocean Parkway: Readings by an Italian American Daughter* (Chicago: University of Chicago Press, 1994).

5. Sharon O'Brien, "Cultural Rights in the United States: A Conflict of Values," *Law and Inequality: A Journal of Theory and Practice* 5(2) (July 1987).

Part I

Race

1

Native Americans, Law, and Land

The difficulty in writing about Native Americans begins with terminology. Today Native Americans constitute more than 500 federally recognized tribes so that even to label them collectively is to distort their cultural and geographical diversity. The commonly used phrase "American Indian" does not reflect their term for themselves. Rather, European explorers, who misunderstood where they were and whom they met, imposed it on them. The terms "Indian" and "Native American" are, then, expedients used to refer to the indigenous peoples of the North American continent.

Historically, these people were, and are today, characterized by a wide range of economic and cultural systems.[1] In spite of real and important differences, however, the many diverse Native American societies shared similar attitudes toward land and nature which they viewed as having "sacred primacy." For Native Americans the land was Mother Earth: They believed that humans had a spiritual relation to the land, and that the land was there to be used, with respect, in perpetuity, and was owned by no one. In the words of Chief Frank Fools Crow, a Lakota medicine man: "We have one law ... to live on this earth with respect for all living things. That means we cannot harm the earth because we have respect for the place of those things in the world. . . . Heart, body, mind and soul all together with the world: that is the Indian way to live. You see, these hills are our church; the rivers and the wind, and the blossoms and the living things—that is our Bible. Nature is God, God is nature."[2]

In this relationship to land lies the most important cultural difference between Native Americans and the Europeans (later the people of the

United States). In contrast to Native American beliefs, in the culture of the United States, land is real estate and has no sacred qualities. Land is a tradeable commodity and a proper source of individual wealth and profit. Drawing upon Western religious ideas, Americans believe nature to be God's gift to man, subject to man's dominion.

These different views on the meaning and use of land created a fundamental conflict as American political institutions resisted acknowledging the right of Native American governments to control their own land and to use it in the traditions of their cultures. The roots of this conflict were exposed in the first encounter between Native Americans and Europeans.

Columbus, and the men who followed him, came with a strongly developed sense of the supremacy of European values, religion, culture, and law. They assumed that they would dominate the land and peoples they encountered in what they called the New World, and were prepared to deal with indigenous peoples only on terms dictated by Europe. The Europeans sought riches, opportunities for trade, land for the expansion of empire, and the chance to bring salvation, through conversion, to Native Americans, uniting them in a universal Christian community, thus, driving out "the demons of difference," that is, those who were not Christians.[3]

Sir Thomas More, among others, in England, in his *Utopia* (1516), promoted this idea of European superiority by claiming that men—in this case European men—have the right to put land to its most efficient use. For the Europeans, Native American land, which was held in common, not used for individual profit and sometimes not used for agriculture, was land used inefficiently, in violation of the European law of nature. Nothing more fundamentally reflected the cultural differences between Europeans and Native Americans than this European view that human beings could only be motivated to work by the promise of individual reward. This view of human nature, written into the earliest law, provided a rationale for the Europeans and later the Americans of the United States, to dispossess Native Americans from their lands.

With the arrival of the British and the French in North America (joining the Spanish), by the early seventeenth century, a competition began among the several European sovereigns and trading companies for access to Native American land and goods, such as animal skins. To secure their investments in land and commerce, the Europeans imported the legal mechanisms that were part of their own cultures: formal deeds and contracts between individuals as well as government-to-government treaties.

When the British colonists organized their own government, first in 1781, under the Articles of Confederation and then in 1789, under the U.S. Constitution, they continued the colonial tradition of dealing with

Native Americans through Anglo-American law. Financially and physically exhausted by the recent revolutionary war against England, concerned about the continuing presence of other European powers in North America, and with its treasury depleted, the leadership of the new Republic of the United States appreciated the value of lawful and diplomatic relations with Native American governments compared with the costs of the warfare and social disorder that would result from continuing conflicts with them. The decision of the United States, then, was to deal with Native American tribes peacefully, as sovereign nations, through internationally binding legal treaties. The degree to which Native Americans understood the nature of these agreements is disputed by scholars; Native American legal concepts differed from those of the Europeans and translation of the proceedings was universally inadequate.

In the first years of these diplomatic relations, Native American governments demonstrated considerable goodwill toward the United States. But it did not take long for Native Americans to realize the implications of white land hunger. By the 1790s, Seneca leader Red Jacket, addressing the United States Senate, spoke sadly of how the Native Americans' faith in white law had been betrayed:

Brother! Listen to what we say. The Great Spirit . . . made . . . [this land] for the use of Indians. . . . But an evil day came upon us. Your forefathers crossed the great waters and landed on this island. Their numbers were small. They found friends and not enemies. . . . They asked for a small seat. We took pity on them, granted their request and they sat down amongst us. We gave them corn and meat. . . . They called us brothers. We believed them and gave them a large seat. At length their numbers had greatly increased. They wanted more land. They wanted our country. Our eyes were opened, and our minds became uneasy.[4]

By the first years of the nineteenth century, with the increasing population of the United States and subsequent scarcity of Native American land on the East Coast, Red Jacket's description became pertinent for more and more Native American nations, though to a different extent depending on the region. The United States was like a patchwork quilt: In the Northeast, much Native American land had been lost by the eighteenth century while in the southeastern part of the continent, Native American nations resisted the pressure from state and federal governments to get their land.

In the 1820s through the mid-1830s, a series of events took place that highlighted the collision course involving land rights and cultural differences between Native American nations and the United States. The allure of fertile farmland and the discovery of gold in the Cherokee Nation (in what is now Georgia) proved a strong magnet attracting both settlers and speculators to Cherokee land. The Cherokee Nation, in the face of the persistent pressure from state and federal governments of the United States to cede its land, realized that no degree of compromise would ever satisfy their American neighbors' hunger for land. As a result, in 1823, in a letter to United States treaty commissioners, the Cherokee National Council expressed "an unalterable determination . . . never again to cede one foot more of land" and refused to sign treaties to that effect.[5]

At the same time, early in the nineteenth century, in an attempt to minimize the cultural differences that whites perceived between themselves and Native Americans, the Cherokee formed themselves into a republic with a constitution based upon that of neighboring governments and the United States. They established public schools and developed a syllabary which made possible the publication of a bilingual newspaper, *The Cherokee Phoenix*. They had become, for the most part, a settled agricultural and commercial people who welcomed Christian missionaries into their community. However, despite Cherokee attempts to accommodate whites by accepting certain aspects of Western culture, their earlier decision "not to cede another foot of land" led to pressure on members of the U.S. Congress to create legislation by which the United States could gain title to the lands of the Cherokee and other southeastern tribes under cover of law.

This legislation, the Indian Removal Act (4 Stat. 411), was passed by Congress in 1830, with the strong support of President Andrew Jackson. This act provided for the *voluntary* removal of Native Americans from their land east of the Mississippi River to lands west of the river. The Louisiana Purchase, in 1803, had encouraged a myth among Americans that there was a vast tract of western land, now under the jurisdiction of the United States, to which the Native Americans could be removed. Expressing sentiments that drew upon More's *Utopia*, President Jackson argued that since people like the Cherokee did not put their land to productive use, they were not entitled to hold it:

Philanthropy could not wish to see this continent restored to the condition in which it was found by our forefathers. What good man would prefer a country covered with forests, and ranged by a few thousand savages to our extensive republic, studded with cities, towns, and prosperous farms; embellished with all the improvements which art can devise, or industry execute . . . and filled with all the blessings of liberty, civilization and religion.[6]

Reluctant supporters of the Indian Removal Act hoped that removal would protect Native Americans from encroaching on whites and their culture; still others saw it as a better alternative to military action against Indians.

The legislation stirred up long and bitter debate. Opponents of the bill included those who did not believe removal would be voluntary, those who believed that the Act violated prior binding treaties and U.S. recognition of Native American sovereignty and property rights, and those who were political opponents of Jackson who wished to embarrass him. Astute observers realized that population in the United States was constantly increasing and that the removal of Native Americans to the West would only be a short-term resolution of the problem, even from the whites' point of view. Furthermore, few members of Congress bothered to consider that these western lands had long been in the possession of other Native American peoples. After a close vote, however, the removal policy became law and a new era of United States–Native American relations began.

THE PROMISE OF LAW: THE CHEROKEE CASES

Even prior to Cherokee removal west in 1838, the increasing tensions between the United States and Native Americans presented an early opportunity for leaders of the Cherokee Republic to test the ideals of the United States which emphasized a commitment to law as a way of resolving conflicts. Even before the Removal Act had been passed, the state of Georgia had passed legislation intended to assert state jurisdiction over Native American societies adjacent to the state, with the intention of eventually incorporating that land. In the face of this hostile state and federal legislation, the Cherokee Nation, unwilling to resort to force, and deciding to take the whites' expressed reverence for law at face value, resolved to test Native American national sovereignty and land rights in court. The Cherokee government hired two of the foremost lawyers in the United States, William Wirt and John Sergeant, to help them bring suit as a foreign nation against the state of Georgia in the U.S. Supreme Court. Through their lawyers, the Cherokee argued to restrain Georgia from executing and enforcing that state's new jurisdiction laws, contending that these laws violated international treaties between the Cherokee Republic and the United States, as well as the Article VI Supremacy Clause of the U.S. Constitution.

In two cases, *Cherokee Nation v. Georgia* [30 U.S. 1 (1831)], and *Worcester v. Georgia* [31 U.S. 515 (1832)], Chief Justice John Marshall established the legal framework that, to this day, broadly governs Native American property and political rights in the eyes of the United States. Marshall wrote that the Cherokee nation was "capable of managing its own affairs and governing itself." But, in order to protect the interests of the United States, he also defined Indian nations as "domestic dependent nations," whose relationship to the United States "resemble[d] that of a ward to his guardian."[7] Regarding land rights, in *Cherokee Nation* Marshall also

attempted to lessen Native Americans' claims to their lands when he
wrote that they "occupy a territory to which we assert a title independent
of their will."[8] A year later in *Worcester*, Marshall provided a doctrine
more sympathetic to Native American sovereignty and land rights. He
described Native American nations as "independent political communities retaining their original natural rights as the undisputed possessors
of the soil."[9] But even here, Marshall did not concede an absolute tribal
title to Native American land, arguing instead that such nations held
occupancy, not fee simple (absolute) title to their land. This meant, in
Marshall's legal confection, that Native American societies had the right
to use the land and live on it as long as they wished, if and until they
willingly consented to extinguish occupancy title, in which case the
United States, as heir to discovery title, would gain full legal possession.

The 1830 Indian Removal Act and the Supreme Court decisions in the
Cherokee cases are significant because they set a pattern in which legal
language appeared to offer protection for Native American rights, yet at
the same time permitted the abrogation of those rights. Both the legislation and the Court decisions established that Native American governments had a land title to be recognized by the United States that could
only be yielded by tribal consent. In fact, however, Native American land
was eagerly sought by whites and both the legislative and executive
branches were willing to respond to political pressure to pursue Indian
land through fraudulent and coerced treaties as well as successful appeals to minority faction leaders within the tribes. Such manipulations
permitted the Cherokee to be removed from their land in 1838 following
the endorsement of a removal treaty by only 75 men in a nation of 15,000
people. The Cherokee name for their journey out of their homeland, the
Trail of Tears, indicates this move was a forced march rather than a
voluntary exodus. With Cherokee removal, the imprimatur of law was
placed, not for the last time, on the expropriation of Native American
land.

THE WHITE PROBLEM DOESN'T GO AWAY

The supporters of the Removal Act hoped—in vain—that it would be
a pragmatic solution to "the Indian Problem." Certainly, for Native
Americans it was not a solution to the "white problem" because the two
groups continued to confront one another as white settlers pushed westward. Many of the problems that had plagued Native Americans in the
East, such as the damaging impact of unscrupulous traders and the sale
of liquor as well as the effects of contagious diseases, followed them, in
the 1840s and 1850s, to the West. In an attempt to address these problems
and to honor binding treaty commitments concerning Native American
land title, the U.S. government embarked upon a wholesale policy of

settling Native Americans, using coercion and force, in precisely defined geographical areas called reservations. Here, ideally, the Native American would be free from what the government considered the damaging effects of some aspects of white culture.

Reservations were not an entirely new idea. Even prior to the creation of the United States, the colonists had attempted to deal with the clash of cultures by creating small reserves of land for Native Americans. This mid-nineteenth-century reservation policy appeared to be the most viable short-term solution, once again, to the "problem that would not go away." By the use of treaties, reservations were established for many Native American tribes from the Mississippi to California (land that came to the United States through the 1803 Louisiana Purchase and the 1848 Treaty of Guadalupe Hidalgo).

While some of the supporters of reservation policy were well-meaning, it is clear that they were also ethnocentric: They wished to save Native Americans physically in order to transform them into Christians, capitalists, and democrats. The reservations provided a way of disarming and controlling Native Americans and making them a captive audience to be taught Western values. While the reservations could help insulate Native Americans from the more violent predations of white society, they would also provide the opportunity for "good people from Christian missions [who] could teach an appreciation for agriculture, manufacture, and the English language."[10] Representatives from the U.S. government called Indian agents, traders, and missionaries, who were permitted within the boundaries of the reservations, would be the agents of change, assisting tribal peoples in the transition from hunter-gatherer societies to American-style agricultural communities. This transition was, for the U.S. government, the linchpin of its Indian policy. While some supporters of the reservation policy hoped to help Native Americans, for other supporters the policy was one more skirmish in a cultural warfare ultimately designed to save the Indian by eradicating Native American cultures.

Within a relatively short time, however, it became clear that the reservation policy did not work. Unwilling subjects of assimilation, most Native Americans resisted acculturation. Furthermore, the centralization of Indian populations on reservations made them even more vulnerable to the purveyors of alcohol. In addition, the reservation system could not and did not protect Native Americans against loss of land. Having lost aboriginal title to eastern lands, Native Americans found treaty title reservation land just as eagerly sought after. Pressure to yield this treaty title reservation land was intense and in various ways including, again, new fraudulent treaties, vast parcels of reservation land came into white ownership. Native Americans continued to be too much in the way of the "march of progress."

By the early 1870s, the inadequacies of the reservation system became apparent. The slow pace of acculturation on reservations combined with continuing assaults by settlers on Native Americans on the frontier, and the negative impact of the transcontinental railroad on the ecology, economy, and social well-being of Native Americans convinced American social reformers and government officials to consider a policy that would result in more rapid Native American assimilation. Reviving an early-nineteenth-century policy, a consensus emerged that the quickest way to turn Native Americans into "good Christians, capitalists and democrats" would be to allot them individually owned sections of land from what had been communally held tribal land. U.S. Senator Henry Dawes expressed a widespread feeling among Americans when he said, in a speech supporting this policy of allotment: "They [the Indians] have got as far as they can go, because they own their land in common . . . under that [system] there is no enterprise to make your home any better than that of your neighbor's. There is no selfishness, which is at the bottom of civilization. Till this people will consent to give up their lands, and divide them among their citizens so that each can own land he cultivates, they will not make much more progress."[11]

In the words of Native American scholars Kirke Kickingbird and Karen Ducheneaux, men like Dawes insisted that, "the magical qualities of individual property would transform the stolid warriors into happy churchgoing farmers."[12] Kickingbird and Ducheneaux aptly capture the spirit of American unwillingness to accept the cultural difference of Native Americans. This unwillingness became law with the passage of the General Allotment (Dawes) Act (24 Stat. 388) in 1887.

As with the earlier Indian Removal Act, the Dawes Act only won congressional support after long and heated debate. It was generally agreed that ultimately, Native Americans would not be able to protect their own cultures against the worst impact of American culture and that only assimilation would save them. There were, however, important disagreements about how long assimilation would and should take, and thus, how law would or should be used to implement a policy of assimilation.

A key issue of the allotment debate centered upon the degree to which Anglo-American law should be applied to Native Americans as they agreed to abandon tribal community and to live like white men and women. Many of those who sought to influence the course of congressional decision making supported a policy of allotment which would also grant full citizenship to Indians—by giving them the vote as well as protecting them by liberal law—in the United States.

The assimilationists considered themselves reformers. They believed that without the protection of American law Native Americans would continue to be both physically and culturally exploited and deprived of "the benefits of civilization." Others argued that "the Indian must live

among us" but was not "yet competent to vote intelligently," and supported a more gradual extension of citizenship rights to Indians. Dr.
Thomas A. Bland, organizer of the National Indian Defense Association,
defended the unpopular view of an "Indian's right to be an Indian." He
argued that earlier assimilation policies had not worked and that any
new assimilation policy should move slowly and take into account gen-
erational differences within Native American communities as well as the
differences between Native American tribes' interest in acculturation.
Unlike other lobbyists, Bland argued for more rather than less Native
American control of their own affairs and less United States interference
in the absence of a specific request by a tribe. Bland's arguments were
the closest that Native Americans came to having a voice in the debate
over their future.

Supporters of immediate Native American assimilation won the day
with the passage of Dawes' General Allotment Act, which provided that,
for the tribes specified in the law, each Native American head of household (and other eligible persons) would be allotted 160 acres of land with
individual, not communal-tribal, title. However, the government forbade
Native American allottees to sell their land for a period of 25 years, a
policy that again emphasized the government's position that Native
Americans were wards in need of paternalistic protection. The Act also
provided that all Native Americans who participated in the allotment,
as well as those who left the land and adopted "civilized life," were
eligible to become American citizens. Another provision of the Act was
that "surplus" land—reservation land left over after each eligible Indian
had received an allotment—could be sold immediately by the U.S. government to non-Indians.

Despite its stated goal of helping the Indians, the Dawes Act was
aimed at destroying tribal societies. By offering individual Native Americans citizenship and individual landholding, the Act made it more difficult for tribal governing bodies to function and, thus, quite intentionally
undercut tribal sovereignty and unity.

As a result of the Dawes Act millions of acres of what was previously
tribal land passed into the hands of whites; some of it by swindle, some
by individual sale, some of it to the U.S. government which sold it as
"surplus" land. It was also ironic that at a time when white farmers and
ranchers were attempting to consolidate landholding in order to make
them more efficient and productive, the Dawes Act required relatively
small allocations to Native Americans. Cherokee DeWitt Clinton Duncan
spoke of this in 1906 before a Senate committee:

I spent the early days of my life on the farm up here of 300 acres, and arranged
to be comfortable in my old age; but the allotment scheme came along. . . . I had
to relinquish every inch of my premises outside of that little [allotment]. . . . I

have exerted all my ability, all industry, all my intelligence . . . to make my living out of that [allotment] . . . and, God be my judge, I have not been able to do it. I am not able to do it. . . . What am I to do? I have a piece of property that doesn't support me and is not worth a cent to me under the cruel provisions of the . . . law that swept away our treaties, our system of nationality, our very existence, and wrested out of our possession our vast territory.[13]

By the 1920s it was apparent that the Dawes Act was a failure. It neither transformed a majority of Native Americans into "happy church-going farmers," nor did it fulfill its supporters' expectations that allot-ment would be "the mighty pulverizing engine for breaking up the tribal mass."[14] Most Native Americans, without a right to be different in the eyes of the United States, nevertheless made it clear that they did not want to be Americanized. For Native Americans the white problem had still not gone away.

THE TWENTIETH CENTURY

Even as the failures of the Dawes Act were acknowledged, the goal of assimilation was not abandoned. In 1924, Congress passed an act ex-tending citizenship to all Native Americans who were not yet citizens. But with the election of Franklin D. Roosevelt as president in 1932, the U.S. government began a reappraisal of its assimilation policy. Led by John Collier, appointed by Roosevelt to head the U.S. Bureau of Indian Affairs, legislation was prepared to address the myriad problems and inequities which the Dawes Act had not in any way resolved and, in-deed, had exacerbated. In 1934 the controversial Indian Reorganization Act (the Wheeler-Howard Act)(48 Stat. 984) was passed, which had the intent of strengthening tribal government, promoting the revival of Na-tive American culture, asserting Indian religious rights, restoring Native American lands to communal holding, and aiding economic develop-ment within tribal communities. Again, in spite of good intentions, albeit informed by a governmental perspective, the end results, from the Na-tive American point of view, were mixed. To begin with, the legislation was written without consultation with Native Americans, and the tribal governments provided for in the Act were based on Western values re-flecting individualism and majoritarianism as opposed to consensual de-cision making. And although tribal landholding increased slightly as a result of the termination of allotment, Native American lives, in fact, did not improve appreciably.

Shortly after World War II, when Dillon Myer (former director of the War Relocation Authority, which had responsibility for the removal of Japanese Americans from the West Coast during the war) became Com-missioner of Indian Affairs, U.S. government policy again shifted back to assimilationism. With the election of Dwight Eisenhower as president this point of view culminated in congressional action aimed at getting the federal government "out of the Indian business." The new policy was colloquially called "termination."

Despite clear evidence that Native Americans had maintained their distinctly different culture—even as many moved to urban areas—in adhering to religious practices, tribal languages, traditional values of community, reciprocity and kinship, and were resistant to assimilation, a basic assertion of termination policy was that no important cultural differences existed between Native Americans and other Americans. The supporters of this policy were political conservatives whose central value was individualism and the priority of private property over group interests, and they refused to acknowledge—or validate—other worldviews.

The intention of the policy was to end both legal and moral obligations by the federal government to Native Americans, an obligation which the government incurred as the legacy of Manifest Destiny and America's march west. Although rarely expressed in explicit terms, many of the services—health, education, law enforcement—that the government had offered Native Americans were in fact necessary to ameliorate the disruptions caused to Native American culture and economy by the incursions of Western culture and subsequent loss of land.

The major thrust of termination policy was the withdrawal of the federal government's trust responsibility to Native American people and their tribes and any special help given to Native Americans as a result of this relationship. In five states, federal and tribal civil and criminal jurisdiction over the tribes within their borders was replaced by state jurisdiction. In addition, termination policy ended the federal prohibition against selling firearms and alcohol to Native Americans, moved responsibility for the Indian Health Service from the Bureau of Indian Affairs (BIA) to the federal agency responsible for health care for all Americans, and began the process of shifting responsibility for the education of Native American children from the BIA to the states.

In addition to its individualistic ideology, termination appealed to American policy makers and the public because a century of federal involvement caused federal leaders to be increasingly impatient and skeptical about the efficacy of the federal trust relationship with tribes, and because termination offered the possibility of decreasing federal spending on Native American communities. Moreover, the rejection by the U.S. Supreme Court, at that time, of the separate-but-equal doctrine in connection with school segregation offered the supporters of termination a convenient rationale for the extension of the idea of equality under law to Native American peoples and communities, despite the completely different history and relationship of the federal government to Native

Americans and African Americans. Thus, in spite of the high tone of the rhetoric of termination, it was in fact yet another government assault on Native American land, sovereignty, culture, and identity.

With the explosion of the African-American civil rights movement in the late 1950s, America embarked on a road of increased self-awareness. Issues of equality and social justice came to dominate the political and social agenda of the nation. Encouraged by the legislative and legal success of the African-American civil rights movement in the 1960s, Native Americans became more vocal and formed new organizations, such as the American Indian Movement (AIM), which protested against the historical injustices to which they had been subject. During the decade of the mid-1960s to the mid-1970s, this Native American protest increased. It was during this time that Native American activists occupied Alcatraz and Wounded Knee, and organized the 1972 march to Washington on the Trail of Broken Treaties, which culminated in the occupation for five days of the Bureau of Indian Affairs. In this political climate, President Richard Nixon signalled the end of the termination era in a 1970 speech requesting that Congress commit resources to strengthen Native American autonomy.

In the 1970s, the apparent openness of the federal government to Native American claims for cultural and religious freedom and economic redress resulted in a major congressional study of the status of the American Indian in the United States,[15] and the establishment of more Native American political and legal organizations. Important among these were two major public interest law firms headed by Native Americans and concerned with Native American legal issues: the Native American Rights Fund and the Indian Law Resource Center. As a result, there was a significant increase in both political lobbying and litigation on issues ranging from religious freedom to hunting, fishing, and water rights. Of all these issues, land claims occupied a central place.

Among land claim litigation, perhaps none achieved the national prominence of *United States v. Sioux* [448 U.S. 371 (1980)]. Familiar to Americans through schoolbooks and films, the Sioux had become emblematic of *the* American Indian. The images portrayed a people—proud, capable, formidable—that, tragically, bore little relation to the contemporary Sioux. Stripped of their land in the last quarter of the nineteenth century, the economy and social and cultural fabric of Sioux society deteriorated under the conditions of restricted reservation life.

It was Gen. George Armstrong Custer who, in 1874, announced to the world that there was gold in the Black Hills, land which belonged to the Sioux Nation. Just six years earlier, the U.S. government had signed, by solemn treaty, the right of the Sioux to "the absolute and undisturbed use" of this land. Custer's announcement set off a clamor among white prospectors to take the Hills away from their Sioux owners. The government responded by first attempting to pressure the Sioux to cede the Black Hills. When that failed, the government forced the Sioux out. Federal agents disarmed the Sioux, took away the ponies without which they were unable to hunt the buffalo, and finally, threatened to cut off the government rations on which the Sioux were largely dependent. In 1876 the United States made one last effort to obtain a legal title to the Black Hills, by attempting to obtain the required signatures of 75 percent of the adult men of the tribe. When only 10 percent gave their consent to the transfer of their land to the United States, Congress passed the Act of 1877, which accomplished the land-grab by fiat.

At this time, the U.S. government justified its extraordinary action in taking the land by claiming that the Sioux were not self-sufficient. This contention was rich in irony, since the 1868 treaty had already seized 48 million acres from the Sioux Nation, virtually eliminating its hunting ground after the buffalo had been decimated by whites. When the army dismounted and disarmed the Sioux, they became totally dependent on the United States for food. In short, the U.S. government took away the ability of the Sioux to be self-sufficient, then pointed to their dependent state as proof of their inability to manage their own affairs and in particular, to control their land.

"THE BLACK HILLS ARE NOT FOR SALE"

Since the late 1880s, Sioux councils had met continuously to discuss their grievances over this taking of the Black Hills.[16] But it was not until the early 1920s that litigation began with a young, non-Indian attorney, Ralph Case, representing the Sioux. Case, sometimes working with other attorneys, framed and filed a legal claim that would give the Sioux money compensation for what the Sioux argued was an illegal taking by the United States of more than seven million acres of land. According to his reading of the law—in particular, the Fifth Amendment's "taking" clause and legislation controlling the U.S. Court of Claims—Case persuaded his Sioux clients that they could not demand that the United States government return the land, but could only hope to get just compensation—market value of the land at the time it was taken, plus interest.

For the next 30 years, Case pursued Sioux claims through a tangle of political and legal pathways, in which he tried to establish a clear history of the government's "double dealing" and coercion in relation to the taking of the Black Hills. But the U.S. Indian Claims Commission, established in 1946, and the several federal courts before which Case argued on behalf of the Sioux, rejected the legal theories upon which he based the Sioux land claims; additionally, they apprised the Sioux that, in their view, the Sioux had no claim because the United States had acted toward them in a "fair and honorable fashion."

By the mid-1950s, little progress appeared to have been made and some Sioux began to explore the possibility of bringing in new attorneys to work on the case. With Case's death in June of 1957, a new team of lawyers from a Washington law firm which had experience in tribal legal issues assumed responsibility for the Sioux claims. For the next two decades these lawyers, led by Arthur Lazarus, Jr. and Marvin Sonosky, used a variety of legal and political stratagems to further a money compensation award to their clients. In 1979, the U.S. Court of Claims, the federal court with jurisdiction for money claims against the U.S. government, awarded the Sioux the long-sought judgment of $17.5 million plus interest for the taking of the Black Hills.

The U.S. government, however, rejected the court's decision. The position of the U.S. Justice Department was that the taking of Sioux land in 1877 was compensated by food and clothing rations that had been sent to the Sioux for many years afterward. In the government's view, the Sioux would have lost the land anyway to the predations of white gold miners and farmers and thus, the United States had not only acted in "perfect good faith" but had actually saved the Sioux from starvation and the loss of their land without *any* compensation. The government argued that there had been no violation of treaties or the Fifth Amendment. It appealed the Court of Claims decision to the U.S. Supreme Court which agreed to hear the case.

Midmorning, Monday, March 24, 1980, lawyers for the Sioux Nation and the U.S. government stood before the justices of the U.S. Supreme Court prepared to argue *United States v. Sioux* (448 U.S. 371), a case which, by that morning, had been in litigation for nearly 60 years. Many thought, and some hoped, the high court's decision would be the final chapter in the ongoing struggle of the Sioux Nation to win redress for the taking of 7.5 million acres of Black Hills land.

That morning Deputy Solicitor General Louis Claiborne presented the government's argument, as expected, that the United States had, in its continual dealings with the Sioux, been motivated solely by a concern for the best interests of the Sioux, claiming that "the Indian tribes have been incapable of prudent management of their communal property" and that the United States had, by necessity, to do it for them.[17]

The attorneys for the Sioux, however, dismissed with contempt the government's argument that it was motivated by concern for Sioux interests, and that the rations proffered over the decades were a fair equivalent of the value of the land. Instead, they argued that the taking of the land in the 1870s violated the Fifth Amendment which says that just compensation must be paid when government takes property for public use.

In an opinion written by Justice Harry Blackmun, with only Justice William Rehnquist dissenting in full, the Supreme Court strongly rejected the government's claim of "fair and honorable dealings," and accepted the Sioux's contention that the rations were in no way fair compensation for the taking of the Black Hills. Indeed, the Court stated, the rations were never intended to be compensation at all. Rather, Justice Blackmun acknowledged that an underlying but critical issue in this land claims case was the U.S. policy of assimilating the Sioux. Blackmun wrote:

It seems readily apparent to us that the obligation to provide rations to the Sioux was undertaken in order to ensure them a means of surviving their transition from the nomadic life of the hunt to the agrarian life style Congress had chosen for them. . . . It is reasonable to conclude that Congress' undertaking of an obligation to provide rations for the Sioux was a *quid pro quo* for depriving them of their chosen way of life, and was not intended to compensate them for the taking of the Black Hills.

The majority of the Court concluded, then, that the government's 1877 Act was a taking of tribal property guaranteed to the Sioux under the 1868 Fort Laramie Treaty and that the government of the United States had an obligation to make just compensation at long last to the Sioux Nation. It affirmed the judgment of the Court of Claims awarding $17.5 million, the value of the land at the time of the taking, plus somewhat less than $100 million in accrued interest.

While Lazarus and Sonosky and some of their Sioux clients were extremely pleased with the Supreme Court decision in their favor, most among the Sioux were not. For many years, while this litigation had been going on, there were Sioux who were determined that the illegal taking of their land by the United States could only be redressed by return of the land itself, and not by money compensation.

While an orally based culture does not, in its nature, tend to create a written archive, from the moment of the taking of *Paha Sapa*, their sacred Black Hills, the Sioux made it clear that they had not parted with their land willingly, that the land was the basis of their spiritual and communal life, and that only fear and the total desperation of their position accounted for their parting with their land. That they devoutly hoped for the return of their land was expressed in many ways, not least in the rapid spread of the Ghost Dance in the 1880s to the Sioux reservations. The Ghost Dance was a messianic, revitalist movement that expressed the vision of, in the words of the Sioux, Kicking Bear, "the promise of a day in which there will be no white man to lay his hand on the bridle of the Indian's horse; when the red man of the prairie will rule the world and not be turned from the hunting grounds by any man."[18] White fear that the Ghost Dance would precipitate Sioux rebellion had led to the tragic massacre of the Sioux at Wounded Knee by the U.S. Army on December 29, 1890. For the next several decades, Sioux elders voiced their deeply felt grievances against the illegal taking of the Black Hills in their tribal councils.

But with the increasing control of Sioux reservations by U.S. government agents, and the imposition of assimilationist policy through, for example, the Dawes Act, factionalism developed among the Sioux in which a new generation of younger, more assimilated Sioux contested the power of the elders and their vision of the future of the Sioux Nation. It was this younger group of Sioux, along with lawyers working on a contingency fee basis, that led to a case framed in terms of money compensation, rather than return of land.

With the shaping of the Sioux claims by attorneys Case, Lazarus, and Sonosky according to a strategy of money compensation rather than return of land, the question arises why a formal statement of claims for *return* of the Black Hills did not emerge until the 1970s. Given the absence of a continuous written record of Sioux debate on the issue, this question cannot be given a definitive answer. However, a review of Sioux history suggests several factors that would support the view that hopes for eventual land return had never ended.

The public silence of the Sioux, in the early twentieth century, immediately after Wounded Knee, was not only a response to the trauma of the massacre but also the result of the intensification of the government's Dawes Act assimilation program that put U.S. government agents firmly in control on the Sioux reservations.

It is also clear that the Sioux, like the Cherokee in the 1830s, were affected by the lack of Native American lawyers trained in the law of the United States. It is logical, then, that the articulation of an alternative legal theory that presented a Sioux case for *return of the land* only occurred in the mid-1970s after the first Pine Ridge Sioux graduated from an American law school and began to practice law. It was this Sioux attorney, Mario Gonzalez, who went before a Sioux tribal council and argued that the Fifth Amendment only permitted the taking of land for *public* use; the Black Hills, he contended, were seized for the private use and benefit of American miners, farmers, and ranchers. Gonzalez maintained that the Sioux should terminate all litigation that did not demand return of the Black Hills. While Gonzalez's position increasingly won support among the Sioux, Sonosky and Lazarus continued arguing the case for money compensation in the Court of Claims and, when the United States appealed, at the Supreme Court. Thus, ironically, at the same time that Gonzalez and his followers were insisting on return of land, U.S. courts were awarding more than $100 million, hoping to quiet Sioux legal title to the Black Hills forever.

The government hope of closing the Sioux land claims case has not been met: The legal struggle over the Black Hills is not over. Virtually all of the members of the Sioux Nation have rejected the "just compensation" awarded by the courts of the United States. The award, now vastly increased in size because of accrued interest, remains untouched at the U.S. Treasury. Holding to their cultural value of the "sacred primacy" of the land, the Sioux continue to argue that, "the Black Hills are not for sale."

NOTES

1. Clark Wissler, *Indians of the United States* (New York: Doubleday, 1966); Harriet J. Kupferer, *Ancient Drums, Other Moccasins: Native American Cultural Adaptation* (Englewood Cliffs, NJ: Prentice-Hall, 1988).

2. Peter Matthiessen, *In the Spirit of Crazy Horse* (New York: Viking, 1983), 519.

3. Robert A. Williams, Jr., *The American Indian in Western Legal Thought* (New York: Oxford University Press, 1990).

4. W. C. Vanderwerth, ed., *Indian Oratory* (New York: Ballantine Books, 1972), 39.

5. Petra T. Shattuck and Jill Norgren, *Partial Justice* (Oxford: Berg, 1991), 39.

6. 7 *Cong. Deb.* App. x (Washington, DC: 1830).

7. *Cherokee Nation v. Georgia*, 30 U.S. 1, 17–18 (1831).

8. *Cherokee Nation v. Georgia*, 44.

9. *Worcester v. Georgia*, 31 U.S. 515, 561 (1832).

10. Francis Paul Prucha, *American Indian Policy in Crisis* (Norman: University of Oklahoma Press, 1976), 21.

11. A. Debo, *And Still the Waters Run* (Norman: University of Oklahoma Press, 1984), 22.

12. Kirke Kickingbird and Karen Ducheneaux, *One Hundred Million Acres* (New York: Macmillan, 1973), 19.

13. Peter Nabokov, ed., *Native American Testimony* (New York: Viking, 1991), 266–67.

14. Prucha, *American Indian Policy*, 257.

15. American Indian Policy Review Commission, *Final Report* (Washington, DC: U.S. Government Printing Office, 1977).

16. Edward Lazarus, *Black Hills/White Justice* (New York: HarperCollins, 1991), 119.

17. For a summary of oral argument in *U.S. v. Sioux*, see Lazarus, *Black Hills/White Justice*, 387–92.

18. Vanderwerth, *Indian Oratory*, 197–98.

2

Trouble in Paradise: Native Hawaiians

The history of cultural clashes, broken promises, violation of legal trust relationships, and loss of land that is so central in relations between Native Americans and the U.S. government is also the source of conflict between the United States and the indigenous people of Hawai'i. Like Native Americans, Native Hawaiian culture stands in contrast to, and sometimes in conflict with, that of the dominant culture of the United States. Native Hawaiians, like Native Americans, value the sacred interdependence of people and nature, the protection and conservation of natural resources, and the inherent value of all living things. Native Hawaiian culture emphasizes the availability, use, and sharing of resources among the *'ohana* (family), the extended kin group, and the community. This worldview contrasts with mainstream American values of dominating nature and developing natural resources, especially land, for individual profit. Hawaiian contact with the West, then, as on the U.S. mainland, has been shaped by cultural clashes and European appropriation of land originally belonging to the Hawaiian people. The struggle for cultural integrity and return of land is at the center of the contemporary efforts of Native Hawaiians to assert their sovereignty and reclaim their rights.[1] From the beginning, law played a key role in these struggles.

In their first incursions into North America, Europeans defined the relationships between themselves and the indigenous peoples they encountered within a (Western) legal framework. In Hawai'i, as in North America, Europeans viewed law as central to their "civilizing" mission and in both ideology and practice, law functioned as the "cutting edge of colonialism" and its accompanying cultural changes.[2] This legal framework has been partly responsible for the widespread denial of America's colonial past with regard to its indigenous peoples.[3]

Understanding the transformative power of Western law in colonial settings is essential in understanding the contemporary Native Hawaiians' quest for sovereignty. While the "law of discovery," rationalizing European appropriation of Native American lands, was not applied to Hawai'i, which was recognized as a fully sovereign nation, the imposition of Western law, particularly regarding land ownership, served equally well to achieve the economic and cultural transformations which permitted European, and later, American dominance.

In this respect, Native Hawaiians were particularly disadvantaged. The exceptions made for collective land rights for Native Americans were based on the special relationship between the American government and Indian "tribes," defined in the Cherokee court cases of the 1830s. Native Hawaiians are in a more ambiguous legal relationship with the United States. Although they are recognized, for some purposes, as an indigenous people owed certain benefits by the state and federal governments, they have not been collectively recognized by Congress as a "tribe." Thus, it has been more difficult for them to get a hearing, either before Congress, or in American courts, for redress of their loss of land and culture. Specifically, and importantly, this lack of tribal status means that Native Hawaiians, unlike Native Americans, are prohibited from suing the federal government and the state of Hawai'i for return of land, reparations, or violations of the trust relationship assumed first by the federal government in annexation, and later by the state government when Hawai'i was made a state.[4] The contemporary Native Hawaiian quest for sovereignty, or "nation within a nation" status, grows out of this historically disadvantaged legal relationship with the American government.

LAW AND LOSS IN HAWAIIAN HISTORY

Sustained Western contact with Hawai'i began with the landing of the English explorer, Captain James Cook, in 1778. Since that time, Western contact, the imposition of Western law, and subsequently, American domination of the islands, almost completely transformed indigenous Hawaiian society, economy, ecology, and demography. European contact had a devastating effect on the survival of the Native Hawaiian population as a result of both a declining birth rate and increased mortality rate. As in North America, the Europeans brought with them venereal disease, tuberculosis, and other bacterial and viral infections; in addition to these causes of death, there were also substantial fatalities from the introduction of guns and alcohol.[5] From a precontact population conservatively estimated at 400,000, by 1859, 70 years after Captain Cook landed, the first reliable census put the population of Native Hawaiians at only 84,000.[6] In the state of Hawai'i today there are only approximately 8,000 pure-blood Native Hawaiians, and about 200,000 part-Hawaiians, out of a population of 1.2 million.[7] European contact led not only to a disastrous decline in the Native Hawaiian population, but also to a loss of land, language, culture, and religion.

The peopling of the Hawaiian Islands began around 300 A.D., when seafaring Polynesians, from the Marquesan Islands in the South Pacific, set sail looking for a new home. Finding the islands they called Hawai'i, they developed a distinctive culture, one related to, but also different from, the Polynesia they had left.[8] This culture includes the Hawaiian language; a rural subsistence economy based on taro (a tropical plant with a starchy, edible root) and fishing; an emphasis on mutuality in human relations expressed through sharing of material goods and cooperative labor; feasting as a source and expression of community; child adoption as an important means of forging kinship relations; and a tradition of government through chiefs and later, monarchs, that ideally rested on a concept of mutual benefit through stewardship and productive labor. Central in traditional Hawaiian culture is the spiritual as well as economic relation to natural resources and land. Because the Hawaiians believe that their gods created the land and sea and all its products, these had to be shared and cared for by the leaders on behalf of the people.[9]

Prior to Western contact, Hawaiian political structure consisted of independent, and frequently warring, chiefdoms. The *ali'i*, or high chiefs, and priests, occupied the highest rung of society. The *ali'i* did not "own" the land, but controlled its distribution, parceling it out to *ahupua'a* or district chiefs who were their relatives or allies. Below the district chiefs were the *konohiki*, or land agents, who were chiefs of independent political units of the *ahupua'a*. At the bottom of the hierarchy were the *maka'ainana*, the common people. Each stratum of society had its obligations, rights, and responsibilities.

The *maka'ainana*, who worked collectively under the direction of chiefs and priests in clearing the land, constructing irrigation systems, cultivating taro, and building fishponds for breeding fish, had liberal rights to use *ahupua'a* resources for their own subsistence. These rights included hunting, gathering wild plants and herbs, offshore fishing, and access to land with sufficient water for taro cultivation. Commoners or *konohiki* who felt they were unfairly treated could move from one district to another, providing them with some leverage to ensure that their rights and needs were met by those higher in the stratification system.[10]

The Hawaiian system of land tenure was based on use rights subject to revocation at the will of the high chief. While chiefs typically reserved some land for their personal use and distributed the remaining land to loyal district chiefs, relatives, or allies, neither the high chief nor those below him owned the land in the Western sense of total and exclusive dominion over it. Use rights in land were not secured by any law of inheritance; when a high chief died or was conquered, his land went not to his heirs, but to the new chief and his allies. This lack of security in land through inheritance became an important source of conflict between Native Hawaiians and Europeans.

Shortly after Captain Cook's landing, with the arrival of traders, missionaries, whaling ships, and investors from many countries, Western contact began in earnest. By 1795, using Western weapons—600 muskets, 20 cannon, 40 swivel guns, and 20 sailing ships—and with European support, the Hawaiian Islands were united under Kamehameha, high chief of Oahu, who became King Kamehameha I, founder of the Hawaiian monarchy.[11] This event benefitted Europeans first, because unified leadership increased stability in the islands by ending warfare, and second, because it was more convenient for Europeans to deal with the Hawaiian people through a single ruler than it would have been to have to negotiate with several autonomous chiefs.

During the reign of Kamehameha I, the European economic presence in Hawai'i expanded considerably, as did the political influence of the British, whose protection Kamehameha I sought both against the demands of other Europeans for land, and to help control the riotous behavior of European sailors who manned the many ships now stopping in Hawaiian ports as part of the fur and sandalwood trade and the whaling industry. Kamehameha I did not alter the Hawaiian land tenure system, but his economic reliance on the Europeans, and the growing involvement of Hawaiian chiefs in European trade, was the opening wedge for subsequent changes to a Western system of private land ownership sanctioned in law.

With the death of King Kamehameha I in 1819, his son, Liholiho, ascended the throne as Kamehameha II, ruling with his mother, Queen Ka'ahumanu, until 1824, when he died of measles contracted while on a state visit to London. During Liholiho's reign, important changes were made both in Hawaiian culture and in the traditional system of land tenure. The traumatic breakdown of the Hawaiian religion occurred in Liholiho's first year on the throne. Hawaiian religion was based on *kapu*, or taboo, which governed every aspect of conduct and social relationships, and regulated the interaction between the people and their environment. The erosion of the *kapu* system had begun with foreign contact, when it was observed that foreigners, who persistently violated taboos, escaped unharmed. In 1819, Queen Ka'ahumanu and Liholiho succeeded in abolishing the *kapu* system altogether, by publicly violating the *kapu* against women and men eating together. Following this event, the king ordered the destruction of temples and images of the gods, and the killing of priests.[12]

This breakdown in the Hawaiian religion occurred just one year before the first organized group of Christian missionaries arrived from the United States, and opened the way for large-scale conversion to Christianity. Missionaries soon became very influential as advisors to the Hawaiian government, and their descendants, who moved from missionary work to business enterprises, would become the major foreign landholders and economic oligarchs in Hawai'i.

During Liloliho's reign, European landholdings increased as Europeans were given land both by the monarch and by many chiefs in exchange for European goods—clothing, rum, weapons, and hardware—and services. Although Liholiho gave land to Europeans with the understanding that it would eventually return to the monarchy, both the Europeans and Hawaiian chiefs pressed him to grant them more permanent rights in land by permitting them to pass their land on to their heirs. Liholiho responded to this pressure by allowing his father's chiefs to keep their land, rather than redistributing it to his own allies. Still, European rights to the lands they had been given remained ambiguous in the absence of explicit rights of inheritance.

When Liholiho died in 1824, his 12-year-old son, Kamehameha III, ascended the throne. The young king, like his father, was very much influenced by Europeans and Western ideas, and he acceded to continued European pressure to alter Hawaiian land tenure so that individual land rights would be protected. Surrounded by a Council of Chiefs, the young king was persuaded to sign The Law of 1825, formally allowing chiefs to retain their lands upon the death of the king and giving them hereditary rights in their land, a major change from the traditional Hawaiian land tenure system.[13]

During the reign of King Kamehameha III, the emerging Hawaiian political structure and land tenure system drew increasingly upon Western liberal ideas about protecting individual property rights. This served the interest of both the foreigners and the chiefs. As the sandalwood trade declined with the depletion of the forests, overharvested by the chiefs to pay their mounting debts for foreign luxury goods, "giving" land to foreigners was another way for the chiefs to pay their bills.

Foreigners, too, and more particularly, Americans, were looking for new investment opportunities, were acquiring more land, and were increasing their investments in large-scale agriculture, which had become a profitable business with the opening of a growing market in California. One American visitor to Hawai'i in 1839 noted that "The Americans alone have at least $572,000 worth of property at stake upon Hawaiian grounds. They have two or three sugar mills . . . and two extensive silk plantations on Kauai Island alone. . . . They will soon have a mill for extracting paint oil from the abundant candle nuts.... At least thirty merchant vessels annually reported to our American Counsel, and not less than fifty whale ships stop annually at Honolulu, for refreshment and repairs."[14]

During the 1820s, 1830s, and 1840s, Western law made inroads among both the Hawaiian elites and the common people, ultimately reshaping the whole of Hawaiian society. While the Hawaiian elites turned to Western law for protection of their growing property rights, the common people were being pulled into the Western legal system through participation in local courts which were set up by mid-century.[15] By the 1820s, many Native Hawaiians, both commoners and chiefs, were leaving their subsistence livelihoods to participate in the new opportunities offered by trading and the emerging cash economy; Native Hawaiians were increasingly employed in menial and marginal service positions in the trading ports of Honolulu and Lahaina (on Maui). The resulting alienation of Native Hawaiians from their kin-based rural communities, the breakdown of the *kapu* system and the social control it enforced, and the need to control the increasingly violent and disruptive behavior of foreigners in the trading ports led to the formulation of the first Hawaiian written criminal law, in 1827. This code reflects the influence of the missionaries who assisted the chiefs in drawing it up: It forbade murder, theft, illicit intercourse between a male and female, the selling of rum, prostitution, and gambling.

In 1842, a system of district courts was set up by the monarchy to handle disputes and punish crimes of both natives and foreigners. These relatively informal courts, conducted in Hawaiian, mainly dealt with theft, property ownership disputes, interpersonal conflicts, and charges of adultery. As Hawaiians left their kin-based rural communities, where theft was rare because an individual's labor and sharing among kin assured survival, conflicts over possession of material goods increased. Urban wage work no longer assured an adequate subsistence and the traditional sanctions of shame, ridicule, and ostracism for theft were no longer effective in the cities. Hawaiians learned to covet Western goods—horses, cattle, clothing, tools, furniture—and cash, accounting for the increase in thefts. Many charges of theft, however, were really conflicts over contracts, illustrating the confusion over property rights in this culturally transitional period. As disputants accepted court judgments reflecting Western legal individualism, a Western legal ideology began to replace the Hawaiian, both reflecting and contributing to the erosion of Hawaiian folk law and culture.[16]

At midcentury, also, with Western advisors now in important positions in the Hawaiian government, Western law regarding land tenure became more deeply entrenched in Hawaiian society. As a result of foreigners continually pressuring the Hawaiian government to legally, permanently, and completely convert traditional Hawaiian land tenure principles to those of absolute ownership, in 1848, the Hawaiian government instituted the Great Mahele, a formal division of land among the king, the chiefs, the Hawaiian people, and the foreign landholders. Under the Mahele, the king held 60 percent of the total land, or 2.5 million acres, while the chiefs received an additional 1.5 million acres. In an attempt to stave off more foreign appropriation of Hawaiian land in the event of some future foreign conquest of the islands, the king then divided his land into two parts: He retained about one million acres for himself and his heirs and successors, which was called the Crown Lands, and "set apart forever to the chiefs and the people" another one million acres of land, called the Government Lands.[17]

The Mahele specified that both the Crown Lands and the Government Lands were subject to "the rights of native tenants," a phrase which was clarified by the passage of the Kuleana Act by the Hawaiian legislature in 1850. This Act awarded fee simple title, or individual ownership, to common people who could prove their claims to living on and cultivating a piece of land. The intent of the Act, which would make "[E]ach man his own *Konohiki* (landlord)" was to ensure the survival of the Native Hawaiian people, albeit in the image of the sturdy, independent New England farmer, with his nuclear family, cultivating his privately owned lands.[18] The assumption of the Kuleana Act's creators that the common Hawaiian people would readily take up this vision by making claims to their individual homesteads was not realized. Of the 30,000 Native Hawaiian males eligible to make these claims, only 8,200 awards were ultimately made. Many Hawaiians were not sufficiently familiar with written law or land claims to understand what they needed to do, others could not afford the survey fees to make their claims, still others were afraid of reprisals from their *konohiki* if they filed. In any case, the king's intention to secure the traditional livelihood of the *maka'ainana* clearly failed and "History . . . transformed the Kuleana Act from an instrument for the confirmation of *maka'ainana* livelihood into one for its undoing."[19]

Like the 1887 Dawes Act, the result of the Great Mahele and the Kuleana Act was the transfer of millions of acres of land from Native Hawaiians to Westerners. By 1890, fewer than 5,000 of the nearly 90,000 Native Hawaiians owned any land at all and what they owned amounted to very little acreage. In contrast, a very small number of Americans and Europeans owned over one million acres. Three quarters of the privately held land in Hawai'i belonged to foreigners.[20] This major land transfer occurred partly because of the enormous acreage already owned by foreigners at the time of the Great Mahele, partly because Hawaiian kings continued to transfer land to Europeans to pay their debts for foreign goods, and partly because commoners often lost their small homesteads to foreigners through debt, coercion, legal technicalities, and the inability of their small, and often marginal, acreage to support a family.

Even after the Great Mahele, the struggle for land continued to dominate the relationship between foreigners and Hawaiians. From the mid-nineteenth century on, the American sugar interests that had largely supplanted European and British advisors and investors in Hawai'i continued to pressure the Hawaiian government to create laws to protect their own wealth and power. Sugar growers, seeing a huge new market with the opening up of the American West, urged legislation in the United States to permit the free export of sugar; when this was achieved, in 1874, the number of sugar plantations expanded enormously and with it the demand for labor. As a result, Native Hawaiians continued to be dispossessed of their land and immigration from Asia increased—between 1877 and 1890, 55,000 new immigrants entered Hawai'i.

As the condition of Native Hawaiians worsened, the Hawaiian monarchs became increasingly resistant to expanding American influence. In return, Americans in Hawai'i sought to restrict the monarchy's power by urging it, under the threat of U.S. military force, to adopt a new constitution favoring American interests. Enacted in 1887, this so-called "Bayonet Constitution," signed under coercion and protest by King David Kalakaua, imposed property and income restrictions as a qualification for voting, disqualifying most ordinary Native Hawaiians; permitted Caucasian (but not other) aliens the right to vote; and expanded the role of American advisors in the Hawaiian government.[21]

In the next several decades, Hawai'i was transformed from a sovereign nation to a colony under the political, economic, and cultural hegemony of the United States. When, in 1891, Hawaiian sugar interests became disadvantaged by a subsidy to U.S. sugar producers, a group of American sugar plantation owners sought the annexation of Hawai'i to the United States as their best chance of keeping the Hawaiian sugar industry highly profitable.

When Queen Lili'uokalani ascended the Hawaiian throne in 1892, conflict between the American "annexationists" and the Hawaiian monarchy increased. In January 1893, the new queen tried to replace the Bayonet Constitution with one less favorable to American sugar interests. John Stevens, the U.S. minister to Hawai'i, and a proponent of annexation, advised President Benjamin Harrison to approve the landing of American marines in Honolulu, claiming that American lives and property needed to be protected from the chaos attending the queen's activities. Harrison approved, and under the coercion of this military force, the queen reluctantly abdicated the throne. The annexationists, led by Sanford Dole, declared a provisional government, which they called the Republic of Hawai'i.

Annexation of Hawai'i had been urged as early as the 1850s, when an American military presence in Hawai'i was perceived by many in Washington as a necessary counterthrust to the many European claims in the Pacific. Indeed, annexation might well have occurred in 1893 itself, had the proannexation Harrison not been replaced by Grover Cleveland as president. The new president questioned the legitimacy of the U.S. role in the overthrow of the monarchy and concluded, after an investigation, that "the landing of the United States forces [occurred] upon false pretexts respecting the danger to life and property" and that the occupation of Honolulu was "lawless."[22] For Native Hawaiians, the illegal overthrow of their monarchy and subsequent annexation of Hawai'i by the United States is a trenchant legal and moral basis of claims for redress from the American government.[23]

Because of the many and conflicting views on the "Hawai'i question," no definitive action was taken by Congress or President Cleveland, either to restore the monarchy, or to annex Hawai'i. In 1896, however, William McKinley was elected president by a nation increasingly supportive of expanding the role of the United States in the Pacific and a Hawai'i "controlled by the United States."[24] By 1898, the U.S. government, already using Pearl Harbor as a port, expanded its role in the Pacific through the acquisition of the Philippines as a result of the treaty settling the 1898 Spanish-American War. With continuing American concern over European expansion in the Far East, the strategic importance of Hawai'i increased. On July 7, 1898, after heated debate in Congress, Hawai'i was annexed to the United States; in 1900, Congress passed the Organic Act, which established Hawai'i as a Territory of the United States and the colonial status of this once sovereign nation became formalized.

With annexation, the United States took title to the Crown Lands, set aside for the monarchy, and the Government Lands, set aside for the chiefs and the people in the Great Mahele. Congress established that these "ceded" public lands, exclusive of the portion that the United States could withdraw from public use for military purposes, would be held in trust by the U.S. government for the benefit of the "inhabitants" of Hawai'i.

The first 20 years of this trust obligation did little to change the dismal physical, educational, and economic condition of the Native Hawaiian people, whose population continued to decline, and whose socioeconomic status and health were deteriorating yearly. Hawaiian culture also continued to disintegrate, as traditional cultural forms, such as the hula, were suppressed by the missionaries. With annexation, the use of the Hawaiian language was also suppressed. Before the overthrow of the monarchy, royalty and their advisors, and the general population, used Hawaiian as their primary language and many Westerners were bilingual. Hawaiian had been the official language of government, and while

English had been the medium of education, after annexation this practice became law. To some extent, the Hawaiian language had also been superseded by a local "pidgin" language, which served as a medium of communication among the many different groups from Asia, and the Portuguese, who came to Hawai'i in large numbers to work on the sugar, and later, pineapple plantations.[25]

Dismayed at the condition of Native Hawaiians, and fearing for their extinction as a people, some territorial representatives and others in Congress claimed that the United States, having annexed Hawai'i, was not fulfilling its trust obligations to its people. In response, in 1921 Congress passed the Hawaiian Homes Commission Act. The Act was similar to the 1850 Hawaiian Kuleana Act, and the 1887 Dawes Act in the United States, in its goal of assimilating Native Hawaiians by transforming them into independent farmers. The Hawaiian Homes Commission Act provided for 200,000 acres of scattered tracts of trust lands throughout the islands to be carved up into homesteading agricultural or ranching plots to be given to Native Hawaiians with 99-year leases at $1.00 a year. The Act also committed the federal government to provide the infrastructure to make these homesteads viable.[26]

The influence of landed American interests in thwarting the stated intention of the Homelands Act was immediately apparent: A Native Hawaiian was defined as any person with 50 percent or more of Hawaiian blood, which excluded from the program the many thousands of Native Hawaiians with more mixed ancestry. Congress also acquiesced to the sugar growers' demands to exclude all sugar producing lands from the acreage set aside for the program. In addition, and partly as a result of the exclusion of sugar plantation land, much of the acreage allotted to the program was virtually useless for agriculture: It was arid and stony, some of it even lava rock. Furthermore, unlike the allotment of land under the Dawes Act, which proceeded with bureaucratic efficiency, the processing of eligible applicants under the Hawaiian Homes Commission Act bogged down from the beginning so that few allotments were actually made.

Thus, in spite of the Act, the steady erosion of the Native Hawaiian land base and culture continued, with legal sanction, up until the mid-twentieth century. But after World War II the pace of change quickened considerably. Statehood was being urged by non–Native Hawaiian political and economic interests and even some Native Hawaiians, who believed they would have more political power if Hawai'i became a state.

Subsequent to a plebiscite, in which Hawaiians were asked to vote "yes" or "no" regarding statehood, Hawai'i became the State of Hawaii in 1959. With this change from territory to state, the federal government transferred the "ceded" lands to the new state government, retaining title to about 400,000 acres, three-quarters of which was used for military activities, and the remainder for national parks. The state now became custodian (with federal oversight retained) for over two million acres of trust land, as well as responsible for implementing the Hawaiian Homes Commission Act. The federal government now considered itself relieved of its trust responsibilities to the Native Hawaiians. The U.S. government considered that with statehood it was no longer appropriate to keep Hawai'i on the United Nations list of "non-self-governing" territories, and Hawai'i was accordingly removed from the list with General Assembly approval.[27]

Now a state, Hawai'i became more attractive to mainlanders as an investment opportunity; with the improvement of air travel, there was an enormous boom in tourism and real estate development, an increased movement of mainland Americans to Hawai'i, and expanded economic investment in the islands by multinational corporations. Yet this almost 40 years of statehood and economic "development" has done little to alleviate the socioeconomic problems of Native Hawaiians, either by land distribution under the Hawaiian Homes Commission Act or through benefits from the state's control over the ceded trust lands.

By 1960, 40 years after passage of the Hawaiian Homes Commission Act, only 1,600 Native Hawaiians had received homesteads; in 1989, fewer than 6,000 Native Hawaiians had received homestead land and 19,000 were on the waiting list.[28] Given the snail's pace at which homeland distribution has taken place, Native Hawaiians are understandably bitter toward the state government, currently responsible for the implementation of the Homes Commission Act.

In a public hearing on the Act in 1989, Daniel Inouye, the senator from Hawai'i, told 91-year-old Henry Afong, who had been on the waiting list since 1952, to "just hang on." Six months later Afong died. He, and many other thousands of Native Hawaiians like him, had not been able to realize the promises of the Hawaiian Homelands Act, while over 60 percent of the allotted land has been rented at very low prices to non–Native Hawaiians, including some of the richest and most powerful families in Hawai'i, or given to other government agencies. The plot of land Afong hoped to get, for example, was leased for many years by the second largest ranching business in the state, Parker Ranch, which pays the state $3.33 an acre for its 27,000 acres. Other land has gone to multinational corporations for mining operations, to the U.S. military, and to local politicians for their own personal estates or private enterprises, such as auto dealerships and shopping malls. Only 17 percent of the land is held by Native Hawaiians and only 3,700 of the tens of thousands of eligible families (about 50,000 Native Hawaiians altogether) live on this land, as the state failed to build the basic infrastructure included in the federal commitment when the Act was signed into law.[29] Without legal recognition as a "tribe," Native Hawaiians cannot sue the state government for failing to implement the Homes Commission Act and Native Hawaiian requests for the federal government to sue the state for trust violations have continually been resisted.[30]

THE NATIVE HAWAIIAN SOVEREIGNTY MOVEMENT

In the 1960s, with the momentum of postwar human rights activism and civil rights and student movements in the United States, long-standing Native Hawaiian resentment over their marginalized position in their own society became organized resistance. Not surprisingly, the beginnings of the current movement grew out of conflicts over land.

Throughout the twentieth century, pockets of Native Hawaiian culture based on subsistence agriculture and fishing had persisted in rural areas and in small communities surrounding urban areas. Because these communities often sat on land of potentially great commercial or recreational value, their residents were becoming subject to evictions by the state and private owners. In the 1970s, Native Hawaiians living on prime ocean-front land who were "forcibly removed" to make way for state parks resisted, and many were arrested. Joined by some university activists, this resistance became the opening wedge in the current Native Hawaiian sovereignty movement.[31]

Widespread public sympathy with the evicted Hawaiians fed into the social activism of the period. In the beginning, these communities identified their struggles as those of "locals," which included both Native Hawaiians and other, long-term residents, against large-scale developers, which included the state of Hawai'i, corporations, and privately owned estates. But by the end of the 1970s, many of these community struggles became more closely identified with asserting the rights of Native Hawaiians alone. Throughout the 1970s, there was a proliferation of activities and organizations directed toward political, social, and economic justice for Native Hawaiians. As new groups formed, the goals of the Native Hawaiian rights movement were broadened beyond the initial goal of improving housing and demanding implementation of the Hawaiian Homes Commission Act to encompass the possibility of reparations and greater self-determination for Native Hawaiians, always with a focus on reclaiming a land base.

Protest took many forms: public confrontations, mainstream political participation, and court challenges. Much of this protest was directed against the state government. From a Native Hawaiian perspective, statehood had neither legitimated U.S. claim to sovereignty over Hawai'i, nor had it resulted in any substantial improvement in the conditions of Native Hawaiians. In 1978, the state of Hawaii enacted a new constitution. In response to Native Hawaiian concerns this included provisions for the creation of the Office of Hawaiian Affairs (OHA), whose members were to be made up of Native Hawaiians and voted on by Native Hawaiians, and for 20 percent of the income from the "ceded" lands to be reserved for the benefit of Native Hawaiians. The OHA was to act as the trustee for Native Hawaiian property and income from the trust lands and designated as a possible vehicle for handling reparations from the federal government, should these be awarded. These provisions have made little impact on Native Hawaiians, and many Native Hawaiian activists reject the Office of Hawaiian Affairs as the voice of their community.[32]

Nor have courts—neither the U.S. Supreme Court nor the Hawai'i Supreme Court—responded very positively to the assertion of Native Hawaiian rights. Of the very few (five) published decisions by the Hawai'i Supreme Court since 1983 dealing with Native Hawaiian rights regarding benefits from trust land, religion, or culture, none expands or advances those rights.[33] Without standing to sue the state and federal governments for trust violations or return of land, Native Hawaiian rights litigation has mainly turned on challenging denial of access to water and land for subsistence purposes, and claiming religious rights involving access to sacred land.

A highly publicized religious rights case occurred in Oahu in the summer of 1982, when *Kahuna* (respected elder) Sam Lono and his followers, members of the Temple of Lono, engaged in a religious retreat in Kualoa Park, an area sacred to Native Hawaiians as the site of an ancient temple to the god Lono, one of the major traditional Hawaiian deities. The purpose of the retreat was to practice *ho'ike kapo* or "the showing of the night," a religious ritual involving meditation and prayer, seeking "advice from the gods."[34] In connection with their four-month retreat, Lono's followers erected a campsite, reconstructed an old *heiau* (temple), and planted melon, corn, taro, and fruit trees.

Because camping is prohibited in Kualoa Park during the summer, Lono's group received over 40 citations for violating park regulations, and late in August 1983, local law enforcement officials, exasperated with the Temple of Lono's refusal to decamp, sent in more than 20 officers, several trucks, a van, and two front loaders, and proceeded to destroy the tents and gardens and to carry away the tables and household goods.[35]

In the initial court proceeding, many of the citations were dismissed and small fines were imposed for the remaining ones. But Lono took his case to District Court, claiming that the destruction of his temple and the imposition of fines violated his religious freedom rights. The District Court found against Lono, holding that "Defendants' religious interest in participating in dreams at Kualoa Regional Park are not indispensable to the Hawaiian religious practices . . . [and] . . . [D]efendants' practices in exercising their religious beliefs at Kualoa Regional Park are philosophical and personal and therefore are not entitled to First Amendment protection."[36]

Lono was determined to test in court the extent to which the state government was willing to stand behind its principles of religious freedom and, along with several of his *haumana* (students) appealed, citing state and national constitutional protection of religious freedom as well as the 1978 American Indian Religious Freedom Act, which commits the federal government to the protection and preservation of the traditional religions of Native Americans and Native Hawaiians, "including but not limited to access to sites, . . . and the freedom to worship through ceremonials and traditional rites."

In testifying to the special sacredness of Kualoa Park and to the indispensability of *ho'ike kapo* to his religion, Lono contrasted traditional Hawaiian spiritual systems with Western religion, saying, "I tell you . . . why, Hawaiians never go to church only Sunday. As soon as they get up it's already god . . . They don't wait until the seventh day. I don't believe in that cause the gods not going wait for you in seven days."[37]

While the District Court, in its findings of fact, had acknowledged that Lono was a bona fide leader of a Native Hawaiian religion, that Kualoa Park has religious significance in the Native Hawaiian religion, and that *pule* is a religious ritual, Lono failed to win his case. Judge David Fong of the Hawai'i Supreme Court affirmed the lower court's opinion that, "Defendants' religious interest in participating in dreams at Kualoa Regional Park are not indispensable to the Hawaiian religious practices" and that the state had a "compelling interest" in enforcing its camping regulations.[38] This decision highlights the vulnerability of the spiritual systems of belief and practice of indigenous peoples in U.S. courts. The American constitution protects religion, not culture, and therefore, non–Judeo-Christian spiritual systems which are totally integrated with culture and with daily activities may find themselves in difficulty. American judges, using Western values and law find it all too easy to characterize such spiritual systems as "philosophical and personal," rather than religious and therefore find them not deserving of legal protection.

In 1987, in *Dedman v. Board of Land & Natural Resources*, the Hawai'i Supreme Court again rejected an attempt by Native Hawaiians to use land in traditional religious ways.[39] A group called "Pele Practitioners" claimed that a decision by the state Board of Land & Natural Resources to develop geothermal power plants in the vicinity of the volcano Mauna Loa, on the island of Hawai'i, violated their religious rights because such development would desecrate an area sacred to the Goddess Pele. All of the phenomena associated with volcanic activity of Mauna Loa—heat, steam, and molten rock, and the surrounding landscape including ferns, shrubs, land, and even the rain—are considered sacred to Pele. The group stated that "any penetration [of the volcano] is a violation. Steam is [Pele's] life blood and sucking out that steam is killing her."[40]

In a heated public controversy, proponents of geothermal development in Hawai'i cited expanding population, the benefits of economic development, and the need for the state to be energy independent.[41] They also argued that geothermal energy reduces the chance of an oil spill with its damaging potential to shorelines. The opponents of geothermal development countered that the increased potential for energy was stimulating *unwanted* development, that much imported oil is used for automobiles, and thus would not be affected by geothermal development, and that the geothermal plant would cause extensive atmospheric and ground pollution. The offer of the geothermal developers to move the site ten miles away threatened the last low-lying rainforest in Hawai'i, and thus was also not acceptable.

In *Dedman*, the court acknowledged the legitimacy and sincerity of the Pele practitioners, but decided against them. Hoping to avoid the politics of energy, the court did not examine whether the state had a "compelling interest" in geothermal development. Rather, the court focused on whether the geothermal development around Mauna Loa would pose a "significant harm" to Hawaiian religious practices. Concluding that it would not, the court pointed to government testimony that "[none] of the witnesses . . . ever conducted or participated in religious ceremonies on this land." The court also held that denying geothermal development because of one religious group's objections would place government in the position of "fostering support of one religion over another."[42]

Another important legal battle involved the U.S. government's use of the Hawaiian island of Kaho'olawe. In 1941, Kaho'olawe was placed under martial law and used as a site for target practice by the military. In 1953, President Eisenhower, by executive order, granted sole use of the island to the navy which used it for war games, artillery practice, laser targeting practice, air-to-ground attacks by jet aircraft and helicopters, and amphibious landings. The navy was instructed to notify the Hawaiian state government when it no longer needed the area, and to make the island safe for human habitation.

In 1976, a group called Protect Kaho'olawe 'Ohana began the struggle to end the use of Kaho'olawe as a military site. The 'Ohana hoped "to set a precedent for a sovereign land base that would eventually come under the jurisdiction of a reestablished Hawaiian nation." They sought recognition for traditional and spiritual Hawaiian beliefs and practices associated with Kaho'olawe and wished to establish protection there for traditional gathering and fishing. Some 'Ohana members occupied Kaho'olawe, which led to arrests and convictions for "unauthorized entry onto a military reservation." The six participating activists were fined, given sentences ranging from probation to six months in prison and were prohibited from returning to the island without the permission of the court. The 'Ohana appealed the district court's decision, claiming that they had a constitutional right to hold religious ceremonies on the island. The Court of Appeals rejected their claim, concluding that "in light of the compelling Government interest . . . in keeping outsiders off danger-ous land, the public interest presently outweighs any burden on the de-fendants' free exercise of religion."[43]

The defendants also claimed that the U.S. government held Ka-ho'olawe illegally because the land was acquired under agreements made in 1898 and 1900 by the "illegal revolutionaries" who overthrew the Hawaiian monarchy and because the annexation of Hawai'i by the United States was also unlawful. The court quickly dismissed this "sov-ereignty defense" as "frivolous," holding that "while the use of an island of apparent religious significance as a bombing target may be regrettable, it cannot be blocked and these convictions cannot be overturned on the ground that the Government was without title to the island."[44]

Where litigation failed, however, the publicity from political action succeeded. On October 22, 1990, President George Bush issued a direc-tive that the U.S. Navy halt all bombing practice on Kaho'olawe, and in May, 1994, the U.S. Navy returned the island to the state of Hawaii.[45]

In 1976, the Hawaiian Supreme Court could dismiss a "sovereignty defense" as "frivolous." Twenty years later, the demand for Hawaiian sovereignty seems anything but frivolous; indeed, some form of Native Hawaiian sovereignty appears inevitable. Legally, sovereignty, or "na-tion within a nation" status, does not seem insurmountable, as Native Hawaiians essentially meet all the legal criteria of an Indian "tribe": They were once a sovereign people; they have suffered as a result of European encroachment and from U.S. seizure and exploitation of their lands; they are an aboriginal group whose ancestors, before the arrival of Europeans, inhabited territory that became part of the United States; and they have had their traditional collective land rights recognized in law. Like Native American tribes, they exercised political authority over their members by council or other governmental forms, namely, through the Hawaiian royal family (before the overthrow of the monarchy in 1893).[46] Hawaiians are already included in the 1978 Native American Religious Freedom Act, and in many other acts which benefit Native Americans as a class.

In spite of this strong basis for sovereignty, the state and federal gov-ernments have not been responsive to Native Hawaiian claims. A bill for reparations died in the 1974 Congress; in December 1980, the govern-ment next responded to Hawaiian claims for reparations by authorizing a major congressional commission report on the culture, needs, and con-cerns of Native Hawaiians. The commission's six non–Native Hawaiian members, perhaps predictably, found that the federal government did not authorize the 1893 overthrow of the Hawaiian monarchy and therefore Native Hawaiians had no legal or moral basis to claim repa-rations.[47] The three Native Hawaiians on the commission dissented, holding that the annexation of Hawai'i had been an illegal "taking" by the U.S. government.[48]

With little progress in the courts or Congress, Native Hawaiian activ-ists moved beyond a call for reparations and began to organize around demands for sovereignty, coupled with demands for return of the ceded, or in their view, stolen, lands. In 1987 a group of several hundred Native Hawaiians representing many Native Hawaiian organizations formed the Hawaiian nation, Ka Lahui Hawai'i. They drafted a constitution for a separate Hawaiian nation within the United States, with a status sim-ilar to that of federally recognized Native American tribes. Ka Lahui Hawai'i proposed that all of the Hawaiian Home Lands and half of the ceded lands be given to their new nation, and toward this end engaged in both political action and litigation.[49]

Frustrated by the lack of response by state and federal legislatures and courts to their claims, Native Hawaiians have turned increasingly to in-ternational legal forums under the aegis of the United Nations, to assert their rights of self-determination as indigenous peoples.[50] In the summer of 1993, Native Hawaiians convened an international tribunal, charging the United States with crimes of genocide, ethnocide, impermissible in-tervention in a sovereign nation, illegal appropriations of land and nat-ural resources, and violations of trust responsibilities established by international law, against Native Hawaiians.[51] The tribunal called for the reinstatement of Hawai'i on the United Nations list of non-self-governing nations slated for decolonization.

In November 1993, the year of the 100th anniversary of the overthrow of the Hawaiian monarchy, the U.S. Congress passed a resolution, signed by President Clinton, acknowledging the illegal overthrow of the Ha-waiian monarchy, the deep connection between the Hawaiian people and their land, the devastation to the Hawaiian people resulting from 200 years of foreign domination, and the resulting loss of language and cul-ture. The resolution expressed "its deep regret to the Hawaiian people" and offered an apology, requesting "the President of the United States . . . to support reconciliation between the United States and the Native Hawaiian people."[52]

In its comment on this event, the *New York Times* noted that in some cases government apologies bring reparations, while in other cases they don't. "It makes you wonder what the native Hawaiians will get?" the *Times* asked. "Hawaii? Probably not."[53]

For Native Hawaiian activists, who rejected the apology as containing "serious historical errors," "damaging misinterpretations," and the "grave deficiency" of making no reference to redress in the form of re-turn of land, the answer to the *Times'* question is not satisfactory.[54] In

1995, Hawai'i will hold a referendum on sovereignty. The outcome of this referendum, and more importantly, the response of the economic and political elites in the state, as well as the federal government, to Native Hawaiian claims for meaningful self-determination based on control of land, will decide the future of this troubled Paradise.

NOTES

1. Haunani-Kay Trask, *From a Native Daughter: Colonialism and Sovereignty in Hawai'i* (Monroe, MA: Common Courage Press, 1993).

2. Sally Merry, "Law and Colonialism," *Law and Society Review* 25(4)(1991): 891–922.

3. D. W. Meinig, "Strategies of Empire," *Culturefront* (Summer 1993), 12–19.

4. Mililani B. Trask, "Historical and Contemporary Hawaiian Self-Determination: A Native Hawaiian Perspective," *Arizona Journal of International and Comparative Law* 8(2) (1991): 77–95.

5. Native Hawaiians Study Commission, Vol. I, *Report on the Culture, Needs, and Concerns of Native Hawaiians (Majority)* (Washington, DC: U.S. Department of the Interior, 1983), 38–40; 558 ff. (hereafter *Commission (Majority)*.

6. *Commission (Majority)*, 102.

7. *The State of Hawai'i Data Book 1993–1994: A Statistical Abstract* (Honolulu, HI: The Department of Business, Economic Development and Tourism, State of Hawai'i, 1994).

8. *Commission (Majority)*. Native Hawaiian activists have contested this source and many other published accounts of Hawaiian history by non–Native Hawaiians; see Trask, *From a Native Daughter*. For the relationship of Hawaiian history to Hawaiian identity see Jonathan Friedman, "The Past is the Future: History and the Politics of Identity," *American Anthropologist* 94 (1992): 837–59, and Marshall Sahlins, "Goodbye to Tristes Tropes: Ethnography in the Context of Modern World History," in *Assessing Cultural Anthropology*, ed. Robert Borofsky (New York: McGraw-Hill, 1994), 377–95.

9. H. Trask, "Lovely Hula Hands: Corporate Tourism and the Prostitution of Hawaiian Culture," in *From a Native Daughter*, 179–200.

10. Melody Kapilialoha MacKenzie, *Native Hawaiian Rights Handbook* (Honolulu, HI: Native Hawaiian Legal Corporation, 1991), 4.

11. Eric Wolf, *Europe and the People Without History* (Berkeley, CA: University of California Press, 1982), 258–59.

12. *Commission (Majority)*, 153; see also Stephenie Seto Levin, "The Overthrow of the *Kapu* System in Hawaii," *Journal of the Polynesian Society* 74 (1968): 402–30, and William Davenport, "The 'Hawaiian Cultural Revolution,'" *American Anthropologist* 71 (1969): 1–19.

13. MacKenzie, *Native Hawaiian Rights Handbook*, 5.

14. Ibid., 6.

15. Mari J. Masuda, "Law and Culture in the District Court of Honolulu, 1844–45: A Case Study of the Rise of Legal Consciousness," *The American Journal of Legal History* 32 (1988): 17–41.

16. Masuda, "Law and Culture."

17. MacKenzie, *Native Hawaiian Rights Handbook*, 6–9.

18. Maivan Clech Lam, "The Kuleana Act Revisited: The Survival of Traditional Hawaiian Commoner Rights in Land," *Washington Law Review* 64 (1989): 233–87.

19. Ibid., 266–67.

20. MacKenzie, *Native Hawaiian Rights Handbook*, 10.

21. Ibid., 11.

22. Native Hawaiians Study Commission, Vol. II, *Claims of Conscience: A Dissenting Study of the Culture, Needs and Concerns of Native Hawaiians* (Washington, DC: Department of the Interior, 1983), 70 (hereafter *Claims of Conscience*). An excellent historical portrayal of the overthrow is found in the film, *Act of War: The Overthrow of the Hawaiian Nation* (1983). For ordering information, contact Na Maka o ka 'Āina, General Delivery, Nā'ālehu, Hawai'i 96772, 808-929-9659.

23. *Claims of Conscience*, 70–79.

24. MacKenzie, *Native Hawaiian Rights Handbook*, 14.

25. Ramon Lopez-Reyes, "The Demise of the Hawaiian Kingdom: A Psychocultural Analysis and Moral Legacy—Something Lost, Something Owed," *Hawaii Bar Journal* 18 (1983): 3–23.

26. MacKenzie, *Native Hawaiian Rights Handbook*, 43.

27. S. James Anaya, "The Native Hawaiian People and International Human Rights Law: Toward a Remedy for Past and Continuing Wrongs," *Georgia Law Review* 28 (1994): 309–64.

28. Susan Faludi, "Broken Promise: How Everyone Got Hawaiians' Homelands Except the Hawaiians," *Wall Street Journal*, September 9, 1991, 1.

29. Ibid.

30. M. Trask, "Historical and Contemporary Hawaiian Self-Determination." In 1988, the passage of the Native Hawaiian Judicial Relief Act permitted Native Hawaiians to sue in state courts for trust violations, but only based on claims arising after 1989. Also, under the Act, courts are not permitted to award successful native plaintiffs either land or money, but must surrender the plaintiffs' award to the state agencies who are responsible for implementing the trust. The irony of this vicious cycle, which makes the very bureaucracies who have been responsible for the problem the solution to the problem, has not been lost on Native Hawaiians.

31. H. Trask, *From a Native Daughter*, 89.

32. M. Trask, "Historical and Contemporary Hawaiian Self-Determination."

33. Melody Kapilialoha MacKenzie, "The Lum Court and Native Hawaiian Rights," *University of Hawai'i Law Review* 14 (1992): 337–94.

34. *State of Hawaii v. Lono* (Oct. 1983), 3.

35. "Lono's Kualoa Park Camp Flattened," *Honolulu Star-Bulletin*, August 27, 1981, A7.

36. *State of Hawaii v. Lono*, Appendix A, 4.

37. *State of Hawaii v. Lono* (1983), 4–5.

38. *State of Hawaii v. Lono*, Memorandum Opinion, 2.

39. *Dedman v. Board of Land and Natural Resources et al*, 69 Haw. 255 (1987).

40. Jacob Kamhis, "Geothermal: Hot Issue," *Hawaii Magazine* (February 1991), 27.

41. Ibid., 28.

42. *Dedman*, 261.

43. *United States v. Mowatt*, 582 F.2d 1194 (1978).

44. Ibid., 1196.

45. "Navy Test Ground Returns to Hawai'i," *New York Times*, May 9, 1994, A12.

46. Richard H. Houghton III, "An Argument for Indian Status for Native Hawaiians: The Discovery of a Lost Tribe," *American Indian Law Review* 14 (1990): 1–55.

47. *Commission, (Majority)*.

48. *Claims of Conscience*, 8.

49. H. Trask, "Kupa'a 'Aina: Native Hawaiian Nationalism in Hawai'i," in *From a Native Daughter*, 87–109.

50. Anaya, "The Native Hawaiian People and International Human Rights Law."

51. See the film, *The Tribunal: Peoples' International Tribunal Hawai'i* (1993), for a Native Hawaiian perspective. Available from Na Maka o ka 'Aina, 3020 Kahaloa Drive, Honolulu, Hawai'i, 96822; for an anthropological interpretation, see Sally Engle Merry, "Legal Vernacularization and Ka Ho' okolokolonui Kanaka Maoli, the People's International Tribunal, Hawai'i 1993," *Polar: Journal of the Association of Political and Legal Anthropology* (1995), forthcoming.

52. S. J. Res. 19, 103d Cong., 1st Sess., 107 Stat. 1510 (1993).

53. "Having to Say You're Sorry," *New York Times Magazine*, November 28, 1993, 46.

54. H. Trask, *From a Native Daughter*, 99.

3

Segregation, Equality, and African Americans

I been 'buked and I been scorned. I'm gonna tell my Lord when I get home just how long you've been treating me wrong.[1]

When Mahalia Jackson sang the words of this traditional spiritual at the 1963 March on Washington, she was expressing African Americans' understanding of their position as the most systematically excluded group in U.S. history. The history of African Americans in America begins with a forced migration, as slaves, to this country. Both the numbers of African Americans brought here as slaves and the prejudice and discrimination they faced is unmatched by any other immigrant group.

While the common initial experience of slavery has great significance in understanding their exclusion, in fact, as local environmental conditions made slavery uneconomic in certain areas, and thus encouraged its abolition, the African-American experience began to diversify. As early as the colonial period, slaves became free individuals, and were subsequently granted citizenship and suffrage in some northern states. In the South, too, a class of free African Americans emerged, who, while being denied the privileges of citizenship, nevertheless developed, in many urban areas, cultures based on literacy and wealth.[2] Thus, regional and economic differences of the American continent influenced the nature and degree of African-American exclusion, and the development of African-American culture, shaping patterns of the interaction of African Americans and members of other racial groups in critically different ways.

Despite these differences, however, the weight of African Americans' historical experience has been one of systematic exclusion. The African-American response to this exclusion has been varied, but historically there has been a persistent effort to break the legal and extralegal barriers that have kept them out of the social, political, economic, religious, and cultural life of the nation.

THE DRED SCOTT CASE [*DRED SCOTT V. SANDFORD* 60 U.S. 393 (1857)]

The most explicit and infamous legal statement of African-American exclusion, and the attempt to overcome it, is the case of the slave, Dred Scott, which was decided by the Supreme Court in 1857. Dred Scott had been taken by his owner to live in Illinois and the Wisconsin Territory where, by an act of Congress, the 1820 Missouri Compromise, slavery was prohibited. Scott lived with his owner for five years on free soil, and then returned to Missouri, which was a slave state. On the basis of his having lived on free soil, in 1846, Scott and his supporters began a suit in state court suing for his freedom. Subsequently, during the 11 years of state and federal litigation, proponents of slavery raised the constitutionality of the Missouri Compromise as an issue. These people also challenged Dred Scott's ability to sue in federal court, raising the issue of all African Americans' right to be citizens of the United States.

The controversial case was argued twice in 1856 before the U.S. Supreme Court. Some evidence suggests that the justices were prepared to exercise judicial restraint and merely affirm the prior Missouri Supreme Court decision declaring Scott a slave. Justices from the slave states, however, led by Justice James Wayne of Georgia, decided to confront the slavery question squarely and supported a full opinion on the merits in which, by a 7–2 vote, the high court struck down the Missouri Compromise as unconstitutional and declared that Dred Scott had not won his freedom by residing in a free territory.[3] Even more critically, the justices stated that *any* person—free or slave—whose ancestors were born in Africa and sold into slavery, was not meant to be, and could never become, a citizen of the United States. The Court emphasized that a slave, such as Dred Scott, was "strictly property, to be used in subserviency to the interests, the convenience, or the will, of his owner" and "that a slave, the . . . property of a master, and possessing within himself no civil or political rights or capacities, cannot be a CITIZEN." The Court argued that since slaves were property, and the Constitution "was pledged" to protect property rights, setting a slave free would be a violation of the rights of his master and, thus, unconstitutional.

Chief Justice Taney began his majority opinion with a comparison of "the Indian races" and "negros [*sic*] of the African race," pointing up the differences. Indians, "although they were uncivilized, they were yet a free and independent people," and, as members of sovereign states, could become citizens, "negros," never. Claiming that "it is not the province of the court to decide upon the justice or injustice . . . of these laws," the Court held that even though free African Americans were citizens and could vote, where qualified, in several states—New Hampshire, New York, New Jersey, North Carolina, and Massachusetts—this did not entitle them to the rights and privileges of citizenship in the nation. Next, Taney argued directly on behalf of the rights of slaveholders as property owners and against the actions of Congress:

The Government of the United States had no right to interfere for any other purpose but that of protecting the rights of the owner, leaving it altogether with the several States to deal with this race, whether emancipated or not.

[T]he right of property in a slave is distinctly and expressly affirmed in the Constitution. The right to traffic in it, like an ordinary article of merchandise and property, was guarantied to the citizens of the United States

. . . the Government in express terms is pledged to protect it in all future time, if the slave escapes from his owner. This is done in plain words—too plain to be misunderstood. And no word can be found in the Constitution which gives Congress a greater power over slave property, or which entitles property of that kind to less protection than property of any other description . . . it is the opinion of the court that the act of Congress which prohibited a citizen from holding and owning property of this kind in the territory of the United States north of the line therein mentioned, is not warranted by the Constitution, and is therefore void; and that neither Dred Scott himself, nor any of his family, were made free by being carried into this territory; even if they had been carried there by the owner, with the intention of becoming a permanent resident.

The Dred Scott case demonstrates the sharply drawn legal and moral perspectives that divided not only the nation, but also the Court. Justices Curtis of Massachusetts and McLean of Ohio systematically rebutted the major points upon which the Court's opinion was based. They not only contended that persons of African descent could be citizens of the United States, but also stated that the Missouri Compromise was constitutional. Referring to earlier federal and state court opinions, the existence of free African-American citizens in many Northern states, and using moral arguments against slavery, Curtis and McLean rejected the arguments of the majority. While admitting the "infamous traffic in slaves" inherited from Great Britain, Justice McLean was more optimistic than the majority about man's ability to throw off "domestic relations [having their source] in so dark a ground." He pointed out that leading men in both the South and the North had hoped that slavery would gradually decline, a hope that was blocked by the increased value of slave labor in the cotton and sugar culture. McLean rejected the majority view that "a slave . . . (is the) same as a horse, or any other kind of property," arguing that, "A slave is not a mere chattel. He bears the impress of his Maker, and is amenable to the laws of God and man; and he is destined to an endless existence." Complementing McLean's moral argument that men of all races share a common humanity, Justice Curtis noted that the Constitution, in its opening declaration, refers not to the Caucasian race, but to "the people" of the United States. He, too, reminded the Court that free persons of African ancestry were citizens in many states, and that therefore slaves of African ancestry such as Dred Scott could indeed become citizens of the United States.

The Dred Scott decision is today often dismissed as no longer important, having been technically reversed by the Thirteenth, Fourteenth, and Fifteenth amendments to the Constitution following the Civil War. But this dismissal underestimates the historical significance of an opinion that established Supreme Court approval for the idea of African-American inferiority and exclusion from all civic rights, a fact of American life that continues to the present day. However dead the law in Dred Scott may be, the attitudes that supported it are very much alive.

HOPES DASHED: THE RISE OF JIM CROW

Despite the depth and persistence of these attitudes in American culture, the period after the Civil War, known as Reconstruction, witnessed some small possibilities for change. The passage of the Thirteenth, Fourteenth, and Fifteenth amendments did provide African Americans with a legal base from which to challenge their continued exclusion from American society. With the formal structure of laws maintaining slavery now banished, new terms of social relations between the races could perhaps develop. In this period much of the racial separatism was informal with a "strong reliance on custom." States avoided passing overtly discriminatory racial laws that would contravene the principle of legal equality established by emancipation. During Reconstruction there were even laws passed in some states that provided African Americans equal access to public facilities, although little, it is true, was done to enforce them. Where discrimination occurred it was often extralegal or even illegal and was not yet accompanied by the legal provision (*de jure*) of separate facilities for African Americans. Thus, the discrimination against African Americans had not hardened into the rigid, systematic, and comprehensive system of enforced separation of African Americans and whites known as Jim Crow.[4] While African-American exclusion, widely practiced in the North, was never as rigidly codified in law as in the South, it nevertheless proved intractable to significant change and, some have argued, was even more powerful in excluding African Americans from mainstream American society.

With the waning of this short period of Reconstruction, after the presidential election of 1876 African Americans became subject to a new, highly structured code of laws that both segregated them and discriminated against them in every area of political, economic, and social life. These "Jim Crow" laws affected African Americans (and, subsequently, in some communities, Asian Americans) from cradle to grave. These laws included: the use of literacy and "character" tests, as well as poll taxes and irregular hours for voter registration to keep African Americans from voting; exclusion of African-American children from the schools attended by white children; segregation of park facilities, health services, and mass transportation. Courts were racially segregated and pains were even taken to prohibit African Americans from swearing on Bibles used by whites.[5]

Several of these state segregation laws, as well as nongovernmental (private) action discriminating against African Americans in quasi-public facilities, such as theaters, were tested before the U.S. Supreme Court, which in an effort to mollify sentiments supporting African-American exclusion, found them constitutional. When, in July of 1890, the Louisiana legislature passed "An act to promote the comfort of passengers" requiring racial segregation in railway cars, a group of middle-class African Americans from New Orleans, alarmed at the growing number of segregation laws, formed the Citizens Committee to Test the Constitutionality of the Separate Car Law. This committee was part of an active African-American civil rights movement that, in 1890 alone, had held five national conventions. The New Orleans Committee, after an unsuccessful attempt to prevent the passage of the law by the Louisiana General Assembly, decided to test its constitutionality before the federal courts. The committee, with funds raised in the African-American community, hired Albion Tourgee, a white northern lawyer who had been active on behalf of former slaves during Reconstruction, to make a test case of Jim Crow.

It was arranged for Homer A. Plessy, a very light-skinned Louisiana African American, to purchase a train ticket and then to take a seat in the coach reserved for whites. (With the knowledge of the railway company which, concerned the law would prove expensive, was anxious for a test case.) When Plessy refused to comply with the conductor's request that he move to the car reserved for people of his race, he was arrested and charged with violation of the Louisiana railway car segregation statute. When Judge Ferguson of New Orleans ruled against Plessy, an appeal was made to the Supreme Court of the United States. By a 7–1 vote the high court turned back the claim made by Plessy that Jim Crow laws were unconstitutional. Rather, the justices established the now famous doctrine of "separate but equal," laying the foundation for a half century more of *de jure* segregation by race. Ironically, the Court's majority opinion upholding Jim Crow was authored by Justice Henry Brown from

Michigan while the sole dissent came from Justice John Harlan, a South-erner, a former slaveholder, "and at heart a conservative."[6]

The majority, as has always been the custom, spoke first:

Plessy v. Ferguson
163 U.S. 537 (1896)

The constitutionality of this act is attacked upon the ground that it conflicts both with the 13th Amendment of the Constitution, abolishing slavery, and the 14th Amendment, which prohibits certain restrictive legislation on the part of the states.

That it does not conflict with the 13th Amendment, which abolished slavery and involuntary servitude, except as a punishment for crime, is too clear for argument.

A statute which implies merely a legal distinction between the white and col-ored races—a distinction which is founded in the color of the two races, and which must always exist so long as white men are distinguished from the other race by color—has no tendency to destroy the legal equality of the two races, or re-establish a state of involuntary servitude.

By the 14th Amendment, all persons born or naturalized in the United States, and subject to the jurisdiction thereof, are made citizens of the United States and of the state wherein they reside; and the states are forbidden from making or enforcing any law which shall abridge the privileges or immunities of citizens of the United States, or shall deprive any person of life, liberty, or property without due process of law, or deny to any person within their jurisdiction the equal protection of the laws.

The object of the amendment was undoubtedly to enforce the absolute equality of the two races before the law, but in the nature of things it could not have been intended to abolish distinctions based upon color, or to enforce social, as distinguished from political, equality, or a commingling of the two races upon terms unsatisfactory to either. Laws permitting, and even requiring their sepa-ration in places where they are liable to be brought into contact do not necessarily imply the inferiority of either race to the other, and have been generally, if not universally, recognized as within the competency of the state legislatures in the exercise of their police power.

So far, then, as a conflict with the 14th Amendment is concerned, the case reduces itself to the question whether the statute of Louisiana is a reasonable regulation, and with respect to this there must necessarily be a large discretion on the part of the legislature. In determining the question of reasonableness it is at liberty to act with reference to the established usages, customs, and traditions of the people, and with a view to the promotion of their comfort, and the pres-ervation of the public peace and good order. Gauged by this standard, we cannot say that a law which authorizes or even requires the separation of the two races in public conveyances is unreasonable.

We consider the underlying fallacy of the plaintiff's argument to consist in the assumption that the enforced separation of the two races stamps the colored race with a badge of inferiority. It this be so, it is not by reason of anything found in the act, but solely because the colored race chooses to put that construction upon it. The argument necessarily assumes that if, as has been more than once the case, and is not unlikely to be so again, the colored race should become the dominant power in the state legislature, and should enact a law in precisely similar terms, it would thereby relegate the white race to an inferior position. We imagine that the white race, at least, would not acquiesce in this assumption. The argument also assumes that social prejudices may be overcome by legislation, and that equal rights cannot be secured to the negro except by an enforced commingling of the two races. We cannot accept this proposition. If the two races are to meet on terms of social equality, it must be the result of natural affinities, a mutual appreciation of each other's merits and a voluntary consent of individuals.... Legislation is powerless to eradicate racial instincts or to abolish distinctions based upon physical differences, and the attempt to do so can only result in accentuating the difficulties of the present situation. If the civil and political rights of both races be equal, one cannot be inferior to the other civilly or politically. If one race be inferior to the other socially, the Constitution of the United States cannot put them upon the same plane.

Two arguments made by Tourgee were dismissed by Justice Brown. To the claim that the Louisiana statute, by explicitly classifying people by race, robbed Plessy of a most valuable property—his near-white skin, and the reputation he traded on because of his previous ability to pass unchallenged in public accommodations—the Court stated that Plessy could not claim this loss of property since, "if he be a colored man . . . he is not lawfully entitled to the reputation of being a white man." In response to Tourgee's claim on behalf of Plessy that the Louisiana law violated Plessy's Thirteenth Amendment right to be free of the disabilities of servitude, Justice Brown caustically stated that this was "running the slavery argument into the ground."

Justice Harlan, in vigorous dissent, accepted Plessy's Thirteenth Amendment argument, as well as that based upon the Fourteenth Amendment's demand of equal protection. Unlike Justice Brown, who refused to acknowledge that government-mandated forced separation of the races stamped "the colored race with a badge of inferiority," Harlan asserted that the U.S. Constitution tolerated no racial classifications as it was "colorblind," and that segregated facilities did impose "a badge of . . . servitude," and thereby violated the Constitution:

In respect of civil rights, common to all citizens, the Constitution of the United States does not, I think, permit any public authority to know the race of those entitled to be protected in the enjoyment of such rights . . . such legislation as that here in question is inconsistent, not only with that equality of rights which pertains to citizenship, national and state, but with the personal liberty enjoyed by every one within the United States.

The 13th Amendment does not permit the withholding or the deprivation of any right necessarily inhering in freedom. It not only struck down the institution of slavery as previously existing in the United States, but it prevents the imposition of any burdens or disabilities that constitute badges of slavery or servitude. It decreed universal civil freedom in this country . . . the 14th Amendment . . . added greatly to the dignity and glory of American citizenship, and to the security of personal liberty. . . . These two amendments, if enforced according to their true intent and meaning, will protect all the civil rights that pertain to freedom and citizenship.

These notable additions to the fundamental law were welcomed by the friends of liberty throughout the world. They removed the race line from our governmental systems. They had, as this court has said, a common purpose, namely, to secure "to a race recently emancipated, a race that through many generations have been held in slavery, all the civil rights that the superior race enjoy." They declared, in legal effect, this court has further said, "that the law in the states shall be the same for the black as for the white; that all persons, whether colored or white, shall stand equal before the laws of the states, and, in regard to the colored race, for whose protection the amendment was primarily designed, that no discrimination shall be made against them by law because of their color." We also said: "The words of the amendment, it is true, are prohibitory, but they contain a necessary implication of a positive immunity, or right, most valuable to the colored race—the right to exemption from unfriendly legislation against them distinctively as colored—exemption from legal discriminations, implying inferiority in civil society, lessening the security of their enjoyment of the rights which others enjoy, and discriminations which are steps towards reducing them to the condition of a subject race."

It was said in argument that the statute of Louisiana does not discriminate against either race, but prescribes a rule applicable alike to white and colored citizens. But this argument does not meet the difficulty. Everyone knows that the statute in question had its origin in the purpose, not so much to exclude white persons from railroad cars occupied by blacks, as to exclude colored people from coaches occupied by or assigned to white persons. . . . No one would be so wanting in candor as to assert the contrary. The fundamental objection, therefore, to the statute, is that it interferes with the personal freedom of citizens. "Personal liberty," it has been well said, "consists in the power of locomotion, of changing situation, or removing one's person to whatsoever places one's own inclination may direct, without imprisonment or restraint, unless by due course of law." If a white man and a black man choose to occupy the same public conveyance on a public highway, it is their right to do so, and no government, proceeding alone on grounds of race, can prevent it without infringing the personal liberty of each.

If a state can prescribe as a rule of civil conduct, that whites and blacks shall not travel as passengers in the same railroad coach, why may it not so regulate the use of the streets of its cities and towns as to compel white citizens to keep on one side of the street and black citizens to keep on the other?

The white race deems itself to be the dominant race in this country. And so it is, in prestige, in achievements, in education, in wealth, and in power. So, I doubt not that it will continue to be for all time, if it remains true to its great heritage and holds fast to the principles of constitutional liberty. But in view of the Constitution, in the eye of the law, there is in this country no superior, dominant, ruling class of citizens. There is no caste here. Our Constitution is color-blind, and neither knows nor tolerates classes among citizens. In respect of civil rights, all citizens are equal before the law. The humblest is the peer of the most powerful. The law regards man as man, and takes no account of his surroundings or of his color when his civil rights as guaranteed by the supreme law of the land are involved. It is therefore to be regretted that this high tribunal, the final expositor of the fundamental law of the land, has reached the conclusion that it is competent for a state to regulate the enjoyment by citizens of their civil rights solely upon the basis of race.

In my opinion, the judgment this day rendered will, in time, prove to be quite as pernicious as the decision made by this tribunal in the *Dred Scott Case.* . . . The present decision, it may well be apprehended, will not stimulate aggressions, more or less brutal and irritating, upon the admitted rights of colored citizens, but will encourage the belief that it is possible, by means of state enactments, to defeat the beneficent purposes which the people of the United States had in view when they adopted the recent amendments of the Constitution, by one of which the blacks of this country were made citizens of the United States. . . . Sixty millions of whites are in no danger from the presence here of eight millions of blacks. The destinies of the two races in this country are indissolubly linked together, and the interests of both require that the common government of all shall not permit the seeds of race hate to be planted under the sanction of law. What can more certainly arouse race hate, what more certainly create and perpetuate a feeling of distrust between these races, than state enactments which in fact proceed on the ground that colored citizens are so inferior and degraded that they cannot be allowed to sit in public coaches occupied by white citizens?

I am of opinion that the statute of Louisiana is inconsistent with the personal liberty of citizens, white and black, in that state, and hostile to both the spirit and letter of the Constitution of the United States. If laws of like character should be enacted in the several states of the Union, the effect would be in the highest degree mischievous. Slavery as an institution tolerated by law would, it is true, have disappeared from our country, but there would remain a power in the states, by sinister legislation, to interfere with the full enjoyment of the blessings of freedom; to regulate civil rights, common to all citizens, upon the basis of race; and to place in a condition of legal inferiority a large body of American citizens, now constituting a part of the political community, called the people of the United States.

THE TWENTIETH CENTURY

African Americans have continued to challenge, in courts, the imposition of discriminatory laws and social practices that have kept them out of the institutions of American society. Along with political lobbying in Congress, in the twentieth century litigation has been a major path by which African Americans have sought redress and the legal changes that would outlaw their exclusion.

In the nineteenth century, African Americans had used litigation to press for their rights, often, as demonstrated by *Dred Scott*, *Plessy*, and other cases, with harsh results. But, for civil rights activists in the early twentieth century, imbued with democratic ideals, and with few alternatives, litigation still offered one hope, however dim, of holding Americans to the spirit of the Constitution. While courts, therefore, were a limited weapon in the battle against African-American exclusion, given the disenfranchisement of African Americans from the political process, African-American and white civil rights activists, some of whom by 1909 had incorporated into the National Association for the Advancement of Colored People (NAACP), had virtually no choice but to employ the strategy of litigation.

For the first half of the twentieth century a continuous battering at the barriers of segregation, led increasingly by African-American lawyers trained at Howard University Law School, was set in motion directed at discriminatory laws restricting access to voting, to housing, to transportation, to education, and against lynching. In the area of education, the initial strategy was directed toward equalizing school facilities for African-American and white children. However, by midcentury, when it became apparent that public education was a major route to success in American society, that the resources the states would use for African-American schools would never permit them to become equal, and finally, that segregated schools, in and of themselves, placed an unfair burden of inferiority on African-American children, the strategy changed to that of a wholesale attack on the "separate-but-equal doctrine" established in *Plessy*.

The confidence to pursue this more far-reaching, though risky, strategy grew out of factors which suggested that there was a changing climate regarding African-American exclusion in America. Above the Mason-Dixon line the Democratic Party increasingly saw political opportunity in attending to rights violations directed toward the growing numbers of urban-dwelling African Americans.[7] Some public officials acknowledged that widespread, government-supported racism in the United States undermined our political credibility with newly independent nations in Africa and Asia. The government's desire to expand markets and curb Soviet influence among these nations also made officials more amenable to the lowering of publicly supported barriers used to exclude African Americans. Thus, with the conclusion of World War II, under President Harry Truman's leadership, the Armed Forces were desegregated, discrimination in federal hiring practices was reduced, and the Federal Housing Authority (FHA) ended its ban on insuring racially mixed housing.[8] Truman called upon Congress to make lynching a federal offense, to end segregation on all interstate transportation, and to outlaw the poll tax.

During these years, the NAACP and other civil rights groups had been laying the foundation in a series of cases, largely involving graduate and professional education, from which to strike down the separate-but-equal doctrine that had been used as the legal basis for segregated schooling. In 1950, in *Sweatt v. Painter* (339 U.S. 629), the Supreme Court signaled a possible change in equal protection law, finding in that case that a segregated law school for African Americans could not provide them equal educational opportunities because it would be "missing those qualities which are incapable of objective measurement but make for greatness in a law school." Such a segregated law school, the Court said, deprived African Americans of Fourteenth Amendment equal protection of the law. Also giving hope that constitutional barriers to desegregation would not be long in coming down was the 1950 decision in *McLaurin v. Oklahoma* (339 U.S. 637). Like *Sweatt*, the case involved the right to education at a desegregated professional school; while not overturning *Plessy*, the Court held that the explicit segregation of African-American students in the classrooms, library, and dining facilities of a white public educational institution violated equal protection guarantees.

At about the same time as the *Sweatt* and *McLaurin* litigation, challenges were brought in several states, including Kansas, Delaware, Virginia, and South Carolina by African-American plaintiffs who argued that segregation was in and of itself discriminatory. All of these claims had been rejected by lower courts. Unlike *Sweatt* and *McLaurin* these cases struck at segregated schooling at the elementary and high school levels. This went more to the heart of American prejudice for two reasons: Clearly an order to desegregate American elementary and secondary schools would involve far greater numbers of students than the desegregation of professional or graduate schools; more pointedly, the creation of racially mixed elementary and high school environments implied a potential for social and sexual interaction that many whites found absolutely unacceptable. These combined school cases reached the Supreme Court on behalf of several plaintiffs, the first of whom was Linda Brown, an African-American student in Topeka, Kansas, who, because of a state law mandating segregated schools, had to walk over a mile to the African-American school, bypassing a whites-only school much nearer to her home.

The Supreme Court that first heard argument on these cases, in the 1952–1953 term, was a court divided by personality and judicial philosophy. Fifteen years after President Franklin D. Roosevelt's attempted court packing plan in which Roosevelt challenged the judicial interference of the Court in the economic recovery legislation of the Depression Era, the justices still had not resolved the role the Court should appropriately play in societal change. Liberals, who in the 1930s had been anxious to further their economic and social agenda through legislative action and who, then, rejected the antidemocratic, nonmajoritarian interference of federal courts, now saw the Court as an essential weapon against legislatures representing popular sentiment which favored the continuing, and to them, unconstitutional injustice of school segregation.

In addition to the philosophical differences among members of the Court, the ineffectual leadership of Chief Justice Fred Vinson further undermined the Court's ability to act conclusively on the school cases. The Court ended its first year of deliberation on *Brown* determined that the issue should be reargued in the new term. Here fate stepped in! A year of turmoil quickly dissipated when, after the death of Chief Justice Vinson, Earl Warren became the new head of the Court. He brought the Court to consensus, insisting that the justices confront the basic issue: "that the doctrine of separate-but-equal rested upon the concept of the inferiority of the colored race." Thus, Warren led the Court to its historical and unanimous decision that *Plessy* had been wrongly decided and that "separate but equal has no place in the field of public education."

Brown v. Board of Education
347 U.S. 483 (1954)

In each of the cases, minors of the Negro race, seek the aid of the courts in obtaining admission to the public schools of their community on a nonsegregated basis. In each instance, they had been denied admission to schools attended by white children under laws requiring or permitting segregation according to race. This segregation was alleged to deprive the plaintiffs of the equal protection of the laws under the Fourteenth Amendment.... [Courts] denied relief to the plaintiffs on the so-called "separate but equal" doctrine announced by this Court in *Plessy v. Ferguson.* Under that doctrine, equality of treatment is accorded when the races are provided substantially equal facilities, even though these facilities be separate.

The plaintiffs contend that segregated public schools are not "equal" and cannot be made "equal," and that hence they are deprived of the equal protection of the laws.

In approaching this problem, we cannot turn the clock back to 1868 when the Amendment was adopted, or even to 1896 when *Plessy v. Ferguson* was written. We must consider public education in the light of its full development and its present place in American life throughout the Nation. Only in this way can it be determined if segregation in public schools deprives these plaintiffs of the equal protection of the laws.

Today, education is perhaps the most important function of states and local governments. Compulsory school attendance laws and the great expenditures for education both demonstrate our recognition of the importance of education to our democratic society. It is required in the performance of our most basic public responsibilities, even service in the armed forces. It is the very foundation of good citizenship. Today it is a principal instrument in awakening the child to cultural values, in preparing him for later professional training, and in helping him to adjust normally to his environment. In these days, it is doubtful that any child may reasonably be expected to succeed in life if he is denied the opportunity of an education. Such an opportunity, where the state has undertaken to provide it, is a right which must be made available to all on equal terms.

We come then to the question presented: Does segregation of children in public schools solely on the basis of race, even though the physical facilities and other "tangible" factors may be equal, deprive the children of the minority group of equal educational opportunities? We believe that it does.

To separate [children in grade and high schools] from others of similar age and qualifications solely because of their race generates a feeling of inferiority as to their status in the community that may affect their hearts and minds in a way unlikely ever to be undone. The effect of this separation on their educational opportunities was well stated by a finding in the Kansas case by a court which nevertheless felt compelled to rule against the Negro plaintiffs:

> Segregation of white and colored children in public schools has a detrimental effect upon the colored children. The impact is greater when it has the sanction of the law; for the policy of separating the races is usually interpreted as denoting the inferiority of the negro group. A sense of inferiority affects the motivation of a child to learn. Segregation with the sanction of law, therefore, has a tendency to [retard] the educational and mental development of negro children and to deprive them of some of the benefits they would receive in a racial[ly] integrated school system.

Whatever may have been the extent of psychological knowledge at the time of *Plessy v. Ferguson,* this finding is amply supported by modern authority. Any language in *Plessy v. Ferguson* contrary to this finding is rejected.

We conclude that in the field of public education the doctrine of "separate but equal" has no place. Separate educational facilities are inherently unequal. Therefore, we hold that the plaintiffs and others similarly situated for whom the actions have been brought are, by reason of the segregation complained of, deprived of the equal protection of the laws guaranteed by the Fourteenth Amendment.

In the initial *Brown* decision the Court did not address the question of remedies, inviting instead, all the parties to the case to submit new memoranda on the question of how to implement desegregation of American schools. It was not until the following year, 1955, in *Brown II* [349 U.S. 294 (1955)], that the Court dealt with this problem. In this opinion, the Court was sensitive to "different local conditions"—the regional culture of the South—as well as the issue of class. It attempted to accommodate the potentially explosive repercussions of its decision by ordering desegregation (not integration) "with all deliberate speed," a decree that appears, from 40 years' hindsight, to have been a strategy of vague generalization. Today, legal historians and civil rights advocates debate the impact of the *Brown* decision on racial justice. Professor Gerald Rosenberg argues that, "there is little evidence that *Brown* helped produce positive change, [and] there is some evidence that it hardened resistance to civil rights among both elites and the white public."[9]

Civil rights lawyer Walter Dellinger refutes these conclusions, writing: "disparagement of *Brown*'s impact is seriously mistaken. . . . The clarion call of the Court's unanimous condemnation of racial segregation as incompatible with our deepest Constitutional principles was to play an indispensable role in the life of the South and the nation."[10] Yet other scholars, Derrick Bell and Harold Cruse among them, insist that the NAACP's strategy in shaping *Brown* reflected the ideals of a "black bourgeoisie" that overemphasized the symbolism of integration and failed to establish greater African-American administrative and intellectual control of integrated schools.[11]

The political response to *Brown* varied greatly. In the six border states and the District of Columbia, *Brown* appears to have promoted desegregation with the number of African-American children attending school with Caucasian children increasing after 1956. In the South, however, stalling and evasion of the desegregation order gave way to massive resistance. The Louisiana legislature, for example, in 1960–1961 alone, enacted 92 laws and resolutions to maintain segregated public schools.[12]

By the 1960s it was clear that Southern school districts were not going to follow through on the spirit of *Brown* without more specific action on the part of the elected branches of the federal government and more specific guidelines from the Supreme Court. Congress responded by enacting the 1964 Civil Rights Act which, in part, barred racial discrimination in schools. The attorney general was given authority under this landmark legislation to bring desegregation suits on behalf of students in segregated schools. The Act also permitted the federal government to withhold federal education aid from school districts that discriminated by race. A year later Congress passed into law the Elementary and Secondary Education Act (ESEA). This legislation provided financial incentives for desegregation.

The U.S. Supreme Court also expanded upon its earlier desegregation rulings and, in the 1971 case of *Swann v. Charlotte-Mecklenburg* (402 U.S. 1), made clear the obligation of local school districts to end state-sanctioned school segregation, if necessary by implementing plans that would result in substantially increasing the numbers of African-American students attending schools with whites. Toward this end, the Court specifically approved controversial methods such as bussing, gerrymandered school districts, and racial quotas to achieve school integration. Chief Justice Warren Burger conceded the necessity of such affirmative methods in a system that previously had been "deliberately constructed and maintained to enforce racial segregation."

While the Court's decisions put an end to legally sanctioned *de jure* segregation in Southern schools, it left *de facto* segregation in both the North and the South largely untouched. In both places, but particularly the North, the exclusion of African Americans had often relied upon subtle forms of discrimination rather than on legal statute. In the 1960s and 1970s, having defeated *de jure* segregation, civil rights groups moved on to attack this next barrier—the *de facto* segregation of schools, housing, and the workplace, testing the limits of courts' willingness to deal with this equally pernicious exclusion of African Americans from the opportunities afforded other Americans. While the Supreme Court has acknowledged the prevalence of *de facto* exclusion of African Americans, through the development of the "intent doctrine" it has resisted meeting, in full, demands for equal participation of African Americans in American society.

Thus, in *Keyes v. School District* [413 U.S. 189 (1973)], where there was a clear showing of intent on the part of the Denver School Board deliberately to segregate the schools by school construction, gerrymandered attendance zones, and excessive use of mobile classrooms, the Supreme Court placed the burden on the local school boards to implement plans resulting in integration. However, the Supreme Court has resisted ordering the amelioration of disparate impact such as *de facto* school segregation where clear evidence of intentional discrimination cannot be demonstrated.

Schools are the site of struggles over rights because of their powerful role in American society. Study after study demonstrates that success in adult life correlates with level of education. In different ways, how children learn in school and what they learn affects life chances. Thus, racial justice, members of the African-American community have argued, extends beyond general issues of school desegregation and integration to specific questions of curriculum. In early curriculum litigation, in a complicated 1970s educational language case brought against the school district of Ann Arbor, Michigan, African-American parents argued that educational agencies must take appropriate action to overcome language barriers that impede equal participation by its students in its instructional programs.[13] In *Martin Luther King Junior Elementary School Children et al. v. Ann Arbor School District Board* [473 F. Supp. 1371 (1979)], African-American plaintiffs drew upon a provision of a 1972 federal school bussing act to support their belief that school curricula must be adapted in ways that would acknowledge Black English, the language of home and community of many African-American children, a language whose syntax is distinct from that of standard English, and to take Black English into account when helping children read in standard English.

Judge Charles W. Joiner, of the U.S. District Court, was persuaded by the expert testimony of sociolinguists that the children spoke a language known as Black English that was different from standard English and did constitute a language barrier that impeded equal participation in instructional programs. Although media distortion and political backlash presented Joiner's decision as a mandate for the schools to teach Black

English, nothing could be further from the truth. In fact, *King* is a continuation of the legal doctrine established in the 1974 *Lau v. Nichols* case (see Chapter 11) and reaffirms the school's responsibility to "open(ing) the doors to the establishment by teaching the children to read in the standard English of the school, the commercial world, the arts, science and the professions." In *King*, Judge Joiner wrote:

> The issue before this court is whether the defendant School Board has violated Section 1703(f) of Title 20 of the United States Code.
>
> A major goal of American education . . . is to train young people to communicate both orally . . . and in writing . . . in the standard vernacular of society. The art of communication among the people of the country in all aspects of people's lives is a basic building block in the development of each individual.
>
> This case is not an effort on the part of the plaintiffs to require that they be taught "black English" or that their instruction throughout their schooling be in "black English," or that a dual language program be provided. . . . It is a straightforward effort to require the court to intervene on the children's behalf to require the defendant School District Board to take appropriate action to teach them to read in the standard English.
>
> [E]xperts . . . testified . . . that efforts to instruct the children in standard English by teachers who failed to appreciate that the children speak a dialect which is acceptable in the home and peer community can result in the children becoming ashamed of their language, and thus impede the learning process. In this respect, the black dialect appears to be different than the usual foreign language because a foreign language is not looked down on by the teachers.
>
> [B]lack children learn to be bilingual. They retain fluency in "black English" to maintain status in the community and they become fluent in standard English to succeed in the general society. They achieve in this way by learning to "code switch" from one to the other depending on the circumstances.

In a far more radical attack on school curriculum, beginning in the late 1980s educators and African-American parents in several American cities proposed "Black Only"—in some instances "Black Male Only"—schools, or schools within schools. Stating that "Most of black America's seven million school age youth are in trouble, particularly those in this nation's central cities," advocates argued the need for special programs with African-American teachers as mentors, an African-centered curriculum, extended hours, school uniforms, and Saturday classes.[14] Using such innovations, proponents hoped to improve the rate of academic success of African Americans in school.

Plans for African-American male-only schools went forward in several American cities in the early 1990s. Ultimately, however, most school boards backed away from the idea in the face of significant criticism or the possibility of lawsuits. Not surprisingly, for example, African American Dr. Kenneth Clark, whose social science research was cited in *Brown v. Board of Education,* spoke against "Black Only" schools saying that they negated everything that he and other civil rights activists fought for in the struggle to end *de jure* school segregation. Other scholars and citizens opposed this new form of segregated schools on the grounds that categorizing children according to race is destructive to the children and to society. These individuals proposed that schools continue to create truly multicultural curricula that can be taught to all students.

Detroit, Michigan, however, "desperate over the wasted lives of its young black men," decided to go ahead with its plan for male academies.[15] After pressure from the Latino community, among others, the school board said that the schools would be open to boys of all races although they would focus on African Americans. Continuing their justification for sex-segregated schools, officials cited the long history of other all-male educational institutions in the United States including military academies and parochial schools.

As soon as Detroit began admitting students for the new male-only academies, a lawsuit was brought by two African-American mothers on behalf of their daughters who, they alleged, were not eligible for the admissions lottery. The mothers contended that the academies' goals of "mastering emotions, maintaining relationships with family and community, accepting responsibility, developing self-esteem—are equally valuable and vital to *all* children" and that the Detroit school board had acknowledged an "equally urgent and unique crisis facing . . . female students."[16] Lawyers from the American Civil Liberties Union and the National Organization for Women Legal Defense and Education Fund arguing the case, *Garrett v. Board of Education of Detroit* [775 F. Supp. 1004 (1991)], challenged the legality of the schools, citing violations of the equal protection clause of the Fourteenth Amendment, Title IX of the Education Amendments of 1972 (requiring equal opportunity in public schools regardless of sex), the Michigan Constitution, and other state statutes. They asked for an injunction. Lawyers for Detroit's school board maintained that the schools could be permitted under the law and referred to Detroit's soaring high school dropout rate among boys.

United States District Court Judge George Woods heard the case and ruled that excluding girls from the new schools did violate the law. Woods acknowledged that while the school system may be failing African-American male students, and while there was "compelling need" to address the "crisis facing African-American males," these facts "fall short of demonstrating that excluding girls is substantially related to the achievement of the Board's objectives. The Board has proffered no evidence that the presence of girls in the classroom bears a substantial relationship to the difficulties facing urban males."[17] Judge Woods also concluded that "male academies improperly use gender as a 'proxy for other, more germane bases of classification,' in this instance, for 'at risk' students. Specifically, the gender-specific data presented in defense of the Academies ignores the fact that all children in the Detroit public schools face significant obstacles to success . . . the Board acknowledged a . . . crisis facing . . . female students. . . . Ignoring the plight of urban females institutionalizes inequality and perpetuates the myth that females are doing well in the current system."[18] He ordered all sides to meet and to work out a schedule under which girls would be admitted. This was done and, by 1995, the three schools at issue in the litigation—Marcus Garvey Academy, Paul Robeson Academy, and Malcolm X Academy—had an enrollment of approximately 20 to 25 percent girls.[19]

The plan to establish all-male, African-centered academies was, of course, an affirmative action program. Affirmative action has been generally defined as "government policies that directly or indirectly award jobs, admissions to [schools], and other social goods and resources to individuals on the basis of membership in designated protected groups, in order to compensate those groups for past discrimination caused by society as a whole."[20] Affirmative action plans to remedy the exclusion of African Americans—among others—from the major economic and educational institutions of the dominant culture raise difficult issues for courts, posing as they do the question of the constitutional permissibility of race-conscious programs that may involve the exclusion of Caucasians as a means of making way for African-American participation. The legitimacy of African-American demands for equal opportunity is borne out by the extensive data indicating persistent and significant gaps between African Americans and Caucasians in income, wealth, employment, education, housing, health, and other measures of well-being. These differences are a function of past and contemporary racial discrimination.[21]

American courts have tried to find their way through the thicket of competing interests by accepting those affirmative action plans initiated in response to an actual finding of discrimination, which do not negatively affect whites already in jobs, or which do not impose utterly inflexible racial quotas. Typical of the latter approach was the U.S. Supreme Court's complicated response in the 1978 case, *Regents of the University of California v. Bakke* (438 U.S. 265).

Alan Bakke, a white male, was denied admission to the medical school at the University of California at Davis in a year when 16 out of 100 places had been set aside for "disadvantaged" minority students. His grade point average and MCAT scores were higher than several of those students accepted under the medical school's affirmative action plan. Bakke challenged the school's program, arguing that it discriminated against him on account of his race. He argued that the quota provision violated the California constitution, Title VI of the 1964 U.S. Civil Rights Act (barring racial discrimination in the federal funding of public and private institutions), and the equal protection clause of the U.S. Constitution's Fourteenth Amendment. The university appealed to the U.S. Supreme Court after a California superior court, and the state's Supreme Court, ruled against the use of such quotas. *Bakke* generated unprecedented interest nationwide and dozens of organizations filed *amicus* briefs stating their views in opposition to, and in support of, affirmative action.

Justice Lewis F. Powell announced the Court's ruling in an opinion that was not signed by the other justices who, deeply divided over statutory and constitutional issues, in five additional opinions, offered their own concurring and dissenting interpretations of the legality of affirmative action plans. The Court's ruling upheld the possibility that affirmative action programs could be legal but it struck down the one used by the Davis campus because it involved a fixed quota. Powell rejected most of the university's arguments on behalf of affirmative action. He did agree, however, that an affirmative action plan that does not employ fixed quotas is permissible at a university because of the need to encourage academic freedom and a diverse student body, actions protected by the First Amendment:

The . . . goal asserted by petitioner is the attainment of a diverse student body. This clearly is a constitutionally permissible goal for an institution of higher education. Academic freedom, though not a specifically enumerated constitutional right, long has been viewed as a special concern of the First Amendment. The freedom of a university to make its own judgments as to education includes the selection of its student body. . . . Physicians serve a heterogeneous population. An otherwise qualified medical student with a particular background—whether it be ethnic, geographic, culturally advantaged or disadvantaged—may bring to a professional school of medicine experiences, outlooks, and ideas that enrich the training of its student body and better equip its graduates to render with understanding their vital service to humanity.

In contrast, Justice Brennan, joined by Blackmun, Marshall, and White, contended that racial quotas are constitutionally permissible remedies for past discrimination. Brennan argued that neither the Constitution nor Title VI prohibited government from taking race into account "when it acts not to demean or insult any racial group, but to remedy disadvantages cast on minorities by past racial prejudice." Referring directly to the fact that Justice Harlan's opinion in *Plessy* was a dissent, Brennan wrote, "no decision of this Court has ever adopted the proposition that the Constitution must be colorblind."

A third bloc, led by Justice Stevens, avoided discussion of the constitutional question, maintaining that a statutory analysis was sufficient. Stevens argued that the medical school's quota plan was barred by "the plain language of the statute (Title VI). . . . A different result cannot be justified unless that language misstates the actual intent of the Congress that enacted the statute." Proponents of Title VI, according to Stevens, "assumed that the Constitution itself required a colorblind standard on the part of government. . . ." Unlike Brennan, Justice Stevens did not acknowledge that the Congress had, subsequent to enacting Title VI, passed affirmative action legislation that provided for racially conscious programs.

The *Bakke* case was much watched and discussed. Because, however, the decision only involved racial quotas in admissions to state-supported universities, and because the Supreme Court was so divided in its views, *Bakke* did not provide a definitive judicial statement on the legality of other affirmative action programs. Since 1978 the U.S. Supreme Court has issued a considerable number of additional opinions on affirmative action and so-called reverse discrimination, most of them having to do with employment and the workplace, rather than education. Among these decisions are *United Steelworkers v. Weber* [443 U.S. 193 (1979)]; *Fullilove v. Klutznick* [448 U.S. 448 (1980)]; *Firefighters v. Stotts* [467 U.S. 561 (1984)]; *Richmond v. Croson* [488 U.S. 469 (1989)]; and *Metro Broadcasting v. FCC* [110 S. Ct. 2997 (1990)]. In these decisions, in addition to approving affirmative action targets and plans that do not negatively affect Caucasians already in jobs or that impose completely fixed quotas, the Supreme Court showed particular deference to affirmative action plans crafted by Congress as compared with racially conscious programs established by state and local governments (unless the latter are designed to redress proven discrimination).

During, and for some years after, the 1960s Civil Rights movement, Congress supported affirmative action and enacted compensatory programs as a means of addressing racial injustice. Affirmative action, however, has always been controversial. In the 1980s and, increasingly, in the 1990s, conservative politicians questioned the legitimacy and efficacy of such programs. The changing social and political climate in the United States, most starkly expressed by the election of conservative Republicans in local, state, and congressional elections in November of 1994, encouraged more officials to go beyond questioning and to repudiate preference programs. Congress, for the first time in decades completely controlled by the Republican party, had the opportunity to make affirmative action a major agenda item. In doing so, opponents of affirmative action argued that preference plans were unfair and unequitable, and that they benefitted people on the basis of membership in a group rather than according to individual achievement. Opponents also maintained that affirmative action "was meant to be a temporary measure and not a way of permanently allocating . . . resource(s)."[22] Those supporting affirmative action, however, recalled the irony that in 1883, *only* eighteen years after the end of slavery, in the *Civil Rights Cases,* the justices of the U.S. Supreme Court wrote: "When a man has emerged from slavery, and by the aid of beneficent legislation has shaken off the inseparable concomitants of that state, there must be some stage in the process of his elevation when he takes the rank of a mere citizen, and ceases to be the special favorite of the laws."[23]

The question of whether affirmative action creates favorites under the law arose again in a 1995 case involving the awarding of federal construction contracts. In this new case, *Adarand v. Pena* [63 U.S.L.W. 4523 (June 12, 1995)], the Court majority, reflecting its increasingly conservative stance on certain social policy issues, withdrew judicial deference for federally mandated affirmative action programs. Justice Sandra Day O'Connor's opinion for the Court calls for the use of a strict judicial scrutiny test in which affirmative action programs will be considered constitutional only if narrowly tailored to accomplish a compelling government interest. While this standard is difficult to meet, the justices did stop short of declaring all government-mandated affirmative action programs to be in violation of equal protection guarantees. Justices Scalia and Thomas, however, argued that affirmative action programs can never be constitutionally justified.

Perhaps more than for any other group, the law has been instrumental in defining the place of African Americans in American society. The Constitution of the United States was the legal source of the enslavement and subsequent exclusion of African Americans from the mainstream of American society and culture for 70 years. But that same document, with its post–Civil War amendments has also provided the foundation of a civil rights litigation strategy aimed at breaking the barriers of African-American exclusion. In spite of the many legal victories, however, America has not fully come to terms with the legacy of slavery and racism. As the United States enters the twenty-first century, important issues stemming from the historic exclusion of African Americans, among them affirmative action, issues of political representation and electoral districts, and the persistence of race-segregated schools, will be debated by lawmakers and ruled upon by judges.

Moreover, important questions remain about the role of law. It is not yet clear to what extent law can modify dominant culture behavior and attitudes so that the extralegal forces that promote African-American exclusion can be overcome. As the 1990s debate over affirmative action so pointedly demonstrates, American willingness to use law not merely to end segregation, but to promote a truly equal status of African Americans within the larger society, remains an open question. This raises the possibility, articulated by African-American law professor Derrick Bell— among others—that the African-American civil rights movement has relied too much on "the leaky boat of litigation."[24] In contrast, not ready to abandon his faith in the law as a weapon in the fight for racial and economic justice, political scientist H. N. Hirsch suggests that we not jettison the law, but rather seek new ways to use it.[25]

NOTES

1. Mahalia Jackson, *Movin' on Up* (New York: Avon, 1966), 198.

2. Arnold Taylor, *Travail and Triumph: Black Life and Culture in the South Since the Civil War* (Westport, CT: Greenwood Press, 1976), 186.

3. See "Scott v. Sandford," in *The Oxford Companion to the Supreme Court of the United States,* ed. Kermit Hall (New York: Oxford University Press, 1992).

4. George M. Fredrickson, *White Supremacy: A Comparative Study in American and South African History* (New York: Oxford University Press, 1981), 261.

5. Taylor, *Travail and Triumph,* 40–41.

6. John A. Garraty, *Quarrels That Have Shaped the Constitution* (New York: Harper and Row, 1962), 156.

7. Edward G. Carmines and James A. Stimson, *Issue Evolution: Race and the Transformation of American Politics* (Princeton, NJ: Princeton University Press, 1989), chapter 2.

8. Richard Kluger, *Simple Justice: The History of Brown v. Board of Education and Black America's Struggle for Equality* (New York: Random House, 1975), 255.

9. Gerald N. Rosenberg, *The Hollow Hope: Can Courts Bring About Social Change?* (Chicago: University of Chicago Press, 1991), 155.

10. Walter Dellinger, "A White Southerner Remembers *Brown,*" *Extensions* (Fall 1994): 5.

11. H. N. Hirsch, "Race and Class, Law and Politics," *Boston University Law Review* 69 (March 1989): 457, 458–59.

12. Data on border and southern states' response may be found in Rosenberg, *The Hollow Hope,* 50–54, 79.

13. For an excellent general reference to various aspects of the case, see John Chambers, Jr., ed., *Black English: Educational Equity and the Law* (Ann Arbor, MI: Karoma, 1983).

14. C. R. Gibbs, "Project 2000: Why Black Men Should Teach Black Boys," *Dollars & Sense* (February/March 1991): 19.

15. Isabel Wilkerson, "To Save Its Men, Detroit Plans Boys-Only Schools," *New York Times,* August 14, 1991, 1.

16. ACLU Letter to Members (September 27, 1991), 1–2.

17. *Garrett v. The Board of Education of Detroit,* 775 F. Supp. 1004, 1007 (E.D.Mich. 1991).

18. Ibid. at 1007.

19. Telephone interview (March 30, 1995) with Mr. Harold Ellis, Executive Assistant to the Detroit Superintendent of Schools.

20. Hall, *The Oxford Companion to the Supreme Court of the United States,* 18.

21. See, e.g., Andrew Hacker, *Two Nations* (New York: Charles Scribner's, 1992). Also, U.S. Congress, *Report of the Federal Glass Ceiling Commission* (March 1995).

22. Richard Bernstein, "Moves Under Way in California to Overturn Higher Education's Affirmative Action Policy," *New York Times,* January 25, 1995, B7.

23. *Civil Rights Cases*, 3 S. Ct. 18, 31(1883).

24. Derrick Bell, *And We Are Not Saved: The Elusive Quest for Racial Justice* (New York: Basic Books, 1987), 71.

25. Hirsch, "Race and Class, Law and Politics," 464–66.

4

100 Percent American: Who Qualifies in a National Emergency? Japanese Americans and the Law

The tolerance, appreciation, and legitimization of cultural differences varies with the historical period. In times of war, rights accorded cultural minorities often become restricted. In the United States this issue was clearly raised in the experiences of the Japanese Americans during World War II. The wartime experiences of Japanese Americans, put under curfew and forcibly evacuated to detention camps, demonstrate the extent to which officials were prepared to go to protect the national security from what many in the government perceived as a dire threat from a portion of the citizenry within its own borders. Upwards of 120,000 Japanese Americans, 70,000 of whom were American citizens, and the rest of whom were resident aliens, were imprisoned for several years during World War II.

By 1941, relations between Japan and the United States had deteriorated, strained by Japan's expansionist policies toward China and Southeast Asia. On December 7 the Japanese attacked the American naval base at Pearl Harbor, Hawai'i. The next day the United States declared war on Japan and several days later entered the European war against Fascist Germany and Italy.

In response to Pearl Harbor, and reflecting a long-standing antagonism toward Asians in the western United States, popular and official sentiment pressed for action to be taken against the perceived threat of sabotage and espionage posed by Americans of Japanese ancestry, including Japanese American citizens, on the West Coast.

Two months later, in February 1942, President Roosevelt announced Executive Order No. 9066. This executive act authorized the secretary of war "to prescribe military areas ... from which any or all persons may be excluded, and . . . subject[ed] to whatever restrictions the Secretary of War . . . may impose." In language that created a smokescreen for the government's actions, the secretary of war was further authorized to provide for residents excluded from restricted areas "such transportation, food, shelter, and other accommodations as may be necessary" to implement the order. President Roosevelt's justification for this measure rested on the assertion that "the successful prosecution of the war requires every possible protection against espionage and . . . sabotage."

Lt. Gen. J. L. DeWitt, Military Commander of the Western Defense Command, became the central figure in implementing the Executive Order with regard to imposing a curfew and evacuating, relocating, and interning Americans of Japanese ancestry from the Pacific Coast of the United States, which he believed was especially vulnerable to acts of espionage and to attack because of its geographical location. Under Executive Order 9066, DeWitt was given authority to "provide for the removal from designated areas of persons whose removal is necessary in the interests of national security" and for their relocation, maintenance, and supervision. In March 1942, Congress enacted legislation ratifying this presidential order and imposing criminal sanctions on those who would not comply.

The attack on Pearl Harbor was the catalyst for transforming long-standing antagonism, even hatred, of the Japanese by whites living on the West Coast into new measures of legally sanctioned discrimination. Legally approved discrimination against Asian immigrants and Asian Americans, however, stretched back into the nineteenth century and was never solely the product of attitudes on the West Coast. Indeed, in spirit and often in wording, legal disabilities applied to Asian immigrants drew upon colonial and early Republic-era laws intended to limit the political and social rights of Native Americans and African Americans. One of the earliest acts of Congress, for example, The 1790 Naturalization Act, restricted American citizenship to "a free white person." This eighteenth-century legislation—elaborated upon by the Naturalization Act of 1870—continued to be an integral part of national policy against the naturalization of persons of Asian ancestry until the 1952 McCarran-Walter Act.[1]

Various nineteenth-century state laws singled out Asians in other ways. Legislation prohibited Asian immigrants and Asian Americans from testifying against a white person, purchasing land, or marrying a Caucasian. Asian heritage defendants were treated more harshly in criminal courts.[2] The national Homestead Act of 1862 tied eligibility for land to citizenship which, thus, excluded Asian immigrants. And, in 1882, the desire to limit labor competition from Chinese workers and to insulate American society from new cultural influences led Congress to enact draconian anti-Asian legislation. Through the 1882 Chinese Exclusion

Act, the federal government barred all Chinese laborers from entering the United States for ten years, specifically prohibited the naturalization of Chinese in the United States for citizenship while requiring them to carry identity papers, and denied entry to the United States to the wives of Chinese laborers already in the country.[3]

Exclusion legislation was extended in the 1917 Immigration Act. In this statute Congress enumerated more than 30 classes of people who were prohibited from entering the United States including those who were residents of the geographic area designated the Asiatic Barred Zone (India, Afghanistan, Burma, Thailand, most of the Polynesian islands, the area then known as Indochina, Indonesia, Malaysia, and the Asiatic parts of Russia).[4] Exclusion legislation applicable to Japanese was enacted in the Immigration Restriction Act of 1924.[5] The rationale for barring Asian peoples drew upon the belief that they were unwilling to assimilate and that Asians were willing to work for low wages. Americans did not stop to consider how American xenophobia, antimiscegenation and school segregation laws directed toward Asians, and court decisions preventing Asian naturalization prevented assimilation.[6]

At the time of the bombing of Pearl Harbor, two groups of people of Japanese ancestry lived in the United States. The first consisted of resident aliens who had qualified as legal immigrants prior to the restrictive 1924 Immigration Act. A second group included Japanese Americans who were citizens because they had been born in the United States. In implementing Executive Order 9066, Lieutenant General DeWitt officially named "all persons of Japanese ancestry, both alien and non-alien" as the subject of his security measures. The discriminatory nature of these orders is revealed in the fact that they applied to Japanese heritage American citizens solely on the basis of their identity and that *no* incidents of espionage or sabotage in the months prior to these orders involved Japanese resident aliens. Indeed, both the Federal Bureau of Investigation (FBI) and the Federal Communications Commission (FCC) stated that no such security threat existed and that the military measures proposed by DeWitt were unnecessary. DeWitt, however, argued otherwise in a February 1942 report to the secretary of war: "The Japanese race is an enemy race and while many second and third generation Japanese born on United States soil, possessed of United States citizenship, have become "Americanized," the racial strains are undiluted." DeWitt concluded his observations with an extraordinary act of reasoning: "The very fact that no [Japanese American] sabotage has taken place to date is a disturbing and confirming indication that such action will be taken."[7]

The discriminatory treatment of Japanese Americans is further underscored by contrasting their treatment with that of German and Italian American citizens and aliens living in the United States at the outbreak of the war. While some German and Italian Americans and aliens were evacuated and imprisoned, there was no systematic internment *by group* of German or Italian Americans. German and Italian Americans subject to evacuation or internment, unlike Japanese Americans, were nearly all afforded prompt loyalty hearings. By late 1942, when most Japanese Americans on the West Coast were beginning a three-year incarceration, German and Italian Americans had benefitted from loyalty proceedings and were free to live where they pleased. The contrasting treatment is all the more remarkable in light of organized pro-German rallies in the late 1930s, the discovery of several German spy rings at the beginning of the war, and reports by the U.S. government that the Nazis conducted "devastating naval warfare . . . along the East Coast" perhaps with aid from people on shore.[8] Despite these facts, the wartime curfew, evacuation, and internment measures as they targeted an entire community on the basis of racial identity fell only on Japanese Americans and resident alien Japanese.

These measures did not go unchallenged. Between 1942 and 1944, four legal appeals testing the constitutionality of the military's regulations as they applied to Japanese Americans and aliens were initiated and reached the U.S. Supreme Court. In the first case to be heard by the Court, *Hirabayashi v. United States* (1943), Japanese American plaintiffs challenged the legality of both the curfew and the evacuation orders. The justices of the Supreme Court avoided the issue of evacuation and addressed only the question of curfew orders, unanimously upholding them. The Court did not question the government's assertion that Japanese Americans maintained their attachment to Japan or that they posed a serious security threat. The justices reasoned that war powers were sufficiently broad to justify the government's actions. On the same day the Court also upheld curfew regulations in *Yasui v. United States* (1943). Six months later a divided court upheld the exclusion order challenged in *Korematsu v. United States* (1944), while refusing to consider the legality of detention. In *Korematsu*, Justice Black wrote, "hardships are a part of war . . . and . . . all citizens . . . feel the impact of war in greater or lesser measure." With these words Black—otherwise a noted civil libertarian—expressed the willingness of the Court, and the country, to impose this burden exclusively on those of Japanese ancestry despite undisputed findings that greater security risks existed within the German and Italian communities in the United States.

Hirabayashi v. United States
320 U.S. 81 (1943)

Mr. Chief Justice Stone delivered the opinion of the Court.

Appellant, an American citizen of Japanese ancestry, was convicted in the district court of violating the Act of Congress of March 21, 1942, which makes it a misdemeanor knowingly to disregard restrictions made applicable by a military commander to persons in a military area prescribed by him as such, all as authorized by an Executive Order of the President.

The questions for our decision are whether the particular restriction violated, namely that all persons of Japanese ancestry residing in such an area be within their place of residence daily between the hours of 8:00 P.M. and 6:00 A.M., was adopted by the military commander in the exercise of an unconstitutional delegation by Congress of its legislative power, and whether the restriction unconstitutionally discriminated between citizens of Japanese ancestry and those of other ancestries in violation of the Fifth Amendment.

The indictment is in two counts. The second charges that appellant, being a person of Japanese ancestry, had on a specified date, contrary to a restriction promulgated by the military commander . . . failed to remain in his place of residence in the designated military area between the hours of 8:00 o'clock P.M. and 6:00 A.M. The first count charges that appellant, on May 11 and 12, 1942, had, contrary to a Civilian Exclusion Order . . . failed to report to the Civil Control Station within the designated area, it appearing that appellant's required presence there was a preliminary step to the exclusion from that area of persons of Japanese ancestry.

[A]ppellant asserted that the indictment should be dismissed because he was an American citizen who had never been a subject of and had never borne allegiance to the Empire of Japan, and also because the Act of March 21, 1942, was an unconstitutional delegation of Congressional power. On the trial to a jury it appeared that the appellant was born in Seattle in 1918, of Japanese parents who had come from Japan to the United States, and who had never afterward returned to Japan; that he was educated in the Washington public schools and at the time of his arrest was a senior in the University of Washington; that he had never been in Japan or had any association with Japanese residing there.

The evidence showed that appellant had failed to report to the Civil Control Station on May 11 or May 12, 1942, as directed, to register for evacuation from the military area. He admitted failure to do so, and stated it had at all times been his belief that he would be waiving his rights as an American citizen by so doing.

We conclude that it was within the constitutional power of Congress and the executive arm of the Government to prescribe this curfew order for the period under consideration and that its promulgation by the military commander involved no unlawful delegation of legislative power.

The war power of the national government is "the power to wage war successfully." It extends to every matter and activity so related to war as substantially to affect its conduct and progress. The power is not restricted to the winning of victories in the field and the repulse of enemy forces. It embraces every phase of the national defense, including the protection of war materials and the members of the armed forces from injury and from the dangers which attend the rise, prosecution and progress of war.

That reasonably prudent men charged with the responsibility of our national defense had ample ground for concluding that they must face the danger of invasion, take measures against it, and in making the choice of measures consider our internal situation, cannot be doubted.

As the curfew was made applicable to citizens residing in the area only if they were of Japanese ancestry, our inquiry must be whether in the light of all the facts and circumstances there was any substantial basis for the conclusion, in which Congress and the military commander united, that the curfew as applied was a protective measure necessary to meet the threat of sabotage and espionage which would substantially affect the war effort and which might reasonably be expected to aid a threatened enemy invasion. The alternative which appellant insists must be accepted is for the military authorities to impose the curfew on all citizens within the military area, or on none. In a case of threatened danger requiring prompt action, it is a choice between inflicting obviously needless hardship on the many, or sitting passive and unresisting in the presence of the threat. We think that constitutional government, in time of war, is not so powerless and does not compel so hard a choice if those charged with the responsibility of our national defense have reasonable ground for believing that the threat is real.

When the orders were promulgated there was a vast concentration, within Military Areas Nos. 1 and 2, of installations and facilities for the production of military equipment, especially ships and airplanes. Important Army and Navy bases were located in California and Washington. Approximately one-fourth of the total value of the major aircraft contracts then let by Government procurement officers were to be performed in the State of California. California ranked second, and Washington fifth, of all the states of the Union with respect to the value of shipbuilding contracts to be performed.

At a time of threatened Japanese attack upon this country, the nature of our inhabitants' attachments to the Japanese enemy was consequently a matter of grave concern. Of the 126,000 persons of Japanese descent in the United States, citizens and non-citizens, approximately 112,000 resided in California, Oregon and Washington at the time of the adoption of the military regulations. Of these approximately two-thirds are citizens because born in the United States. Not only did the great majority of such persons reside within the Pacific Coast states but they were concentrated in or near three of the large cities, Seattle, Portland and Los Angeles, all in Military Area No. 1.

There is support for the view that social, economic and political conditions which have prevailed since the close of the last century, when the Japanese began to come to this country in substantial numbers, have intensified their solidarity and have in large measure prevented their assimilation as an integral part of the white population.

In addition, large numbers of children of Japanese parentage are sent to Japanese language schools outside the regular hours of public schools in the locality. Some of these schools are generally believed to be sources of Japanese nationalistic propaganda, cultivating allegiance to Japan. Considerable numbers, estimated to be approximately 10,000, of American-born children of Japanese parentage have been sent to Japan for all or a part of their education.

Congress and the Executive, including the military commander, could have attributed special significance, in its bearing on the loyalties of persons of Japanese descent, to the maintenance by Japan of its system of dual citizenship. Children born in the United States of alien Japanese parents, and especially those children born before December 1, 1924, are under many circumstances deemed, by Japanese law, to be citizens of Japan.

The large number of resident alien Japanese, approximately one-third of all Japanese inhabitants of the country, are of mature years and occupy positions of influence in Japanese communities. The association of influential Japanese residents with Japanese Consulates has been deemed a ready means for the dissemination of propaganda and for the maintenance of the influence of the Japanese Government with the Japanese population in this country.

As a result of all these conditions affecting the life of the Japanese, both aliens and citizens, in the Pacific Coast area, there has been relatively little social intercourse between them and the white population. The restrictions, both practical and legal, affecting the privileges and opportunities afforded to persons of Japanese extraction residing in the United States, have been sources of irritation and may well have tended to increase their isolation, and in many instances their attachments to Japan and its institutions.

Appellant does not deny that, given the danger, a curfew was an appropriate measure against sabotage.

But appellant insists that the exercise of the power is inappropriate and unconstitutional because it discriminates against citizens of Japanese ancestry, in violation of the Fifth Amendment.

Distinctions between citizens solely because of their ancestry are by their very nature odious to a free people whose institutions are founded upon the doctrine of equality. For that reason, legislative classification or discriminations based on race alone has often been held to be a denial of equal protection. We may assume that these considerations would be controlling here were it not for the fact that the danger of espionage and sabotage, in time of war and of threatened invasion, calls upon the military authorities to scrutinize every relevant fact bearing on the loyalty of populations in the danger areas. Because racial discriminations are in most circumstances irrelevant and therefore prohibited, it by no means follows that, in dealing with the perils of war, Congress and the Executive are wholly precluded from taking into account those facts and circumstances which are relevant to measures for our national defense and for the successful prosecution of the war, and which may in fact place citizens of one ancestry in a different category from others. . . . The adoption by Government in the crisis of war and of threatened invasion, of measures for the public safety, based upon the recognition of facts and circumstances which indicate that a group of one national extraction may menace that safety more than others, is not wholly beyond the limits of the Constitution and is not to be condemned merely because in other and in most circumstances racial distinctions are irrelevant. . . . We cannot close our eyes to the fact, demonstrated by experience, that in time of war residents having ethnic affiliations with an invading enemy may be a greater source of danger than those of a different ancestry. Nor can we deny that Congress, and the military authorities acting with its authorization, have constitutional power to appraise the danger in the light of facts of public notoriety. In this case it is enough that circumstances within the knowledge of those charged with the responsibility for maintaining the national defense afforded a rational basis for the decision which they made. Whether we would have made it is irrelevant.

Though the opinion of the Court, which employed a rational relation test, was ultimately unanimous, in the preliminary voting Justice Murphy had dissented. Under strong pressure from Justice Frankfurter, Murphy agreed to change his vote and to side with the majority.[9] He wrote a concurring opinion, however, which barely veiled his distaste for the court's holding:

It does not follow, however, that the broad guarantees of the Bill of Rights and other provisions of the Constitution protecting essential liberties are suspended by the mere existence of a state of war. It has been frequently stated and recognized by this Court that the war power, like the other great substantive powers of government, is subject to the limitations of the Constitution.

Distinctions based on color and ancestry are utterly inconsistent with our traditions and ideals. They are at variance with the principles for which we are now waging war. We cannot close our eyes to the fact that for centuries the Old World has been torn by racial and religious conflicts and has suffered the worst kind of anguish because of inequality of treatment for different groups. There was one law for one and a different law for another. Nothing is written more firmly into our law than the compact of the Plymouth voyagers to have just and equal law. To say that any group cannot be assimilated is to admit that the great American experiment has failed, that our way of life has failed when confronted with the normal attachment of certain groups to the lands of their forefathers. As a nation we embrace many groups, some of them among the oldest settlements in our midst, which have isolated themselves for religious and cultural reasons.

Today is the first time, so far as I am aware, that we have sustained a substantial restriction of the personal liberty of citizens of the United States based upon the accident of race or ancestry. Under the curfew order here challenged no less than 70,000 American citizens have been placed under a special ban and deprived of their liberty because of their particular racial inheritance. In this sense it bears a melancholy resemblance to the treatment accorded to members of the Jewish race in Germany and in other parts of Europe. The result is the creation in this country of two classes of citizens for the purposes of a critical and perilous hour—to sanction discrimination between groups of United States citizens on the basis of ancestry. In my opinion this goes to the very brink of constitutional power.

Except under conditions of great emergency a regulation of this kind applicable solely to citizens of a particular racial extraction would not be regarded as in accord with the requirement of due process of law contained in the Fifth Amendment. We have consistently held that attempts to apply regulatory action to particular groups solely on the basis of racial distinction or classification is not in accordance with due process of law as prescribed by the Fifth and Fourteenth Amendments.

In the *Hirabayashi* case, the Court sidestepped the issue of the exclusion of Japanese Americans from their residential communities, now designated military areas. The constitutionality of these orders was finally taken up in *Korematsu v. United States*. In its decision the justices established that the use of racial classifications by government is suspect and, when legally challenged, must be subject to "the most rigid" judicial scrutiny. Employing this standard, a majority of the high court's members nevertheless concluded that "pressing public necessity" justified the racial classification used to evacuate Japanese Americans from their homes. Justice Black delivered the opinion of the majority:

Korematsu v. United States
323 U.S. 214 (1944)

The petitioner, an American of Japanese descent, was convicted in a federal district court for remaining in San Leandro, California, a "Military Area," contrary to Civilian Exclusion Order No. 34 . . . of the U.S. Army, which directed that after May 9, 1942, all persons of Japanese ancestry should be excluded from that area. No question was raised as to petitioner's loyalty to the United States.

It should be noted, to begin with, that all legal restrictions which curtail the civil rights of a single racial group are immediately suspect. That is not to say that all restrictions are unconstitutional. It is to say that courts must subject them to the most rigid scrutiny. Pressing public necessity may sometimes justify the existence of such restrictions; racial antagonism never can.

In the light of the principles we announced in the *Hirabayashi* case, we are unable to conclude that it was beyond the war power of Congress and the Executive to exclude those of Japanese ancestry from the West Coast war area at the time they did. . . . [E]xclusion from a threatened area, no less than curfew, has a definite and close relationship to the prevention of espionage and sabotage.

In this case the petitioner challenges the assumptions upon which we rested our conclusions in the *Hirabayashi* case. He also urges that by May 1942, when Order No. 34 was promulgated, all danger of Japanese invasion of the West Coast had disappeared. After careful consideration of these contentions we are compelled to reject them.

In doing so, we are not unmindful of the hardships imposed by it upon a large group of American citizens. But hardships are part of war, and war is an aggregation of hardships. All citizens alike, both in and out of uniform, feel the impact of war in greater or lesser measure. Citizenship has its responsibilities as well as its privileges, and in time of war the burden is always heavier. Compulsory exclusion of large groups of citizens from their homes, except under circumstances of direst emergency and peril, is inconsistent with our basic governmental institutions. But when under conditions of modern warfare our shores are threatened by hostile forces, the power to protect must be commensurate with the threatened danger.

It is said that we are dealing here with the case of imprisonment of a citizen in a concentration camp solely because of his ancestry, without evidence or inquiry concerning his loyalty and good disposition towards the United States. Our task would be simple, our duty clear, were this a case involving the imprisonment of a loyal citizen in a concentration camp because of racial prejudice. Regardless of the true nature of the assembly and relocation centers—and we deem it unjustifiable to call them concentration camps with all the ugly connotations that term implies—we are dealing specifically with nothing but an exclusion order. To cast this case into outlines of racial prejudice, without reference to the real military dangers which were presented, merely confuses the issue.

Korematsu was not excluded from the Military Area because of hostility to him or his race. He *was* excluded because we are at war with the Japanese Empire, because the properly constituted military authorities feared an invasion . . . because they decided that the military urgency of the situation demanded that all citizens of Japanese ancestry be segregated from the West Coast temporarily, and finally, because Congress, reposing its confidence in this time of war in our military leaders—as inevitably it must—determined that they should have the power to do just this. There was evidence of disloyalty on the part of some, the military authorities considered that the need for action was great, and time was short. We cannot—by availing ourselves of the calm perspective of hindsight—now say that at that time these actions were unjustified.

Despite the pressures of wartime, or, perhaps, because an Allied victory was beginning to appear likely, three of the justices dissented from the opinion of the majority in *Korematsu*. Justice Roberts wrote of a "clear violation of constitutional rights" in which a citizen was convicted "for not submitting to imprisonment in a concentration camp, based on his ancestry . . . without evidence or inquiry concerning his loyalty . . . toward the United States." Justice Jackson, too, dissented, arguing:

Korematsu was born on our soil, of parents born in Japan. The Constitution makes him a citizen of the United States by nativity and a citizen of California by residence. No claim is made that he is not loyal to this country.

A citizen's presence in the locality, however, was made a crime only if his parents were of Japanese birth. Had Korematsu been one of four—the others say, a German alien enemy, an Italian enemy alien, and a citizen of American-born ancestors, convicted of treason but out on parole—only Korematsu's presence would have violated the order. The difference between their innocence and his crime would result, not from anything he did, said, or thought, different than they, but only in that he was born of different racial stock.

Now, if any fundamental assumption underlies our system, it is that guilt is personal and not inheritable. Even if all of one's antecedents had been convicted of treason, the Constitution forbids its penalties to be visited upon him, for it provides that "no attainder of treason shall work corruption of blood, or forfeiture except during the life of the person attained." But here is an attempt to make an otherwise innocent act a crime merely because this prisoner is the son of parents as to whom he had no choice, and belongs to a race from which there is no way to resign.

Much is said of the danger to liberty from the Army program for deporting and detaining these citizens of Japanese extraction. But a judicial construction of the due process clause that will sustain this order is a far more subtle blow to liberty than the promulgation of the order itself. A military order, however unconstitutional, is not apt to last longer than the military emergency. Even during that period a succeeding commander may revoke it all. But once a judicial opinion rationalizes such an order to show that it conforms to the Constitution, or rather rationalizes the Constitution to show that the Constitution sanctions such an order, the Court for all time has validated the principle of racial discrimination in criminal procedure and of transplanting American citizens. The principle then lies about like a loaded weapon ready for the hand of any authority that can bring forward a plausible claim of an urgent need.

A military commander may overstep the bounds of constitutionality, and it is an incident. But if we review and approve, that passing incident becomes the doctrine of the Constitution. There it has a generative power of its own, and all that it creates will be in its own image. Nothing better illustrates this danger than does the Court's opinion in this case.

Even more than Jackson, Justice Murphy's dissent confronted the racial issue head-on, arguing that, under judicial standards set by the Court, the evacuation order failed to justify itself:

This exclusion of "all persons of Japanese ancestry, both alien and non-alien" goes over "the very brink of constitutional power" and falls into the ugly abyss of racism.

In dealing with matters relating to the prosecution and progress of a war, we must accord great respect and consideration to the judgments of the military authorities.

At the same time, however, it is essential that there be definite limits to military discretion, especially where martial law has not been declared. Individuals must not be left impoverished of their constitutional rights on a plea of military necessity that has neither substance nor support. Thus, like other claims conflicting with the asserted constitutional rights of the individual, the military claim must subject itself to the judicial process of having its reasonableness determined and its conflicts with other interests reconciled.

Being an obvious racial discrimination, the order deprives all those within its scope of the equal protection of the laws as guaranteed by the Fifth Amendment. It further deprives these individuals of their constitutional rights to live and work where they will, to establish a home where they choose and move about freely. In excommunicating them without benefit of hearings, this order also deprives them of all their constitutional rights to procedural due process.

It must be conceded that the military and naval situation in the spring of 1942 was such as to generate a very real fear of invasion of the Pacific Coast, accompanied by fears of sabotage and espionage in that area. . . . [I]t is necessary only that the action have some reasonable relation to the removal of the dangers of invasion, sabotage and espionage. But the exclusion, either temporarily or permanently, of all persons with Japanese blood in their veins has no such reasonable relation. And that relation is lacking because the exclusion order necessarily must rely for its reasonableness upon the assumption that *all* persons of Japanese ancestry may have a dangerous tendency to commit sabotage and espionage. . . . That this forced exclusion was the result in good measure of this erroneous assumption of racial guilt rather than bona fide military necessity is evidenced by the Commanding General's Final Report on the evacuation from the Pacific Coast area. In it he refers to all individuals of Japanese descent as "subversive," as belonging to "an enemy race" whose "racial strains are undiluted," and as constituting "over 112,000 potential enemies . . . at large today" along the Pacific

Coast. In support of this blanket condemnation of all persons of Japanese descent, however, no reliable evidence is cited to show that such individuals were generally disloyal. . . . Individuals of Japanese ancestry are condemned because they are said to be "a large, unassimilated, tightly knit racial group, bound to an enemy nation by strong ties of race, culture, custom and religion." They are claimed to be given to "emperor worshipping ceremonies" and to "dual citizenship." Japanese language schools and allegedly pro-Japanese organizations are cited as evidence of possible group disloyalty . . . charged or proved, that persons of Japanese ancestry were responsible for three minor isolated shellings and bombings of the Pacific Coast area, as well as for unidentified radio transmissions and night signaling.

The main reasons relied upon by those responsible for the forced evacuation, therefore, do not prove a reasonable relation between the group characteristics of Japanese Americans and the dangers of invasion, sabotage, and espionage. The reasons appear, instead, to be largely an accumulation of much of the misinformation, half-truths and insinuations that for years have been directed against Japanese Americans by people with racial and economic prejudices—the same people who have been among the foremost advocates of the evacuation. A military judgment based upon such racial and sociological considerations is not entitled to the great weight ordinarily given the judgments based upon strictly military considerations. . . . [T]o infer that examples of individual disloyalty prove group disloyalty and justify discriminatory action against the entire group is to deny that under our system of law individual guilt is the sole basis for deprivation of rights. Moreover, this inference, which is at the very heart of the evacuation orders, has been used in support of the abhorrent and despicable treatment of minority groups by the dictatorial tyrannies which this nation is now pledged to destroy. To give constitutional sanction to that inference in this case, however well-intentioned may have been the military command on the Pacific Coast, is to adopt one of the cruelest of the rationales used by our enemies to destroy the dignity of the individual and to encourage and open the door to discriminatory actions against other minority groups in the passions of tomorrow.

I dissent, therefore, from this legalization of racism. Racial discrimination in any form and in any degree has no justifiable part whatever in our democratic way of life. It is unattractive in any setting but it is utterly revolting among a free people who have embraced the principles set forth in the Constitution of the United States. All residents of this nation are kin in some way by blood or culture to a foreign land. Yet they are primarily and necessarily a part of the new and distinct civilization of the United States. They must accordingly be treated at all times as the heirs of the American experiment and as entitled to all the rights and freedoms guaranteed by the Constitution.

On the same day that the court handed down its opinion in the *Korematsu* case, it announced its decision in the fourth major challenge to the denial of constitutional rights of Japanese Americans. This case was *Ex parte Endo* [323 U.S. 283 (1944)]. For the first and only time in this sequence of litigation the Court conceded wartime rights of Japanese Americans, agreeing that a concededly loyal American of Japanese ancestry could not be detained beyond the period needed to determine her loyalty. The decision in *Endo*, unanimously authorizing a writ of habeas corpus, was a hollow victory given the court's prior ruling in *Korematsu*. While free to leave the detention center, Ms. Endo was not permitted, under the *Korematsu* decision (upholding evacuation), to return to her home in California which the army still classified as a restricted military zone, and thus off-limits to Japanese Americans. As in *Korematsu*, it was again Justice Murphy, in his concurrence, who most forcefully took issue with the government's unconstitutional use of racial classification in these cases: "Detention in Relocation Centers of persons of Japanese ancestry regardless of loyalty is not only unauthorized by Congress or the Executive but is another example of the unconstitutional resort to racism inherent in the entire evacuation program.... Racial discrimination of this nature bears no reasonable relation to military necessity and is utterly foreign to the ideals and traditions of the American people."

In historical perspective, it is difficult to see how the Court upheld the use of this racial classification, a classification which, in the Court's own words, is suspect and demands the most rigid scrutiny. It is also difficult to understand how, given the flimsiness of the evidence presented by the military and disputed by other government agencies like the FBI, the Court justified its decisions as ones grounded in "military necessity." For example, the Court appeared to accept without question DeWitt's contention that internment of Japanese Americans was necessary because there was no efficient way to "separate out the loyal from the disloyal," in spite of the widespread knowledge that the British had successfully carried out such a clearance program and that the United States had employed loyalty hearings for German and Italian Americans as early as 1942.

The inescapable conclusion is that these Supreme Court decisions must be understood in the context of the extreme anti-Asian racial prejudice, exacerbated by economic competition on the West Coast as well as national wartime concerns. Japanese Americans were included in the general prejudice against Asians, which began with the immigration of Chinese laborers in the mid-nineteenth century. The Japanese, in fact, came to supplant the Chinese as targets of racial hatred after the Chinese Exclusion Act, as the number of Japanese on the West Coast increased and their economic position improved.

Although the Japanese never exceeded 2 percent of the population of California, and although during the period in which anti-Japanese sentiment grew, farms owned by Japanese occupied only 1 percent of cultivated land in California, their considerable economic success was perceived as threatening to Caucasian Californians, increasingly reluctant to share the wealth made possible by irrigation and an ever-expanding population. The ability of Japanese farmers in California to produce farm goods whose value far exceeded that of white farmers, along with the more general race prejudice, led to an organized movement on the part of California farm interests to pass laws limiting Japanese land ownership and even excluding them altogether.

Despite anti-Asian and specifically anti-Japanese legislation, such as the 1924 Immigration Restriction Act, the fears of Caucasians on the West Coast did not diminish. With the attack on Pearl Harbor, representatives from white business organizations, such as the Farm Growers Association, renewed their anti-Japanese lobbying. As Austin Anson, managing secretary of the Salinas Vegetable Grower-Shipper Association frankly admitted:

We are charged with wanting to get rid of the Japs for selfish reasons. . . . We do. It's a question of whether the white man lives on the Pacific Coast or the brown men. They came into this valley to work, and they stayed to take over. . . . They undersell the white man in the markets . . . they work their women and children while the white farmer has to pay wages for his help. If all the Japs were removed tomorrow, we'd never miss them in two weeks, because the white farmer can take over and produce everything the Jap does. And we don't want them back when the war ends, either.[10]

Wartime fears about the loyalty of Japanese Americans and their subsequent internment provided an ideal opportunity for Anglo farmers to remove competition and to buy some of the best farmland in California at less than fair market value.

In addition to the prejudice against the Japanese based on economic competition, the belief that Japanese Americans resisted assimilation intensified discrimination against them. DeWitt's final report asserted that mechanisms for maintaining Japanese American ethnic identity—native language schools, voluntary ethnic associations, and dual citizenship—posed permanent and insoluble problems of national security; he did not feel that similar mechanisms among Germans and Italians posed the same threat. The undocumented and unfair nature of this allegation was commented upon by Justice Murphy, as he correctly noted that "where assimilation is a problem, it is largely the result of certain social customs and laws of the American general public." Justice Murphy further pointed out that the retention of ethnic customs "by some persons" was not evidence of disloyalty. The charge of disloyalty based on dual citizenship, he wrote, reflects a misunderstanding of the true situation, in which Japan claimed as her citizens all persons born of Japanese nationals wherever located. By World War II, Japan had modified this doctrine, and allowed all Japanese born in the United States to renounce any claim of dual citizenship and released her political claim to all those born in the United States after 1925.[11]

The belief that Japanese Americans did not assimilate fed widespread fear in the months after Pearl Harbor that they were disloyal and would engage in espionage and sabotage. The United States did not give Japanese Americans the opportunity to prove their loyalty through government hearings prior to incarceration in detention centers. Justice Jackson focuses upon this issue of due process in his *Korematsu* dissent, arguing that, given the extremely important constitutional questions involved, and the severe consequences of incarceration for the Japanese Americans, such hearings could and should have been ordered by government leaders.

Today, in peacetime, it is difficult to understand so sweeping a deprivation of individual rights on so little and such contested factual evidence.

The pervasive belief that these wartime cases represented an egregious denial of due process and equal protection, in violation of constitutional guarantees, prompted an immediate protesting of these decisions. After the war, this opposition coalesced into action for redress to which Congress made only the most minimal response. In 1948 that body passed the Japanese American Claims Act, giving persons of Japanese ancestry the right to claim from the government real and personal property losses (e.g., for homes, land, store leases, and stock), but not income. The Act required, however, such elaborate proof that the resulting awards totaled only $37 million (out of $131 million claimed) which was far below what would have been full and fair compensation for actual economic losses.[12] Executive Order 9066 itself was not, in fact, repealed until 1976 when President Gerald R. Ford publicly acknowledged Japanese American wartime loyalty.

THE MODERN REDRESS MOVEMENT

The modern redress movement began in the late 1970s, taking shape slowly, with members of the Japanese American community disagreeing on the nature of an appropriate response from the national government. Some individuals argued that the United States need only offer a formal apology for its discriminatory wartime policies, while other activists insisted upon monetary reparations, an antidiscrimination education campaign, and the vacating of (to annul or to void) wartime criminal convictions of Japanese Americans who had resisted curfew and evacuation. This modern movement has focused its efforts upon legislative and judicial forums and has been driven, in part, by the discovery that the White House and the military had suppressed evidence and made false statements in its legal briefs in *Hirabayashi* and *Korematsu*.

In 1980, Congress took a step toward meeting demands for redress when it established the Commission on the Wartime Relocation and Internment of Civilians (CWRIC), a body empowered to determine whether any wrong was committed against those American citizens and permanent resident aliens affected by Executive Order 9066, and if so, to recommend to Congress appropriate remedies. In its 1983 report, *Personal Justice Denied*, the members of this government commission concluded that the detention of the Japanese Americans was not justified by military necessity and that "the broad historical causes which shaped these decisions were race prejudice, war hysteria and a failure of political leadership."[13] The CWRIC characterized the incarceration as a "grave injustice." The commission subsequently recommended offering a national apology to the victims of Executive Order 9066, a presidential pardon of persons convicted of disobeying this order, favorable review by executive agencies of applications by Japanese Americans for restitution of "positions, status or entitlements, lost as a consequence of the order," an appropriation of 1.5 billion dollars to provide compensatory payments of $20,000 to each surviving victim, and support for a foundation for social education on issues of civil liberties.[14]

In the summer of 1988, Congress passed the "Civil Liberties Act," also known as "The Japanese Reparations Act" (Public Law 100–383). This legislation enacted the commission's 1983 recommendations. President Ronald Reagan, who had previously opposed government-sponsored redress, signed the bill on August 10, opening the way for the Department of Justice to establish the administrative mechanism for certification of the $20,000 compensatory payment to survivors of the internment camps. The first reparation checks were issued in October 1990. The Office of Redress Administration reports that, by the end of 1994, 79,515 individuals had qualified for the $20,000 payment.[15]

In the courts, modern redress litigation originally took two directions: The original wartime plaintiffs, Yasui, Korematsu, and Hirabayashi, sought to have their convictions vacated thereby clearing their names. The three men argued that the evidence suppressed by the executive branch in 1943 and 1944 tainted the government's arguments before the Supreme Court and that it was possible, under the common law writ of error *coram nobis*, to reopen their cases in the federal courts in which they had first been heard.[16] In another quite different case, 19 named Japanese American plaintiffs filed suit in *Hohri v. United States* on behalf of a potential class of 120,000 victims. They sought billions of dollars in monetary damages for confiscation of property and deprivation of liberty during the war for all who were incarcerated, or their heirs.

A federal judge first dismissed the *Hohri* suit in May of 1984, holding that the six-year statute of limitations for actions against the United States barred hearing the case. In his opinion, Judge Louis Oberdorfer wrote that the plaintiffs had circumstantial evidence that internment was not justified by "military necessity" as early as 1949, and should have brought legal action against the United States in the 1950s. Plaintiff William Hohri responded: "We had just come out from behind barbed wire and had been intimidated by losing four major cases in the Supreme Court based on what we now recognize as fraudulent evidence of 'military necessity.' Given those problems, the political climate of the early 1950s, and the need to start rebuilding our broken lives, how could we have been expected to mount a major lawsuit of this kind?"[17] Appeals in the *Hohri* case, which continued to turn on technical issues of jurisdiction and statute of limitations proceeded for much of the 1980s until, in October of 1988, the U.S. Supreme Court denied the last writ of *certiorari*.[18]

Litigation in the 1980s to clear the names of Yasui, Korematsu, and Hirabayashi proceeded with more success. Korematsu's conviction was rendered void and a finding was made of misconduct on the part of the government. Yasui won a vacating of his conviction, but did not get a finding of governmental misconduct. He appealed this as a civil suit and lost the appeal on a technicality. When he died, in November 1986, the Court ruled that the case could not continue. Gordon Hirabayashi also saw his wartime conviction vacated. Quietly, many Japanese Americans and civil libertarians had hoped that at least one of the *Yasui*, *Korematsu*, or *Hirabayashi* appeals would go to the U.S. Supreme Court. Had this happened, the justices might have considered whether *Korematsu* should be overruled "to assure that in a comparable future emergency, the balance between individual rights and perceived national security would not again be struck as it was during World War II."[19] None of the appeals did go to the Supreme Court, thus preventing this outcome.

The most recent legal action connected to the redress movement has been a challenge, on the part of a number of individuals, to the federal government's denial of certification for the $20,000 compensatory payments. Claims have been filed, for example, by Japanese Americans who, as children, were neither taken to nor born in the internment camps, but who state that they were "deprived of liberty or property" as the result of wartime "racial prejudice, wartime hysteria, and a failure of political leadership."[20] These children, it is argued in legal briefs, "solely because of their Japanese ancestry, were involuntarily excluded from their homes and forbidden to return during the war by federal law."[21] They moved with their families, who sold their belongings and left their jobs, to regions outside the designated military areas, at the urging of the government and as an involuntary alternative to internment. Most families suffered severe economic hardships, trading skilled jobs and professions for irregular, minimum-wage work. They were, it is claimed, in exile in their native country.

The outcome of these lawsuits, which are expected to be in federal appeals courts until the early years of the twenty-first century, will turn on the courts' interpretation of the language used by Congress in the 1988 Civil Liberties Act. Individuals eligible for redress under the Act have been defined as follows:

any individual of Japanese ancestry [or spouse or parent] who is living on the date of enactment of this Act, and who, during the evacuation, relocation and internment period . . . was confined, held in custody, relocated, or otherwise deprived of liberty or property as a result of . . . [specified government actions].[22]

Japanese American plaintiffs argue that Congress intended the 1988 Civil Liberties Act to be remedial and to benefit an entire broad class of victims of racial prejudice who suffered material and intangible damages and endured significant suffering. In two separate cases on this particular question of certification, the United States Court of Federal Claims has issued conflicting decisions.[23] Years of appeals will determine whether Congress intended to benefit a broad class of victims or, as lawyers for the U.S. Department of Justice contend, only those "most directly affected" by the evacuation and internment orders.[24]

The Japanese Americans, as a racially visible group, have long experienced social, economic, and political discrimination in the United States. At the national level this has been expressed by exclusionary immigration and naturalization legislation and wartime actions that were based on their visibility. Historically, at a local level, Japanese Americans, on the West Coast particularly, have been the victims of newspaper propaganda, economic discrimination, and organized lobbying designed to undermine their status as Americans and even to remove them from American soil. While the justification for these actions was often rationalized by the so-called cultural differences and "clannishness" of the Japanese Americans, in fact, members of this community have demonstrated a consistent willingness to assimilate. And indeed, many of the cultural values maintained by Americans of Japanese heritage, especially patterns of hard work, saving, achievement orientation, lawfulness, family solidarity, and personal discipline, are time-honored values of the dominant American culture. Yet, in a country where racial differences have always mattered, powerful government and economic interests were able to use wartime concerns to manipulate this prejudice and to cast Japanese Americans into an unchosen status as outsiders from which, during the war, even the highest court of the land would not rescue them. Subsequent legislative and judicial actions suggest that redress is possible. While reparations have been paid and convictions made void, *Hirabayashi* and *Korematsu* have not been overruled, suggesting that, in wartime, military necessity might be argued to supersede individual due process and equal protection rights. Thus, the final test of the Supreme Court's decision in *Endo,* and congressional intent in enacting the 1988 Civil Liberties Act, will be whether, in the future, the United States will prohibit racial and ethnic prejudice when promulgating policies necessary for wartime military security.

NOTES

1. Hyung-chan Kim, *A Legal History of Asian Americans, 1790–1990* (Westport, CT: Greenwood Press, 1994), 33. The right of the United States, on the basis of this legislation, to deny Asian Americans the right of naturalization was upheld by the U.S. Supreme Court in *Ozawa v. United States*, 260 U.S. 178 (1922). The McCarran-Walter Act, an otherwise conservative legislative initiative, ended earlier restrictive immigration and naturalization laws that targeted Asians.

2. See, for example, John R. Wunder, "The Chinese and the Courts in the Pacific Northwest: Justice Denied?" *Pacific Historical Review* 52 (1983): 191–211.

3. The Chinese Exclusion Act, 22 Stat. 58. In 1892, Congress extended the period of exclusion for an additional ten years. 27 Stat. 25. Merchants and teachers were permitted to settle. Legal restriction upon Japanese immigration to the United States was initiated in the so-called "Gentleman's Agreement of 1908" signed by the governments of the United States and Japan.

4. Kim, *A Legal History of Asian Americans*, 105. 39 Stat. 874.

5. The Immigration Restriction Act, 43 Stat. 153.

6. See, e.g., *Ozawa v. United States*, 260 U.S. 178 (1922); *Yamashita v. Hinkle*, 260 U.S. 199 (1922); and *United States v. Bhagat Singh Thind*, 262 U.S. 204 (1923).

7. Lt. Gen. John L. DeWitt, *Final Recommendation of the Commanding General, Western Defense Command and Fourth Army, to the Secretary of War* (February 14, 1942)(Final Recommendation)(Joint Appendix), 109–10.

8. "Raskin Replies," *The Nation* (April 1, 1991), 398. See also, Joel B. Grossman, Shirley Castelnuovo, and Randal Boe, "*Korematsu* after 40 Years: Can It Happen Again?" Paper presented at the Midwest Political Science Association Meeting (Chicago: April 18, 1985).

9. Grossman, Castelnuovo, and Boe, "*Korematsu* after 40 Years," 17ff.

10. *Korematsu v. United States*, 323 U.S. 214, 239 (1944). Interned Japanese Americans were permitted to leave the camps if they could demonstrate they had the ability to live and support themselves outside of the military exclusion zones. Given the hostility of white farmers in California, it is ironic that more than 2,000 interned Japanese Americans were released to work in one of the country's largest vegetable processing plants in Seabrook, New Jersey, which was experiencing a wartime labor shortage. Jon Nordheimer, "Remembering a Haven from Shame," *New York Times*, July 20, 1994, B1.

11. *Korematsu v. United States*, 323 U.S. 214, 237 (1944).

12. Philip Tajitsu Nash, "Moving for Redress," *Yale Law Journal* 94 (January 1985): 747.

13. Ibid., 749.

14. Ibid., 749, 750.

15. Conversation with staff of the Office of Redress Administration, December 1994. Payments have been made to Japanese Americans as well as 127 former Peruvian-Japanese who were interned in the United States during World War II

as the result of international agreements among the Allied powers to bring Japanese resident aliens from South and Latin America for imprisonment in this country.

16. Roger Daniels, *Prisoners Without Trial: Japanese Americans in World War II* (New York: Hill and Wang, 1993), 99.

17. Nash, "Moving for Redress," 751.

18. See, for example, *Hohri v. United States*, 586 F. Supp. 796 (1984), and *Hohri v. United States*, 782 F.2d 227 (D.C. Cir. 1986).

19. Grossman, Castelnuovo, and Boe, "*Korematsu* After 40 Years," 9.

20. Appellant's Brief in the U.S. Court of Appeals for the Federal Circuit at 5, 7, *Ishida v. United States*, 94–5151 (December 15, 1994).

21. Brief for Amicus Curiae, National Coalition for Redress and Reparations in the U.S. Court of Appeals for the Federal Circuit, *Ishida v. United States* (December 5, 1994), 1.

22. The Civil Liberties Act, 102 Stat. 903, Sections 1989b-3 through b-5; 1989b-7(2).

23. See *Ishida v. United States*, 31 Fed. Cl. 280 (1994), and *Consolo v. United States*, 31 Fed. Cl. 447 (1994).

24. Defendant-Appellee's Brief in the U.S. Court of Appeals for the Federal Circuit at 10–15, *Ishida v. United States*, 94–5151 (January 17, 1995).

Part II

Religion

5

The Mormons

The Church of Jesus Christ of Latter-day Saints, most commonly known as Mormons, is one of the wealthiest and politically well-connected groups in the United States today. This could be expected given the Mormons' stress on thrift and personal industry but it might well have not occurred because of the early history of persecution of Mormons in many American communities.

Mormonism originated in the religious experience of a young man named Joseph Smith. Smith lived in western New York state during the period of the great religious revival of the 1820s in which revelation and emotion regained their place in American Protestantism. At the age of 14, Smith experienced his first revelation. Three years later, he discovered (through divine direction), and later translated, new scriptures called the Book of Mormon. The Book of Mormon is a large and complex text. It describes the dispersion of Israelites, sometime after 600 B.C., to North America where Jesus appeared to the deserving, taught, and established his church. In varied contexts, using stories in which the dark-skinned Lamanites fight the lighter Nephites, the Book of Mormon illustrates a central theme: the cycle of good and evil, human pride, and divine forgiveness.

From the beginning, Smith was attacked because of the extravagant nature of his claims of seeing God and angels, which were denounced as heresy by more established Christian sects. Harassment followed Smith and his growing number of believers, among whom was Brigham Young, as they moved continually westward to escape persecution and arrest. Smith and his followers believed the Native Americans were from a portion of one of the Lost Tribes and that Mormons were religiously obligated to redeem them by conversion. For this reason, and to avoid increasing troubles, Joseph Smith and his followers continued their move west to their "promised land" in Missouri, and then to a place on the banks of the Mississippi River, which Smith named Nauvoo. At first Smith's group was welcomed and they set up a virtually autonomous religious community. It was at Nauvoo that Smith claimed to have received the revelation sanctioning polygamy. The Mormon church endorsed only the form of polygamy known as polygyny, the marriage of one man to more than one wife, which Smith and a few trusted leaders began to practice. The announcement of this revelation had a heavy price; it led to a schism within the Mormon community and ultimately to Smith's arrest and jailhouse murder by an anti-Mormon mob in 1844.[1]

Polygamy was central to Smith's understanding of the way Mormonism would restore the true order of the ancient Church of Christ. He presented it as an important principle of the religion, the restoration of the sacred and binding marriage patterns of Abraham, Issac, and Jacob. For Smith, polygamy strengthened the patriarchical nature of Mormon marriage and enhanced the status of the exclusively male priesthood through a new pattern of family network created by plural marriage. Plural unions reinforced the Mormon emphasis on community, family, and stability over individualism. Its earthly purpose was procreation. Marriage, however, was also critical to the entrance of the faithful into the kingdom of God after this life. In Mormonism, "celestial marriage" bound husbands and wives for time and all eternity in an endless union providing both parties lived the covenants. The "sealing" of a union in a Mormon temple was the final way by which Mormon faithful could obtain glory and exaltation in the highest kingdom of God, the highest degree of the celestial kingdom. In the theology of the Saints (as they called themselves), polygamy became an exalted form of "celestial marriage."

As a result of ongoing persecution by non-Mormons, and internal division, in 1847 Brigham Young and Herbert Kimbal decided a move was necessary. They led an advance group of 150 Mormons out of the several thousand at Nauvoo even farther west and established a colony, which they called Deseret, in the Great Salt Lake Valley on July 24, 1847. Under Young's vigorous leadership, the Mormons set up a communitarian economy and a highly controlled theocracy which prospered aided, in part, by the immigration of thousands of English working men, whom Mormon missionaries had converted. Young was appointed territorial governor when Congress organized Deseret as the Utah Territory in 1850.

This early recognition of Mormonism's legitimacy soon foundered on the political, economic, and cultural differences between the Mormons and the rest of the United States. In Deseret, the Mormons had established a communalistic theocracy whose principles ran counter to the dominant American value of capitalism. Their theocracy was also in explicit contravention of the First Amendment's "no establishment of religion" clause. The Mormons thought that by fleeing west of the Mississippi to the Great Salt Lake Basin, which was, at the time, Mexican territory and, therefore, legally inaccessible to the reach of federal administration and the hostile culture of the United States, they could escape the reach of the Constitution and the criminal laws of the United States. But just two years after the founding of Deseret, the Salt Lake Valley became part of U.S. territory as a result of a war with Mexico, and Mormon troubles began again.

The people of the United States feared the Mormon theocracy as a threat to its own expanding sovereignty. Hostility toward the Mormons, who engaged in secret ceremonies and recruited converts abroad, drew upon a larger anti-Masonic, anti-alien, and anti-Catholic spirit in America. The presence of Latter-day Saint communities in the West also renewed concern, voiced earlier in Illinois and Missouri, about Mormon bloc voting. Although most Saints did not practice polygamy and, in many ways, their lives resembled those of other Western pioneers, Mormons were identified as having rejected important tenets of American culture, namely, secularism, monogamy, and individualism. As their long, difficult, and dangerous flight westward demonstrated, church members were tenaciously committed to their own social and religious institutions, possibly strengthened by persistent opposition. Popular outrage against the Mormons grew, fueled by newspaper stories about polygamy. Censure was encouraged by other incendiary public statements such as that of the new Republican Party in 1856 that polygamy in Utah should be equated with Southern slavery as the "twin relics of barbarism." American officials regarded polygamists as criminals and said that civilized society looked upon the plural wife as a concubine and her children as illegitimate.[2] In 1857, President Buchanan sent 5,000 troops to occupy the Salt Lake Valley to serve notice to the Mormons that flouting the law of the United States could not and would not be allowed.

Although federal attention to Mormon opposition lessened during the Civil War, in 1862, Congress passed the Morrill Antibigamy Act. This act turned out to be unenforceable. By the early 1870s, however, interest in the economic resources of the Utah Territory, and continued outrage at polygamy, revived federal determination to undermine the power of the Mormon Church. Using a legal rather than a military strategy, the U.S. government began a 20-year campaign against the religious, economic, and political activities of the Saints.

The new assault began with the Poland Act of 1874, establishing federal control over the courts and juries of the Utah Territory, which—composed largely of Mormons—had been refusing to convict polygamists under the Morrill Antibigamy Act. Next, in 1879, the Supreme Court, in the case of *Reynolds v. United States,* upheld the constitutionality of the federal antibigamy legislation, asserting the sanctity of monogamy and its central place in American culture against the Saints' claims that the law violated First Amendment religious rights and that it was an *ex post facto* law. The centerpiece of the Court's decision rested upon the new belief-action doctrine. According to the justices, the First Amendment guaranteed the right to hold whatever religious opinion one wished but not necessarily the right to act according to that belief or faith.

Four years later, encouraged by various economic interests and moral reformers from the temperance and woman suffrage movements, Congress again attempted to curb Mormon elective power in the territory of Utah through provisions of the Edmunds Act. This legislation prohibited polygamy and unlawful cohabitation and established a federal commission to administer test oaths requiring voters to swear they were neither bigamists nor polygamists. Those Mormons who would not take the oath were barred from public service and voting. An Idaho statute compelling a similar oath had the purpose of limiting Mormon participation in territorial and county government as well as eliminating Mormon control of local schools. In Utah, Arizona, and Idaho, the surveillance, arrest, and imprisonment of polygamous men and women intensified. Arizona prisons became so overcrowded that convicted polygamists there were transported 2,000 miles to Detroit to serve their sentences. The authorities targeted, in particular, the church leadership, convicting and imprisoning many of them. During the 1880s, more than 1,300 Mormon men and women were imprisoned because of their religious practice of polygamy.

The effects of the federal Edmunds Act caused a group of Mormons, in 1885, to petition President Grover Cleveland for an end to the national antipolygamy campaign. The petition described a double standard as well as family and personal duress:

The paramour of mistresses and harlots, secure from prosecution, walks the streets in open day. No United States official puts a spotter on his "trail," or makes an effort to drag his deeds in guilt and shame before a judge and jury. ... But (with respect to the Mormon people) "Spotters" and spies dog their footsteps. Delators [informers] thrust themselves into bedchambers and watch at windows. Children are questioned upon the streets as to the marital relations of their parents. Families are dragged before Commissioners and grand juries, and on pain of punishment for contempt, are compelled to testify against their fathers and husbands. Modest women are made to answer shamefully indecent questions as to the sexual relations of men and women. Attempts are made to bribe men to work up cases against their neighbors. Notoriously disreputable characters are employed to spy into men's family relations.[3]

In these years, Idaho Mormons also initiated a challenge in the U.S. Supreme Court of that territory's 1885 oath test. In the 1889 case of *Davis v. Beason*, Samuel Davis argued that his conviction for obstructing the law, in the territorial district court, violated the First Amendment's admonition that there be no law respecting an establishment of religion. As in the *Reynolds* case, the weight of the Court's opinion came down most strongly upon the "odious" institution of polygamy. In this attack on their civil rights, the Mormons did attract limited support among Eastern politicians. Congressman Zebulon Vance of North Carolina, for example, made the wry observation (referring to Biblical polygamy) that, "If alive today, Moses, the great lawgiver, could not be mayor of a crossroads town. . . . King Solomon in all his glory could not serve a warrant for 50 cents, and King David . . . the man after God's own heart, could not serve the warrants. The rabbis of the temple could not sit upon the jury to try the case."[4]

Congressional and judicial efforts to bring Mormon social institutions in line with the dominant American culture largely failed, however, until Congress decided upon truly drastic legislation. In 1887, the Edmunds–Tucker Act was passed: This statute withdrew women's suffrage in Utah; disinherited the children of plural marriages; prescribed another test oath for those wanting to vote, hold political office, and serve on juries; stipulated that legal wives could testify against their husbands; vested all political, military, and legal powers in federal appointees; placed all Utah schools under the control of a court-appointed commissioner; required all marriages to be certified in the probate courts; eliminated all existing electoral districts; and dissolved the church militia. The Act also disenfranchised Mormons who advocated polygamy even if the church member did not engage in the practice.

Affecting the Church even more directly, the Edmunds–Tucker Act repealed the charter of the Mormon Church, and provided for the confiscation of its most valuable holdings, resulting in a loss of over $1 million in cash and property.[5] Church leaders immediately challenged the constitutionality of this statute but without success. In the 1889 case of *Romney v. United States*, the Supreme Court rejected the Mormons' arguments, once again asserting the absolute right of the United States to regulate a church committed to polygamy, a practice the Court characterized as "a crime against the laws, and abhorrent to the sentiments and feelings of the civilized world."

Reynolds v. United States
98 U.S. 146 (1879)

Mr. Chief Justice Waite delivered the opinion of the court. The assignments of error . . . present the following questions. . . . Should the accused have been acquitted if he marries a second time, because he believed it to be his religious duty? Did the court err in that part of the charge which directed the attention of the jury to the consequences of polygamy?

As to the defense of religious belief or duty . . . the accused proved that at the time of his alleged second marriage he was, and for many years before had been, a member of the Church of Jesus Christ of Latter-Day Saints, commonly called the Mormon Church, and a believer in its doctrines; that it was an accepted doctrine of that church "that it was the duty of male members of said church, circumstances permitting, to practice polygamy . . . that this duty was enjoined by different books which the members of said church believed to be of divine origin, and among others the Holy Bible, and also that the members of the church believed that the practice of polygamy was directly enjoined upon the male members thereof by the Almighty God, in a revelation to Joseph Smith, the founder and prophet of said church; that the failing or refusing to practice polygamy by such male members of said church, when circumstances would admit, would be punished, and that the penalty for such failure and refusal would be damnation in the life to come."

[T]he question is raised, whether religious belief can be accepted as a justification of an overt act made criminal by the law of the land. The inquiry is not as to the power of Congress to prescribe criminal laws for the Territories, but as to the guilt of one who knowingly violates a law which has been properly enacted, if he entertains a religious belief that the law is wrong.

Congress cannot pass a law for the government of the Territories which shall prohibit the free exercise of religion. The first amendment to the Constitution expressly forbids such legislation. Religious freedom is guaranteed everywhere throughout the United States, so far as congressional interference is concerned. The question to be determined is, whether the law now under consideration comes within this prohibition.

The word "religion" is not defined in the Constitution. We must go elsewhere, therefore, to ascertain its meaning, and nowhere more appropriately, we think, than to the history of the times in the midst of which the provision was adopted. The precise point of the inquiry is, what is the religious freedom which has been guaranteed.

After summing up a history of eighteenth-century debate on the nature of religious freedom, the Chief Justice turned to the words of Thomas Jefferson:

Believing with you that religion is a matter which lies solely between man and his God; that he owes account to none other for his faith or his worship; that the legislative powers of the government reach actions only, and not opinions,—I contemplate with sovereign reverence that act of the whole American people which declared that their legislature should "make no law respecting an establishment of religion or prohibiting the free exercise thereof," thus building a wall of separation between Church and State. Adhering to this expression of the supreme will of the nation in behalf of the rights of conscience, I shall see with sincere satisfaction the progress of those sentiments which tend to restore man to all his natural rights, convinced he has no natural right in opposition to his social duties.

The Chief Justice continued in his own words:

Coming as this does from an acknowledged leader of the advocates of the measure, it may be accepted almost as an authoritative declaration of the scope and effect of the amendment thus secured. Congress was deprived of all legislative power over mere opinion, but was left free to reach actions which were in violation of social duties or subversive of good order.

Polygamy has always been odious among the northern and western nations of Europe, and, until the establishment of the Mormon Church, was almost exclusively a feature of the life of Asiatic and of African people. At common law, the second marriage was always void and from the earliest history of England polygamy has been treated as an offence against society.

We think it may safely be said there never has been a time in any State of the Union when polygamy has not been an offence against society, cognizable by the civil courts and punishable with more or less severity. In the face of all this evidence, it is impossible to believe that the constitutional guaranty of religious freedom was intended to prohibit legislation in respect to this most important feature of social life. Marriage, while from its very nature a sacred obligation, is nevertheless, in most civilized nations, a civil contract, and usually regulated by law. Upon it society may be said to be built, and out of its fruits spring social relations and social obligations and duties, with which government is necessarily required to deal. In fact, according as monogamous or polygamous marriages are allowed, do we find the principles on which the government of the people, to a greater or lesser extent, rests . . . polygamy leads to the patriarchal principle, and which, when applied to large communities, fetters the people in stationary despotism, while that principle cannot long exist in connection with monogamy. . . . In our opinion, the statute immediately under consideration is within the legislative power of Congress. It is constitutional and valid as prescribing a rule of action for all those residing in the Territories, and in places over which the United States have exclusive control. This being so, the only question which remains is, whether those who make polygamy a part of their religion are excepted from the operation of the statute. If they are, then those who do not make polygamy a part of their religious belief may be found guilty and punished, while those who do, must be acquitted and go free. This would be introducing a new element into criminal law. Laws are made for the government of actions, and while they cannot interfere with mere religious belief and opinions, they may with practices. Suppose one believed that human sacrifices were a necessary part of religious worship, would it be seriously contended that the civil government under which he lived could not interfere to prevent a sacrifice? Or if a wife religiously believed it was her duty to burn herself upon the funeral pyre of her dead husband, would it be beyond the power of the civil government to prevent her carrying her belief into practice?

So here, as a law of the organization of society under the exclusive dominion of the United States, it is provided that plural marriages shall not be allowed.

Can a man excuse his practices to the contrary because of his religious belief? To permit this would be to make the professed doctrines of religious belief superior to the law of the land, and in effect to permit every citizen to become a law unto himself. Government could exist only in name under such circumstances.

But when the offence consists of a positive act which is knowingly done, it would be dangerous to hold that the offender might escape punishment because he religiously believed the law which he had broken ought never to have been made. No case, we believe, can be found that has gone so far.

As to that part of the charge which directed the attention of the jury to the consequences of polygamy.

The passage complained of is as follows: "I think it not improper, in the discharge of your duties in this case, that you should consider what are to be the consequences to the innocent victims of this delusion. As this contest goes on, they multiply, and there are pure-minded women and there are innocent children,—innocent in the sense even beyond the degree of the innocence of childhood itself. These are to be the sufferers; and as jurors fail to do their duty, and as these cases come up in the Territory of Utah, just so do these victims multiply and spread themselves over the land."

Congress, in 1862 saw fit to make bigamy a crime in the Territories. This was done because of the evil consequences that were supposed to flow from plural marriages. . . . Upon the showing made by the accused himself, he was guilty of a violation of the law under which he had been indicted.

A decade later the Supreme Court ruled against Samuel Davis and other Idaho Mormons challenging the territory's oath test. In a far-reaching opinion, Justice Stephen J. Field ignored the implications of withdrawing civic rights from citizens. Instead, his majority opinion emphasized the right of the government to criminalize the practice of polygamy *as well as* "the teaching, advising or counseling" of the practice in the name of the peace, morality, and prosperity of American society.

Davis v. Beason
133 U.S. 333 (1889)

In his opening notes Mr. Justice Field outlined the facts and issues in the case.

In April, 1889, the appellant, Samuel D. Davis [and others] was indicted in the District Court of the Third Judicial District of the Territory of Idaho . . . for a conspiracy to unlawfully pervert and obstruct the due administration of the laws of the Territory in this, that they would unlawfully procure themselves to be admitted to registration as electors of said County of Oneida for the general election then next to occur in that county, when they were not entitled to be admitted to such registration . . . and [that they swore] oath prescribed by the Statute of the State, in substance as follows: "I do swear (or affirm) that I am a male citizen of the United States of the age of twenty-one years . . . and I do further swear that I am not a bigamist or polygamist; that I am not a member of any order, organization or association which teaches, advises, counsels or encourages its members, devotees or any other person to commit the crime of bigamy or polygamy, or any other crime defined by law as a duty arising or resulting from membership in such order, organization or association, or which practices bigamy, polygamy or plural or celestial marriage as a doctrinal right of such organization; that I do not and will not, publicly or privately, or in any manner whatever, teach, advise, counsel or encourage any person to commit the crime of bigamy or polygamy, or any other crime defined by law, either as a religious duty or otherwise; that I do regard the Constitution of the United States and the laws thereof and the laws of this Territory, as interpreted by the courts, as the supreme laws of the land, the teachings of any order, organization or association to the contrary notwithstanding, so help me God," when, in truth, each of the defendants was a member of . . . the Church of Jesus Christ of Latter-Day Saints, commonly known as the Mormon Church, which they knew taught, advised, counseled and encouraged its members and devotees to commit the crimes of bigamy and polygamy.

On the trial which followed on the 12th of September, 1889, the jury found the defendant Samuel D. Davis guilty as charged in the indictment. . . . The Defendant applied to the court . . . and obtained a writ of habeas corpus alleging . . . that [the oath] is a "law respecting an establishment of religion," in violation of the First Amendment of the Constitution and void.

In his majority opinion, Justice Field rejected the claim that the oath violated the Establishment Clause, writing:

Bigamy and polygamy are crimes by the laws of all civilized and Christian countries. They are crimes by the laws of the United States, and they are crimes by the laws of Idaho. They tend to destroy the purity of the marriage relation, to disturb the peace of families, to degrade woman and to debase man. Few crimes are more pernicious to the best interests of society and receive more general or more deserved punishment. To extend exemption from punishment for such crimes would be to shock the moral judgment of the community. To call their advocacy a tenet of religion is to offend the common sense of mankind. If they are crimes, then to teach, advise and counsel their practice is to aid in their commission, and such teaching and counseling are themselves criminal and proper subjects of punishment, as aiding and abetting crime are in all other cases.

The term "religion" has reference to one's views of his relations to his Creator, and to the obligations they impose of reverence for his being and character, and of obedience to his will. It is often confounded with the *cultus* or form of worship of a particular sect, but is distinguishable from the latter. The First Amendment to the Constitution, in declaring that Congress shall make no law respecting the establishment of religion, or forbidding the free exercise thereof, was intended to allow everyone under the jurisdiction of the United States to entertain such notions respecting his relations to his Maker and the duties they impose as may be approved by his judgment and conscience, and to exhibit his sentiments in such form of worship as he may think proper, not injurious to the equal rights of others, and to prohibit legislation for the support of any religious tenets, or the modes of worship of any sect. The oppressive measures adopted, and the cruelties and punishments inflicted by the governments of Europe for many ages, to compel parties to conform in their religious beliefs and modes of worship to the views of the most numerous sect, and the folly of attempting in that way to control the mental operations of persons and enforce an outward conformity to a prescribed standard, led to the adoption of the Amendment in question. It was never intended or supposed that the Amendment could be invoked as a protection against legislation for the punishment of acts inimical to the peace, good order and morals of society. With man's relations to his Maker and the obligations he may think they impose, and the manner in which an expression shall be made by him of his belief on those subjects, no interference can be permitted, provided always the laws of society, designed to secure its peace and prosperity, and the morals of its people, are not interfered with. However free the exercise of religion may be, it must be subordinate to the criminal laws of the country, passed with reference to actions regarded by general consent as properly the subjects of punitive legislation. There have been sects which denied as a part of their religious tenets that there should be any marriage tie, and advocated promiscuous intercourse of the sexes as prompted by the passions of their members. And history discloses the fact that the necessity of human sacrifices, on special occasions, has been a tenet of many sects. Should a sect of either of these kinds ever find its way into this country, swift punishment would follow the carrying into effect of its doctrines, and no heed would be given to the pretense that, as religious beliefs, their supporters could be protected in their exercise by the Constitution of the United States. Probably never before in the history of this country has it been seriously contended that the whole punitive power of the government, for acts recognized by the general consent of the Christian world in modern times as proper matters for prohibitory legislation, must be suspended in order that the tenets of a religious sect encouraging crime may be carried out without hindrance . . . and in *Murphy v. Ramsey*, referring to the Act of Congress excluding polygamists and bigamists from voting or holding office, the court, speaking by Mr. Justice Matthews, said: "Certainly no legislation can be supposed more wholesome and necessary in the founding of a free, self-governing commonwealth, fit to take rank as one of the coordinate States of the Union, than that which seeks to establish it on the basis of the idea of the family, as consisting in and springing from the union for life of one man and one woman in the holy estate of matrimony—the sure foundation of all that is stable and noble in our civilization; the best guaranty of that reverent morality which is the source of all beneficent progress in social and political improvement. And to this end no means are more directly and immediately suitable than those provided by this Act, which endeavors to withdraw all political influence from those who are practically hostile to its attainment."

It is assumed by counsel of the petitioner that, because no mode of worship can be established or religious tenets enforced in this country, therefore any form of worship may be followed and any tenets, however destructive of society, may be held and advocated, if asserted to be a part of the religious doctrines of those advocating and practicing them. But nothing is further from the truth. Whilst legislation for the establishment of a religion is forbidden, and its free exercise permitted, it does not follow that everything which may be so called can be tolerated. Crime is not less odious because sanctioned by what any particular sect may designate as religion.

In the same year, the U.S. Supreme Court handed down its opinion in the *Romney* case, ruling that the Edmunds–Tucker Act did not violate religious rights guaranteed in the First Amendment. The majority opinion penned by Justice Joseph Bradley broke little new legal ground, instead revisiting the moral themes of earlier decisions. The impact of the Edmunds–Tucker Act and the *Romney* decision, however, cannot be understated. In both, the United States gave clear notice of the scope of government regulation that it would sanction, under the belief-action doctrine announced in *Reynolds,* when religious groups did not conform to dominant culture norms or, in the justices' words, "the enlightened sentiments of mankind."

Romney v. United States
136 U.S. 1 (1889)

Notwithstanding the stringent laws which have been passed by Congress—notwithstanding all the efforts made to suppress this barbarous practice—the sect or community composing the Church of Latter-Day Saints perseveres, in defiance of law, in preaching, upholding, promoting and defending [polygamy]. It is a matter of public notoriety that its emissaries are engaged in many countries in propagating this nefarious doctrine, and urging its converts to join the community in Utah. The existence of such a propaganda is a blot on our civilization. The organization of a community for the spread and practice of polygamy is, in a measure, a return to barbarism. It is contrary to the spirit of Christianity and of the civilization which Christianity has produced in the Western World. The question, therefore, is whether the promotion of such a nefarious system and practice, so repugnant to our laws and to the principles of civilization, is to be allowed to continue by the sanction of the government itself; and whether the funds accumulated for that purpose shall be restored to the same unlawful uses as heretofore, to the detriment of the true interests of civil society.

It is unnecessary here to refer to the past history of the sect, to their defiance of the government authorities, to their attempt to establish an independent community, to their efforts to drive from the territory all who were not connected with them in communion and sympathy. The tale is one of patience on the part of the American government and people, and of contempt of authority and resistance to law on the part of the Mormons. Whatever persecutions they may have suffered in the early part of their history, in Missouri and Illinois, they have no excuse for their persistent defiance of law under the government of the United States.

One pretense for this obstinate course is, that their belief in the practice of polygamy, or in the right to indulge in it, is a religious belief, and, therefore, under the protection of the constitutional guaranty of religious freedom. This is altogether a sophistical plea. No doubt the Thugs of India imagined that their belief in the right of assassination was a religious belief; but their thinking so did not make it so. The practice of suttee by the Hindu widows may have sprung from a supposed religious conviction. The offering of human sacrifices by our own ancestors in Britain was no doubt sanctioned by an equally conscientious impulse. But no one, on that account, would hesitate to brand these practices, now, as crimes against society, and obnoxious to condemnation and punishment by the civil authority.

The State has the perfect right to prohibit polygamy, and all other open offences against the enlightened sentiment of mankind, notwithstanding the pretense of religious conviction by which they may be advocated and practised . . . and . . . finding [Church] funds without legal ownership . . . to cause them to be seized and to be devoted to objects of undoubted charity and usefulness—such for example as the maintenance of schools.

The confiscation of church property divided the Court. Justice Melville Fuller, joined by Justices Lamar and Field, dissented:

I am constrained to dissent from the opinion and judgment just announced . . . I agree that the power to make needful rules and regulations for the Territories necessarily comprehends the power to suppress crime; . . . even though that crime assumes the form of a religious belief or creed. Congress has the power to extirpate polygamy in any of the Territories, by the enactment of a criminal code directed to that end; but it is not authorized under the cover of that power to seize and confiscate the property of persons, individuals, or corporations, without office found, because they may have been guilty of criminal practices.

The language of the Supreme Court decisions leaves no doubt as to the implacable hostility of the United States and its adamant refusal to accommodate Mormon communitarianism, theocracy, and its "peculiar" custom of polygamy. While the Saints' commitment to a theocratic, communalistic society ranked as an important reason for government action against them, challenging Mormon religious culture as it was expressed through polygamy also provided a strong focus for political and legal attack. After losing these several important legal battles, the Saints' leaders clearly understood that in order to gain statehood, the Church would have to renounce polygamy, dissolve the church party, and refashion aspects of its communalistic economy. In October of 1890, following the announcement of an instructive revelation received by Mormon leader Wilford Woodruff, the Church formally repudiated the practice of polygamy.

Given this unswerving legal and political harassment in the nineteenth century, the successful adaptation of the Church to a set of values so in opposition to its original theology is striking. Moreover, having defeated the Mormons in the courts, federal politicians quickly extended the glad hand of political fellowship. In the unsettled political climate at the turn of the century, the Republican Party sought Utah's votes in order to control the U.S. Congress.

Similarly, Eastern investors, seeking outlets for their capital, turned toward Utah, where they found a troubled and declining Mormon economy and leaders ready to make alliances. Although these economic partnerships resulted in the loss of Mormon financial control over various business enterprises, their ultimate effect was to integrate the Saints into a burgeoning national capitalist economy. Through this move from a parochial, regional economy to corporate capitalism, many individual Mormons became very wealthy. The theology of the Church demonstrated its flexibility to accommodate, and even embrace, the capitalistic values of capital accumulation, private ownership of property, and individual profit-taking. Not only did individual Mormons become wealthy, but the Church itself prospered through the religious obligation of tithing (10 percent of a church member's income must be given to the Church) and its subsequent investments. Today, the Church of Jesus Christ of Latter-day Saints ranks among the richest religious organizations in the United States. Besides temples, meeting houses, and other religious real estate worth billions of dollars, the Church owns a portfolio of stocks and bonds valued at hundreds of millions of dollars, television and radio stations, a newspaper, insurance companies, and other businesses.[6]

Beginning in the 1950s, Mormons also moved into national political prominence. The examples of Ezra Taft Benson, a church leader who was secretary of agriculture under President Dwight D. Eisenhower, and George Romney, a candidate for president, have been followed by an increasing number of Mormons on the White House staff, in federal bureaucracies, and in the U.S. Congress. The Central Intelligence Agency and the Federal Bureau of Investigation find young Mormons particularly attractive candidates because of their foreign missionary experience and strict morality.

The Church of Latter-day Saints has undergone a dramatic transformation, in the eyes of non-Mormon Americans, from an institution of infamy to one of influence. The Mormons, once seen as a people opposed to the U.S. government and much of American culture, are now portrayed as a model of American capitalistic enterprise and moral respectability.[7] As we will see later, this experience has been distinctly different from that of the Amish, who made no accommodation to the demands of politics or industrialization and who therefore have no political or economic influence in contemporary America.

MODERN-DAY FUNDAMENTALISTS ON TRIAL

There have been, however, Mormons who, in the twentieth century, refused to make this accommodation to American courts, legislatures, and mainstream values. Certain Mormons have resisted the 1890 renunciation of polygamy. Although the Mormon Church excommunicates members for polygamy, practitioners of polygamy continue to consider themselves members of the church of Joseph Smith. These Mormon fundamentalists reject the idea that polygamy is anti-Christian or that they are promiscuous as charged in *Reynolds*. The principle of polygamy remains at the center of what church leaders condemn as the fundamentalists' apostate understanding of Mormon religious doctrine, identity, and community. Fundamentalists defend polygamy as a "straighter line to God," part of the path to eternal life, that is, salvation.[8] The willingness of fundamentalist Mormons, now estimated to number more than 30,000 to 50,000 in the United States, to live their religious belief in polygamy has meant ongoing legal confrontation.

After the formal abandonment of the principle of polygamy by the Mormon Church in 1890, polygamous families became few in number. Fundamentalists were scattered. By the early 1930s, however, small communities of families who followed "The Principle" (polygamy) had begun to come together in small isolated Western towns as well as at certain Mormon meetings in Salt Lake City and other larger communities. Fundamentalist religious interpretations found voice in a magazine named *Truth*. The growing numbers of fundamentalists and their visibility proved too much of a threat to civic authorities, and to the Mormon Church. In 1935 arrests of polygamous Mormon men and women began anew. Initially, only a handful of people were tried and convicted. The threat of imprisonment was enough, however, to revive the practice—common in the 1880s—of families going into hiding or becoming extraordinarily private in the conduct of their lives. And then, in early March of 1944, in the middle of the Second World War, federal and local officials declared a war of their own against the polygamists.

U.S. Attorney General John S. Boyden and Utah State Attorney General Brigham E. Roberts believed that the polygamists could be stopped once and for all with a massive roundup and criminal prosecution of polygamous couples. FBI agents, U.S. marshals, deputy sheriffs, Salt Lake City police, support units from several Utah and Arizona counties as well as sheriffs from Idaho served warrants for the arrest of fundamentalists charged with various categories of state and federal offenses. In state prosecutions, officials filed charges under unlawful cohabitation and criminal conspiracy laws. On behalf of the federal government, prosecutors also charged a number of fundamentalists with mailing obscene literature, kidnapping (under the federal Lindbergh Act), and white slave act violations (under the federal Mann Act).[9]

The fundamentalists won an important victory 11 days after the raid when Federal District Court Judge J. Foster Symes agreed that an indictment which charged 12 men with the mailing of obscene materials should be dismissed. The 12 fundamentalists had written for the magazine *Truth*. The federal government argued that their articles and editorials advocating plural marriage constituted criminally obscene, lewd, and lascivious matter. In *United States v. Barlow et al.* [56 F. Supp. 795 (1944)], Judge Symes, however, rejected the government's argument in an opinion clearly sympathetic to the fundamentalists:

A careful reading of the editorial discloses no obscene or filthy word or expression of lewd suggestion. . . . It is restrained and nothing more than an argument in favor of a practice that for many years was a tenet of the Mormon Church. . . . I cannot see how . . . these editorials . . . can be denominated as lascivious, or of a nature to excite erotic feelings or thoughts in the mind of the ordinary reader, or as tending to deprave public morals, or lead to impure purposes or practices.

The court takes judicial notice that the Mormon Church for many years advocated polygamy, and in so doing used the mails to disseminate its literature, advocating "celestial or plural marriages." Such a use of the mails has continued for many years without molestation. . . . In the interpretation of a doubtful and ambiguous statute a uniform administration practice by the authorities in respect thereto over a considerable period of time carries weight with the court, especially where, as here, thousands of good citizens sincerely and honestly believe in it as part of their religion.

Judge Symes concluded his opinion with the observation, one long made by fundamentalists, that American law and culture contained an openly double standard and that prosecution of Mormons was a form of harassment:

[O]ne cannot pick up a national magazine, or go to the theatre or movie without being confronted with illustrations and advertisements that tend more to incite sexual desire than do any of the publications in this magazine that have been called to our attention. . . . In fact sex incitement is a selling point of innumerable publications and advertisements that pass without comment or prosecution.

A 1946 decision of the U.S. Supreme Court also supported the fundamentalists by refusing to accept the appropriateness of a federal prosecution under the Federal Kidnapping (Lindbergh) Act. The defendant had been convicted of kidnapping when he transported a plural wife across state lines. In the appeal, *Chatwin v. United States* (326 U.S. 455), Justice Frank Murphy argued for the Court that "the broadness of the statutory language does not permit us to tear the words out of their context, using the magic of lexigraphy to apply them to unattractive or immoral situations lacking the involuntariness of seizure and detention." But ten months later, in *Cleveland v. United States* [329 U.S. 14 (1946)], Justice Murphy was not able to convince other members of the Supreme Court that the language of another federal statute, the Mann ("White Slave Traffic") Act, was not intended by Congress to include the transportation of polygamous wives across state lines. In *Cleveland*, Justice

William O. Douglas (a man who, in his personal life, engaged in serial monogamy) wrote for the majority that polygamy was a practice with pervasive influences in society and that "the establishment of polygamous households is a notorious example of promiscuity . . . branded as immoral in the law." Douglas argued that Congress intended, and earlier Supreme Court decisions had upheld, that the Mann Act not only prohibited the transportation in interstate commerce of "any woman or girl for the purpose of prostitution" or other forms of sex commercialism, but also immoral purposes that did not involve economic profit. The Mann Act, in the majority's view, applied to polygamous families moving across state borders, although the statute did not explicitly mention polygamy. The opinion thus reaffirmed the *Reynolds* doctrine that religious polygamy did not have constitutional protection under the First Amendment's free exercise clause.

In his opinion, the normally liberal Douglas made no effort to understand the culture of fundamentalist Mormons or to place their beliefs in a historical context. In contrast, Justice Murphy did. His dissent argues with the conclusion "that polygamy is 'in the same genus' as prostitution and debauchery and hence within the phrase [of the Mann Act] 'any other immoral purpose' simply because it has sexual connotations and has 'long been branded as immoral in the law' of this nation." He goes on to write that while it is not his intention "to defend the practice of polygamy or to claim that it is morally the equivalent of monogamy . . . it is essential to understand what it is, as well as what it is not." Polygamy, Justice Murphy stated:

was quite common among ancient civilizations and was referred to many times by the writers of the Old Testament; even today it is to be found frequently among certain pagan and non-Christian peoples of the world. We must recognize then, that polygyny, like other forms of marriage, is basically a cultural institution rooted deeply in the religious beliefs and social mores of those societies in which it appears. It is equally true that the beliefs and mores of the dominant culture of the contemporary world condemn the practice as immoral and substitute monogamy in its place. To those beliefs and mores I subscribe, but that does not alter the fact that polygyny is a form of marriage built upon a set of social and moral principles. It must be recognized and treated as such.

Writing from this cultural perspective, Justice Murphy outlined possibly the fairest and most neutral words ever offered by a high court jurist about Mormon polygamy. It was a dissent, however, and did not save the fundamentalists from their punishment as Mann Act criminals.

While these federal court cases moved forward, fundamentalists also fought local charges, stemming from the raids, that they had violated cohabitation and criminal conspiracy laws. The local trials raised fundamental issues of fairness as many of the eligible judges and prospective jurors in the tightly knit Mormon communities were members of the Church of Latter-day Saints, the church that had openly and willingly excommunicated the men whose cases were to be heard. In one trial, 200 individuals were interviewed during the *voir dire* before the defense and prosecution could reach agreement on jurors.

The cases resulting from the 1944 raids also demonstrate the vagaries of the law. In one Utah trial, *State v. Barlow et al.* [153 P.2D 647 (1944)], 15 fundamentalists charged with unlawful cohabitation were found guilty and sentenced to a maximum of five years' imprisonment in the state penitentiary. Their argument that the free exercise clause protected the religiously based practice of polygamy was rejected with the state prosecutor asserting that when the law of God and the law of the government conflict, citizens must obey the law of government.[10] But in a second, closely allied proceeding, *State v. Musser et al.* [175 P.2D 724 (1946)], 33 men and women convicted of criminal conspiracy to commit polygamy and unlawful cohabitation—"acts injurious to public morals"—won a dismissal of the case before the Utah State Supreme Court on remand from the U.S. Supreme Court. The state high court ruled that the cohabitation section of the conspiracy statute, under which the group was convicted, was "vague and indefinite under the Fourteenth Amendment to the Federal Constitution," and as such failed to give sufficient definition of the crime or reasonable standards for determining guilt.[11] The law could also present ironies. When one of the 15 convicted fundamentalists from the *Barlow* proceedings challenged a prison rule permitting inmates to send only two one-page letters weekly, officials granted special permission for the man—imprisoned for practicing polygamy—to write six letters a week because he had six wives.[12]

Despite the mixed public response to the 1944 raids, as well as the prosecutors' failure to win convictions in all of the cases against polygamists, public officials remained interested in the use of court action as a means of stamping out Mormon fundamentalism. In 1953, the state of Arizona carried out what was to become the last major raid on polygamous communities. In the early morning of Sunday, July 26, state highway patrolmen, deputy sheriffs, national guardsmen, and liquor control agents enlisted for the raid, swept down on the rural community of Short Creek. Arrest warrants were served on 36 men and 86 women who were variously charged with rape, statutory rape, carnal knowledge, polygamous living, unlawful and notorious cohabitation, bigamy, and adultery.[13] The state also took 153 of the children of Short Creek into custody, making them wards of the state.

The raid on Short Creek revealed ongoing revulsion with the idea of polygamy and, in particular, with the marriage of young girls to older fundamentalist men. Arizona governor Howard Pyle who, perhaps, envisioned the raid as an aid to his neophyte political career, revived the use of nineteenth-century rhetoric, describing polygamy as a form of degrading female slavery. New themes also emerged as part of the rationale for the expensive government action at Short Creek. Local taxpayers were indignant about the school taxes needed to educate fundamentalist children. Officials also said that an increasing number of fundamentalist mothers with large families were applying for child welfare. The plight of the children themselves became a central theme in justifying the raid. Where earlier condemnation had focused, in Justice Field's words, on the tendency of polygamy "to destroy the purity of the marriage relation . . . to degrade woman and to debase man," much of the justification for the state's action at Short Creek concentrated upon the perceived need to save the children of polygamous unions from the immoral socializing influence of their parents. The raid demonstrated the willingness and the power of modern government to assert itself as an alternative agent of socialization. The fact that Short Creek families were often poor and that the fundamentalists were communal in some of their economic arrangements only enhanced the appeal of a "good samaritan" operation in which the state would show fundamentalist children how to live a "decent" life.

Several years were required to try the hundreds of cases arising from the Short Creek raid. Most of the arrested polygamous husbands were convicted in Arizona courts. Many of these convictions, however, were reversed on the grounds that the Arizona legislature had never enacted a statute providing for the prosecution of violations of the state constitution's antipolygamy clause. Legal action involving Short Creek's plural wives with dependent children was, in some ways, more dramatic and complex. Immediately after the raid, the women and children were taken, in large groups, to Phoenix. It was a nearly day-long bus journey, later described by a state senator as an unsavory "deportation."[14] In Phoenix, the children were placed in government-supported foster homes where "wholesome values" could be learned. It has been suggested that this socialization included unconstitutional state involvement in teaching the children an alternative religion.

In order to stay by their children, fundamentalist mothers joined them in the foster homes. As each turn came, the mothers had to argue at a juvenile court hearing that she was fit to regain independent custody of her children. For many families this involved a two-to four-year ordeal during which they were required to live with strangers and not see the fathers of their children, as well as to endure requests to give their children up for adoption. Eventually, all of the children were given back to their mothers who promised to—but did not—renounce polygamy. This process was repeated in Utah in other well-publicized cases.

The Short Creek raid and subsequent prosecutions did not end the fundamentalists' assertion that they had a First Amendment right to practice polygamy. It did, however, lead polygamous families and communities to shroud themselves in secrecy until the 1980s when, left alone by law enforcement officials, fundamentalists began a slow campaign to win public acceptance. Aided by the social revolution occurring in the United States, fundamentalists began to grant interviews and to appear on television talk shows. They sought tolerance of their manner of living and explored, with public interest legal organizations such as the American Civil Liberties Union (ACLU), new ways to challenge the 100-year-old statutes and court decisions criminalizing polygamy. In 1991, the ACLU national board declared, "The ACLU believes that criminal and civil laws prohibiting or penalizing the practice of plural marriage violate constitutional protections of freedom of expression and association, freedom of religion, and privacy for personal relationships among consenting adults."[15]

Fundamentalists and the ACLU took one step in the legal challenge of *Reynolds* in a late 1980s case involving the right of a polygamous family to adopt children. Following the decision of a Utah Family Court judge that the polygamous Vaughn Fischer family was not eligible to adopt because "practice of polygamy is a crime and constitutes immoral conduct," the ACLU, in an amicus brief, argued that polygamy should be permitted and asked the Utah Supreme Court to consider whether *Reynolds* was still good law. The ACLU lawyers maintained that *Reynolds* was decided in the nineteenth century, a very different era, and contended that the Supreme Court has, in recent years, adopted a different standard for determining the constitutionality of regulations which burden religious conduct. In a close but important 3–2 decision in this case, the Utah Supreme Court ruled that polygamous families cannot be stripped of civil rights without due process, and that the Fischer family could not automatically be ruled ineligible to adopt because the adults were practicing plural marriage.

The question remains whether these polygamists will pursue legalization of religious polygamy or whether they will settle for the current willingness of state officials to look the other way. As Utah's Attorney General observed in 1991: "We all know what's going on. But trying to do anything about it legally would be opening one Pandora's box after another." Reflecting, no doubt, upon the larger American society in which so many young couples live together without marrying, he continued, "Once you start going after people for cohabitation, or adultery, where do you stop?"[16]

The issue of polygamy also prompts the question of the rights of American Muslims, another religion that sanctions polygyny. Muslims who wish to practice plural marriage experience the same legal restrictions as Mormon fundamentalists. Unlike the Mormons, however, Muslims face the additional problem of being identified with a religion characterized as non-Western and "exotic."[17] Exclusion of fundamentalist Mormons, and Muslims, from the civic privilege of legal plural marriage reflects the American preference for monogamy and the willingness to limit constitutional rights in order to enforce this preference.

NOTES

1. Although the Mormons only practice the form of polygamy known as polygyny, we have used the term *polygamy* throughout the chapter, as it is used in the court cases and popular culture. The discussion of the place of polygamy in the theology of the Church of Jesus Christ of Latter-day Saints draws upon the explanation offered by Martha Sonntag Bradley, *Kidnapped from That Land: The Government Raids on the Short Creek Polygamists* (Salt Lake City: University of Utah Press, 1993), 1–3. Although historians differ in their estimates, at best 20 percent of Mormons and perhaps as few as 5 percent of males and 12 percent of females have practiced polygyny since the 1850s. Id., 214, note 9.

2. Merle Wells, *Anti-Mormonism in Idaho, 1872–92* (Provo, Utah: Brigham Young University Press, 1978), 26. Historians have argued that "Contrary to public opinion, polygamy was not especially popular among Mormons. Most men had to be called, cajoled, and almost threatened into practicing it.... Despite outward appearances, it was a trial to all parties. They ... schooled themselves to bear its discomforts as a sort of religious penance." Maria S. Ellsworth, *Mormon Odyssey: The Story of Ida Hunt Udall, Plural Wife* (Urbana: University of Chicago Press, 1992), 45–46.

3. Wells, *Anti-Mormonism in Idaho*, 63–64.

4. U.S. Congress, Senate, *Congressional Record*, 51st Cong., 1st Sess., 1890, 51, pt. 7:6833. Quoted in Wells, *Anti-Mormonism in Idaho*, 147.

5. Mark P. Leone, *Roots of Modern Mormonism* (Cambridge: Harvard University Press, 1979), 151.

6. Robert Lindsey, "The Mormons," *New York Times Magazine*, January 12, 1986.

7. Some scholars argue that historians have overemphasized the impact of the 1890 Manifesto renouncing polygyny in causing a dramatic transformation in Mormon life and the way Mormons relate to the larger American culture. Grant Underwood suggests that there is not yet sufficient information on "the degree to which ordinary Latter-day Saints were actually affected by plural marriage, theocratic politics, and economic communalism" and that sweeping generalizations about "transformation" are premature. Grant Underwood, "Re-visioning Mormon History," *Pacific Historical Review* (August 1986): 406.

8. Bradley, *Kidnapped from That Land*, 34.

9. Ibid., 68–73.

10. Ibid., 80.

11. *State v. Musser et al.*, 175 Pacific Reporter, 2d Series, 724, 734 (1946).

12. Bradley, *Kidnapped from That Land*, 88.

13. This account of the 1953 raid draws upon Bradley, *Kidnapped from That Land*, chapters 8 and 9.

14. Ibid., 153.

15. American Civil Liberties Union, *Board Minutes*, April 6–7, 1991.

16. Dirk Johnson, "Polygamists Emerge from Secrecy, Seeking Not Just Peace but Respect," *New York Times*, April 9, 1991, A22.

17. Muslim foreigners applying for resident alien status must, under the Immigration Act of 1891 (26 Stat. 1084), swear that they are not polygamists or be denied admission to the United States.

6

Religion and Schools: The Amish

The Old Order Amish are an Anabaptist religion, which, in 1693 under the leadership of Jakob Amman, broke with their Swiss Mennonite brethren over matters of theology. The Amish faced severe persecution, even death, for practicing their religious beliefs in Europe, and the opportunity to practice their faith "unmolested and undisturbed" was an important factor in their migration to North America in the early eighteenth century. Today there are approximately 130,000 Amish in the United States, mainly living in Ohio, Pennsylvania, and Indiana, with other settlements in Michigan, Missouri, New York, and Wisconsin.[1]

The central value in Amish life is submission to a higher authority, which entails resignation to God's will, yielding to others, self-denial, contentment, and a quiet spirit. This value, modeled after the suffering Jesus who refused to resist his adversaries, clashes with the American cultural value that individuals have a legitimate right to exercise force to protect their rights and interests. The Amish spirit also clashes with the coercive nature of the state, which must sometimes use force to achieve its goals. Thus, the Amish, although enjoined not to "resist, despise, or condemn" the state, are also not permitted to participate in it.[2]

The Amish universe is divided into the "world," which is the non-Amish society representing vanity, vice, greed, and force, and their own "community of piety." This separation between the two worlds is essential not only for the continuity of the Amish as a group, but also for the salvation of the individual. The Amish are therefore "in the world but not of it" and a "congregation of the righteous," a "peculiar people," organizing their lives around obedience to God, as expressed by conformity to the community's rules.[3] In their attempts to keep the world of God separate from that of the state, Amish do not use the law to protect their rights or to force others to comply with contractual obligations, although they do allow themselves to be represented in court by non-Amish attorneys and friendly third parties. The Amish are allowed to vote, though they generally do not do so except occasionally in local elections, and are forbidden to hold political office, to serve on juries, or to serve in the armed forces.

Amish religion is woven into the fabric of everyday life: Religion, culture, and community are inseparable. Thus, while Amish conflicts with the state are expressed in the language of religious liberty, the underlying issue is that of cultures in conflict—that of the modern, secular, bureaucratized, technologically complex, individualistic rights-oriented culture of the United States with that of pietistic Christian religious principles, the importance of the local community, and the simple, nonacquisitive, noncoercive, communal culture of the Amish.

Amish separateness is manifest in their speech, dress, social customs, and their agricultural life. For the Amish, the soil has spiritual significance, and farming is a moral obligation. The Amish farm not merely to live, but rather to fashion a life which will permit them independence from the surrounding, ungodly world. They reject power machinery, including cars, tractors, electrical tools and appliances, and telephones. Their religion requires economic self-sufficiency, as commanded in I Timothy 5:8: "if any provide not for his own, and especially those of his own house, he hath denied the faith, and is worse than an infidel."

The Amish desire to avoid unnecessary contact with the outside world became increasingly difficult as government in the United States grew more bureaucratic and regulatory. By the nineteenth century, and throughout the twentieth, the Amish were increasingly drawn into legal conflicts with the state over what they regarded as impermissible intrusions into the exercise of their religion. In some of these conflicts, like mandatory contributions to Social Security, which violated their religious principle of self-sufficiency, or pacifism, which brought them in conflict with local draft boards, no compromise for the Amish was possible. On other matters, however, such as traffic, zoning, pollution, and land use regulations, the Amish have negotiated successfully with local communities and have been able to compromise, such as in their willingness to use flashing lights on their carriages when required by state law. In some areas, state and federal governments have accommodated the Amish; in response to their informational campaign before Congress, for example, in 1965, the Amish were granted an exemption from mandatory contributions to Social Security.

Unlike the Jehovah's Witnesses, the Amish do not proselytize; this may be one reason why, nationally, they have a generally favorable image. Local communities, however, have frequently been unfriendly to the

Amish. As the Amish expanded into new areas, as newcomers and as a "peculiar people" who were pacifists as well, they often became targets of hostility, particularly of the xenophobia which flourished when the United States was at war. This hostility was sometimes expressed by aggressive enforcement of state laws requiring compulsory education until the age of 16, which the Amish hold are incompatible with their religiously mandated separation from the larger society.

The Amish are not opposed to all formal education. Traditionally, they sent their children to local, one-room schools, whose remoteness permitted the isolation of Amish children from "English" children and the teaching of a curriculum that did not violate Amish religious tenets. As the twentieth century progressed, however, and school organization and curricula reflected the urban and technological development in the United States, the one-room schoolhouse gave way, in the school consolidation movement, to larger institutions mixing children from diverse cultural backgrounds. In these years, the age of compulsory education was also extended.

The Amish resisted these educational developments which exposed Amish children too much to the outside world and undermined the community's ability to maintain control over its younger members. The Amish created and controlled "vocational" schools were regarded as substandard academically and not acceptable. The Amish were also generally unsuccessful in resisting state education laws in courts, where they claimed (represented by non-Amish lawyers) that such laws violated the free exercise of their religion.

In 1972, when three Amish fathers who had refused to enroll their teenage children in a Wisconsin high school were arrested, the long-simmering controversy between the Amish and the state reached the U.S. Supreme Court. In *Wisconsin v. Yoder,* the Court was asked whether the state's interest in universal education was more compelling than the Amish First Amendment claim to the right of free exercise of their religion. In its decision the Court held, for the first time in American history, the right of an individual to be exempt from compulsory education laws on the basis of religious freedom. Chief Justice Burger wrote the opinion of the Court:

Wisconsin v. Yoder
406 U.S. 205 (1972)

Respondents Jonas Yoder and Wallace Miller are members of the Old Order Amish religion, and respondent Adin Yutzy is a member of the Conservative Amish Mennonite Church. They and their families are residents of Green County, Wisconsin. Wisconsin's compulsory school-attendance law required them to cause their children to attend public or private school until reaching age 16 but the respondents declined to send their children, ages 14 and 15, to public school after they completed the eighth grade. The children were not enrolled in any private school, or within any recognized exception to the compulsory-attendance law, and they are conceded to be subject to the Wisconsin statute.

On complaint of the school district administrator for the public schools, respondents were charged, tried, and convicted of violating the compulsory-attendance law in Green County Court and were fined the sum of $5 each. Respondents defended on the ground that the application of the compulsory-attendance law violated their rights under the First and Fourteenth Amendments. The trial testimony showed that respondents believed, in accordance with the tenets of Old Order Amish communities generally, that their children's attendance at high school, public or private, was contrary to the Amish religion and way of life. They believed that by sending their children to high school, they would not only expose themselves to the danger of the censure of the church community, but, as found by the county court, also endanger their own salvation and that of their children. The State stipulated that respondents' religious beliefs were sincere.

In support of their position, respondents presented as expert witnesses scholars on religion and education whose testimony is uncontradicted. They expressed their opinions on the relationship of the Amish belief concerning school attendance to the more general tenets of their religion, and described the impact that compulsory high school attendance could have on the continued survival of Amish communities as they exist in the United States today. The history of the Amish sect was given in some detail, beginning with the Swiss Anabaptists of the 16th century who rejected institutionalized churches and sought to return to the early, simple, Christian life de-emphasizing material success, rejecting the competitive spirit, and seeking to insulate themselves from the modern world. As a result of their common heritage, Old Order Amish communities today are characterized by a fundamental belief that salvation requires life in a church community separate and apart from the world and worldly influence. This concept of life aloof from the world and its values is central to their faith.

A related feature of Old Order Amish communities is their devotion to a life in harmony with nature and the soil, as exemplified by the simple life of the early Christian era that continued in America during much of our early national life. Amish beliefs require members of the community to make their living by farming or closely related activities. Broadly speaking, the Old Order Amish religion pervades and determines the entire mode of life of its adherents. Their conduct is regulated in great detail by the *Ordnung*, or rules, of the church community. Adult baptism, which occurs in late adolescence, is the time at which Amish young people voluntarily undertake heavy obligations, not unlike the Bar Mitzvah of the Jews, to abide by the rules of the church community.

Amish objection to formal education beyond the eighth grade is firmly grounded in these central religious concepts. They object to the high school, and higher education generally, because the values they teach are in marked variance with Amish values and the Amish way of life; they view secondary school education as an impermissable exposure of their children to a "worldly" influence in conflict with their beliefs. The high school tends to emphasize intellectual and scientific accomplishments, self-distinction, competitiveness, worldly success, and social life with other students. Amish society emphasizes informal learning-through-doing; a life of "goodness," rather than a life of intellect; wisdom, rather than technical knowledge; community welfare, rather than competition; and separation from, rather than integration with, contemporary worldly society.

Formal high school education beyond the eighth grade is contrary to Amish beliefs, not only because it places Amish children in an environment hostile to Amish beliefs with increasing emphasis on competition in class work and sports and with pressure to conform to the styles, manners, and ways of the peer group, but also because it takes them away from their community, physically and emotionally, during the crucial and formative adolescent period of life. During this period, the children must acquire Amish attitudes favoring manual work and self-reliance and the specific skills needed to perform the adult role of an Amish farmer or housewife. They must learn to enjoy physical labor. Once a child has learned basic reading, writing, and elementary mathematics, these traits, skills, and attitudes admittedly fall within the category of those best learned through example and "doing" rather than in a classroom. And, at this time in life, the Amish child must also grow in his faith and his relationship to the Amish community if he is to be prepared to accept the heavy obligations imposed by adult baptism. In short, high school attendance with teachers who are not of the Amish faith—and may even be hostile to it—interposes a serious barrier to the integration of the Amish child into the Amish religious community. Dr. John Hostetler, one of the experts on Amish society, testified that the modern high school is not equipped, in curriculum or social environment, to impart the values promoted by Amish society.

The Amish do not object to elementary education through the first eight grades as a general proposition because they agree that their children must have basic skills in the "three R's" in order to read the Bible, to be good farmers and citizens, and to be able to deal with non-Amish people when necessary in the course of daily affairs. They view such a basic education as acceptable because it does not significantly expose their children to worldly values or interfere with their development in the Amish community during the crucial adolescent period. While the Amish accept compulsory elementary education generally, wherever possible they have established their own elementary schools in many respects like the small local schools of the past. In the Amish belief higher learning tends to develop values they reject as influences that alienate man from God.

On the basis of such considerations, Dr. Hostetler testified that compulsory high school attendance could not only result in great psychological harm to Amish children, because of the conflicts it would produce, but would also, in his opinion, ultimately result in the destruction of the Old Order Amish church community as it exists in the United States today. The testimony of Dr. Donald A. Erickson, an expert witness on education also showed that the Amish succeed in preparing their high school age children to be productive members of the Amish community. He described their system of learning through doing the skills directly relevant to their adult roles in the Amish community as "ideal" and perhaps superior to ordinary high school education. The evidence also showed that the Amish have an excellent record as law-abiding and generally self-sufficient members of society. . . .

There is no doubt as to the power of a State, having a high responsibility for education of its citizens, to impose reasonable regulations for the control and duration of basic education. Providing public schools ranks at the very apex of the function of a State. Yet even this paramount responsibility was, in *Pierce*, made to yield to the right of parents to provide an equivalent education in a privately operated system. . . . Thus, a State's interest in universal education, however highly we rank it, is not totally free from a balancing process when it impinges on fundamental rights and interests, such as those specifically protected by the Free Exercise Clause of the First Amendment, and the traditional interest of parents with respect to the religious upbringing of their children so long as they, in the words of *Pierce*, "prepare [them] for additional obligations. . . ." We can accept it as settled, therefore, that, however strong the State's interest in universal compulsory education, it is by no means absolute to the exclusion or subordination of all other interests. . . .

We come then to the quality of the claims of the respondents concerning the alleged encroachment of Wisconsin's compulsory school-attendance statute on their rights and the rights of their children to the free exercise of the religious beliefs they and their forebears have adhered to for almost three centuries. In evaluating those claims we must be careful to determine whether the Amish religious faith and their mode of life are, as they claim, inseparable and inter-dependent. A way of life, however virtuous and admirable, may not be inter-posed as a barrier to reasonable state regulation of education if it is based on purely secular considerations; to have the protection of the Religion Clauses, the claims must be rooted in religious belief. Although a determination of what is a "religious" belief or practice entitled to constitutional protection may present a most delicate question, the very concept of ordered liberty precludes allowing every person to make his own standards on matters of conduct in which society as a whole has important interests. Thus, if the Amish asserted their claims be-cause of their subjective evaluation and rejection of the contemporary secular values accepted by the majority, much as Thoreau rejected the social values of his time and isolated himself at Walden Pond, their claims would not rest on a religious basis. Thoreau's choice was philosophical and personal rather than re-ligious, and such belief does not rise to the demands of the Religion Clauses.

Giving no weight to such secular considerations, however, we see that the record in this case abundantly supports the claim that the traditional way of life of the Amish is not merely a matter of personal preference, but one of deep religious conviction, shared by an organized group, and intimately related to daily living. That the Old Order Amish daily life and religious practice stem from their faith is shown by the fact that it is in response to their literal inter-pretation of the Biblical injunction from the Epistle of Paul to the Romans, "be not conformed to this world. . . ." This command is fundamental to the Amish faith. Moreover, for the Old Order Amish, religion is not simply a matter of theocratic belief. As the expert witnesses explained, the Old Order Amish religion pervades and determines virtually their entire way of life, regulating it with the detail of the Talmudic diet through the strictly enforced rules of the church com-munity.

The record shows that the respondents' religious beliefs and attitude toward life, family, and home have remained constant—perhaps some would say static—in a period of unparalleled progress in human knowledge generally and great changes in education. The respondents freely concede, and indeed assert as an article of faith, that their religious beliefs and what we would today call "life style" have not altered in fundamentals for centuries. Their way of life in a church-oriented community, separated from the outside world and "worldly" influences, their attachment to nature and the soil, is a way inherently simple and uncomplicated, albeit difficult to preserve against the pressure to conform. Their rejection of telephones, automobiles, radios, and television, their mode of dress, of speech, their habits of manual work do indeed set them apart from much of contemporary society; these customs are both symbolic and practical.

As the society around the Amish has become more populous, urban, industrialized, and complex, particularly in this century, government regulation of human affairs has correspondingly become more detailed and pervasive. The Amish mode of life has thus come into conflict increasingly with requirements of contemporary society exerting a hydraulic insistence on conformity to majoritarian standards. So long as compulsory education laws were confined to eight grades of elementary basic education imparted in a nearby rural schoolhouse, with a large proportion of students of the Amish faith, the Old Order Amish had little basis to fear that school attendance would expose their children to the worldly influence they reject. But modern compulsory secondary education in rural areas is now largely carried on in a consolidated school, often remote from the student's home and alien to his daily home life. As the record so strongly shows, the values and programs of the modern secondary school are in sharp conflict with the fundamental mode of life mandated by the Amish religion; modern laws requiring compulsory secondary education have accordingly engendered great concern and conflict. The conclusion is inescapable that secondary schooling, by exposing Amish children to worldly influences in terms of attitudes, goals, and values contrary to beliefs, and by substantially interfering with the religious development of the Amish child and his integration into the way of life of the Amish faith community at the crucial adolescent stage of development, contravenes the basic religious tenets and practices of the Amish faith, both as to the parent and the child.

The impact of the compulsory-attendance law on respondents' practice of the Amish religion is not only severe, but inescapable, for the Wisconsin law affirmatively compels them, under threat of criminal sanction, to perform acts undeniably at odds with fundamental tenets of their religious beliefs. Nor is the impact of the compulsory-attendance law confined to grave interference with important Amish religious tenets from a subjective point of view. It carries with it precisely the kind of objective danger to the free exercise of religion that the First Amendment was designed to prevent. As the record shows, compulsory school attendance to age 16 for Amish children carries with it a very real threat of undermining the Amish community and religious practice as they exist today; they must either abandon belief and be assimilated into society at large, or be forced to migrate to some other and more tolerant region.

In sum, the unchallenged testimony of acknowledged experts in education and religious history, almost 300 years of consistent practice, and strong evidence of a sustained faith pervading and regulating respondents' entire mode of life support the claim that enforcement of the State's requirement of compulsory formal education after the eighth grade would gravely endanger if not destroy the free exercise of respondents' religious beliefs.

Neither the findings of the trial court nor the Amish claims as to the nature of their faith are challenged in this Court by the State of Wisconsin. Its position is that the State's interest in universal compulsory formal secondary education to age 16 is so great that it is paramount to the undisputed claims of respondents that their mode of preparing their youth for Amish life, after the traditional elementary education, is an essential part of their religious belief and practice. Nor does the State undertake to meet the claim that the Amish mode of life and education is inseparable from and a part of the basic tenets of their religion—indeed, as much a part of their religious belief and practices as baptism, the confessional, or a sabbath may be for others.

Wisconsin concedes that under the Religion Clauses religious beliefs are absolutely free from the State's control, but it argues that "actions," even though religiously grounded, are outside the protection of the First Amendment. But our decisions have rejected the idea that religiously grounded conduct is always outside the protection of the Free Exercise Clause. It is true that activities of individuals, even when religiously based, are often subject to regulation by the States in the exercise of their undoubted power to promote the health, safety, and general welfare, or the Federal Government in the exercise of its delegated powers. But to agree that religiously grounded conduct must often be subject to the broad police power of the State is not to deny that there are areas of conduct protected by the Free Exercise Clause of the First Amendment and thus beyond the power of the State to control, even under regulations of general applicability. This case, therefore, does not become easier because respondents were convicted for their "actions" in refusing to send their children to the public high school; in this context belief and action cannot be neatly confined in logic-tight compartments.

Nor can this case be disposed of on the grounds that Wisconsin's requirement for school attendance to age 16 applies uniformly to all citizens of the State and does not, on its face, discriminate against religions or a particular religion, or that it is motivated by legitimate secular concerns. A regulation neutral on its face may, in its application, nonetheless offend the constitutional requirement for governmental neutrality if it unduly burdens the free exercise of religion. The Court must not ignore the danger that an exception from a general obligation of citizenship on religious grounds may run afoul of the Establishment Clause, but that danger cannot be allowed to prevent any exception no matter how vital it may be to the protection of values promoted by the right of free exercise. By preserving doctrinal flexibility and recognizing the need for a sensible and realistic application of the Religion Clauses

> we have been able to chart a course that preserved the autonomy and freedom of religious bodies while avoiding any semblance of established religion. This is a 'tight rope' and one we have successfully traversed.

We turn, then, to the State's broader contention that its interest in its system of compulsory education is so compelling that even the established religious practices of the Amish must give way. Where fundamental claims of religious freedom are at stake, however, we cannot accept such a sweeping claim; despite its admitted validity in the generality of cases, we must searchingly examine the interests that the State seeks to promote by its requirement for compulsory education to age 16, and the impediment to those objectives that would flow from recognizing the claimed Amish exemption.

The State advances two primary arguments in support of its system of compulsory education. It notes, as Thomas Jefferson pointed out early in our history, that some degree of education is necessary to prepare citizens to participate effectively and intelligently in our open political system if we are to preserve freedom and independence. Further, education prepares individuals to be self-reliant and self-sufficient participants in society. We accept these propositions.

However, the evidence adduced by the Amish in this case is persuasively to the effect that an additional one or two years of formal high school for Amish children in place of their long-established program of informal vocational education would do little to serve those interests. Respondents' experts testified at trial, without challenge, that the value of all education must be assessed in terms of its capacity to prepare the child for life. It is one thing to say that compulsory education for a year or two beyond the eighth grade may be necessary when its goal is the preparation of the child for life in modern society as the majority live, but it is quite another if the goal of education be viewed as the preparation of the child for life in the separated agrarian community that is the keystone of the Amish faith.

The State attacks respondents' position as one fostering "ignorance" from which the child must be protected by the State. No one can question the State's duty to protect children from ignorance but this argument does not square with the facts disclosed in the record. Whatever their idiosyncrasies as seen by the majority, this record strongly shows that the Amish community has been a highly successful social unit within our society, even if apart from the conventional "mainstream." Its members are productive and very law-abiding members of society; they reject public welfare in any of its usual modern forms. The Congress itself recognized their self-sufficiency by authorizing exemption of such groups as the Amish from the obligation to pay social security taxes.

It is neither fair nor correct to suggest that the Amish are opposed to education beyond the eighth grade level. What this record shows is that they are opposed to conventional formal education of the type provided by a certified high school because it comes at the child's crucial adolescent period of religious development. Dr. Donald Erickson, for example, testified that their system of learning-by-doing was an "ideal system" of education in terms of preparing Amish children for life as adults in the Amish community, and that "I would be inclined to say they do a better job in this than most of the rest of us do." As he put it, "These people aren't purporting to be learned people, and it seems to me the self-sufficiency of the community is the best evidence I can point to—whatever is being done seems to function well."

We must not forget that in the Middle Ages important values of the civilization of the Western World were preserved by members of religious orders who isolated themselves from all worldly influences against great obstacles. There can be no assumption that today's majority is "right" and the Amish and others like them are "wrong." A way of life that is odd or even erratic but interferes with no rights or interests of others is not to be condemned because it is different.

The State, however, supports its interest in providing an additional one or two years of compulsory high school education to Amish children because of the possibility that some such children will choose to leave the Amish community, and that if this occurs they will be ill-equipped for life. The State argues that if Amish children leave their church they should not be in the position of making their way in the world without the education available in the one or two additional years the State requires. However, on this record, the argument is highly speculative. There is no specific evidence of the loss of Amish adherents by attrition, nor is there any showing that upon leaving the Amish community Amish children, with their practical agricultural training and habits of industry and self-reliance, would become burdens on society because of educational shortcomings. Indeed, this argument of the State appears to rest primarily on the State's mistaken assumption, already noted, that the Amish do not provide any education for their children beyond the eighth grade, but allow them to grow in "ignorance." To the contrary, not only do the Amish accept the necessity for formal schooling through the eighth grade level, but continue to provide what has been characterized by the undisputed testimony of expert educators as an "ideal" vocational education for their children in the adolescent years.

There is nothing in this record to suggest that the Amish qualities of reliability, self-reliance, and dedication to work would fail to find ready markets in today's society. Absent some contrary evidence supporting the State's position, we are unwilling to assume that persons possessing such valuable vocational skills and habits are doomed to become burdens on society should they determine to leave the Amish faith, nor is there any basis in the record to warrant a finding that an additional one or two years of formal school education beyond the eighth grade would serve to eliminate any such problem that might exist.

Insofar as the State's claim rests on the view that a brief additional period of formal education is imperative to enable the Amish to participate effectively and intelligently in our democratic process, it must fall. The Amish alternative to formal secondary school education has enabled them to function effectively in their day-to-day life under self-imposed limitations on relations with the world, and to survive and prosper in contemporary society as a separate, sharply identifiable and highly self-sufficient community for more than 200 years in this country. In itself this is strong evidence that they are capable of fulfilling the social and political responsibilities of citizenship without compelled attendance beyond the eighth grade at the price of jeopardizing their free exercise of religious belief. When Thomas Jefferson emphasized the need for education as a bulwark of a free people against tyranny, there is nothing to indicate he had in mind compulsory education through any fixed age beyond a basic education. Indeed, the Amish communities singularly parallel and reflect many of the virtues of Jefferson's ideal of the "sturdy yeoman" who would form the basis of what he considered as the ideal of a democratic society. Even their idiosyncratic separateness exemplifies the diversity we profess to admire and encourage.

The requirement for compulsory education beyond the eighth grade is a relatively recent development in our history. Less than 60 years ago, the educational requirements of almost all of the States were satisfied by completion of the elementary grades, at least where the child was regularly and lawfully employed. The independence and successful social functioning of the Amish community for a period approaching almost three centuries and more than 200 years in this country are strong evidence that there is at best a speculative gain, in terms of meeting the duties of citizenship, from an additional one or two years of compulsory formal education. Against this background it would require a more particularized showing from the State on this point to justify the severe interference with religious freedom such additional compulsory attendance would entail.

We should also note that compulsory education and child labor laws find their historical origin in common humanitarian instincts, and that the age limits of both laws have been coordinated to achieve their related objectives. In the context of this case, such considerations, if anything, support rather than detract from respondents' position. The origins of the requirement for school attendance to age 16, an age falling after the completion of elementary school but before completion of high school, are not entirely clear. But to some extent such laws reflected the movement to prohibit most child labor under age 16 that culminated in the provisions of the Federal Fair Labor Standards Act of 1938. It is true, then, that the 16-year child labor age limit may to some degree derive from a contemporary impression that children should be in school until that age. But at the same time, it cannot be denied that, conversely, the 16-year education limit reflects, in substantial measure, the concern that children under that age not be employed under conditions hazardous to their health, or in work that should be performed by adults.

The requirement of compulsory schooling to age 16 must therefore be viewed as aimed not merely at providing educational opportunities for children, but as an alternative to the equally undesirable consequence of unhealthful child labor displacing adult workers, or, on the other hand, forced idleness. The two kinds of statutes—compulsory school attendance and child labor laws—tend to keep children of certain ages off the labor market and in school; this regimen in turn provides opportunity to prepare for a livelihood of a higher order than that which children could pursue without education and protects their health in adolescence.

In these terms, Wisconsin's interest in compelling the school attendance of Amish children to age 16 emerges as somewhat less substantial than requiring such attendance for children generally. For, while agricultural employment is not totally outside the legitimate concerns of the child labor laws, employment of children under parental guidance and on the family farm from age 14 to age 16 is an ancient tradition that lies at the periphery of the objectives of such laws. There is no intimation that the Amish employment of their children on family farms is in any way deleterious to their health or that Amish parents exploit children at tender years. Any such inference would be contrary to the record before us. Moreover, employment of Amish children on the family farm does not present the undesirable economic aspects of eliminating jobs that might otherwise be held by adults.

Finally, the State, on authority of *Prince v. Massachusetts,* argues that a decision exempting Amish children from the State's requirement fails to recognize the substantive right of the Amish child to a secondary education, and fails to give due regard to the power of the State as *parens patriae* to extend the benefit of secondary education to children regardless of the wishes of their parents. Taken at its broadest sweep, the Court's language in *Prince* might be read to give support to the State's position. However, the Court was not confronted in *Prince* with a situation comparable to that of the Amish as revealed in this record. . . .

This case [in contrast to *Prince*], of course, is not one in which any harm to the physical or mental health of the child or to the public safety, peace, order, or welfare has been demonstrated or may be properly inferred. The record is to the contrary, and any reliance on that theory would find no support in the evidence.

Contrary to the suggestion of the dissenting opinion of Mr. Justice Douglas, our holding today in no degree depends on the assertion of the religious interest of the child as contrasted with that of the parents. It is the parents who are subject to prosecution here for failing to cause their children to attend school, and it is their right of free exercise, not that of their children that must determine Wisconsin's power to impose criminal penalties on the parent. The dissent argues that a child who expresses a desire to attend public high school in conflict with the wishes of his parents should not be prevented from doing so. There is no reason for the Court to consider that point since it is not an issue in the case. The children are not parties to this litigation. The State has at no point tried this case on the theory that respondents were preventing their children from attending school against their expressed desires, and indeed the record is to the contrary. The State's position from the outset has been that it is empowered to apply its compulsory-attendance law to Amish parents in the same manner as to other parents—that is, without regard to the wishes of the child. That is the claim we reject today.

Our holding in no way determines the proper resolution of possible competing interests of parents, children and the State in an appropriate state court proceeding in which the power of the State is asserted on the theory that Amish parents are preventing their minor children from attending high school despite their expressed desires to the contrary. Recognition of the claim of the State in such a proceeding would, of course, call into question traditional concepts of parental control over the religious upbringing and education of their minor children recognized in this Court's past decisions. It is clear that such an intrusion by a State into family decisions in the area of religious training would give rise to grave questions of religious freedom comparable to those raised here and those presented in *Pierce v. Society of Sisters*. On this record we neither reach nor decide those issues.

The State's argument proceeds without reliance on any actual conflict between the wishes of parents and children. It appears to rest on the potential that exemption of Amish parents from the requirements of the compulsory-education law might allow some parents to act contrary to the best interests of their children by foreclosing their opportunity to make an intelligent choice between the Amish way of life and that of the outside world. The same argument could, of course, be made with respect to all church schools short of college. There is nothing in the record or in the ordinary course of human experience to suggest that non-Amish parents generally consult with children of ages 14–16 if they are placed in a church school of the parents' faith.

Indeed it seems clear that if the State is empowered, as *parens patriae*, to "save" a child from himself or his Amish parents by requiring an additional two years of compulsory formal high school education, the State will in large measure influence, if not determine, the religious future of the child. Even more markedly than in *Prince*, therefore, this case involves the fundamental interest of parents, as contrasted with that of the State, to guide the religious future and education of their children. The history and culture of Western civilization reflect a strong tradition of parental concern for the nurture and upbringing of their children. This primary role of the parents in the upbringing of their children is now established beyond debate as an enduring American tradition. If not the first, perhaps the most significant statements of the Court in this area are found in *Pierce v. Society of Sisters*, in which the Court observed:

> Under the doctrine of *Meyer v. Nebraska*, we think it entirely plain that the Act of 1922 unreasonably interferes with the liberty of parents and guardians to direct the upbringing and education of children under their control. As often heretofore pointed out rights guaranteed by the Constitution may not be abridged by legislation which has no reasonable relation to some purpose within the competency of the State. The fundamental theory of liberty upon which all governments in this Union repose excludes any general power of the State to standardize its children by forcing them to accept instruction from public teachers only. The child is not the mere creature of the State; those who nurture him and direct his destiny have the right, coupled with the high duty, to recognize and prepare him for additional obligations.

The duty to prepare the child for "additional obligations," referred to by the Court, must be read to include the inculcation of moral standards, religious beliefs, and elements of good citizenship. *Pierce*, of course, recognized that where nothing more than the general interest of the parent in the nurture and education of his children is involved, it is beyond dispute that the State acts "reasonably" and constitutionally in requiring education to age 16 in some public or private school meeting the standards prescribed by the State.

However read, the Court's holding in *Pierce* stands as a charter of the rights of parents to direct the religious upbringing of their children. And, when the interests of parenthood are combined with a free exercise claim of the nature revealed by this record, more than merely a "reasonable relation to some purpose within the competency of the State" is required to sustain the validity of the State's requirement under the First Amendment. To be sure, the power of the parent, even when linked to a free exercise claim, may be subject to limitation under *Prince* if it appears that parental decisions will jeopardize the health or safety of the child, or have a potential for significant social burdens. But in this case, the Amish have introduced persuasive evidence undermining the arguments the State has advanced to support its claims in terms of the welfare of the child and society as a whole. The record strongly indicates that accommodating the religious objections of the Amish by forgoing one, or at most two, additional years of compulsory education will not impair the physical or mental health of the child, or result in an inability to be self-supporting or to discharge the duties and responsibilities of citizenship, or in any other way materially detract from the welfare of society.

In the face of our consistent emphasis on the central values underlying the Religion Clauses in our constitutional scheme of government, we cannot accept a *parens patriae* claim of such all-encompassing scope and with such sweeping potential for broad and unforeseeable application as that urged by the State.

For the reasons stated we hold, with the Supreme Court of Wisconsin, that the First and Fourteenth Amendments prevent the State from compelling respondents to cause their children to attend formal high school to age 16. . . . It cannot be overemphasized that we are not dealing with a way of life and mode of education by a group claiming to have recently discovered some "progressive" or more enlightened process for rearing children for modern life.

Aided by a history of three centuries as an identifiable religious sect and a long history as a successful and self-sufficient segment of American society, the Amish in this case have convincingly demonstrated the sincerity of their religious beliefs, the interrelationship of belief with their mode of life, the vital role that belief and daily conduct play in the continued survival of Old Order Amish communities and their religious organization, and the hazards presented by the State's enforcement of a statute generally valid as to others. Beyond this, they have carried the even more difficult burden of demonstrating the adequacy of their alternative mode of continuing informal vocational education in terms of precisely those overall interests that the State advances in support of its program of compulsory high school education. In light of this convincing showing, one that probably few other religious groups or sects could make, and weighing the minimal differences between what the State would require and what the Amish already accept, it was incumbent on the State to show with more particularity how its admittedly strong interest in compulsory education would be adversely affected by granting an exemption to the Amish.

Nothing we hold is intended to undermine the general applicability of the State's compulsory school-attendance statutes or to limit the power of the State to promulgate reasonable standards that, while not impairing the free exercise of religion, provide for continuing agricultural vocational education under parental and church guidance by the Old Order Amish or others similarly situated. The States have had a long history of amicable and effective relationships with church-sponsored schools, and there is no basis for assuming that, in this related context, reasonable standards cannot be established concerning the content of the continuing vocational education of Amish children under parental guidance, provided always that state regulations are not inconsistent with what we have said in this opinion.

In his concurring opinion, joined by Justices Brennan and Stewart, Justice White took up a point which he felt the court had insufficiently emphasized:

Cases such as this one inevitably call for a delicate balancing of important but conflicting interests. I join the opinion and judgment of the Court because I cannot say that the State's interest in requiring two more years of compulsory education in the ninth and tenth grades outweighs the importance of the concededly sincere Amish religious practice to the survival of that sect.

This would be a very different case for me if respondents' claim were that their religion forbade their children from attending any school at any time and from complying in any way with the educational standards set by the State. Since the Amish children are permitted to acquire the basic tools of literacy to survive in modern society by attending grades one through eight and since the deviation from the State's compulsory-education law is relatively slight, I conclude that respondents' claim must prevail, largely because "religious freedom—the freedom to believe and to practice strange and, it may be, foreign creeds—has classically been one of the highest values of our society."

The importance of the state interest asserted here cannot be denigrated, however:

> Today, education is perhaps the most important function of state and local governments. Compulsory school attendance laws and the great expenditures for education both demonstrate our recognition of the importance of education to our democratic society. It is required in the performance of our most basic public responsibilities, even service in the armed forces. It is the very foundation of good citizenship. Today it is a principal instrument in awakening the child to cultural values, in preparing him for later professional training, and in helping him to adjust normally to his environment.

As recently as last Term, the Court re-emphasized the legitimacy of the State's concern for enforcing minimal educational standards ... lends no support to the contention that parents may replace state educational requirements with their own idiosyncratic views of what knowledge a child needs to be a productive and happy member of society; in *Pierce,* both the parochial and military schools were in compliance with all the educational standards that the State had set, and the Court held simply that while a State may posit such standards, it may not pre-empt the educational process by requiring children to attend public schools. In the present case, the State is not concerned with the maintenance of an educational system as an end in itself, it is rather attempting to nurture and develop the human potential of its children whether Amish or non-Amish: to expand their knowledge, broaden their sensibilities, kindle their imagination, foster a spirit of free inquiry, and increase their human understanding and tolerance. It is possible that most Amish children will wish to continue living the rural life of their parents, in which case their training at home will adequately equip them for their future role. Others, however, may wish to become nuclear physicists, ballet dancers, computer programmers, or historians, and for these occupations, formal training will be necessary. There is evidence in the record that many children desert the Amish faith when they come of age. A State has a legitimate interest not only in seeking to develop the latent talents of its children but also in seeking to prepare them for the life style that they may later choose, or at least to provide them with an option other than the life they have led in the past. In the circumstances of this case, although the question is close, I am unable to say that the State has demonstrated that Amish children who leave school in the eighth grade will be intellectually stultified or unable to acquire new academic skills later. The statutory minimum school attendance age set by the State is, after all, only 16.

Decision in cases such as this and the administration of an exemption for Old Order Amish from the State's compulsory school-attendance laws will inevitably involve the kind of close and perhaps repeated scrutiny of religious practices, as is exemplified in today's opinion, which the Court has heretofore been anxious to avoid. But such entanglement does not create a forbidden establishment of religion where it is essential to implement free exercise values threatened by an otherwise neutral program instituted to foster some permissible, nonreligious state objective. I join the Court because the sincerity of the Amish religious policy here is uncontested, because the potentially adverse impact of the state require-ment is great, and because the State's valid interest in education has already been largely satisfied by the eight years the children have already spent in school.

In his separate opinion, Justice Douglas indicated that he joined the decision of the court with respect to reversing the conviction of Jonas Yoder because Yoder's daughter Frieda had testified that she agreed with the decision to withdraw from school on the basis of religious belief. Concerned, however, with the impact of the majority's opinion on those Amish children who might not share the community's view on the un-acceptability of education after the eighth grade, Douglas dissented on behalf of the Yutzy and Miller children, who were not called to testify, and whose views were not therefore known, and on behalf of all other Amish children whose views might be contrary to those of their parents:

I agree with the Court that the religious scruples of the Amish are opposed to the education of their children beyond the grade schools, yet I disagree with the Court's conclusion that the matter is within the dispensation of the parents alone. The Court's analysis assumes that the only interests at stake in the case are those of the Amish parents on the one hand, and those of the State on the other. The difficulty with this approach is that, despite the Court's claim, the parents are seeking to vindicate not only their own free exercise claims, but also those of their high-school-age children.

It is argued that the right of the Amish children to religious freedom is not presented by the facts of the case, as the issue before the Court involves only the Amish parents' religious freedom to defy a state criminal statute imposing upon them an affirmative duty to cause their children to attend high school.

First, respondents' motion to dismiss in the trial court expressly asserts, not only the religious liberty of the adults, but also that of the children, as a defense to the prosecutions. It is, of course, beyond question that the parents have stand-ing as defendants in a criminal prosecution to assert the religious interests of their children as a defense. Although the lower courts and a majority of this Court assume an identity of interest between parent and child, it is clear that they have treated the religious interest of the child as a factor in the analysis.

Second, it is essential to reach the question to decide the case, not only because the question was squarely raised in the motion to dismiss, but also because no analysis of religious-liberty claims can take place in a vacuum. If the parents in this case are allowed a religious exemption, the inevitable effect is to impose the parents' notions of religious duty upon their children. Where the child is mature enough to express potentially conflicting desires, it would be an invasion of the child's rights to permit such an imposition without canvassing his views. As in

Prince v. Massachusetts it is an imposition resulting from this very litigation. As the child has no other effective forum, it is in this litigation that his rights should be considered. And, if an Amish child desires to attend high school, and is mature enough to have that desire respected, the State may well be able to override the parents' religiously motivated objections.

Religion is an individual experience. It is not necessary, nor even appropriate, for every Amish child to express his views on the subject in a prosecution of a single adult. Crucial, however, are the views of the child whose parent is the subject of the suit. Frieda Yoder has in fact testified that her own religious views are opposed to high-school education. I therefore join the judgment of the Court as to respondent Jonas Yoder. But Frieda Yoder's views may not be those of Vernon Yutzy or Barbara Miller. I must dissent, therefore, as to respondents Adin Yutzy and Wallace Miller as their motion to dismiss also raised the question of their children's religious liberty.

On this important and vital matter of education, I think the children should be entitled to be heard. While the parents, absent dissent, normally speak for the entire family, the education of the child is a matter on which the child will often have decided views. He may want to be a pianist or an astronaut or an ocean-ographer. To do so he will have to break from the Amish tradition.

It is the future of the student, not the future of the parents, that is imperiled by today's decision. If a parent keeps his child out of school beyond the grade school, then the child will be forever barred from entry into the new and amazing world of diversity that we have today. The child may decide that that is the preferred course, or he may rebel. It is the student's judgment, not his parents', that is essential if we are to give full meaning to what we have said about the Bill of Rights and of the right of students to be masters of their own destiny. If he is harnessed to the Amish way of life by those in authority over him and if his education is truncated, his entire life may be stunted and deformed. The child, therefore, should be given an opportunity to be heard before the State gives the exemption which we honor today.

The views of the children in question were not canvassed by the Wisconsin courts. The matter should be explicitly reserved so that new hearings can be held on remand of the case.

Wisconsin v. Yoder resolved an important question of constitutional rights: whether the state's interest in the schooling of young children can be subordinate to the free exercise of religion. Given the central role of education in twentieth century urban, industrial, and postindustrial America, it is important to look at the court's reasoning in exempting future generations of Americans from this critical institution of economic and political socialization.

The text of the *Yoder* decision makes it clear that the court held for the Amish first, because the Amish only requested exemption from ninth and tenth grades. The same text also leaves no doubt, however, that factors beyond the constitutional question were involved. The Supreme Court read, accepted, and reasoned from, expert testimony which presented the Amish as self-sufficient, law-abiding, productive, and morally righteous, and therefore "deserving" of consideration that, by implication, other groups were not. In his partial dissent Justice Douglas spoke specifically to this point:

> I think the emphasis of the Court on the "law and order" record of this Amish group of people is quite irrelevant. A religion is a religion irrespective of what the misdemeanor or felony records of its members might be. I am not at all sure how the Catholics, Episcopalians, the Baptists, Jehovah's Witnesses, the Unitarians, and my own Presbyterians would make out if subjected to such a test.

The weight given by the majority of the court to the 300-year history of the Amish as a Christian sect, as well as to their contemporary "goodness," raises, as Douglas notes, a central question of constitutional law: whether rights pertain to individuals and groups according to, or regardless of, their law-abidingness, economic success, and social behaviors. When comparing, for example, the Supreme Court's treatment of the Amish, the Mormons, and the Japanese Americans, it appears that the dominant culture's perceptions of the social and economic behaviors of different groups, in different historical periods, do indeed matter. For example, the Mormons were as self-sufficient as the Amish. But because their self-sufficiency was communal and socialistic, and was allied with such repugnant practices as polygamy, the dominant culture felt the need to repress it. Similarly, the economic self-sufficiency of Japanese Americans, achieved in part through the use of family labor similar to that of the Amish, was turned against them by large commercial agricultural interests, who portrayed them as "exploitative and un-American," a portrayal that was not entirely without influence on the Court.

The highly positive and even romantic view of the Amish in the larger society is abetted by the nonintrusive, self-contained nature of their religiously based life style which conforms to the dominant American sense of what is respectable behavior. The Court's opinion, while making much of the Constitution's ability to accommodate cultural pluralism, in fact rested more upon the similarities between the Amish and the larger society. The Court's sympathy with the Amish is reflected in their letting pass the fact, noted only by Douglas, that the Amish children had not all been heard from. Further, the Court's acceptance of the Amish position that the community did prepare its children adequately for life *within* the community ignored statistics which the Court itself cited that there was significant out-migration of Amish young people.[4] Read in the context of this outmigration, the Court's opinion denies those children who leave the Amish agricultural community the protection of the state in providing adequate educational preparation which is otherwise widely accepted in American law. This contrasts with the Court's adamant assertion of state authority over that of the family in the 1944 Jehovah's Witness case, *Prince v. Massachusetts.*

Unlike the Mormons, the Amish have resisted any major changes in their culture or their theology in order to accommodate the many changes in values and technology in American society. Because the Amish have resisted these changes they are a model, ready at hand, of an idealized picture of rural, moral, self-sufficient America, which is fast disappearing, and yet which still plays an important role in our identity and history. The dominant culture, through social practice and law, has unabashedly accommodated the Amish, supporting the continuation of their subculture and the "mythology" they represent to an urban, competitive, materialistic, secular society.

NOTES

1. John A. Hostetler, *Amish Society*, 3d ed. (Baltimore, MD: Johns Hopkins University Press, 1980), 98–102.
2. Donald B. Kraybill, ed., *The Amish and the State* (Baltimore, MD: Johns Hopkins University Press, 1993), 24.
3. Hostetler, *Amish Society*, 22.
4. *Wisconsin v. Yoder*, 406 U.S. 205, 240 (1972).

7

Religion and Schools: The Satmar Hasidim

With the many social changes that have occurred in the last three decades in the United States, the clash between religious and secular values, always simmering in our pluralistic society, has reemerged. This clash grows out of two fundamentally opposed worldviews, that of conservative, often fundamental Christianity, on the one hand, and that of a liberal and progressive social philosophy, sometimes called secular humanism, on the other.[1]

Secular humanism grew out of the eighteenth-century Enlightenment's rejection of religion as the irrefutable and authoritative source of all knowledge. It emphasizes human freedom and dignity, and its emphasis on the rights of the individual underlies political democracy in the United States, as incorporated into the Constitution, particularly the Bill of Rights, and specifically the religious rights guaranteed by the First Amendment. According to Christian fundamentalists, secular humanism, by its insistence on the separation of church and state, and by its acceptance of personal choice in sexual behavior, undermines the integrity of traditional American family life and the Christian values and practices upon which they believe this country should be based.

Historically, and currently, one aspect of the cultural clash between fundamental Christianity and secular humanism is "war" over control of the public schools, as the attempts of the religious to impose their religious values and practices in schools are resisted by civil libertarians equally determined to protect nonsectarian public education from the intrusions of religion.[2] The importance of schools in this culture clash stems from their importance in political socialization. Public schools are a major institutional means of reproducing American values and national identity and are as central today as they have been historically, in the assimilation of culturally different groups in the United States.

The "separation of church and state" as mandated in the First Amendment emerges in both Free Exercise and Establishment issues. The Free Exercise Clause protects religious groups from unwarranted government interference in religion. The Amish and the Jehovah's Witnesses cases established that where secular public education imposes an undue burden on the free exercise of a group's religion, and where the government cannot demonstrate a compelling interest, groups may be exempted from general laws and regulations governing public education. The Establishment Clause is designed to prevent any religious group from gaining control of state institutions, or from the state favoring one religion over another, or favoring religion over nonreligion. Applied to education, the Establishment Clause essentially means that the public schools will be as secular as possible and that public funds will not be used to support private religious (sectarian) schools.

Conflicts between fundamentalist religious groups and civil libertarians have emerged over curriculum, particularly the teaching of evolution and later, of "creation-science"; censorship of textbooks and library books; prayer in the schools; sex education; access of religious groups to school sites; and public aid to students in sectarian schools.[3] Attempts by religious groups to lower the wall between church and state, whether by legislation seeking to infuse religious beliefs and practices into the public schools or seeking public aid for religious schools, most frequently run aground on the Establishment Clause. When considering whether such legislation violates the Establishment Clause, courts use the three-pronged test established in *Lemon v. Kurtzman* [403 U.S. 602 (1971)], which holds that in order to be constitutional, a statute (1) must have a secular legislative purpose; (2) must not, as its principal or primary effect, advance or inhibit religion; and (3) must not foster an excessive government entanglement with religion.

Although the *Lemon* test has proved useful in federal courts for turning back religious fundamentalist efforts over the past 20 years to establish religious beliefs and practices in public schools, constitutional scholar Lawrence H. Tribe cautioned that "these [court] decisions take some of the wind out of their [fundamentalist] sails . . . but [they don't] sink the ship."[4] Tribe's note of warning has been more than justified by the growing political clout of religious conservatives, as the result of a highly organized effort, in local government, state legislatures, governors' mansions, and, as a result of the Reagan/Bush appointments to federal district courts and to the Supreme Court. This has led to renewed attacks by religious groups on the "wall of separation between church and state," and public education, as in the past, has again become a central battleground in the "culture war." It is in this context that litigation involving, ironically, a small, little-known Jewish, not Christian, sect in New York State, the Satmar Hasidim, reached the Supreme Court and attracted national attention.

THE SATMAR HASIDIM

The Satmar Hasidim are an Orthodox Jewish sect, who, like the Amish, are a "community of piety."[5] Satmar believe in a literal interpretation of Scripture and the teachings of the *Torah* (the first five books of the Hebrew Testament). The *Talmud* (the interpretive book of Jewish law and tradition) guides every aspect of Satmar life, from diet to dress. Satmar religious beliefs both symbolize and maintain their separation from the rest of society. For example, their religiously based sexual code requires strict separation of the sexes (except within the immediate family and in the case of children with disabilities) to avoid "impure thoughts" which might lead to sinful acts. This means that Satmar avoid public transportation if possible, and travel in private busses.

The Satmar, again like the Amish, strenuously resist interaction outside their community. They view such contact as furthering assimilation, which they see as a severe threat to the survival of American Jewry. The principal Satmar language is Yiddish and they make little use of English-language television, radio, and print media. In addition to sex segregation, there is a mandated male and female dress code. Boys wear long side curls, head coverings, and distinctive garments; girls dress modestly in long sleeved dresses and thick stockings. Satmar religious schools are essential in maintaining Satmar culture and warding off outside influences: In addition to teaching secular academic subjects, boys are educated in Torah and girls mainly in cooking, sewing, and other tasks they will need to know as adults in the community. The center of the Satmar social order is the religious leader, or *Rebbeh,* who is the ultimate decision maker, exercising his religious authority over all aspects of the life of the members of his "court," or followers. Any challenges to this authority may result in ostracism and expulsion from the community.[6] New Satmar communities are led by a *Rov* or "town rabbi," who is appointed by the Rebbeh.

The Satmar, led by Joel Teitelbaum, the sect's founder and rabbi, came to the United States after World War II. They settled in Brooklyn, New York, and flourished, mainly finding work in the diamond and needle trades. As their religious prohibitions against birth control and abortion encourage large families, the Satmar outgrew their Brooklyn neighborhoods and began to establish other communities in Brooklyn and upstate New York.

In the early 1970s, a group of Brooklyn Satmar moved to an approved but undeveloped subdivision of the Town of Monroe, in Orange County,

New York. A bitter contest ensued as the Satmar sought to oppose the Town of Monroe's efforts to enforce its zoning regulations regarding the number of families permitted in single-family residences, and the prohibition of portions of such residences being used as synagogues and schools. At this point, the Satmar utilized a general New York State statute to legally incorporate their community as Kiryas Joel—the Village of Joel (named after their Rabbi), within the Town of Monroe. This enabled them to evade Monroe's zoning regulations. Residents of the area who did not wish to secede with the Satmar protested vigorously, and after arduous negotiations, the proposed boundaries of Kiryas Joel were drawn to include just the 320 acres owned and inhabited entirely by Satmars. The village was incorporated in 1977 and today has a population of 12,000 persons.

The Satmar had been involved in litigation both in Brooklyn and in Monroe, with both cases growing out of their strict, religiously based practice of sex segregation. In *Parents' Assn. of P.S. 16 v. Quinones* [803 F.2d 1235 (2d Cir. 1986)], the Satmar attempted to use public funds to provide remedial education for Satmar girls only, in nine classrooms separated out from the rest of the local public school, and closed to other students in the school. In the litigation, the Satmar said, "[We] struggle very hard to maintain [our] belief and our culture . . . [we] want [our] children separate. . . . The issue goes to the heart of the Orthodox tradition, which requires the separation of males and females for . . . every activity, including schooling, and encourages isolation from other cultures. If we have our kids learning with them, they'll be corrupted. . . . We don't hate these people, but we don't like them. We want to be separate."[7]

In another case, in Monroe, the Satmar litigated to require the local school bus company to provide only male drivers on the school busses which transported male Satmar children, claiming that using female bus drivers violated their free exercise of religion.[8] The Satmar lost both these cases, with the courts holding that both the separate classrooms and the bus company's attempt to accommodate Satmar religious views impermissibly advanced Satmar religious beliefs and entangled the government in religion.

In 1993 litigation involving the Satmar reached the U.S. Supreme Court.[9] This litigation, which was part of a long and complex process of conflict, litigation, negotiation, and legislation, involved the providing of educational services to disabled Satmar children. While virtually all Kiryas Joel children attend the private, religious schools in the village, until 1985 the handicapped children of the village, pursuant to the federal Individuals with Disabilities Act and New York State Education Law, which entitles handicapped children to a public education "in the least restrictive environment," were educated in special classes at an annex adjacent to and educationally identifiable with the girl's religious school.

They were taught by public school teachers from the Monroe–Woodbury Central School District in which Kiryas Joel is included and were paid by public funds. Children with disabilities from other Hasidic communities in a neighboring county also attended the school.

In 1985, however, the U.S. Supreme Court handed down two important decisions, in *Aguilar v. Felton* (473 U.S. 402) and *Grand Rapids v. Ball* (473 U.S. 373), which held that state-financed special education services could only be held on the site of a public school, and not on the site of a religious school. Subsequent to these decisions, the Monroe–Woodbury public school district stopped providing special education services to the Satmar at the private school site. The district interpreted state and federal laws regarding children with disabilities to require that handicapped Satmar children be placed in the district's public schools, where they would be integrated with other children rather than isolated from them. Monroe–Woodbury was prepared to hire Yiddish-speaking teachers and provide parents with bilingual reports on their children.

Satmar parents refused to accept these placements, claiming that their children experienced "fear and trauma" when leaving their own community and being with others whose ways were so different. They insisted that the bilingual and cultural needs of their children could only be met within their own community, and a few Satmar parents engaged private services for their children. At this point, the Monroe Board of Education and the Satmar parents filed countersuits in Orange County court. The Monroe Board of Education sought judicial affirmation of its policy of public school placements for the handicapped Satmar children. Satmar parents sought a ruling to have their children educated within the village, preferably at an annex to their religious school, but if necessary, at a "neutral" site.

In the initial litigation in the state courts, the Satmar did not claim that the public school placements of their children violated their free exercise of religion rights. They insisted at the trial court that they should be exempted from public school placements only for nonreligious reasons which they defined as the "traumatic psychological impact" upon the children of travelling out of the sheltered environment of the village; the psychological harm of being thrust into a strange environment; the fact that their physical appearance, dress, and language differences set the Satmar children apart from the other students; and the necessity for bilingual/bicultural programs specially adapted to meet the children's social, psychological, and cultural needs. The Satmar claimed that the emotional toll of sending their children to public school outweighed the benefits of the special educational services and that they were financially unable to pay for the costly services, which as taxpayers, they were entitled to for their children.

Thus, unlike the Amish, who based their claims for exemption from a general education law on a violation of their free exercise of religious rights, the Satmar claimed their right to state-supported special education was a legitimate accommodation to the *secular* needs of a *culturally* distinctive group that "happened" to be of the same religion. Also, unlike the Amish, who went to great lengths to convince the courts that their religion and culture were inseparable, the Satmar went to great lengths to assert that their culture and religion were separable.

The court held, in *Monroe–Woodbury CSD v. Wieder*, that Monroe–Woodbury could, and must, provide the necessary services to the handicapped Satmar children outside the district public schools, but at a "neutral site," that is, a location not physically or educationally identified with the village but accessible to the children.[10] The Monroe–Woodbury School Board appealed, voicing doubt that any so-called "neutral site" could "ever be a genuinely neutral, public site, free of identification with [Satmar] beliefs" because any truly neutral site would not address the Satmar parents' concerns about the fear and trauma of their children having to mix with others whose language and lifestyle was so different from their own.

The Appellate Division of the New York State Supreme Court reversed the lower court's decision and found for the Monroe–Woodbury School Board, ruling that Monroe–Woodbury could provide the required services *only* within its public school facilities.[11] Providing the educational services in a separate environment addressed parental concerns for Satmar religious and social practices, rather than secular factors such as the children's disability, the Court said, and thereby violated the Establishment Clause. The Court further noted that the distinctive culture of the Satmar was based on their religion, that the "apparent over-all goal" of the Satmar was that "children should continue to live by the religious standards of their parents," and that "Satmarer want their school to serve primarily as a bastion against undesirable acculturation."

The Satmar appealed, now claiming that the placement of their children in public schools, rather than in their own schools or schools at a "neutral site," "interfered with the free exercise of their sincere religious beliefs." They emphasized the "compelling" analogy between their case and that of the Amish in *Yoder*, but the New York Court of Appeals refused to consider this constitutional issue because the Satmar had not asserted this free exercise claim in the initial litigation. In considering the narrower question of whether New York State's Education Law *required* services to handicapped Satmar children only at the public schools, or whether it *required* some "neutral site location," the court found the law *required* neither, and that the services *could* be offered at either site. This decision left the dispute back where it had begun.[12]

Satmar parents continued to refuse public school placements for their handicapped children, and in an attempt to resolve the problem, the

New York state legislature enacted a law, Chapter 748, in June 1989, which established a separate public school district coterminous with the village of Kiryas Joel for the expressed purpose of providing special education services to the handicapped village children. As these services would now be offered as part of a public school district, the school was to be entirely nonreligious and subject to all the regulations of the state's public schools. The Monroe–Woodbury Central School district, in an attempt to end the conflict and litigation, passed a resolution supporting the bill. On July 25, 1989, then governor of New York Mario Cuomo, a lawyer by training, perhaps in a bid for political support from the Hasidic community in his upcoming gubernatorial race, signed Chapter 748 creating the Kiryas Joel Village Public School District, in spite of warnings by the New York State Commissioner of Education that the statute might well be unconstitutional.

In response, Louis Grumet, Executive Director of the New York State School Boards Association, and Albert Hawk, acting as citizen-taxpayers, brought suit against the School District of Kiryas Joel and the Monroe–Woodbury School District in the New York Supreme Court, Albany County, challenging the statute as violating the Establishment Clause of the United States and New York State Constitutions.[13] Grumet and Hawk contended that the statute creating a school district serving only Hasidic children had both the intent and the effect of furthering the Hasidim's desire, based on their religious beliefs, to insulate their children from the larger, diverse outside society and thus failed the first two prongs of the *Lemon* test. Grumet and Hawk also contended that the statute violated the third prong of the *Lemon* test because it would require state officials, who would have to monitor the implementation of the statute, to become excessively entangled in religion.

The New York State Supreme Court ruled that the law indeed failed all three prongs of the *Lemon* test: It had a sectarian rather than a secular purpose in that it created a governmental unit, a school, to meet a group's religious needs; it had the primary effect of advancing the religious beliefs of Kiryas Joel; and it impermissibly entangled the state in religion. In holding that the law violated the Establishment Clause of the U.S. Constitution, Judge Lawrence E. Kahn noted that "[T]he legislation is an attempt to camouflage, with secular garments, a religious community as a public school district." While praising the attempts of the legislature and the governor to meet "the parochial needs of a religious group," he also chided them and the Satmar for trying to circumvent the First Amendment with constitutionally forbidden legislation, which could "jeopardize the very religious freedom that they now enjoy." Judge Kahn noted that "[T]he strength of our democracy is that a multitude of religious, ethnic and racial groups can live side by side with respect for each other [and while] the uniqueness of religious values, as observed by the Satmar Sect, is especially to be admired as non-conformity becomes increasingly more difficult to sustain," laws which advance and endorse such parochial needs violate our deep-rooted principle of separation of church and state.[14] The Court's decision was upheld in the Appellate Division.[15]

The Satmar again appealed. On July 6, 1993, in a 4–2 decision, the New York State Court of Appeals affirmed the Appellate Division's decision, holding that Chapter 748 violated the second prong of the *Lemon* test because its primary effect was not to provide the village's handicapped children with educational services, "but to yield to the demands of a religious community whose separatist tenets create tension between needs of students and religious practices."[16]

In response to the Court of Appeals decision, the School Board of Monroe–Woodbury, the Board of Education of the Kiryas Joel Village School District, and the Attorney General of the State of New York, together appealed to the Supreme Court of the United States. Their appeal questioned not merely the lower courts' decisions, but also the validity of the *Lemon* test, which they considered overrestrictive, arguing that "the Constitution requires accommodation, not merely tolerance of all religions, and forbids hostility toward any." Indeed, they claimed, "callous indifference would violate the idea of free exercise of religion." The petitioners criticized the New York State Court of Appeals' application of the second prong of *Lemon* to invalidate Chapter 748 as amounting to a position that any accommodation to concerns of the Satmar as a religious group was an impermissible advancement, promotion and favoritism of [their] religion. Such a position, the Satmar and their allies contended, "leaves behind the freedoms intended to be preserved" and "evinces a hostility to the group's way of life and a denigration and diminution of their secular concerns, which centered on the emotional trauma of the children and the negative effect on their educational progress."[17]

Kiryas Joel claimed that the fact that Chapter 748 permits the Satmar to isolate themselves from outside communities was incidental to the legislation, and should not be grounds for rejecting a wholly secular solution to a social problem. Rather, they said, Chapter 748 exhibits a "tolerance of a minority view, a healthy and constitutional respect for religious diversity." The petitioners also claimed that the court was making the assumption that because the distinctive lifestyle of the Satmar has its basis in religion, the Satmar therefore have no legitimate secular interests, an assumption that the petitioners claimed was invalid. In fact, the petitioners asserted, "the courts' disparaging of the Satmar's secular claim impermissibly entangled the courts in fact-finding regarding the true nature of Satmar religious doctrine."

In attempting to demonstrate that Chapter 748 neither advances religion nor advances the Satmar religion over others, the petitioners pointed out that both the Monroe–Woodbury School District and the Satmar found the solution acceptable. They also cited *Yoder* in arguing that to force the Satmar to choose between their separatist lifestyle and the free appropriate public education to which they are entitled is neither acceptable nor necessary. They attempted to persuade the Supreme Court that Chapter 748 enhances nonconformity rather than conformity of religion, and thus preserves the very diversity of society that the respondents claim to champion in their arguments that schools should consist of a diverse population. In concluding, the petitioners pressed their case for the importance of accommodation of religious minorities by again citing *Yoder* where the Court held, regarding the Amish, that "Even their idiosyncratic separateness exemplifies the diversity we profess to admire and encourage."[18]

The respondents, Grumet and Hawk, supported by many civil liberties organizations who submitted *amicus* briefs, argued that Chapter 748 violated the Establishment Clause because it failed all three prongs of the *Lemon* test. They asserted that the statute is not one of general applicability, but was enacted expressly to help the Satmar, and runs counter to the goal of New York State to "maintain[ing] diversity . . . and [to] ensure that school district boundaries are not drawn in a manner that segregates pupils along ethnic, racial or religious lines." It also runs counter to New York State education laws which historically have promoted consolidation of smaller school districts. Chapter 748 clearly contravened the standard of separation of church and school established in earlier Supreme Court opinion which held that "public schools must discharge their public function of training students for citizenship in a heterogeneous democratic society . . . 'in an atmosphere free of parochial, divisive, or separatist influences of any sort.' "[19]

Emphasizing the history of the law, the respondents claimed that the New York legislature was certainly aware of the religious nature of both the dispute and the solution, and stated that "the statute's alleged secular purpose is a sham." Rejecting the petitioners' claims that an important aim of Chapter 748 was "to end long years of strife and litigation," the respondents noted for the Court that the long-standing conflict was based upon Satmar religious beliefs and traditions. The respondents contrasted the legal *form* of Kiryas Joel as just another incorporated New York State community, with the reality: that Kiryas Joel is in fact "a religious enclave under the control and supervision of the Satmar religious leadership which exercises its religious authority over all aspects of daily life." They gave as example the recent conflict in Kiryas Joel, where a Satmarer who challenged the Rabbi's leadership in the election for the newly created school district board was, as a result, ostracized by the community, expelled from the congregation, and had his children expelled from the village's religious schools.[20]

On June 27, 1994, the Supreme Court of the United States affirmed the earlier New York State courts' rulings that Chapter 748, creating a public school district for Kiryas Joel, was an impermissible government establishment of religion, violating the First Amendment. In delivering the opinion for the Court, Justice David Souter characterized this "unusual act," which "carved out a separate district, following village lines, to serve this distinctive population . . . tantamount to an allocation of political power on a religious criterion."[21] He cited precedent which holds that "a State may not delegate its civic authority to a group chosen according to a religious criterion," and further noted that "Authority over public schools belongs to the State, and cannot be delegated to a local school district defined by the State in order to grant political control to a religious group."

Although the majority opinion acknowledged that the delegation of the civic power in Chapter 748 was "to the qualified voters of the village," and not the religious leader or religious institution, Justice Souter found that in Kiryas Joel, they amounted to the same thing. He saw the legislation not as "denying groups of religious people . . . their rights as citizens because of their religious affiliations," which would violate their religious free exercise, but as the deliberate delegation by the state of discretionary power to a community on the ground of religious identity. Because the school district boundaries were created to exactly coincide with village boundaries, drawn on religious lines, Justice Souter rejected the petitioners' claim that Chapter 748 was only the incidental delegation of power to a group who happen to be of the same religion.

He also rejected the petitioners' argument that the legislation had a secular purpose. The opinion noted, for example, that the New York State Assembly sponsor of the legislation three times described its beneficiaries as "the *Hasidic* children or community, rather than referring to all groups similarly situated. Central to the Court's concerns was whether the special benefits awarded to the Satmar would be equally provided to other religious and nonreligious groups, a question that could not come before the courts, since a legislature's failure to act is not open to judicial review. This would leave the legislature open to preferring one religion over another. And, the opinion emphasized (in response to a point made by Justice Scalia in dissent), the state aiding "a single, small religious group causes no less a constitutional problem" of establishment of religion than if the group were large, or if the state were aiding religion in general.[22]

The opinion acknowledged that the Constitution does allow the state to accommodate religious needs by alleviating special burdens. "But accommodation is not a principle without limits," Justice Souter said, and the Court could not countenance the Satmar's religiously grounded preferences. He then outlined alternative routes for providing bilingual and bicultural special education to Satmar children that would be constitutionally permissible. Since the Satmar have claimed their separatism is not religiously grounded, Justice Souter suggested they reconsider the public school option previously offered by the Monroe School District.

Finally, Justice Souter concluded that "the statute before us fails the test of neutrality. It delegates a power [i.e., public education] this Court has said (citing *Yoder*) "ranks at the very apex of the function of a State, to an electorate defined by common religious belief and practice, in a manner that fails to foreclose religious favoritism. It therefore crosses the line from permissible accommodation to impermissible establishment."[23]

In the 6–3 decision, there were many concurrences. Several justices took this opportunity to reconsider or endorse the validity of the *Lemon* test as the standard for interpreting violations of the Establishment Clause. Indeed, it was this opportunity that may have been responsible for the Supreme Court accepting the case in the first place. Justice Blackmun explicitly disagreed with any attempts to depart from *Lemon*, and noted that Justice Souter's opinion was essentially based on *Lemon*'s second and third criteria. Justice Stevens' concurrence, with Justices Blackmun and Ginsburg joining, addressed Satmar concerns about their children's emotional trauma if required to leave their village:

To meet these concerns, the State could have taken steps to alleviate the children's fear by teaching their schoolmates to be tolerant and respectful of Satmar customs. Action of that kind would raise no constitutional concerns and would further the strong public interest in promoting diversity and understanding in the public schools.

Instead, the State responded with a solution that affirmatively supports a religious sect's interest in segregating itself and preventing its children from associating with their neighbors. The isolation of these children, while it may protect them from "panic, fear and trauma," also unquestionably increased the likelihood that they would remain within the fold, faithful adherents of their parents' religious faith. By creating a school district that is specifically intended to shield children from contact with others who have "different ways," the State provided official support to cement the attachment of young adherents to a particular faith. It is telling, in this regard, that two thirds of the school's full-time students are Hasidic handicapped children from *outside* the village; the Kiryas Joel school thus serves a population far wider than the village—one defined less by geography than by religion.[24]

These three justices agreed that Chapter 748 was more accurately characterized as establishing, rather than "merely accommodating," religion.

In another concurrence, Justice Sandra Day O'Connor saw the crux of the case as the following question: "What may the government do, consistent with the Establishment Clause, to accommodate people's religious beliefs? She viewed the Satmar case as particularly instructive because of their past involvement in litigation requesting accommodations involving remedial education and bussing. Justice O'Connor noted that Satmar religious needs, such as in the original zoning conflicts with the Town of Monroe, could be accommodated through laws which are neutral regarding religion, in this case, the general New York state law regarding incorporation of villages. She also cited with approval the general accommodations made for religious groups, for example, permitting those religiously opposed to taking oaths to affirm instead. She emphasized the important American legal principle that "one's religion ought not affect one's legal rights or duties or benefits," and held that there is nothing wrong with the government accommodating a group's deeply held religious belief, so long as it does not discriminate "based on sect."[25]

It was this commitment to neutrality, or *equal treatment* in accommodating religious groups that was central to Justice O'Connor's concurrence. Because, like Justice Souter, Justice O'Connor was concerned that another religious group might not be accommodated by the legislature, she suggested an alternative law the New York legislature might pass, allowing all villages, for example, to operate their own school district, or setting forth neutral criteria, like size, that would not discriminate on a religious basis.

Justice O'Connor, like Justice Kennedy in his concurrence, and Justice Scalia in a dissent, noted that "The Establishment Clause does not demand government hostility to religion, religious ideas, religious people, or religious schools," but does demand neutrality. In this connection, she thought *Aguilar* had been wrongly decided (as did Justice Kennedy), and also that *Lemon* was due for a judicial reconsideration. Claiming that as a unitary test for all religious establishment cases, *Lemon* was becoming more of a burden than a source of clarity, Justice O'Connor held that the Establishment Clause "cannot easily be reduced to a single test" and that "different categories of Establishment Clause cases . . . may call for different approaches." In contrast to Justice Blackmun, Justice O'Connor viewed the present case as a "[further] slide away from *Lemon*'s unitary approach" and welcomed a new approach which would "still have to [ask the hard questions], but [will ask them] within a more carefully tailored and less distorted framework."[26]

Justice Kennedy's concurring opinion also emphasized that it was not the fact, but the *manner* of New York accommodating the Satmar that created the constitutional problem. He viewed the New York legislature's intent to accommodate the Satmar as a perfectly valid attempt to alleviate a special burden on their religious practices, and citing *Oregon v. Smith*, noted that legislatures may go beyond courts in granting religious accommodations. He viewed Chapter 748 as typical of the unique responses legislatures make to problems as they arise, and saw nothing threatening to religious liberty in the special treatment of the Satmar.[27] Like the majority of the Court, however, Justice Kennedy did find fault with the school district for having been drawn along the religious lines of the village, which impermissibly involved the state directly "in accomplishing the religious segregation." He contrasted this with the situation in which a town or state

whose boundaries are derived according to neutral historical and geographic criteria [happened to consist of] . . . People who share a common religious belief or lifestyle [who] may live together without sacrificing the basic rights of self-governance that all American citizens enjoy, so long as they do not use those rights to establish their religious faith. Religion flourishes in community, and the Establishment Clause must not be construed as some sort of homogenizing solvent that forces unconventional religious groups to choose between assimilating to mainstream American culture or losing their political rights. There is more than a fine line, however, between the voluntary association that leads to a political community comprised of people who share a common religious faith, and the forced separation that occurs when the government draws explicit political boundaries on the basis of peoples' faith. In creating the Kiryas Joel Village School District, New York crossed that line, and so we must hold the district invalid.[28]

Justice Scalia's dissent, joined by Chief Justice Rehnquist and Justice Thomas, was partly based on their acceptance of the Satmar claim that Chapter 748 validly addressed cultural concerns, which were not based on religion. Ignoring the previous Satmar litigation, the religious basis of the creation of the Village of Kiryas Joel, and the context of the passage of the legislation, Justice Scalia's dissent held that in enacting Chapter 748, the New York legislature properly addressed the secular concerns of a group that happened also to have a common religion. In his opinion this case did not involve aid to religiously based private schools but only concerned a public school providing a public secular education to handicapped students.

Noting an increasing hostility in the Court toward religion in the United States, Justice Scalia surmised that

Justice Souter would laud this humanitarian legislation if all of the distinctiveness of Kiryas Joel were attributable to the fact that their parents were nonreligious commune-dwellers, or American Indians, or gypsies. The creation of a special, one-culture school district for the benefit of those children would pose no problem. The neutrality demanded by the Religion Clauses requires the same indulgence towards cultural characteristics that *are* accompanied by religious belief. The Establishment Clause does not license government to treat religion and those who teach or practice it . . . as . . . subject to unique disabilities.[29]

Scalia criticized the Court's interpretation of the Establishment Clause as exhibiting government hostility to religion, and said that even if Chapter 748 was passed for the Satmar *because* of their religion, it would still be a permissible accommodation, and one that "follows the best of our traditions." He saw the Court, in contrast, as "uncomfortable with this aspect of our constitutional tradition," qualifying its endorsement by saying "it is not a principle without limits." He also criticized Justice Stevens' opinion as "a manifesto of secularism . . . surpass[ing] mere rejection of accommodation and announc[ing] a positive hostility to religion" and expressed agreement with Justices Kennedy and O'Connor that *Aguilar* and *Lemon* should be reconsidered, as they are "so hostile to our national tradition of accommodation [to religion]."

The dissent in this case has important implications given the reinvigorated agenda of the fundamentalist religious right for control of public education and the receptiveness to that agenda by the Court's conservative justices. Indeed, the national interest in the case stems from the Court's revisiting, in its questioning of *Lemon*, what had been assumed to be settled doctrine with regard to interpretation of the Free Exercise and Establishment Clauses.

The *Kiryas Joel* litigation is also interesting because it provokes comparison with the treatment of the Amish in *Yoder*. The Satmar and the Amish are similar in many ways: Both are authentic and historically old "communities of piety," whose unique cultures are based on deeply held religious beliefs; both groups reject many of the ideas, institutions, and commodities of modern life; both groups resist assimilation and attempt to isolate themselves from the larger society, which they see as corrupting; both groups have experienced hostility in their local communities; and both groups have a history of conflict with the government over education because of their wish to educate their children separately from others, thereby binding them more closely to their religion. From the standpoint of the Amish and the Satmar, both the diversity of the student body of the public school and the assimilating effect of its curriculum are an anathema.

Why, then, were the Amish able to prevail in their wish to be exempted from state education law, whereas Kiryas Joel failed in its attempt to have the state lift a burden on the free exercise of their religion by passing a state law creating a public school district coterminus with their village? Asked this way, the question perhaps answers itself: It is not the nature of the two groups that explains the different outcomes, but rather the claims each group made on the state. The Amish were asking for an *exemption* from a general law, whereas the legislative solution to the Kiryas Joel conflict required an affirmative involvement of the state in religion, in the passage of the law, in the resulting use of public funds for sectarian education, and in the monitoring of the district by state officials that would be required.

In its *Yoder* decision, the Supreme Court acknowledged the importance of religious nonconformity and the decision appears to support cultural diversity, although the Court was careful to state that a group claiming such an exemption from state law on the basis of its *culture*, rather than its religion, would not prevail. The First Amendment does not protect culture, but only religion. The *Kiryas Joel* decision is ambiguous regarding cultural diversity. The opinions of the lower courts, and the many opinions in the Supreme Court refer to the importance of cultural diversity, including religious diversity, in our society, but appear to differ on how this ideal can be furthered. It may be, as Justice Scalia mockingly suggested in his dissent, that the majority of the Court would have been more accommodating to a "cultural" group than a religious group; but the fact is that just as the First Amendment protects only religious, and not cultural groups, so the Establishment Clause forbids government support only of religious groups, and not cultural groups.

Justice Scalia's dissent brings us back to where we began this chapter—with the conflict in today's society between a conservative religious view and the secular humanist view that underlies the religious clauses in the Constitution. This case—the attempts of a small, religious minority to use public funds to serve religious ends—attracted national attention because it raised deeper issues about the separation of church and state, particularly as this involves public schools, in a climate of growing political power of the religious right. In this context, the Supreme Court decision was an important victory for those who wish to keep a wall between church and state, and a defeat for the fundamentalist religious agenda for public education.

But the case does not end here. Taking up the suggestion of Justices O'Connor and Kennedy that a general New York state law would be a constitutionally acceptable solution to the Satmar need, the New York legislature crafted Chapter 241, which adds a mechanism to the New York State Educational Law whereby new school districts may be established for qualifying municipalities without legislative intervention. The legislation only applies to municipalities currently in existence, and contains five very specific geographical, numerical, and financial criteria for eligibility. After applying each one of the criteria to the potentially eligible 57 cities, 932 towns, and 557 villages in New York State, the only municipality to survive eligibility under all five criteria is the Village of Kiryas Joel!

Almost immediately after its passage, Louis Grumet and Albert Hawk, appearing as plaintiffs, contested this new legislation, asserting that the new law is a sham intended to circumvent the Supreme Court decision.[30] They noted that the legislature authorized the Kiryas Joel school district to continue operating until the New York state courts implement the Supreme Court decision, *"or until such school district is reconstituted,"* (emphasis in the original) indicating that it clearly envisioned this would occur. The plaintiffs also noted the speed with which the legislation was crafted, in contrast to the legislature's prior record of having missed the constitutional deadline for approving a state budget in almost all of the past 15 years. They cited as evidence that the new law was addressed specifically to the needs of the Satmar by quoting a statement from the office of the assemblyman who sponsored the legislation: "The trick for negotiators [was] to craft legislation so Kiryas Joel would be virtually the only village to take advantage of the opportunity to create a district—even though many others technically could."[31]

The New York State Constitution, in a provision which explicitly excludes public funding for "any school . . . wholly or in part under the control or direction of any religious denomination," reflects New York's history of conflicts over education and is aimed at precluding *de facto* religious control over the state's public schools. Chapter 241, Grumet claims, thus violates the New York State Constitution and the Establishment Clause in the same way as its predecessor, Chapter 748, in favoring the Satmar over other religious groups and nonreligious communities.

On March 9, 1995, Judge Lawrence E. Kahn of the New York State Supreme Court held that the new law was constitutional, stating that it was religiously neutral and not a sham. He acknowledged that the new law was created with Kiryas Joel in mind, but held that the law was religiously neutral and, while accommodating the Satmar, did not single them out for favorable treatment.[32] Grumet is appealing the case.

Kiryas Joel, unlike the Amish, another religiously based culture that attempts to isolate itself from the dominant society, has no hesitation in using the legal institutions of that same society to protect its religious rights. In doing so, it has attracted national attention. In the current climate of increasing political power of American fundamentalist religious groups the *Kiryas Joel* litigation takes on a significance beyond this one small community. As it may be the occasion for the Supreme Court to indicate a new direction in deciding issues involving the Establishment Clause, the *Kiryas Joel* litigation is one more battle in the ongoing "culture wars."

NOTES

1. James Davison Hunter, *Culture Wars: The Struggle to Define America* (New York: Basic, 1991).

2. Ibid., 197.

3. Marc D. Stern, *Religion and the Public Schools: A Summary of the Law* (New York: American Jewish Congress, 1993).

4. William K. Stevens, "Despite Defeats, Fundamentalists Vow to Press Efforts to Reshape Schools," *New York Times*, August 29, 1987, 6.

5. Sanford Pinsker, "Piety as Community: The Hasidic View," *Social Research* 42 (Summer 1975): 230–46; Israel Rubin Satmar, *An Island in the City* (New York: Quadrangle, 1972).

6. Robert Hennelly, "Shtetl and State," *Village Voice*, April 12, 1994, 4; Joseph Berger, "Public School Leadership Fight Tearing a Hasidic Sect," *New York Times*, January 3, 1993, A15.

7. *Parents' Assn. of P.S. 16 v. Quinones*, 1236–38.

8. *Bollenbach v. Bd. of Education of the Monroe–Woodbury Central School District*, 659 F. Supp. 1450 (S.D.N.Y. 1987), 1464–66.

9. *Kiryas Joel v. Grumet*, 512 US __, 129 L. Ed. 2d 546 (1994).

10. *Board of Education of the Monroe–Woodbury CSD v. Wieder*, 134 Misc. 2d 658 (1987).

11. Ibid.

12. *Board of Education of the Monroe–Woodbury CSD v. Wieder*, 72 N.Y.2d 174 (1988).

13. *Louis Grumet and Albert Hawk v. New York State Education Department et al*, 579 N.Y.S.2d 1004 (Supp. 1992).

14. *Grumet v. NYS Education Dept. et al*, 1007.

15. *Louis Grumet et al v. Bd. of Education of Kiryas Joel et al*, 187 A.D.2d 16, 592, N.Y.S.2d 123 (1992).

16. *Louis Grumet et al v. Board of Education of the Kiryas Joel Village School District et al*, 601 N.Y.S.2d 61 (Ct. App. 1993), 68.

17. *The Attorney General of the State of New York et al v. Louis Grumet and Albert W. Hawk*, 512 US __, 129 L. Ed. 2d 546 (1994). Subsequently cited as *Kiryas Joel v. Grumet*, Brief for Petitioner.

18. *Kiryas Joel v. Grumet*, Brief for Petitioner.

19. Ibid.

20. Berger, "Public School Leadership Fight."

21. *Kiryas Joel v. Grumet*, 552.

22. Ibid., 562.

23. Ibid., 565.

24. Ibid., 566.

25. Ibid., 566–68.

26. Ibid., 569–71.

27. Ibid., 574.

28. Ibid., 578.

29. Ibid., 585.

30. *Louis Grumet and Albert W. Hawk v. Mario Cuomo et al*, State of New York Supreme Court, Albany County, Index No. 4210-94, Brief for Plaintiffs, 18.

31. Ibid., 14.

32. Joseph Berger, "Court Affirms Public School for Hasidim," *New York Times*, March 9, 1995, B1.

8

Religious Practice and Drug Use:
The Rastafari and the
Native American Church

No issue is better suited to challenge the limits of cultural pluralism in the United States than that of the use of drugs, even in connection with religious practice. The use of substances declared illegal by states and the federal government has put such groups as the Rastafarians and the Native American Church on a collision course with not only their local communities, but with the entire criminal justice system. Religious practices different from those of the mainstream of America have always invited hostility, often leading to government prohibition and prosecution. The current widespread scourge of drug use has intensified the prosecution of drug use, even in religious contexts.

THE SACRAMENTAL USE OF MARIJUANA: THE RASTAFARIANS

43 Star Island, an estate on the quiet, exclusive island community of Miami Beach, Florida, seems an unlikely setting for a confrontation on the issue of religious use of marijuana, a confrontation whose reverberations drew the attention of politicians in Washington, the venerable national media program *60 Minutes*, and a number of important East Coast lawyers. In the late 1970s, the estate at 43 Star Island, owned by Jacquelyn Renee Town, was used by the Ethiopian Zion Coptic Church as a place of meeting and daily worship. This church is one of the many denominations of the Rastafarians, a religious community that originated in the 1930s on the Caribbean island of Jamaica. Rastafarianism blends elements of Christianity with an African consciousness.

For more than 200 years Jamaica had been colonized by the British.

During this period the rise of a white society, built on capitalism and bourgeois respectability, left the black peasantry, descendants of African slaves, in a condition of economic and social oppression. In the 1920s, the teachings of Marcus Garvey, a Jamaican, emphasizing social reform and repatriation to Africa, stirred hopes among this peasantry for a more just life. Attuned to the importance of Africa, an event occurred, in 1934, that mobilized a part of that peasantry. This event, widely reported in the Jamaican press, was the coronation of Ras Tafari as Haile Selassie I, King of Ethiopia. The photographic images of this black African king, whose coronation was attended by European dignitaries, intensified the importance of Africa in the Jamaican black identity. Within a few years, Rastafarian preachers emerged proclaiming the divinity of Haile Selassie, and groups began to form to discuss the connection between Haile Selassie as the messiah and the hopes of black people.

As economic conditions worsened during the depression of the 1930s, many peasants found themselves landless and moved to Kingston and other cities, where they became part of an urban underclass. The message of the Rastafarian preachers found a wide audience among this group. By the late 1930s, harassment of Rasta leaders began, as the British colonial government realized the revolutionary implications of a spiritual movement that venerated an African king above the British crown, and that rejected the individualistic work ethic of exploitative capitalism.[1]

In spite of hostility from the colonial government, the Rastafarian movement continued to gain followers and in 1940, Leonard Howell, one of the original Rastafarian prophets, set up a commune which was called "The Pinnacle." During the 14 years that the commune was in existence, before it was disbanded by Jamaican authorities, the ritual codes and theology of the Rastas were further developed. Many of the central Rastafarian characteristics—the communal sharing of property, the wearing of dreadlocks, sacramental use of marijuana, and particular dietary customs, all of which set the Rastas in opposition to the larger society—developed in this period.

In 1954, after The Pinnacle was disbanded, the Rastas moved again to the cities and their membership among the urban underclass continued to grow. Shortly afterward, reggae music, which is antiestablishment and inflammatory to authorities, and now is most popularly associated with the late Bob Marley, became identified with the Rastafari, provoking yet more hostility from the larger society.

Concerned with their growing bad press, in 1960 the Rastas took the initiative and invited scholars from the University of the West Indies to visit their Kingston communes. The positive report from these academic fieldworkers, disseminated through the Jamaican press, did indeed alter the previous negative image of the Rastas as "ganja smoking, good-for-nothing rascals" and the Rastas' relations with the government, now independent from England since 1962, improved for a number of years. In 1972, the People's National Party (PNP) candidate, Michael Manley, successfully campaigned for the post of prime minister on a platform that incorporated Rasta ideals and symbols. He even used reggae music to popularize this reformist economic program. This gave him widespread appeal among the poor. Much of the middle class, however, remained uncomfortable with the Rasta lifestyle, including their use of marijuana, and with the Rasta ideology that so firmly rejected the individualist, profit-oriented basis of emerging Jamaican capitalism.

Throughout the 1970s, the processes of formalization and sectarianism took place within the Rasta movement. Just as the Methodist church, for example, following its prophet, John Wesley, split off from the larger Protestant movement in Europe, so too, did the Ethiopian Zion Coptic Church split off from the other Rastafarian churches, developing a somewhat different ritual and theology. In spite of sectarian differences, however, there is a common core to Rastafarianism: Haile Selassie is the living God, at least of African people and he is revealed only to true believers; black African people, who are the reincarnation of the ancient Israelites, are considered superior to whites, although individual whites who are able to put aside racist beliefs are accepted into Rasta congregations. Ethiopia, which stands for all of Africa, is Heaven; in opposition stands Babylon, the corrupt, secular world outside. Enjoined by Haile Selassie to liberate their own societies from oppression and social injustice, Rastafarians live "in the white-dominated world, without becoming part of it." Like the Amish, the Rastafarians engage in a delicate balancing between a life of opposition to the values and practices of the larger society and the need to interact with that society.

Like all fundamentalist religious communities, the Rastafarian theology creates an encompassing, highly structured lifestyle and a traditional morality. Rastafarian ritual observances are syncretic and largely based on the Old Testament: They follow the dietary laws of Leviticus (similar to the kosher practices of orthodox Jews) and, based on Leviticus 21:5, Rastafarian men do not shave or cut their hair. Following their central belief that Babylon is Hell, Rastas resist the institutions of Babylon, including marriage, sending their children to public schools, and the payment of taxes. Women, according to Corinthians 1:4, do not expose their hair and eschew the use of cosmetics. In both daily life and religious practices Rasta women engage in different activities and have different responsibilities than men. Women do not hold leadership positions in the religious community and are not permitted in "reasoning sessions."

Reasoning sessions are the heart of Rasta spiritualism. In worship services that occur mornings, afternoons, and evenings, Rastafarian men recite biblical passages and discuss their "reasonings" or understandings of them. The smoking of marijuana is essential to these sessions. Cannabis is described by Rastafarians as the mystical body and blood of "Jesus." It enhances enlightenment, permits him to find the spirit of love, unity, and justice within himself, and serves to bring him closer to God. For the Rastas, ganja as a sacrament is legitimated by many references to biblical scripture: from Genesis 1:11–12, "and God said, let the earth bring forth grass, the herb yielding seed, and . . . God saw that it was good." For Rastas, ganja is the only true sacrament. Rasta theology holds that wine alcohol is a dead spirit, distilled by corrupted man, the false sacrament of the white man's Christendom, causing drunkenness and crime and is, therefore, not the symbol of the body and blood of Christ. Ganja, on the other hand, is a natural substance, and coming from God directly, must be good and true.[2] For this reason, Rastafarians challenge the labelling of ganja as a drug; similarly, they also abjure not only what our society calls "hard drugs" such as processed heroin and cocaine, but also synthetic and manufactured medicines.

Although law enforcement agents have characterized the Rastafarians' use of marijuana as "freewheeling," in part because Rastafarian religious services do not conform to the scheduled nature of religious services most Americans are used to, in fact, Rasta religious services, including the use of ganja, do conform to specific rules and doctrines. The ganja pipes, for example, are considered holy objects and ganja use is preceded by specific prayers. Indeed, the Rastas might easily be ignored as another of the many fundamentalist Christian sects that have frequently emerged in Western history, were it not for their use of ganja. It is the Rastas' practice of using ganja that has joined them in conflict with the government in the United States, despite the ostensible protection of the First Amendment which holds that "Congress shall make no law . . . prohibiting the free exercise [of religion]."

"HOLY SMOKE": LITIGATION AND THE ETHIOPIAN ZION COPTIC CHURCH

The most widely known litigation involving the religious use of marijuana centered on the Rasta congregation that gathered at 43 Star Island, Miami Beach. The beginnings of this litigation actually reach back into the early 1970s when several members of the Ethiopian Zion Coptic Church were arrested in connection with the confiscation of large quantities of marijuana in several locations in central Florida. The Florida locale is not surprising given its proximity to Jamaica which is both the origin point of the church and a major source of marijuana production. Furthermore, the Star Island congregation of the Ethiopian Zion Coptic Church had had close links with the Jamaican Rastafarians since the 1960s. During this period, Coptic Church members first found their way to Rasta communes as part of a generation of American counterculture youth searching for more congenial environments in which to practice alternative lifestyles. Of the many young white people who went to Jamaica, a small number professed a sincere conversion to Rastafarianism and were accepted by Jamaican Rastas as part of their community. Some of these people later returned to the United States and established the Ethiopian Zion Coptic Church in Miami, keeping active personal and spiritual relationships with Rasta leaders in Jamaica, among them Keith Gordon, who was to later figure in the litigation.

In the late 1970s, following phone calls by neighbors, Janet Reno, then a prosecutor for the state of Florida, along with officials representing the City of Miami Beach, filed a complaint against the members of the Ethiopian Zion Coptic Church, charging them with a violation of local zoning ordinances that prevent a religious congregation from holding services in a residential neighborhood. The complaint against them also charged the illegal use of marijuana in violation of Florida public nuisance statutes. These charges, minor as they might seem, became part of a strategy by state and local law enforcement agents to rid Florida of a group that officials saw as a drug enterprise and not as a genuine religion. According to *Miami Herald* reporter Joe Oglesby's informant, "The idea is to put [the Coptics] out of business."[3]

The trial and appeals courts found, however, that the Coptic church was a bona fide religion of long standing, and that the use of marijuana was a genuine religious sacrament essential to religious practice. In this aspect of the case, the courts did not lend support to the government strategy to close down the Church. However, both courts ultimately ruled against church members on the public nuisance charge because the ganja sacrament was offered to children and to adult nonmembers. The justices also pointed out that Coptics used cannabis throughout the day and did not limit its use to the church facility.

On the zoning issue, too, the courts found against the Coptics. While the trial judge had offered what undoubtedly seemed to him the compromise that the owner, Renee Town, could worship at 43 Star Island with her family and friends, both local and appeals courts nevertheless held that the property could not be used for church meetings.

What would have happened after the Supreme Court of Florida upheld the trial court's injunction against the Coptics, and the U.S. Supreme Court refused to hear the case on appeal, became a moot question when, on October 28, 1979, the television news show *60 Minutes* aired a feature piece entitled "Holy Smoke," describing the 43 Star Island Coptic community. The prime time, nationwide broadcast, showing the open and frequent use of marijuana by the Coptics, prompted Florida Governor Graham to urge the U.S. government to bring a "massive" federal case—one that would revive the earlier smuggling and possession and use charges—against the Coptics. The U.S. Justice Department agreed to explore this possibility and subsequently instructed the U.S. Attorney in Miami to bring a case.

As a result, in the early hours of the morning, three weeks after the *60 Minutes* broadcast, federal and local police raided the 43 Star Island compound. In an attempt to obtain evidence of large caches of marijuana, a Drug Enforcement Administration tow truck, accompanied by armed agents, rammed the gates, interrupting the morning prayer service. Although no marijuana was found, a six-count indictment was issued charging 19 members of the Coptic church with conspiracy to violate the federal Controlled Substances Act. In addition, Keith Gordon, the Coptic spiritual leader from Jamaica, and two members of the Star Island community, Thomas Reilly, known as "Brother Louv," and Clifton Middleton, were charged with conducting a criminal enterprise. The government alleged that the street value of marijuana seized in previous raids involving Coptics totalled $80 to $100 million. As one of the lawyers for the Coptics, Milton M. Ferrell, Jr., later explained, the U.S. Attorney's office was able to construct the case that Governor Graham wanted by stringing together all the previous Florida cases, that had been up to now unsuccessfully prosecuted, as a federal conspiracy case.

The defense mounted by attorneys for the Coptics in this federal prosecution pursued a dual strategy. Offering evidence from a number of internists, psychiatrists, nutritionists, and anthropologists, the defense claimed that the classification of marijuana as a harmful and dangerous drug was arbitrary and irrational and therefore violated Fifth Amendment due process and equal protection guarantees. But the lawyers for the Coptics also argued that since marijuana was an indispensable part of the Coptic religion, prohibiting its use violated the First Amendment free exercise rights of church members.

First attempting to prove the irrationality of the classification of marijuana as harmful and dangerous, defense witnesses, on the basis of prior research as well as clinical examinations of both Jamaican and American Coptics, testified that they found no physically or psychologically harmful effects of marijuana use, even among those persons who had been using it for a long time.

Dr. Lester Grinspoon, a psychiatrist from the Harvard Medical School and Director of the Massachusetts Mental Health Center, testified that the effects of marijuana use are "limited and mild," that they disappear when the high is over, and that they "are not medically harmful to the user."[4] Dr. Grinspoon, and Dr. J. Thomas Ungerleider, of the UCLA Medical Center, citing a 1972 report of the National Commission on Marijuana and Drug Abuse, further testified that the allegedly harmful effects of long-term use of marijuana—that it leads to addiction, causes crime and other aggressive behavior, leads to brain damage and the use of other drugs, and is potentially lethal—are all "myths . . . without any valid empirical foundation."[5] Dr. Grinspoon also stated that the negative pulmonary effects of marijuana are not as severe as those from tobacco smoke. Dr. Ungerleider concluded his testimony by citing the commission finding that there is "no significant harm to the marijuana user and no significant danger to the public health or welfare from the use of marijuana."[6]

Several other expert witnesses, all medical doctors, examined several dozen Coptics in Jamaica and at Star Island. These physicians testified that there were no negative physical or mental health effects in these individuals that could be attributed to the long-term and continual use of marijuana. Dr. Brian L. Weiss did observe that some of the American Coptics that he examined had prior histories of alcohol and drug use; he also noted, however, that in his opinion, the American Coptics were functioning at a much better level than before joining the Church.[7]

In challenging the classification of marijuana as a dangerous drug, still other witnesses pointed to the empirical evidence that marijuana has therapeutic properties in the treatment of glaucoma, neurological disorders, and nausea induced by chemotherapy.[8] Indeed, Dr. Grinspoon capped the testimony with the provocative statement that "the single greatest danger encountered by the marijuana user is that of being arrested by law enforcement personnel."[9]

The defense strategy did not work. And, despite earlier court findings that the Coptics were a sincere and long-established religious group, the jury found all but one of the defendants guilty as charged. Four months later, U.S. District Judge William Hoeveler imposed sentences ranging from seven to fifteen years. With nine of the Coptics in jail, and ten others fugitives from the law, Florida officials got their wish to put this Coptic Church out of business! In this case, the constitutional issue of free exercise of religion could not withstand the determination of the government to prosecute the Coptic Church on a drug conspiracy charge.

THE PEYOTE WAY AND AMERICAN JUSTICE

American courts have not responded in the same way to all groups that use controlled substances in their religious rituals. Much depends upon the period in which a case comes before the court, the particular group involved, as well as the specific nature of the ritual, and the substance in question. In the 1964 California case *People v. Woody* (61 Cal. 2d 716), for example, Native Americans successfully litigated the right to use peyote in Native American Church ritual.

The sacramental use of peyote by indigenous peoples in North America dates back thousands of years. Spanish explorers in the 1600s observed the religious use of peyote by Native Americans in Mexico and the American Southwest.[10] The peyote cactus grew in abundance south of the Rio Grande and was used as a sacrament by native priests for inducing visions. In the nineteenth century, unorganized and varied forms of this peyote religion spread to some North American tribes from the Southwest as far as California and Oklahoma, although at the same time, Spanish priests attempted to suppress it, fearing it would inhibit conversion to Catholicism.[11] Because peyote induces visions, it was branded by the Spanish as an evil that would impair both the physical and mental health of the Indians. Despite this attempted suppression of native religion, peyotism continued to travel north where it again provoked hostility among Catholic and Protestant missionaries, as well as agents of the U.S. Bureau of Indian Affairs.

Denouncing it as a "heathenish" practice, the U.S. government and missionaries attempted to prohibit peyotism as part of an explicit assimilationist policy on the part of the United States intended to transform Native Americans into good democrats, Christians, and farmers. While penalties were both threatened and inflicted upon Native Americans who engaged in peyote rituals, it was not until 1899 that a statute was enacted, in the territory of Oklahoma, specifically controlling the use of peyote.[12] Subsequently, over several decades, a number of states passed statutes criminalizing the use of peyote even in religious rituals. At the national level, despite more than a half century of lobbying, antipeyotists did not win congressional approval for legislation making peyote illegal until passage of the Drug Abuse Control Act of 1965.

During the period of antipeyotist harassment in the early twentieth century, it became clear to peyotists and their supporters that gaining protection under the First Amendment would be easier if they organized as a legally incorporated church with a recognized name, officials, and established rules. And so, in 1918, in Oklahoma, a group of peyotists met and signed articles of incorporation as the Native American Church (NAC). Their church charter clearly acknowledged the importance of Christianity in belief and practice: "The purpose for which this corporation is formed is to foster and promote the religious belief of the several tribes of Indians in the State of Oklahoma, in the Christian religion with the practice of the Peyote Sacrament as commonly understood and used among the adherents of this religion in the several tribes . . . and to teach the Christian religion with morality, sobriety, industry, kindly charity and right living and to cultivate a spirit of self-respect and brotherly union among the members of the Native Race of Indians."[13] This incorporation of Christian elements proved critical in the *Woody* case.

Peyote is a non-habit-forming, hallucinogenic drug derived from a small, spineless cactus growing principally in northern Mexico and southern Texas. Peyote buttons, which are generally dried, and then eaten, are extremely bitter and often produce vomiting. Peyote has psychedelic properties that produce feelings of friendliness, pleasant eu-

phoria, relaxation, timelessness, and visual images of bright and kalei-
doscopic colors or scenes involving animals or humans. In some cases it
produces hallucinatory symptoms similar to those observed in paranoic
schizophrenia.[14]

The cornerstone of the peyote religion is a ceremony that is marked
by the sacramental use of peyote. The ceremony is usually led by men;
traditionally, women were excluded but today they may participate. The
ritual usually lasts from sundown Saturday night to dawn on Sunday.
A church member will sponsor a meeting to give thanks for past good
fortune, to find guidance for future conduct, or because he is worried
about his own or a family member's ill health. Although peyotism in-
fuses the daily life of peyotists in the form of singing and the possession
of household ritual paraphernalia (peyote rattle and drum), the monthly
meetings are especially important and attract peyotists from long dis-
tances, specially and carefully dressed for the occasion. During the ten-
hour ceremony, peyote buttons are passed and eaten; much of the night
is spent in singing and prayer. The meeting sponsor supervises the ceremony, deciding the order of events and the amount of peyote to be
consumed.

Peyotists believe that peyote is a divine plant revealed to the Native
Americans and capable of working miracles; the ceremonial taking of
peyote establishes communion with God or the spiritual world in general. Unlike marijuana for the Rastafarians, peyote is more than a sacrament; it is itself an object of worship and prayers are directed to it.
Also in contrast to marijuana use among Rastafarians, peyote use outside
the ritual meeting is considered sacrilegious.

PSYCHEDELIC BUTTONS: THE NATIVE AMERICAN
CHURCH AND THE COURTS

On April 28, 1962, a group of Navajo Native American Church (NAC)
members met in a hogan (a Navajo dwelling made of earth supported
by timbers) in the desert near Needles, California. As with the Rastafarians, local law enforcement officials were aware of drug use during religious ceremonies and had the hogan under surveillance. Members of
the congregation, who were participating in a peyote ceremony, were
arrested and subsequently convicted of violating the California Health
and Safety Code which prohibits the unauthorized use of peyote. Unlike
many other states, and the federal government, California, at the time of
this arrest, did not grant a religious exemption for peyote use.

The convicted NAC members appealed to the California Supreme
Court, arguing that since peyote is an integral part of their religious faith,
invoking the Code against them abridged their right to free exercise of
religion and was, therefore, unconstitutional. The California Supreme

Court agreed, and overturned the lower court conviction on the grounds that criminalizing the use of peyote would remove the "theological heart" of the religion.

In his opinion in *People v. Woody*, California Supreme Court Justice Tobriner did first acknowledge that for many people strict enforcement of drug laws was more important than "carv[ing] out an ... exception for a few believers in a strange faith," as peyotism had been described in the attorney general's brief for the state. But, Tobriner argued, the religious use of peyote posed little danger to the state, and the state's interest in its prohibition was, therefore, outweighed by the First Amendment interest in religious freedom held by NAC members.

In affirming the religious rights of this subculture, Justice Tobriner wrote, "In a mass society, which presses at every point toward conformity, the protection of the self-expression, however unique, of the individual and the group becomes ever more important. The varying currents of the subcultures that flow into the mainstream of our national life give it depth and beauty. We preserve a greater value than an ancient tradition when we protect the rights of the Indians who honestly practiced an old religion in using peyote one night at a meeting in a desert hogan near Needles, California."

These widely quoted and inspiring words require close examination and raise the question of the degree to which Judge Tobriner's opinion was a significant voice for American multiculturalism. First, peyotism was not, in fact, the "strange faith" the state attorney general claimed. As Judge Tobriner himself noted in his opinion, the NAC incorporated many familiar elements of Christianity; indeed, in their articles of incorporation they explicitly referred to themselves as a Christian church. Second, at the time of this decision, 1964, the drug culture which so concerned American courts at a later time was not yet perceived by the nation as a major problem. Third, the qualities of peyote—which include extreme bitterness and a strong tendency to induce vomiting—would appear to place limits on its widespread use as a recreational drug.

Finally, the NAC has no political or social agenda perceived as threatening to the dominant American culture. Unlike the Indian Ghost Dance of the late nineteenth century, and some other Native American revitalization movements, peyotism does not emphasize a change in the social order. Although it is an attempt to continue significant aspects of native religion, it is not informed by a vision of whites disappearing and the land once again in possession of Native Americans. Unlike the mass energy released through the Ghost Dance, peyotism is quietistic, with each individual seeking his own road of enlightenment and self-awareness.

On balance, then, the Tobriner decision yielded, at best, a narrow point. Religious exemption for use of a drug would be permitted where the ritual was highly controlled and for the most part limited to a small, quietistic Christian subculture—little enough danger in all this. Thus, the case of *People v. Woody*, although hailed as an important affirmation of cultural pluralism, can, in retrospect, only be regarded as a partial victory.

Although *Woody* was a state supreme court decision, it was widely cited and influential in state and federal courts addressing issues of First Amendment free exercise rights. Native Americans considered the issue of religious use of peyote by NAC members a settled matter of law. They were wrong. In the 1990 case of *Oregon v. Smith*, the U.S. Supreme Court ruled that the First Amendment did not protect NAC members engaged in peyote ritual. The case involved two NAC members in Oregon, both of whom were fired from their jobs and denied unemployment benefits after participating in a sacramental peyote rite. Oregon state law disqualified employees discharged for work-related "misconduct" from receiving compensation. The men argued that the "misconduct" was, in fact, constitutionally protected religious activity. After several rounds of technical legal skirmishes, the state of Oregon sought to resolve the case in the U.S. Supreme Court. Given the large number of states (23), along with the federal government, which exempted peyote use from criminalization, and the principles expounded in *Woody*, no one was prepared for the Supreme Court decision which, finding against the Native American Church members, considerably curtailed religious freedom in general, and ritual use of peyote in particular.

Justice Antonin Scalia's opinion for the Court held that constitutional protection for religious rights only prevents government from coercing religious beliefs and does not compel it to support all religious practice. His opinion broke new ground by abandoning the use of the compelling state interest test by which government is required to demonstrate the most significant of reasons to deny First Amendment religious rights. Scalia argued that the compelling interest test offered too much protection for religious liberty and that, in particular, the religious diversity found in the United States was a "luxury" that the nation "could not afford."

Following this legal reasoning, the Scalia decision narrowed constitutional protection for religious conduct that would otherwise be punishable under criminal law. Critically, the opinion left to state legislatures the decision of what religious conduct would be permitted. Under Scalia's interpretation, these legislatures could, if they wished, exempt otherwise proscribed conduct—such as religious drug use—but Scalia's opinion did not hold that there was a constitutional requirement that they do so.

Anticipating that his opinion would throw religious groups upon the mercies of majoritarian legislatures, Scalia acknowledged that "leaving accommodation to the political process will place at a relative disadvantage those religious practices that are not widely engaged in." He defended this position—which seemed to many as utterly contrary to the very rights that the First Amendment was designed to protect—by writing that "[this] unavoidable consequence of democratic government must be preferred to a system in which each conscience is a law unto itself or in which judges weigh the social importance of all laws against the centrality of all religious beliefs."[15] Such an interpretation, Scalia wrote, would "be courting anarchy, [a] danger which increases in direct proportion to the society's diversity of religious beliefs."[16]

Justice Sandra Day O'Connor, while joining in the result of the majority, strongly disagreed with Scalia's reasoning, in particular, abandoning the compelling interest test. Acknowledging that no right is absolute, she nevertheless underscored the Supreme Court's long-standing commitment to the preferred position of religious rights even when the exercise of these rights conflicts with other laws, unless such laws are "required by clear and compelling governmental interests 'of the highest order.' "[17]

The dissenting justices, Blackmun, Brennan, and Marshall, took strong exception to the result and opinion of the Court as diminishing religious rights. In several revealing comments, however, the dissenters also made clear that their openness to the religious use of peyote by members of the Native American Church specifically would not extend to religious use of marijuana by members of the Ethiopian Zion Coptic Church.[18] These justices cited several reasons for distinguishing religious peyote use from other drugs, including marijuana: They believed that the unpleasant physiological qualities of peyote made it "self-limiting" and discouraged casual, social use; they noted that drug trafficking in substances such as marijuana and heroin involved "greed and violence" and was far more extensive than peyote (the total amount of illegal peyote seized by federal authorities between 1980 and 1987 was 19.4 pounds, in contrast to the more than 15 million pounds of marijuana seized in that same period); and they distinguished between the restricted "ceremonial context" of peyote use in the Native American Church and the teaching of the Ethiopian Zion Church that "marijuana is properly smoked 'continually all day.' "

In both the *Oregon v. Smith* opinion and dissent, a strong signal was given to the Ethiopian Zion Coptic Church and other groups which seek to use marijuana openly in their religious life that such religious conduct will not be protected. In *Oregon v. Smith*, it is implicit that the state of Oregon, as well as the majority of the Court accepted the Federal Drug Enforcement's classification of marijuana with the most dangerous drugs, for example, heroin and LSD. And while the dissenting justices did forcefully challenge the similar classification of peyote, which they claim "rests on no evidentiary foundation at all," even they did not extend this challenge to marijuana. Thus, these dissenting justices also implicitly accepted the government's view that marijuana is harmful and dangerous.

Justice Scalia's opinion produced a firestorm of anger and reaction. Working through members of Congress, the Native American Church in coalition with the nation's major religious denominations, human rights groups, and Native American tribes and national organizations successfully lobbied for two corrective laws.[19] The first, the 1993 Religious Freedom Restoration Act (Pub. L. 103–141, 107 Stat. 1488), restored the compelling government interest test in free exercise litigation. A year later, in 1994, President Bill Clinton signed additional legislation (Pub. L. 103–344, 108 Stat. 3125) amending the American Indian Religious Freedom Act of 1978 (42 USC, sec. 1996) to guarantee legal protection for Native Americans to use, possess, and transport peyote "for religious purposes."

The 1994 amendments negate the *Oregon v. Smith* decision and provide federal legal protection for members of the Native American Church in their religious use of peyote. In contrast, it is difficult to imagine that in the near future, the Ethiopian Zion Coptic Church will be likely to win even the limited acceptance that is expressed by government exemptions for the NAC. A consideration of the two religious groups indicates many specific reasons why we would expect the Rastafarians to fare less well than the Native American Church under American law. As cited in the Florida decisions, the willingness of the Coptic Church to offer the marijuana sacrament to children and to adult nonmembers inhibits courts from granting them the right to a religious exemption from the drug laws, even as the courts acknowledge the centrality of the marijuana sacrament to their religion. The Rastafarians' very open and frequent use of marijuana, as well as their willingness to sell it, also militates against their success in gaining further religious rights. In addition, Rastafarian dress and hairstyle distance them from a majority of the American population, even more so than Native American Church members, whose religion does not require culturally distinct symbols. The perception of Rastas as a group that condemns wage labor also sets them in opposition to dominant American society. In addition, the general perception of Rastafarianism as an "imported" religion increases the difficulty of their acceptance, compared, for example, to the Native American Church. Finally, in contrast, for example, to alcohol and tobacco, drugs which are legal because they are broadly used across the dominant culture from the working class to the corporate class, marijuana and peyote have generally been associated with people outside, and in some cases, in opposition to, the dominant culture.

Members of the Native American Church and the Ethiopian Zion Coptic Church who claim the right to use controlled substances in religious ritual assert one of the most cherished American values: that of the free exercise of religion. In particular, they raise the question of whether religious practices that are not widely engaged in and are perceived as threatening to the dominant culture can find protection under the First Amendment.

Justice Scalia's view that majoritarian legislatures are the proper arena in which religious groups must seek to win their rights—in these cases, to win a religious exemption for drug use—imposes a heavy burden on groups that are often small and outside the mainstream. Members of the Native American Church finally succeeded in 1994, in part because the impact of the Scalia opinion reached far beyond the NAC, into the heart of American religion and, in part because of the special legal relationship of Native Americans and the government of the United States. It appears unlikely that, in the face of the specter of substance abuse, majoritarian legislatures will either reclassify nonaddictive drugs such as marijuana so that it is no longer considered "harmful and dangerous," or will, in the absence of such reclassification, nevertheless, permit religious exemptions for Rastafarians.

NOTES

1. See Leonard E. Barrett, Sr., *The Rastafarians: Sounds of Cultural Dissonance,* rev. ed. (Boston: Beacon Press, 1988), and William F. Lewis, *Soul Rebels: The Rastafari* (Prospect Heights, IL: Waveland Press, 1993).

2. *Town v. Florida ex rel. Reno,* Brief for the Appellant to the Supreme Court of the United States (March 31, 1980), 13a.

3. Joe Oglesby, "Probe Aims at Shutting Down Coptics," *Miami Herald,* December 6, 1978.

4. *United States v. Morrison,* Motion to Dismiss the Indictment (Case No. 79-379-CR-WMH), 3.

5. Ibid., 10.

6. Ibid., 8.

7. *United States v. Morrison,* Documentary Evidence, 48ff.

8. *New York Times,* May 1, 1991, B22.

9. *United States v. Morrison,* Motion to Dismiss Indictment, 6.

10. Native American Rights Fund, *Legal Review* 20 (Winter/Spring 1995): 7.

11. Alice Beck Kehoe, *The Ghost Dance: Ethnohistory and Revitalization* (Fort Worth: Holt, Rinehart and Winston, 1989), 108.

12. Omar Stewart, *Peyote Religion* (Norman: University of Oklahoma Press, 1987), 130–31.

13. Ibid., 224.

14. Ibid., 3.

15. *Oregon v. Smith,* 494 U.S. 872, 890 (1990).

16. Ibid., 888.
17. Ibid., 895.
18. Ibid., 917–18.
19. Native American Rights Fund, *Legal Review*, 19.

Part III

Gender

9

Gays and the Law: Status and Conduct

Among the most significant changes in American society is the emergence of homosexual men and women into the public and political life of the nation. Homosexuality as a practice, of course, has always been acknowledged in Western culture; usually disparaged and stigmatized, and always regulated by law, the degree of its public approval varied in different historical periods. The Greeks, for example, considered homosexuality quite as natural as heterosexuality. Christianity, in contrast, embraced celibacy as the highest form of good, and homosexuality was condemned as animal lust, sinful, and unnatural.[1] One expression of Christian disapproval of homosexuality was the pressure for laws criminalizing sodomy. This influence was incorporated into English common law and subsequently into the law of the United States as well.

The widespread social disapproval of homosexuality, expressed in law, religious injunction, and social discrimination in the United States, created an environment in which most homosexuals chose to be invisible. The documentation of homosexual subcultures in pre-twentieth century America is scanty; in the latter part of the nineteenth century it appears, however, that there were certain places and activities which formed what might be called an incipient male homosexual subculture. Indications of a male homosexual subculture were homosexual houses of prostitution, homosexual bars and saloons, and public urban places such as the Loop in Chicago, known for homosexual transactions.[2]

Clearly, growing urbanization was critical for the development of first, a male homosexual, and then, some decades later, a lesbian subculture in the United States. The subcultures of male homosexuals in cities often have spatial dimensions; lesbians are more of a "sociopsychological" community.[3] Lesbian subcultures have historically been even more invisible than male homosexual subcultures. This is partly reflected in the dearth of laws regulating lesbianism compared to those regulating male homosexuality, for example, sodomy laws.

It was not until the 1950s and particularly, the 1960s, that a changing climate of social norms and increased political activism on the part of many minorities paved the way for the emergence of these previously underground homosexual subcultures. Today, the existence of gay male and lesbian communities, supporting distinctive subcultures, is clearly established. Gay men and lesbians participate in gay institutions such as churches and political groups; organized channels of formal and informal communication; and special norms of dress, gesture, means of identification, beliefs, values, and behaviors; and hold a group identity based on both a knowledge of a shared sexual preference and the experience of being an oppressed minority. The power and pride generated by the growing numbers of men and women openly acknowledging their gay identities and openly participating in the gay subculture led to a political agenda calling for the removal of legal and social barriers against homosexuals in American society.

An important item on the gay legal agenda is challenging state statutes criminalizing sodomy. Litigation efforts on a state-by-state basis are paralleled by efforts to have the United States Supreme Court declare such statutes unconstitutional. The importance of striking down sodomy statutes is twofold. In the first place, sodomy statutes symbolically denigrate an activity that is at the heart of male homosexual relationships. In addition, although such statutes are seldom enforced, their existence makes every homosexual potentially subject to criminal sanctions. Although the language of sodomy laws is general, and therefore includes heterosexual activity, such laws have been primarily enforced against homosexuals.

An early case in which the Supreme Court summarily affirmed the lower court's opinion, *Doe v. Richmond* (425 U.S. 901, 1976), attempted to invalidate Virginia's statute criminalizing sodomy. The plaintiffs contended that the sodomy statute deprived adult males engaging in "regular homosexual relations consensually and in private," of their constitutional rights to freedom of expression, privacy, and due process. In stressing the regular, consensual, and private nature of the relationship, Doe sought to have homosexual relationships accepted as equal to marriage, and therefore to the privacy rights enjoyed by a married couple, as recognized by the Supreme Court in *Griswold v. Connecticut* (381 U.S. 479, 1965). The court disagreed, holding that "the Constitution [only] condemns State legislation that trespasses upon the privacy of the incidents of marriage, upon the sanctity of the home, or upon the nature of family life," and emphasized that *Griswold* applied only to *marital* rights of heterosexual couples. The district court sustained the state's contention that homosexuality is likely to contribute to, if not result in, moral delinquency, and therefore the state had a right to prohibit homosexual sodomy.

Pursuing litigation in the face of earlier defeats, the gay community continued to challenge state sodomy laws. The most recent case which came before the United States Supreme Court was that of *Bowers v. Hardwick*, challenging a Georgia statute criminalizing oral and anal sex. The case arose when an Atlanta police officer, attempting to serve a warrant for an unpaid fine, was admitted to the home of Michael Hardwick, a member of Atlanta's gay community, and given permission to find him. The police officer found Mr. Hardwick in his bedroom, having sexual relations with another man. He was arrested, but not prosecuted. Mr. Hardwick, however, brought suit in court on the grounds that the law violated his constitutional right to privacy, specifically claiming that his homosexual activity was a private and intimate association beyond the reach of state regulation. A sharply divided court rejected Hardwick's claim. Justice Byron White wrote the opinion for the majority:

Bowers v. Hardwick
478 U.S. 186 (1986)

In August 1982, respondent was charged with violating the Georgia statute criminalizing sodomy by committing that act with another adult male in the bedroom of respondent's home. After a preliminary hearing, the District Attorney decided not to present the matter to the grand jury unless further evidence developed.

Respondent then brought suit in the Federal District Court, challenging the constitutionality of the statute insofar as it criminalized consensual sodomy. He asserted that he was a practicing homosexual, that the Georgia sodomy statute, as administered by the defendants, placed him in imminent danger of arrest, and that the statute for several reasons violates the Federal Constitution.

This case does not require a judgment on whether laws against sodomy between consenting adults in general, or between homosexuals in particular, are wise or desirable. It raises no question about the right or propriety of state legislative decisions invalidating those laws on state constitutional grounds. The issue presented is whether the Federal Constitution confers a fundamental right upon homosexuals to engage in sodomy and hence invalidates the laws of the many States that still make such conduct illegal and have done so for a very long time. The case also calls for some judgment about the limits of the Court's role in carrying out its constitutional mandate.

We first register our disagreement with the Court of Appeals and with respondent that the Court's prior cases have construed the Constitution to confer a right of privacy that extends to homosexual sodomy and for all intents and purposes have decided this case . . . we think it is evident that none of the rights announced in those cases bears any resemblance to the claimed constitutional right of homosexuals to engage in acts of sodomy that is asserted in this case.

No connection between family, marriage, or procreation on the one hand and homosexual activity on the other has been demonstrated, either by the Court of Appeals or by respondent. Moreover, any claim that these cases nevertheless stand for the proposition that any kind of private sexual conduct between consenting adults is constitutionally insulated from state proscription is unsupportable.

Precedent aside, however, respondent would have us announce, as the Court of Appeals did, a fundamental right to engage in homosexual sodomy. This we are quite unwilling to do. It is true that despite the language of the Due Process Clauses of the Fifth and Fourteenth Amendments, which appears to focus only on the processes by which life, liberty, or property is taken, the cases are legion in which those Clauses have been interpreted to have substantive content, subsuming rights that to a great extent are immune from federal or state regulation or proscription. Among such cases are those recognizing rights that have little or no textual support in the constitutional language.

Striving to assure itself and the public that announcing rights not readily identifiable in the Constitution's text involves much more than the imposition of the Justices' own choice of values on the States and the Federal Government, the Court has sought to identify the nature of the rights qualifying for heightened judicial protection . . . this category includes those fundamental liberties that are "implicit in the concept of ordered liberty," such that "neither liberty nor justice would exist if [they] were sacrificed" . . . [and] those liberties that are "deeply rooted in this Nation's history and tradition."

It is obvious to us that neither of these formulations would extend a fundamental right to homosexuals to engage in acts of consensual sodomy. Proscriptions against that conduct have ancient roots. Sodomy was a criminal offense at common law and was forbidden by the laws of the original thirteen States when they ratified the Bill of Rights. In 1868, when the Fourteenth Amendment was ratified, all but 5 of the 37 States in the Union had criminal sodomy laws. In fact, until 1961, all 50 States outlawed sodomy, and today, 24 States and the District of Columbia continue to provide criminal penalties for sodomy performed in private and between consenting adults. Against this background, to claim that a right to engage in such conduct is "deeply rooted in this Nation's history and tradition" or "implicit in the concept of ordered liberty" is, at best, facetious. . . .

Even if the conduct at issue here is not a fundamental right, respondent asserts that there must be a rational basis for the law and that there is none in this case other than the presumed belief of a majority of the electorate in Georgia that homosexual sodomy is immoral and unacceptable. This is said to be an inadequate rationale to support the law. The law, however, is constantly based on notions of morality, and if all laws representing essentially moral choices are to be invalidated under the Due Process Clause, the courts will be very busy indeed. Even respondent makes no such claim, but insists that majority sentiments about the morality of homosexuality should be declared inadequate. We do not agree, and are unpersuaded that the sodomy laws of some 25 States should be invalidated on this basis.

Two concurring opinions were entered. Chief Justice Burger wrote a separate opinion to underscore his view that "in constitutional terms there is no such thing as a fundamental right to commit homosexual sodomy." He went on to say:

[T]he proscriptions against sodomy have very "ancient roots." Decisions of individuals relating to homosexual conduct have been subject to state intervention throughout the history of Western Civilization. Condemnation of those practices is firmly rooted in Judeo-Christian moral and ethical standards. Homosexual sodomy was a capital crime under Roman law. During the English Reformation when powers of the ecclesiastical courts were transferred to the King's Courts, the first English statute criminalizing sodomy was passed. Blackstone described "the infamous crime against nature" as an offense of "deeper malignity" than rape, an heinous act "the very mention of which is a disgrace to human nature," and "a crime not fit to be named." The common law of England, including its prohibition of sodomy, became the received law of Georgia and the other Colonies. In 1816 the Georgia Legislature passed the statute at issue here, and that statute has been continuously in force in one form or another since that time. To hold that the act of homosexual sodomy is somehow protected as a fundamental right would be to cast aside millennia of moral teaching.

This is essentially not a question of personal "preferences" but rather the [sic] of the legislative authority of the State. I find nothing in the Constitution depriving a State of the power to enact the statute challenged here.

In his concurrence, Justice Powell agreed with the Court that there was no fundamental right, as claimed by Hardwick, to be free from prosecution for sodomy. He did feel, however, that the Georgia statute contested by Hardwick imposed a penalty—potential imprisonment up to twenty years—that created a serious Eighth Amendment (cruel and unusual punishment) issue. Since Hardwick had not, however, been tried and sentenced, this issue was not presently before the court.

Justice Blackmun's dissent argued that the majority was incorrect in analyzing the rights at issue in the narrow terms of homosexuality, and sought to place the decision within the larger arena of the right to privacy of all people, regardless of their sexual orientation.

This case is [not] about "a fundamental right to engage in homosexual sodomy," as the Court purports to declare.... Rather, this case is about "the most comprehensive of rights and the right most valued by civilized men," namely, "the right to be let alone."

The statute at issue denies individuals the right to decide for themselves whether to engage in particular forms of private, consensual sexual activity. The Court concludes that [the statute] is valid essentially because "the laws of ... many States ... still make such conduct illegal and have done so for a very long time." But the fact that the moral judgments expressed by [these] statutes may be "natural and familiar ... ought not to conclude our judgment upon the question whether statutes embodying them conflict with the Constitution of the United States." Like Justice Holmes, I believe that "[i]t is revolting to have no better reason for a rule of law than that so it was laid down in the time of Henry IV. It is still more revolting if the grounds upon which it was laid down have vanished long since, and the rule simply persists from blind imitation of the past." I believe we must analyze respondent's claim in the light of the values that underlie the constitutional right to privacy. If that means anything, it means that, before Georgia can prosecute its citizens for making choices about the most intimate aspects of their lives, it must do more than assert that the choice they have made is an "abominable crime not fit to be named among Christians."

In its haste to reverse the Court of Appeals and hold that the Constitution does not "confe[r] a fundamental right upon homosexuals to engage in sodomy," the Court relegates the actual statute being challenged to a footnote and ignores the procedural posture of the case before it. A fair reading of the statute and of the complaint clearly reveals that the majority has distorted the question this case presents.

First, the Court's almost obsessive focus on homosexual activity is particularly hard to justify in light of the broad language Georgia has used. Unlike the Court, the Georgia Legislature has not proceeded on the assumption that homosexuals are so different from other citizens that their lives may be controlled in a way that would not be tolerated if it limited the choices of those other citizens.

Rather, Georgia has provided that "[a] person commits the offense of sodomy when he performs or submits to any sexual act involving the sex organs of one person and the mouth or anus of another. . . ." The sex or status of the persons who engage in the act is irrelevant as a matter of state law. I therefore see no basis for . . . Georgia's attempt, both in its brief and at oral argument, to defend [the statute] solely on the grounds that it prohibits homosexual activity. Michael Hardwick's standing may rest in significant part on Georgia's apparent willingness to enforce against homosexuals a law it seems not to have any desire to enforce against heterosexuals. But his claim that [the statute] involves an unconstitutional intrusion into his privacy and his right of intimate association does not depend in any way on his sexual orientation. . . .

The Court's cramped reading of the issue before it makes for a short opinion, but it does little to make for a persuasive one.

. . . The Court concludes today that none of our prior cases dealing with various decisions that individuals are entitled to make free of governmental interference "bears any resemblance to the claimed constitutional right of homosexuals to engage in acts of sodomy that is asserted in this case." While it is true that these cases may be characterized by their connection to protection of the family, the Court's conclusion that they extend no further than this boundary ignores the warning in *Moore v. East Cleveland* (plurality opinion), against "clos[ing] our eyes to the basic reasons why certain rights associated with the family have been accorded shelter under the Fourteenth Amendment's Due Process Clause." We protect those rights not because they contribute, in some direct and material way, to the general public welfare, but because they form so central a part of an individual's life. "[T]he concept of privacy embodies the 'moral fact, that a person belongs to himself and not others nor to society as a whole.' " And so we protect the decision whether to marry precisely because marriage "is an association that promotes a way of life, not causes; a harmony in living, not political faiths; a bilateral loyalty, not commercial or social projects." We protect the decision whether to have a child because parenthood alters so dramatically an individual's self-definition, not because of demographic considerations or the Bible's command to be fruitful and multiply. And we protect the family because it contributes so powerfully to the happiness of individuals, not because of a preference for stereotypical households. The Court recognized in *Roberts* that the "ability independently to define one's identity that is central to any concept of liberty" cannot truly be exercised in a vacuum; we all depend on the "emotional enrichment of close ties with others."

Only the most willful blindness could obscure the fact that sexual intimacy is "a sensitive, key relationship of human existence, central to family life, community welfare, and the development of human personality." The fact that individuals define themselves in a significant way through their intimate sexual relationships with others suggests, in a Nation as diverse as ours, that there may be many "right" ways of conducting those relationships, and that much of the richness of a relationship will come from the freedom an individual has to choose the form and nature of these intensely personal bonds.

In a variety of circumstances we have recognized that a necessary corollary of giving individuals freedom to choose how to conduct their lives is acceptance of the fact that different individuals will make different choices. For example, in holding that the clearly important state interest in public education should give way to a competing claim by the Amish to the effect that extended formal schooling threatened their way of life, the Court declared: "There can be no assumption that today's majority is 'right' and the Amish and others like them are 'wrong.' A way of life that is odd or even erratic but interferes with no rights or interests of others is not to be condemned because it is different." The Court claims that its decision today merely refuses to recognize a fundamental right to engage in homosexual sodomy; what the Court really has refused to recognize is the fundamental interest all individuals have in controlling the nature of their intimate associations with others.

The behavior for which Hardwick faces prosecution occurred in his own home, a place to which the Fourth Amendment attaches special significance. The Court's treatment of this aspect of the case is symptomatic of its overall refusal to consider the broad principles that have informed our treatment of privacy in specific cases. Just as the right to privacy is more than the mere aggregation of a number of entitlements to engage in specific behavior, so too, protecting the physical integrity of the home is more than merely a means of protecting specific activities that often take place there. Even when our understanding of the contours of the right to privacy depends on "reference to a 'place,' " "the essence of a Fourth Amendment violation is 'not the breaking of [a person's] doors, and the rummaging of his drawers,' but rather is 'the invasion of his indefensible right of personal security, personal liberty and private property. . . . ' " Indeed, the right of an individual to conduct intimate relationships in the intimacy of his or her own home seems to me to be the heart of the Constitution's protection of privacy.

The Court's failure to comprehend the magnitude of the liberty interests at stake in this case leads it to slight the question whether petitioner, on behalf of the State, has justified Georgia's infringement of these interests. I believe that neither of the two general justifications for [the statute] that petitioner has advanced warrants dismissing respondent's challenge for failure to state a claim.

First, petitioner asserts that the acts made criminal by the statute may have serious adverse consequences for "the general public health and welfare," such as spreading communicable diseases or fostering other criminal activity. Inasmuch as this case was dismissed by the District Court on the pleadings, it is not surprising that the record before us is barren of any evidence to support petitioner's claim. In light of the state of the record, I see no justification for the Court's attempt to equate the private, consensual sexual activity at issue here with the "possession in the home of drugs, firearms, or stolen goods," to which *Stanley* refused to extend its protection. None of the behavior so mentioned can properly be viewed as "[v]ictimless," drugs and weapons are inherently dangerous, and for property to be "stolen," someone must have been wrongfully deprived of it. Nothing in the record before the Court provides any justification for finding the activity forbidden by [the statute] to be physically dangerous, either to the persons engaged in it or to others.

The core of petitioner's defense of [the statute] however, is that respondent and others who engage in the conduct prohibited by [it] interfere with Georgia's exercise of the " 'right of the Nation and of the States to maintain a decent society.' " Essentially, petitioner argues, and the Court agrees, that the fact that the acts described in [the statute] "for hundreds of years, if not thousands, have been uniformly condemned as immoral" is a sufficient reason to permit a State to ban them today.

I cannot agree that either the length of time a majority has held its convictions or the passions with which it defends them can withdraw legislation from this Court's scrutiny. As Justice Jackson wrote so eloquently for the Court in *West Virginia Board of Education v. Barnette*, "we apply the limitations of the Constitution with no fear that freedom to be intellectually and spiritually diverse or even contrary will disintegrate the social organization . . . [F]reedom to differ is not limited to things that do not matter much. That would be a mere shadow of freedom. The test of its substance is the right to differ as to things that touch the heart of the existing order." It is precisely because the issue raised by this case touches the heart of what makes individuals what they are that we should be especially sensitive to the rights of those whose choices upset the majority.

The assertion that "traditional Judeo-Christian values proscribe" the conduct involved cannot provide an adequate justification for [the statute]. That certain, but by no means all, religious groups condemn the behavior at issue gives the State no license to impose their judgments on the entire citizenry. The legitimacy of secular legislation depends instead on whether the State can advance some justification for its law beyond its conformity to religious doctrine. Thus, far from buttressing his case, petitioner's invocation of Leviticus, Romans, St. Thomas Aquinas, and sodomy's heretical status during the Middle Ages undermines his suggestion that [the statute] represents a legitimate use of secular coercive power. A state can no more punish private behavior [because] of religious intolerance than it can punish such behavior because of racial animus. "The Constitution cannot control such prejudices, but neither can it tolerate them. Private biases may be outside the reach of the law, but the law cannot, directly or indirectly give them effect." No matter how uncomfortable a certain group may make the majority of this Court, we have held that "[m]ere public intolerance or animosity cannot constitutionally justify the deprivation of a person's physical liberty."

Nor can [the statute] be justified as a "morally neutral" exercise of Georgia's power to "protect the public environment." Certainly, some private behavior can affect the fabric of society as a whole. Reasonable people may differ about whether particular sexual acts are moral or immoral, but "we have ample evidence for believing that people will not abandon morality, will not think any better of murder, cruelty and dishonesty, merely because some private sexual practice which they abominate is not punished by the law." Petitioner and the Court fail to see the difference between laws that protect public sensibilities and those that enforce private morality. Statutes banning public sexual activity are entirely consistent with protecting the individual's liberty interest in decisions concerning sexual relations: the same recognition that those decisions are intensely private which justifies protecting them from governmental interference can justify protecting individuals from unwilling exposure to the sexual activities of others. But the mere fact that intimate behavior may be punished when it takes place in public cannot dictate how States can regulate intimate behavior that occurs in intimate places.

This case involves no real interference with the rights of others, for the mere knowledge that other individuals do not adhere to one's value system cannot be a legally cognizable interest, let alone an interest that can justify invading the houses, hearts, and minds of citizens who choose to live their lives differently.

It took but three years for the Court to see the error in its analysis in *Minersville School District v. Gobitis* (1940), and to recognize that the threat to national cohesion posed by a refusal to salute the flag was vastly outweighed by the threat of those same values posed by compelling such a salute. I can only hope that here, too, the Court soon will reconsider its analysis and conclude that depriving individuals of the right to choose for themselves how to conduct their intimate relationships poses a far greater threat to the values most deeply rooted in our Nation's history than tolerance of nonconformity could ever do. Because I think the Court today betrays those values, I dissent.

In another dissent, Justice Stevens focused on whether it was constitutional for a law, which included heterosexuals, to be differentially applied to homosexuals.

Like the statute that is challenged in this case, the rationale of the Court's opinion applies equally to the prohibited conduct regardless of whether the parties who engage in it are married or unmarried, or are of the same or different sexes. Sodomy was condemned as an odious and sinful type of behavior during the formative period of the common law. That condemnation was equally damning for heterosexual and homosexual sodomy. Moreover, it provided no special exemption for married couples. The license to cohabit and to produce legitimate offspring simply did not include any permission to engage in sexual conduct that was considered a "crime against nature."

The history of the Georgia statute before us clearly reveals this traditional prohibition of heterosexual, as well as homosexual, sodomy. Indeed, at one point in the 20th century, Georgia's law was construed to permit certain sexual conduct between homosexual women even though such conduct was prohibited between heterosexuals. The history of the statutes cited by the majority as proof for the proposition that sodomy is not constitutionally protected . . . similarly reveals a prohibition on heterosexual, as well as homosexual, sodomy.

Because the Georgia statute expresses the traditional view that sodomy is an immoral kind of conduct regardless of the identity of the persons who engage in it, I believe that a proper analysis of its constitutionality requires consideration of two questions: First, may a State totally prohibit the described conduct by means of a neutral law applying without exception to all persons subject to its jurisdiction? If not, may the State save the statute by announcing that it will only enforce the law against homosexuals? The two questions merit separate discussion.

Our prior cases make two propositions abundantly clear. First, the fact that the governing majority in a State has traditionally viewed a particular practice as immoral is not a sufficient reason for upholding a law prohibiting the practice; neither history nor tradition could save a law prohibiting miscegenation from constitutional attack. Second, individual decisions by married persons, concerning the intimacies of their physical relationship, even when not intended to produce offspring, are a form of "liberty" protected by the Due Process Clause of the Fourteenth Amendment. Moreover, this protection extends to intimate choices by unmarried as well as married persons.

In consideration of claims of this kind, the Court has emphasized the individual interest in privacy, but its decisions have actually been animated by an even more fundamental concern. As I wrote some years ago:

> These cases do not deal with the individual's interest in protection from unwarranted public attention, comment, or exploitation. They deal, rather, with the individual's right to make certain unusually important decisions that will affect his own, or his family's, destiny. The Court has referred to such decisions as implicating basic values; as being 'fundamental,' and as being dignified by history and tradition. The character of the Court's language in these cases brings to mind the origins of the American heritage of freedom—the abiding interest in individual liberty that makes certain state intrusions on the citizen's right to decide how he will live his own life intolerable. Guided by history, our tradition of respect for the dignity of individual choice in matters of conscience and the restraints implicit in the federal system, federal judges have accepted the responsibility for recognition and protection of these rights in appropriate cases.

Society has every right to encourage its individual members to follow particular traditions in expressing affection for one another and in gratifying their personal desires. It, of course, may prohibit an individual from imposing his will on another to satisfy his own selfish interests. It also may prevent an individual from interfering with, or violating, a legally sanctioned and protected relationship, such as marriage. And it may explain the relative advantages and disadvantages of different forms of intimate expression. But when individual married couples are isolated from observation by others, the way in which they voluntarily choose to conduct their intimate relations is a matter for them—not the State—to decide. The essential "liberty" that animated the development of the law in cases like *Griswold, Eisenstadt,* and *Carey* surely embraces the right to engage in nonreproductive, sexual conduct that others may consider offensive or immoral.

Paradoxical as it may seem, our prior cases thus establish that a State may not prohibit sodomy within "the sacred precincts of marital bedrooms," or, indeed, between unmarried heterosexual adults. In all events, it is perfectly clear that the State of Georgia may not totally prohibit the conduct proscribed by [the statute] of the Georgia Criminal Code.

If the Georgia statute cannot be enforced as it is written, if the conduct it seeks to prohibit is a protected form of liberty for the vast majority of Georgia's citizens—the State must assume the burden of justifying a selective application of its law. Either the persons to whom Georgia seeks to apply its statute do not have the same interest in "liberty" that others have, or there must be a reason why the State may be permitted to apply a generally applicable law to certain persons that it does not apply to others.

The first possibility is plainly unacceptable. Although the meaning of the principle that "all men are created equal" is not always clear, it surely must mean that every free citizen has the same interest in "liberty" that the members of the majority share. From the standpoint of the individual, the homosexual and the heterosexual have the same interest in deciding how he will live his own life, and, more narrowly, how he will conduct himself in his personal and voluntary associations with his companions. State intrusion into the private conduct of either is equally burdensome.

The second possibility is similarly unacceptable. A policy of selective application must be supported by a neutral and legitimate interest—something more substantial than a habitual dislike for, or ignorance about, the disfavored group. Neither the State nor the Court has identified any such interest in this case. The Court has posited as a justification for the Georgia statute "the presumed belief of a majority of the electorate in Georgia that homosexual sodomy is immoral and unacceptable." But the Georgia electorate has expressed no such belief— instead, its representatives enacted a law that presumably reflects the belief that *all sodomy* is immoral and unacceptable. Unless the Court is prepared to conclude that such a law is constitutional, it may not rely on the work product of the Georgia Legislature to support its holding. For the Georgia statute does not single out homosexuals as a separate class meriting special disfavored treatment.

Nor, indeed, does the Georgia prosecutor even believe that all homosexuals who violate this statute should be punished. This conclusion is evident from the fact that the respondent in this very case has formally acknowledged in his complaint and in court that he has engaged, and intends to continue to engage, in the prohibited conduct, yet the State has elected not to process criminal charges against him. As JUSTICE POWELL points out, moreover, Georgia's prohibition on private, consensual sodomy has not been enforced for decades. The record of nonenforcement, in this case and in the last several decades, belies the Attorney General's representations about the importance of the State's selective application of its generally applicable law.

Both the Georgia statute and the Georgia prosecutor thus completely fail to provide the Court with any support for the conclusion that homosexual sodomy, *simpliciter,* is considered unacceptable conduct in that State, and that the burden of justifying a selective application of the generally applicable law has been met.

The Court orders the dismissal of respondent's complaint even though the State's statute prohibits all sodomy; even though that prohibition is concededly unconstitutional with respect to heterosexuals; and even though the State's *post hoc* explanations for selective application are belied by the State's own actions. At the very least, I think it clear at this early stage of the litigation that respondent has alleged a constitutional claim sufficient to withstand a motion to dismiss. I respectfully dissent.

Justice Powell's vote is particularly interesting as he was undecided when the justices initially met to discuss the case. Justice Powell was not quite in agreement with Justice Blackmun's sweeping arguments about the right to privacy, although he also believed that sodomy laws were unenforced, unenforceable, and generally useless. Justice Powell finally decided to vote with Justice Blackmun, but several days later changed his mind.[4] Had Georgia actually enforced the law against Hardwick, Justice Powell said he would have voted to throw the law out. But because this was a civil suit, he did not wish to use this case to overturn all sodomy statutes.

Four years after *Bowers,* Justice Powell expressed second thoughts on his vote. "I think I probably made a mistake," he said.[5] He now views the Court's decision as inconsistent with *Roe v. Wade,* a case in which he joined the majority in holding that the right to privacy embedded in liberty gave women a constitutional right to obtain abortions.

Within a year of the decision in *Bowers,* Justice Powell retired and two new justices, Antonin Scalia and Anthony Kennedy, joined the Court. There is little doubt that Justice Scalia would have rejected the privacy argument raised in *Bowers,* a case which has been cited in more than 100 state and federal court decisions as authority for refusing to find a right to privacy in a number of different contexts, in addition to those of gay rights. As we shall see below, *Bowers* had a particularly significant negative impact on cases involving gays and the military.

GAYS AND THE MILITARY

Homosexuality is incompatible with military service. The presence in the military environment of persons who engage in homosexual conduct or who, by their statements, demonstrate a propensity to engage in homosexual conduct, seriously impairs the accomplishment of the military mission. The presence of such members adversely affects the ability of the Military Services to maintain

discipline, good order, and morale; to foster mutual trust and confidence among service members; to ensure the integrity of the system of rank and command; to facilitate assignment and worldwide deployment of service members who frequently must live and work under close conditions affording minimal privacy; to recruit and retain members of the Military Services; to maintain the public acceptability of military service; and to prevent breaches of security.
Department of Defense Directive 1332.14 and 1332.30, 1982

The military gave me a medal for killing two men, but it wants to give me a discharge for loving one.

> Leonard Matlovitch,
> Technical Sergeant, United States Air Force
> (Dismissed for being homosexual)[6]

For the past 20 years, the military ban on gays serving in the U.S. armed forces has presented a major gay civil rights issue for the courts, the Pentagon, and elected officials. Although gay men and lesbians have served in the military since our country was founded, they were never welcomed, and a sodomy conviction while in the service resulted in court-martial and dishonorable discharge. Banning individuals from the military for merely *being* homosexual, however, was not codified in American military law until World War I. At that time, in consultation with the new field of psychiatry, military policy pronounced that homosexuals were not only dangerous, but also ineffective fighters, and in the 1920s and 1930s many gays were purged from the service.[7]

In World War II, the military, faced with a huge task of recruitment and screening, formulated regulations banning those with "homosexual tendencies" from all branches of the armed forces. These regulations, and their rationales, cited in the directive above, remained fundamentally unchanged until 1993, although they have been inconsistently implemented. In wartime, when military personnel were most needed, dismissals of gays decreased, and unless they engaged in misconduct, gays were quietly accepted by their field commands. When wartime crises passed, purges of gay men and especially lesbians increased.[8] At all times, however, thousands of gay men and lesbians have served, often with great distinction, in all branches of the armed services.

In different eras, different rationales were emphasized in barring gays from the military. During and just after World War II, although homosexuals as a class were considered "unfit for military service," the military ban permitted exceptions for individual homosexuals who could be "reclaimed" after a period of hospitalization or whose homosexuality would be overlooked if they were exceptionally outstanding personnel. During the McCarthy period, the most frequently used rationale was that gays were security risks because they could be subject to blackmail. No evidence was ever found to support this claim, and the primary rationale barring gays then shifted to the negative effects their service would have on morale, and thus on military effectiveness.

This rationale, which was the basis of the military ban until President Clinton's "don't ask, don't tell" policy, initiated in November 1993, reflects several assumptions: that service personnel would not have confidence in or respect for homosexual officers; that homosexuals would be unable to perform their duties effectively because of their emotional involvement with other homosexuals and fear of disclosure; that homosexual relationships between subordinates and superiors would disrupt the chain of command structure; that heterosexuals would be discouraged from enlisting in the service; and that there would be adverse foreign reaction to homosexual military personnel serving abroad.

Critics of the present antigay military policy point out that many government studies indicate there is no sociological or scientific evidence for these rationales.[9] They also note that all of these arguments were used by the military in resisting racial integration of the armed forces, ordered by President Truman in 1948. At that time, the Pentagon claimed that it did not endorse racism but was merely acquiescing to American popular opinion. This argument justly failed on the basis that the U.S. Constitution prohibits discrimination by the government against one minority group in order to acquiesce to the prejudices of a majority, a prohibition now central to challenges of the military's ban on homosexuals in the services. And, indeed, the anticipated dire effects of integrating African Americans into the military were never realized. In fact, racial integration of the armed forces is generally viewed as successful, due partly to the military's own sensitivity training programs.

Supporters of the Pentagon policy resist the analogy between racial segregation and barring gays from the military: They claim that while skin color does not imply any particular kind of behavior, a homosexual orientation implies sodomy, a behavior which is unnatural, disruptive, and abhorrent to most Americans, and, in addition, illegal.[10] This relationship between status (what one is) and behavior (what one does, or can be presumed to do) is central in recent legal challenges to military policy.

At the heart of gay litigation is the challenge to the reasonableness and legitimacy of the government policy; in legal terms, does the military ban on gays have some rational relationship to government interests, or is it merely based on ignorance of the nature of homosexuality, fears concerning gay sexual practices, and the long history of antigay prejudice in American culture? If the military ban on gays is based on prejudice, then a classification according to sexual orientation can only legally stand if the government demonstrates a compelling interest in such a classification. Thus, in early gay litigation, courts sought more explicit rationales from the armed services for their ban on gays. When Ensign Vernon Berg III challenged his dismissal from the navy for homosexuality, the navy responded to the court's request by claiming, among other things, that homosexuals "might force their desires on others resulting in sexual assaults," and that the "emotional relationships with other individuals" might disrupt the chain of command.[11] That these rationales are based on inaccurate and pernicious stereotypes about gays' inability to control their sexuality, and that "emotional relationships" which might disrupt the command structure were already covered by more general military regulations on fraternization, was simply ignored by the navy.

Department of Defense policy barring gays was discredited by reports commissioned by the armed services themselves, and which the Pentagon attempted, unsuccessfully, to suppress. As early as 1957 the Crittenden Report and later, the 1988 PERSEREC study and the 1993 RAND study all contradicted the DOD rationales.[12] The Crittenden Report concluded that "There is no correlation between homosexuality and either ability or attainments," and found no empirical evidence for the naval policy that gays could not acceptably serve. Indeed, the report pointed out, many did so serve, indicating clearly that preinduction screening for gays was unsuccessful. The report also concluded that the security risk argument had no factual basis. The PERSEREC Report came to the same conclusions, holding that official fears about the disruption to the military's "good order, discipline and morale" were unfounded. It suggested that the same kind of training programs which successfully achieved racial integration of the services could also be applied to the successful integration of homosexuals by the military in the 1990s.

As the government was unsuccessful in marshalling any evidence supporting the DOD regulations and as evidence contradicting the basis of the military policy piled up, the military shifted its rationale, now emphasizing that the ban against gays was necessary to conform with prevailing social prejudices—in short, that a sufficient reason for barring homosexuals was that heterosexuals would not want to serve with them. Thus, in 1975, the navy rationalized its ban on gays by stating "[P]arents would be more than reluctant, to say the least, to permit their sons and daughters to join the Navy if the Navy had the reputation as a haven for homosexuals."[13] In fact, there is no evidence for this claim; quite the contrary: Armed forces induction screenings which ask an individual if he or she is homosexual are clearly not keeping gays out, and once in the service, most gays are quietly accepted with little fanfare.

Legal Challenges to Military Policy

Military dismissals for homosexuality (between about 700 and 2000 each year for the past ten years), have not been initiated by heterosexuals who refuse to serve with gays, but by military investigations with an interest in "purging" gays from the armed forces. Few gays are dismissed on sodomy charges, which require conclusive evidence of misconduct. Rather, most gay dismissals result from administrative fact-finding hearings based on a serviceperson's "confession" that he or she is gay or lesbian. These "confessions" generally resulted from having been named by others in interrogations frighteningly similar to the duplicitous and coercive techniques of the McCarthy era.[14]

Prior to the 1970s, these men and women, many of whom had exemplary records, for the most part went quietly, frightened by threats of military investigators to make their sexual orientations public and feeling totally powerless to do anything about their treatment and dismissal. But in the 1970s, after a decade of civil rights activism, confrontation, and social change, and particularly with the rise of the gay activist movement, gays in the military became more assertive of their rights. They began to challenge their dismissals from the military in the federal courts, with the aim of ultimately getting a ruling from the U.S. Supreme Court that the Department of Defense regulations were unconstitutional.

The early cases, drawing in part on the right to privacy delineated in *Roe v. Wade*, were uniformly rejected by the courts, and after the *Bowers* decision in 1986, violation of privacy rights no longer appeared to be a basis for a successful constitutional challenge. The traditional deference of courts to military opinion on matters involving the military, which could, in some cases, legitimately limit the constitutional rights of service personnel, was another obstacle to successful gay challenges to the military ban.[15] At the same time, however, some federal judges, even when ruling against the gays' challenges, or in dissent, questioned the wisdom, rationality, and constitutionality of the regulations, and even appealed to the military to change its policies.[16] Yet, despite the presence of judges willing to question the military policy banning gays, in 1982, the Department of Defense rewrote regulation 1332.14 (regarding homosexuals), to eliminate any possibility of exceptions and to require the dismissal of any serviceperson who admitted to being gay, that is, having a gay "sexual orientation." In spite of this, and the changed political climate ushered in by the election of Ronald Reagan as president, gay civil rights activists were still optimistic about a legal strategy and continued to challenge the DOD regulations in court.[17]

In 1984, gays' optimism about winning their rights through the courts was significantly set back by a U.S. Appeals Court decision which rejected the right to privacy and equal protection claims of James Dronenburg, who unlike most gays dismissed from the armed services for *saying* they were homosexuals, admitted to having had sex with a sailor.[18] Writing the opinion for the majority in *Dronenberg*, Judge Robert Bork defended not only sodomy laws but all regulations proscribing homosexuality. Bork viewed the military's regulation as "plainly a rational means of advancing a legitimate, indeed a crucial, interest" of the armed forces. "The effects of homosexual conduct within a Naval or military unit are almost certain to be harmful to morale and discipline," he said, and "[T]he Navy is not required to produce social science data . . . to prove what *common sense and common experience* (emphasis added) demonstrate." Judge Bork cited Dronenburg's admission of sex as evidence that allowing homosexuals to serve in the military would "enhance the possibility of homosexual seduction." Bork also noted that the "revolution in sexual mores" should arrive through the "moral choices of the people and their elected representatives," not through the courts.[19]

Bork's opinion was castigated by other judges on the Appeals Court. Chief Judge Spottswood W. Robinson III took Bork to task for accepting the government rationale for the gay policy which, he said, presented "a patently inadequate justification in a Navy that includes personnel of both sexes and places no parallel ban on all types of heterosexual conduct . . . [T]his disparity in treatment calls for serious equal protection analysis."[20] Bork dismissed Judge Robinson's objections as "moral relativism," and countered that Robinson's willingness to accept gays was not the moral position of most naval personnel.

In spite of the setback in *Dronenberg,* legal challenges to the DOD policy continued, as gays continued to hope for a Supreme Court ruling on the issue; they also intensified their lobbying efforts in Washington. Their optimism on the political and legal fronts was stimulated, perhaps, by some decisions in federal appeals courts which seemed to seriously undermine the government's position. After nine years of litigation, for example, in 1988, in San Francisco, an Appeals Court ruling reinstated Perry Watkins, an openly gay sergeant who had been dismissed from the army after 14 years of service. In his opinion for the majority, Judge William Norris noted the clear analogy between gays and other minority groups, particularly African Americans, when he wrote, "Discrimination faced by homosexuals in our society is plainly no less pernicious or intense than the discrimination faced by other groups. . . . Laws that limit the acceptable focus of one's sexual desires to members of the opposite sex, like laws that limit one's choice of a sexual partner to members of the same race, cannot withstand constitutional scrutiny absent a compelling governmental justification." In addition, Norris dismissed the army's claims that barring gays was necessary to maintain army morale. He noted that "For much of our history, the military's fear of racial tension kept black soldiers separated from whites. Today it is unthinkable that the judiciary would defer to the Army's prior 'professional' judgment that black and white soldiers had to be segregated to avoid interracial tensions. To use this rationale to support an anti-gay policy," Norris said, was to "illegitimately cater to private biases."[21]

Judge Stephen Reinhardt felt constrained to dissent in the Watkins case because of the Supreme Court decision in *Bowers*, but he stated his basic agreement with the majority that the army's antigay regulations were unconstitutional. He characterized the *Bowers* decision as "egregious" and compared it to the majority decision in *Plessy v. Ferguson*, giving as his opinion that *Bowers* would most likely be overturned by "a wiser and more enlightened court."[22] Because the Watkins case was ultimately decided on narrow, technical grounds of fairness (Watkins had been previously reenlisted by the army even though he had openly declared himself a homosexual), the U.S. Supreme Court refused to hear the army's appeal; this in effect let the federal appeals court decision to reinstate Watkins stand. But because the case was not decided on constitutional issues, it did not establish broad constitutional precedent.

Judge Reinhardt's dissent in the Watkins case, reluctant as it was, indicated that the gay challenge to the unequal enforcement of the prohibitions on sodomy against homosexuals under DOD regulations, and the gays' assertions to a right to privacy, had little chance of success as long as the ruling in *Bowers* stood. But Judge Norris's opinion for the majority in the Watkins case, which explicitly emphasized the analogy between gays and African Americans, did pave the way for a new legal strategy several years later.

In December 1988, Joseph C. Steffan challenged his dismissal from the U.S. Naval Academy on the grounds of his admitted homosexuality.[23] Steffan claimed that his dismissal, which was based not on prohibited *conduct* (as in *Dronenberg*), but on *statements* about his sexual orientation, violated his rights of equal protection under the Fourteenth and Fifth Amendments. Echoing Judge Norris in the Watkins case, Steffan claimed that government classifications according to sexual orientation, like those based on race and national origin, should be subject to "strict" judicial scrutiny, requiring the government to demonstrate a compelling, rather than merely legitimate or rational, government interest. In spite of a strong showing that gays fit all of the criteria of other minority groups, for whose classifications the government had to demonstrate a compelling interest, Steffan's challenge was rejected.

Although Steffan's case did not succeed, it raised an issue that became central in later cases which were successful. These new cases challenged the aspect of DOD policy that related to homosexual "orientation," that is, the military's assumption of the inherent connection between status and behavior. In 1993, in *Meinhold v. U.S. Dept. of Defense* [808 F. Supp. 1455 (C.D.Cal. 1993)], a U.S. District Court in California ordered the navy to reinstate Keith Meinhold, a naval officer dismissed for announcing on an ABC news show that he was gay. In his opinion, Judge Hatter held that the Department of Defense must establish, through a factual record, that its policy is "rationally related to permissible goals" and that the court "cannot merely defer to the 'military judgment' " as an acceptable rationale. Citing the many research studies contradicting the DOD policy, Judge Hatter rejected the government's position that the rationale for the gay ban is "not capable of being determined authoritatively by scientific means or proven studies," a conclusion reached by the government based on the claim [that] "military judgment [is] inherently subjective in nature [and not susceptible to] scientific or sociological analysis."[24] Judge Hatter further cited the experience of foreign nations, specifically those in NATO, none of which, with the exception of the United States and Great Britain, had a ban on gays in their military. In support of his decision, Judge Hatter expressed his hope that "[Our] military leaders will come to realize that [w]e are not an assimilative, homogeneous society, but a facilitative, pluralistic one, in which we must be willing to abide someone else's unfamiliar or even repellant practice because the same tolerant impulse protects our own idiosyncracies."

Yet more recently, in June 1994, Margarethe Cammermeyer, a former colonel in the National Guard who was discharged from the army for acknowledging she was a lesbian, successfully challenged the government in court, claiming that the DOD regulations violated her equal protection rights and her substantive due process rights under the Fifth Amendment.[25] Judge Thomas Zilly's opinion in this case emphasized the distinction between homosexual orientation or status, and homosexual conduct, claiming the former could not be assumed to indicate anything about the latter and was therefore an impermissible basis for discrimination. Noting previous legal opinion (as in *Steffan*) that homosexuals did not constitute a suspect or quasi-suspect class, Judge Zilly indicated that the court's decision on whether DOD policy violated Cammermeyer's equal protection rights would be based on whether the government military policy was *rational* and served a *legitimate* government interest, a standard of review accepted by Cammermeyer. Judge Zilly cited the evidence contrary to government policy in the Crittenden, PERESEC, and RAND reports and found that DOD regulations were based "solely on prejudice against homosexuals." He called attention to public opinion polls which indicated that the level of public disapproval of gays serving in the military is much lower than that claimed by the army. In any case, Judge Zilly held, "to the extent that public disapproval of homosexual service in the military is based on prejudice, such disapproval would not be a legitimate basis for the government policy." In ordering the reinstatement of Colonel Cammermeyer, Judge Zilly wrote that her dismissal was based on a government policy founded "solely on prejudice" and that "[P]rejudice, whether founded on unsubstantiated fears, cultural myths, stereotypes or erroneous assumptions, cannot be the basis for a discriminatory classification."[26] The Ninth Circuit Court affirmed this decision, and the army chose not to appeal.

When Bill Clinton ran for president in 1992, a much discussed issue of his campaign was his expressed determination to change the ban on gays serving in the military. In connection with this pledge, after he entered the White House, congressional hearings and research reports on the antigay military policy were initiated to help shape a new policy. A major study by the RAND Corporation, a conservative research group with long-standing ties to the military, concluded that there was no scientific or sociological basis for the government policy and suggested that the main obstacle to removing the ban on gays came not from the universal opposition of those in the military, but rather from the resistance of the Joint Chiefs of Staff. The Rand report included a detailed proposal for allowing gay men and lesbians to serve openly in the armed forces, but the insistence of the Joint Chiefs that open homosexuality "simply could not fit into the military culture" led to the compromise policy, "Don't ask, don't tell." This policy, which dropped the induction questions on sexual orientation, and which sanctioned gays and lesbians serving in the military as long as they did not reveal their sexual orientation, was only reluctantly accepted by the military and angrily rejected by many gay activist groups, who began mounting legal challenges. On March 31, 1995, Eugene H. Nickerson, judge of the federal court in Brooklyn, declared the military's policy unconstitutional, in violating the First and Fifth Amendments and in catering to the fears and prejudices of heterosexual troops.[27] Although this court decision only affects the six plaintiffs, because it is the first ruling on the policy it will carry significant weight, although it is expected that the case will eventually reach the Supreme Court as the government is going to appeal.

Barring gays and lesbians from the military denies them the important economic opportunity of a military career and also the opportunity to make a civic contribution to their country. It both results from and maintains a stigma, which has deep roots in the American cultural definition of masculinity and the cultural connections of manhood to warfare.[28] Challenges to this long-held cultural construction seriously began with the integration of African Americans into combat roles in the military, and later with the integration of women into many military roles they were formerly denied. Given the overwhelming evidence of effective, even exemplary performance by many homosexuals in the military, it may well be that the strong resistance to reforming military policy is our culture's last defense against a myth of manhood which is being seriously questioned in many sectors of our society.

NOTES

1. Vern L. Bullough, *Sexual Variance in Society and History* (Chicago: University of Chicago Press, 1976); but see also John Boswell, *Christianity, Social Toler-*

ance, and Homosexuality: Gay People in Western Europe from the Beginning of the Christian Era to the Fourteenth Century (Chicago: University of Chicago Press, 1980).

2. Bullough, *Sexual Variance in Society and History*, 609–10.

3. Denyse Lockard, "The Lesbian Community: An Anthropological Approach," *Journal of Homosexuality* 11 (Summer 1985): 85–86.

4. Randy Shilts, *Conduct Unbecoming: Gays in the Military* (New York: St. Martin's Press, 1993), 523.

5. Linda Greenhouse, "When Second Thoughts in Case Come Too Late," *New York Times*, November 5, 1990, A14.

6. Leonard Matlovich ordered these words carved on his gravestone. In Shilts, *Conduct Unbecoming*, 582. Also see Martin Duberman, "The Case of the Gay Sergeant," *New York Times Magazine*, November 9, 1975, 16.

7. Shilts, *Conduct Unbecoming*, 14.

8. Ibid., 70.

9. See Crittenden Report, "Report to the Board Appointed to Prepare and Submit Recommendations to the Secretary of the Navy for the Revision of Policies, Procedures and Directives Dealing with Homosexuals" (December 21, 1956–March 15, 1957); PERSEREC Report, Theodore R. Sarbin and Kenneth E. Karols, *Nonconforming Sexual Orientations and Military Suitability* (Monterrey, CA: Defense Personnel Security Research and Education Center, December 1988); David F. Burelli, "Homosexuals and U.S. Military Personnel Policy," Washington, D.C.: Congressional Research Service (CRS), Library of Congress Report for Congress, 1993; RAND Report, *Sexual Orientation and U.S. Military Personnel Policy: Options and Assessment* (Santa Monica, CA: National Defense Research Institute, 1993).

10. Burelli, "Homosexuals and U.S. Military Personnel Policy," 26, 59.

11. Shilts, *Conduct Unbecoming*, 281.

12. Ibid., 281–83.

13. Ibid., 213.

14. This is repeatedly documented in Shilts, *Conduct Unbecoming*.

15. *Beller v. Middendorf*, 632 F.2d 788, 811 (9th Cir. 1980), cited in Shilts, *Conduct Unbecoming*, 366.

16. Shilts, *Conduct Unbecoming*, 367.

17. Ibid., 455.

18. *Dronenberg v. Zech*, 741 F.2d 1388 (D.C. Cir. 1984).

19. Shilts, *Conduct Unbecoming*, 451.

20. Ibid., 452.

21. Ibid., 641.

22. Ibid.

23. *Joseph C. Steffan v. Richard Cheney, Secretary of Defense*, 780 F. Supp. 1 (D.D.C. 1991); see also Marc Wolinsky and Kenneth Sherrill, eds., *Gays and the Military: Joseph Steffan versus the United States* (Princeton, NJ: Princeton University Press, 1994).

24. *Meinhold v. U.S. Dept. of Defense* (808 F. Supp. 1455 [C.D.Cal. 1993]), 1458.

25. *Cammermeyer v. Les Aspin* (850 F. Supp. 910, 1994).

26. *Cammermeyer v. Les Aspin*, U.S. Dis. Ct., Western District of Washington at Seattle, Order (No. C92-942Z) 50, Decided June 1, 1994.

27. Eric Schmitt, "Pentagon Keeps Silent on Rejected Gay Troop Plan," *New*

York Times, July 22, 1993, A12; Eric Schmitt, "The New Rules on Gay Soldiers: A Year Later, No Clear Results," *New York Times*, March 13, 1995, A1; Eric Schmitt, "Judge Overturns Pentagon Policy on Homosexuals," *New York Times*, March 31, 1995, A1.

28. Michael Lerner, "Curing Homophobia and Other Conservative Patholo-gies," *Tikkun* 8(5)(September/October 1993): 5.

10

Women's Nature, Women's Lives, Women's Rights

American law has been based on gender stereotypes defining the woman's world as that of home and hearth. Constrained by the view of women as made by nature for childbirth and child care, women's lives were shaped into a subculture whose sole criterion was gender, though this was modified by race and class. The myth of women as fragile, dependent, childlike creatures formed the basis of laws which created and maintained a reality in which women, often under the guise of protective law, were denied access to political power and economic resources. Carried forward by a growing middle-class culture, this myth created an even heavier burden for minority and working-class women, who, unlike middle-class women, did not even have access to power through their husbands.

LIMITS ON CIVIC PARTICIPATION

The image of woman as child eased the way for a broad denial of her political rights. Thus, although the franchise has been regarded as fundamental to a democratic republic, armed with these images, lawmakers denied women a constitutionally guaranteed right to vote until the passage of the Nineteenth Amendment in 1920.

By 1872 the women's movement supported litigation brought by Virginia Minor, claiming that the state of Missouri violated the "privileges and immunities of citizenship" granted by the recently adopted Fourteenth Amendment by prohibiting women from voting. In this case, *Minor v. Happersett* [21 Wall. 162 (1875)], the U.S. Supreme Court held that the right to vote was not necessarily one of the privileges or immunities of citizenship, and specifically that suffrage was not coextensive with citizenship. The heart of the Court's reasoning in this extraordinary decision lay in two conclusions: first, that since virtually all women in all jurisdictions had historically been denied the right to vote, it was not inappropriate, nor indeed unconstitutional, for state governments to continue that which they had always done, even in light of this new civil rights amendment. The Court also concluded that sex was merely another perfectly reasonable criterion, along with age, property-holding status, being of "quiet and reasonable behavior," and length of residence, by which states might grant or withhold the right to vote.

Perhaps smarting under the plaintiff's accusation that the denial of the vote to women was an egregious violation of the spirit of the Republic, Chief Justice Morrison Waite wrote that given the long-standing history of women's political exclusion, "it is certainly now too late to contend that a government is not republican within the meaning of this guaranty in the Constitution, because women are not made voters. No argument as to women's need of suffrage can be considered. We can only act upon her rights as they exist. It is not for us to look at the hardship of withholding. Our duty is at an end if we find it is within the power of a State to withhold."

Consistent with the view that women's domain was home and children, virtually all local governments similarly exempted women from jury duty, unless they specifically volunteered. This was a double burden; it not only excluded women from full participation in the civic culture, but it also denied women plaintiffs and defendants a jury of their peers. The U.S. Supreme Court upheld this practice until 1975 when it struck down, citing the Sixth Amendment, a jury registration statute that permitted but did not obligate women to serve on juries. In this case, *Taylor v. Louisiana*, the justices explained that "Restricting jury service to only special groups or excluding identifiable segments playing major roles in the community cannot be squared with the constitutional concept of jury trial."[1]

While the issues of women's right to vote, as well as sex discrimination in jury duty and jury selection, have been resolved, women's full participation in the service of their country is still circumscribed by national law. National policy obligates men but not women to register for a military draft and has long prohibited women from serving in combat positions. The 1980 Supreme Court decision in *Rostker v. Goldberg* [453 U.S. 57 (1981)] upheld the constitutional right of Congress to exclude women from even having to *register* for any future military draft. Writing for the majority, Justice William Rehnquist stressed judicial deference to congressional authority over matters of national defense and military affairs. His opinion accepted the congressional view, rejected by a lower federal court, that since the "purpose of military registration was to prepare for a draft of *combat troops,"* registering women was not worth the effort.

Rejection of women for combat service reinforces the stereotype of women as physically weak and in need of male protection. However, the successful performance of 35,000 women in the Persian Gulf war in 1991, a number of them in "indirect" combat work, encouraged Defense Department officials as well as members of Congress to review long-standing restrictions on women in combat positions. While change is occurring, all of the army's proposals for change, for example, continue to bar women from "direct" combat including infantry, armor, and many field artillery positions that are essential for promotion to senior ranks. In upholding restrictions on women's full participation in the military, American lawmakers fail to consider whether such limitations on full political participation hinder the ability of women to change their status in society.

LEGAL LIMITS ON EMPLOYMENT

Many people argue that the burdens of second-class citizenship are balanced by the high regard in which wives and mothers are held in American cultural ideology. This high—even noble—regard does not, unfortunately, translate into fair and equal economic currency. This is true for women in the domestic sphere, and even more so when they seek participation in the public sphere.

Economically, the formal laws and informal practices discriminating against women have been countless. A view of women as only wives and mothers, and less capable by their nature of intellectual reasoning, meant that they did not require higher education. Women were consistently kept out of educational institutions necessary for economic success. Only recently have such educational opportunities for women in colleges and professional schools opened up to them in relation to their numbers in the population. It is true that, beginning in the last quarter of the nineteenth century, an increasing number of women from affluent families found educational opportunities at both coeducational universities and newly opened women's colleges. The degrees these women received created professional opportunities for this select group; some went into traditional male careers such as medicine and law, while others created new forms of community involvement and were central to the development of the Progressive social reform movement at the beginning of the twentieth century.

Recent studies demonstrate that school is still a place of unequal opportunity for girls and women. In a 1992 report, *How Schools Shortchange Women,* researchers assert that teachers call on girls less frequently in class and offer them less constructive criticism, that girls must cope with ongoing sexual harassment from boys, that textbooks are less oriented to girls or stereotype them, and that tests remain biased against girls, damaging their chances of obtaining scholarships and getting into college.[2] Moreover, although Title IX of the 1972 Higher Education Amendments barred sex discrimination in schools and colleges that receive federal aid, the Supreme Court's 1984 decision in *Grove City College v. Bell* (465 U.S. 555) limited the scope of that legislation. In response, in 1988 Congress passed the Civil Rights Restoration Act, legislation intended to clarify the application of Title IX and thus lessen the future impact of the *Grove City* decision.

Even when women overcame the formidable obstacles to higher education, informal hiring practices and formal law often prevented them from practicing their professions and establishing professional status equal to that of men. Women educated as lawyers in the nineteenth century, for example, were told by the Supreme Court that it was not a violation of their Fourteenth Amendment rights to be barred from practice by state law.

In 1872, Mrs. Myra Bradwell, a resident of Illinois, was refused a license to practice law on the grounds that "as a married woman [she] would be bound neither by her express contracts nor by those implied contracts which it is the policy of law to create between attorney and client." The U.S. Supreme Court held in *Bradwell v. Illinois* [83 U.S. 130 (1873)] that although not expressly excluded, it was never the intention of the Illinois legislature to allow women to practice law. Writing for the majority in *Bradwell*, Justice Samuel Miller held:

God designed the sexes to occupy different spheres of action, and that it belonged to men to make, apply, and execute the laws, was regarded as an almost axiomatic truth.

In view of these facts, we are certainly warranted in saying that when the legislature gave to this court the power of granting licenses to practice law, it was with not the slightest expectation that this privilege would be extended to women.

While Justice Miller emphasized the right of state governments to control and regulate professional licenses, Justice Joseph Bradley, in a concurring opinion, emphasized the relationship between "women's place" and the economic limitations imposed upon them:

the civil law, as well as nature herself, has always recognized a wide difference in the respective spheres and destinies of man and woman. Man is, or should be, woman's protector and defender. The natural and proper timidity and delicacy which belongs to the female sex evidently unfits it for many of the occupations of civil life. The constitution of the family organization, which is founded in the divine ordinance, as well as in the nature of things, indicates the domestic sphere as that which properly belongs to the domain and functions of woman-hood. The harmony, not to say identity, of interests and views which belong, or should belong, to the family institution is repugnant to the idea of a woman adopting a distinct and independent career from that of her husband. So firmly fixed was this sentiment in the founders of the common law that it became a maxim of that system of jurisprudence that a woman had no legal existence separate from her husband, who was regarded as her head and representative in the social state; and, notwithstanding some recent modifications of this civil status, many of the special rules of law flowing from and dependent upon this cardinal principle still exist in full force in most States. One of these is, that a married woman is incapable, without her husband's consent, of making contracts which shall be binding on her or him. This very incapacity was one circumstance which the Supreme Court of Illinois deemed important in rendering a married woman incompetent fully to perform the duties and trusts that belong to the office of an attorney and counselor.

It is true that many women are unmarried and not affected by any of the duties, complications, and incapacities arising out of the married state, but these are exceptions to the general rule. The paramount destiny and mission of woman are to fulfill the noble and benign offices of wife and mother. This is the law of the Creator.

It is the prerogative of the legislator to prescribe regulations founded on nature, reason, and experience for the due admission of qualified persons to professions and callings demanding special skill and confidence. This fairly belongs to the police power of the State.

In nonprofessional occupations, it was accepted that women would be workers, as indeed they were, in many unskilled and semiskilled positions. At the turn of the century, a growing reform movement resulted in legislation which improved conditions for all workers. However, to the extent that some of these protective labor laws were directed specifically at women, exempting them, for example, from certain hazardous or strenuous work, these laws reinforced the stereotypes of women as weaker and less capable than men, and resulted in excluding them from a wide range of blue-collar work. The feminist movement of the time varied in its response to these laws. While the mid-nineteenth-century feminist movement had "staked its claim" to women's rights on the basis of women being more like men than unlike them, later in the nineteenth century the greater majority of feminists had reversed their position. These feminists now argued that women had special sensibilities—compassion, nurturance, a better developed sense of morality—and that these unique attributes should be preserved and protected, something not possible in the competitive world of economic struggle.[3]

In 1903 the Oregon state legislature passed an act limiting the number of hours women could be employed "in any mechanical establishment, or factory, or laundry" to ten hours during any one day. This protective legislation was resisted by employers. One disgruntled laundry owner,

Curt Muller, after having been convicted of violating the law, brought suit, charging that the law, by restricting the right to contract, violated the Fourteenth Amendment Due Process and Equal Protection rights of employers and employees.

Mr. Muller undoubtedly expected a sympathetic hearing from the U.S. Supreme Court that had, only three years before in *Lochner v. New York* (198 U.S. 45, 1905), invalidated a New York law regulating the number of hours that any worker, male or female, could be required to work in bakeries. The Court's reasoning was that the law was not a legitimate exercise of state police power, but "an unreasonable, unnecessary and arbitrary interference with the right and liberty of the individual to contract in relation to his labor," and thus unconstitutional. In *Muller,* however, the Court found that the difference between the sexes was sufficient legal reason to uphold the state's use of its regulatory powers. The language of the Court in this decision paved the way for a variety of sex-based discriminatory laws that were subsequently upheld.[4] Justice David Brewer wrote for the court:

Muller v. Oregon
208 U.S. 412 (1908)

[*Lochner*] is invoked by plaintiff in error as decisive of the question before us but this assumes that the difference between the sexes does not justify a different rule respecting a restriction of the hours of labor.

That woman's physical structure and the performance of maternal functions place her at a disadvantage in the struggle for subsistence is obvious. This is especially true when the burdens of motherhood are upon her. Even when they are not, by abundant testimony of the medical fraternity continuance for a long time on her feet at work, repeating this from day to day, tends to injurious effects upon the body, and, as healthy mothers are essential to vigorous offspring, the physical well-being of woman becomes an object of public interest and care in order to preserve the strength and vigor of the race.

Still again, history discloses the fact that woman has always been dependent upon man. He established his control at the outset by superior physical strength, and this control in various forms, with diminishing intensity, has continued to the present. As minors, though not to the same extent, she has been looked upon in the courts as needing especial care that her rights may be preserved. Education was long denied her, and while now the doors of the schoolroom are opened and her opportunities for acquiring knowledge are great, yet even with that and the consequent increase of capacity for business affairs it is still true that in the struggle for subsistence she is not an equal competitor with her brother. Though limitations upon personal and contractual rights may be removed by legislation, there is that in her disposition and habits of life which will operate against a full assertion of those rights. . . . Differentiated by these matters from the other sex, she is properly placed in a class by herself, and legislation designed for her protection may be sustained, even when like legislation is not necessary for men, and could not be sustained. It is impossible to close one's eyes to the fact that she still looks to her brother and depends upon him . . . to protect her from the greed as well as the passion of man.

While today the language in *Muller* stands as a remnant of the Victorian age, the idea of women expressed in this decision persisted well into midcentury. In 1948, in the case of *Goesaert v. Cleary*, the U.S. Supreme Court upheld a Michigan law forbidding any female to act as a bartender unless she was the wife or daughter of a male owner. Justice Felix Frankfurter, in his opinion for the majority, dismissed in a humorous aside what many, including Justices Rutledge, Douglas, and Murphy, in their dissent, held as central—the notion that the Michigan law was nothing more than a veiled attempt to limit a profitable occupation to men. Justice Frankfurter wrote:

Goesaert v. Cleary
335 U.S. 464 (1948)

We are, to be sure, dealing with a historic calling. We meet the alewife, sprightly and ribald, in Shakespeare, but centuries before him she played a role in the social life of England. The Fourteenth Amendment did not tear history up by the roots, and the regulation of the liquor traffic is one of the oldest and most untrammeled of legislative powers. Michigan could, beyond question, forbid all women from working behind a bar. This is so despite the vast changes in the social and legal position of women. The fact that women may now have achieved the virtues that men have long claimed as their prerogatives and now indulge in vices that men have long practiced, does not preclude the States from drawing a sharp line between the sexes, certainly in such matters as the regulation of the liquor traffic.

Since bartending by women may, in the allowable legislative judgment, give rise to moral and social problems against which it may devise preventive measures, the legislature need not go to the full length of prohibition. Michigan evidently believes that the oversight assured through ownership of a bar by a barmaid's husband or father minimizes hazards that may confront a barmaid without such protecting oversight. This Court is certainly not in a position to gainsay such belief by the Michigan legislature. If it is entertainable, as we think it is, Michigan has not violated its duty to afford equal protection of its laws. We cannot cross-examine either actually or argumentatively the mind of Michigan legislators nor question their motives. Since the line they have drawn is not without a basis in reason, we cannot give ear to the suggestion that the real impulse behind this legislation was an unchivalrous desire of male bartenders to try to monopolize the calling.

The lack of a highly organized women's movement during the 1950s and early 1960s resulted in few significant changes in the legal view of women's employment rights. For example, courts upheld local laws and regulations which mandated that women, even in the earliest stages of pregnancy, leave positions as schoolteachers and, until litigated in the late 1960s and early 1970s, women airline stewardesses were not allowed to continue their jobs past the age of 35 or if they got married. In many occupations women, of course, were never or barely considered at all, relegated, for example, to the lower-status and lower-paying jobs of nurse rather than physician, matron rather than police officer, secretary rather than corporate executive, and waitress rather than bartender.

National legislative efforts to provide redress and prevent further discrimination against women in employment—reinforced by state and local initiatives—finally met success when Congress passed the Equal Pay Act of 1963 forbidding sex discrimination in wages, and Title VII of the 1964 Civil Rights Act barring an employer from discriminating against any employee because of sex in hiring, firing, promoting, compensating, or in any other aspects of employment. Title VII did not specifically address questions of employment discrimination arising from pregnancy. Thus, in 1978, to overturn the effects of the Supreme Court's ruling in *General Electric Co. v. Gilbert* [429 U.S. 125 (1976)] stating that discrimination on the basis of pregnancy was not sex discrimination under Title VII, Congress passed the Pregnancy Discrimination Act (PDA). This law amends Title VII by prohibiting employment discrimination against pregnant women.

An important test of the Pregnancy Discrimination Act, and California civil rights law, occurred several years later. This case, *California Federal Savings and Loan v. Guerra* [479 U.S. 272 (1987)], expressed women's concern that pregnancy, which fulfills critical personal and societal needs, not impede women's careers. The litigation also demonstrated a major division within the women's movement. On one side were women's organizations which argued that women have special biological needs that should receive special treatment in law. Other feminist groups, however, contended that preferential treatment, harkening back to the era of *Muller*, leads to job segregation, lower wages, and the stereotyping of women as childbearers. These feminists insisted that all laws must be sex-neutral and that such neutrality was the intent of Congress in passing Title VII. Groups such as the National Organization for Women, the American Civil Liberties Union, and the National Women's Political Caucus argued in favor of disability leave for male and female workers.

In *Guerra* the U.S. Supreme Court ruled that requiring an employer to provide unpaid pregnancy leave and to guarantee a comparable job upon return to the workplace did not violate Title VII's antidiscrimination mandate because of the amendment to Title VII provided by Congress in the Pregnancy Discrimination Act.

The critical role of Congress in helping women, and men, balance family responsibilities with the demands of employment was again demonstrated when, in 1993, national lawmakers passed the much debated Family and Medical Leave Act. This legislation mandates that companies with more than 50 employees provide up to 12 weeks' unpaid leave for workers to care for a newborn or adopted child or a critically ill family member.

Even with the passage of these many acts, it has become clear that the mere passage of legislation demanding equal treatment in employment for women, as in the case of racial minorities, was not sufficient to overcome widely held and deeply ingrained attitudes that kept women out of many occupations or prevented women from receiving equal or comparable pay.[5] Armed with legislation, executive orders, and the Constitution itself, women followed the lead of the African-American civil rights movement in pressing for affirmative plans in both public and private employment which would incorporate them into the labor force at all levels consistent with their numbers in the population and their skills and training.

By the 1980s men began responding to affirmative action for women, as they had to affirmative action claims on behalf of African Americans, by taking their grievances to court. Holding that such affirmative action plans violated both the equal protection provisions of the Constitution and the intent of Title VII to bar all discrimination, Paul E. Johnson, a transportation worker passed over in favor of a woman for promotion to the position of road dispatcher with the Santa Clara, California Transportation Agency as a result of a voluntary affirmative action plan, sued the agency. The U.S. Supreme Court decided against Mr. Johnson. In the 1987 decision in *Johnson v. Santa Clara County Transportation Agency* (480 U.S. 616), the Court upheld voluntary affirmative action plans instituted by employers, including employers who had not previously been cited in court for discriminating against women, as long as these plans were flexible, gradual, and limited in their adverse effects on other groups. In its ruling, the Court made clear that qualified individuals *could* benefit from such affirmative action plans even where they could not prove that they were personally victims of past discrimination.

A scathing dissent written by Justice Antonin Scalia, joined by Chief Justice William Rehnquist, and partly by Justice Byron White, attacked the opinion as "converting [Title VII] from a guarantee that race or sex will not be the basis for employment determination, to a guarantee that it often will . . . we [now] effectively replace the goal of a discrimination-free society with the quite incompatible goal of proportionate representation by . . . sex in the workplace." Justice Scalia held that the traditional absence of women in road maintenance jobs was due primarily to "[the absence] of women eager to shoulder pick and shovel," and stated that he found it unacceptable to use Title VII to overcome the effect of "societal attitudes that have limited the entry of . . . a particular sex, into certain jobs." Ignoring the historical facts of past discrimination in employment against women, Justice Scalia added that "the only losers [by this decision] . . . are the Johnsons of the country."

MARRIAGE, MONEY, AND THE LAW

Discrimination in employment has not meant, of course, that women have not worked. Not only were women limited in their choice of occupations, however, but in compensation, responsibilities, and benefits they were clearly viewed and treated as secondary wage earners. In spite of the fact that many working-class and minority women were indeed the primary family wage earners, both law and social custom supported the male view that women could not and should not be relied upon for family economic security. This reaffirmed the role of the male as major breadwinner, serving as a rationale for further discrimination against women who would compete for jobs and promotions needed by male family heads.[6]

As a result of the efforts of the modern women's movement since the early 1970s, there have been major changes in virtually all aspects of the laws and practices used to discriminate against women in the economic sphere. Fighting the assumption that the family is dependent only upon male earnings and benefits, women attacked administrative practices and social security laws that denied them equal benefits. In *Frontiero v. Richardson*, the U.S. Supreme Court ruled that the army's regulations permitting males in the armed services an automatic dependency allowance for their wives but requiring servicewomen to prove that their husbands were dependent, violated women's equal protection rights.[7] In his decision for the Court, Justice William Brennan, Jr., stated:

Frontiero v. Richardson
411 U.S. 677 (1973)

[O]ur nation has had a long and unfortunate history of sex discrimination. . . . Traditionally, such discrimination was rationalized by an attitude of "romantic paternalism" which, in practical effect, put women not on a pedestal, but in a cage.

As a result of notions such as these, [statutes] became laden with gross, stereotypical distinctions between the sexes and, indeed, throughout much of the nineteenth century the position of women in our society was, in many respects, comparable to that of blacks under the pre-Civil War slave codes. Neither slaves nor women could hold office, serve on juries, or bring suit in their own names, and married women traditionally were denied the legal capacity to hold or convey property or to serve as legal guardians of their own children. And although blacks were guaranteed the right to vote in 1870, women were denied even [that] until adoption of the Nineteenth Amendment half a century later.

Moreover, since sex, like race and national origin, is an immutable character-istic [the] imposition of special disabilities [would] seem to violate "the basic concept of our system that legal burdens should bear some relationship to in-dividual responsibility" (*Weber*). And what differentiates sex from such nonsus-pect statuses as intelligence or physical disability [is] that the sex characteristic frequently bears no relation to ability to perform or contribute to society. As a result, statutory distinctions between the sexes often have the effect of invidi-ously relegating the entire class of females to inferior legal status without regard to the actual capabilities of its individual members.

[The] Government [maintains] that, as an empirical matter, wives in our society frequently are dependent upon their husbands, while husbands rarely are de-pendent upon their wives. Thus, the Government argues that Congress might reasonably have concluded that it would be both cheaper and easier simply con-clusively to presume that wives of male members are financially dependent upon their husbands, while burdening female members with the task of establishing dependency in fact.

The Government offers no concrete evidence, however, tending to support its view that such differential treatment in fact saves the Government any money. [And any] statutory scheme which draws a sharp line between the sexes, *solely* [for] administrative convenience [violates equal protection].

In the subsequent cases of *Weinberger v. Wiesenfeld* [420 U.S. 636 (1975)] and *Califano v. Goldfarb* [430 U.S. 199 (1977)], the Supreme Court contin-ued to strike down social security laws which the Court argued were based on a traditional way of thinking about females as dependents. Private sector pension plans and payment schemes that discriminate against women have also been successfully challenged in the courts.

Law has not only differentiated married men from married women with respect to employment benefits, such as pensions, but, for most of American history, undermined women's economic independence by lim-iting a married woman's property rights. The historical position of mar-ried women as dependents in American law grows out of English common law, itself based on biblical notions about the "unity of the flesh of man and wife." Under this notion, a woman's husband assumed con-trol over her property, her wages, if she earned any, and indeed, over much of her legal responsibilities and identity. Despite the passage in the nineteenth century of "Married Women's Property Acts" in a number of states which ensured a woman control over her own property, nu-merous restrictions continued into the 1970s. Maryland placed limits on a married woman's right to sue and be sued in her own name; several states did not permit a woman to serve in positions of trust, including the right to administer a descendant's estate; other states would not let a woman mortgage her property unless her husband demonstrated knowledge and involvement in the transactions; and numerous states restricted women's rights to engage independently in their own busi-nesses, or to make contracts.[8]

These laws reflected a view that men better understood the world of law and business and that it was woman's nature only to look after home and children. Ironically, however, until children became an economic liability, as was increasingly the case with the growth of urbanization and industrialization and the imposition of child labor laws, men—not women—were awarded custody of children in divorce cases. These laws which gave men control, of course, also gave responsibility for all dependents, including the wife, to the man of the house. Thus, in the United States, law developed which on the one hand made women dependents, and on the other hand obligated men to support them. Many people would claim that the law has been more successful in its first aspect than in its second. Responding to cultural norms and female socialization, many women—particularly middle-class women—have accepted the role of homemaker with its dependent status. As dependent homemakers they lack the most fundamental protections available to most salaried workers; homemakers are not eligible for disability payments; if divorced or widowed they do not get unemployment compensation; they are not eligible to receive social security payments on their husband's account until the age of 60; and if, at the time of a divorce, a woman has been married less than 10 years she has no claim to any part of her husband's social security. Neither she nor her husband may make payments to create a social security account in her name.[9] Without a "salary" the homemaker is also limited to a level of support "that provides the minimum for survival." No matter how much money her husband makes, the courts have denied her the right to legally claim anything more than this minimum from her husband.

The presumption of the economic dependency for women implicit in the marriage bond has been recognized by courts to extend into the relationship of divorce through the laws of alimony and child support. In the United States, partly because of the publicity surrounding large alimony awards, there has been a popular myth that all divorced women receive alimony. In fact, government statistics indicate that only a small number—sometimes as little as 15 percent—of divorced wives are awarded alimony. The general amount of such awards also contradicts the popular myth of alimony creating "an army of alimony drones who neither toil nor spin and become a drain on society and a menace to themselves."[10] The amounts of such awards are generally exceedingly modest, barely equalling welfare or social security payments. Coupled with equally modest child support awards, the obligations historically intended to "nourish and sustain" the family are hardly adequate and have instead contributed to the continuing impoverishment of women and female-headed households. Compounding the meagerness of alimony awards and property division granted by courts is the high degree of noncompliance in paying these awards. Not one study in the United

States has found even half of the assessed men complying with court orders for child support.[11] Thus, a multidecade study in California revealed that "just a year after legal divorce, men experience a 42 percent increase in their postdivorce standard of living, while women experience a 73 percent decline."[12]

Many changes in the laws regarding payments to divorced women, while attempting to establish equitable solutions to historic problems of gender discrimination, have in fact had the unanticipated result of further burdening women, particularly older housewives, young mothers, and women who have had weak employment experiences. In its attempt to be gender-neutral and with perhaps all good intentions to reform divorce, alimony, and property laws, "the abiding lesson ... is this: To grant equal rights in the absence of equal opportunity is to strengthen the strong and weaken the weak."[13]

THE STRUGGLE FOR REPRODUCTIVE AUTONOMY

The creation and maintenance of a subculture of female dependency and powerlessness have been both expressed and furthered by laws criminalizing birth control and abortion, which denied women control over their own bodies. Women have been socialized to believe that their proper world is that of home and children: These laws provided the policing function necessary to shore up this "proper world."

Understanding that the cultural definition of woman's nature as childbearer and nurturer restricted her opportunities in the larger society, in recent years many women were eager to unburden themselves of the laws criminalizing birth control and abortion—laws which not only resulted in unwanted pregnancies, but which also denied women the right to make these important personal decisions for themselves, without the aid of the state.

Early litigation in the line of cases brought to establish women's reproductive freedom included that of *Poe v. Ullman* [367 U.S. 497 (1961)], challenging the constitutionality of the Connecticut statute providing that "Any person who uses any drug, medicinal article or instrument for the purpose of preventing conception shall be fined not less than fifty dollars or imprisoned not less than sixty days ... and that [a]ny person who assists, abets, counsels, causes, hires or commands another to commit any offense may be prosecuted and punished as if he were the principal offender." Although the majority opinion of the Court dismissed the appeal because of "the lack of immediacy" of any threat of prosecution, Justice Brennan, in his concurrence, pointed to the central but unspoken issue in the case: "The true controversy in this case is over the opening of birth-control clinics on a large scale; it is that which the State has prevented in the past, not the use of contraceptives by isolated and individual married couples." The Connecticut prohibition fell disproportionately on poor women, and it was generally acknowledged that middle-class women received birth control information and could purchase birth control supplies in Connecticut.

Leaving aside for the moment this issue of class equity, and returning to the main issue of reproductive freedom, the extensive dissents in *Poe*, introduced by Justices Douglas and Harlan, advanced much of the reasoning subsequently used in *Griswold v. Connecticut* [381 U.S. 479 (1965)], which, four years later, struck down the contested Connecticut statute. Specifically, in *Poe*, Douglas and Harlan spoke of a zone of privacy that protected the *marital* bedroom from state intrusion regarding the use of birth control:

> The regulation as applied in this case touches the relationship between man and wife. It reaches into the intimacies of the marriage relationship. If we imagine a regime of full enforcement of the law in the manner of an Anthony Comstock, we would reach the point where search warrants issued and officers appeared in bedrooms to find out what went on. It is said that this is not that case. And so it is not. But when the State makes "use" of a crime and applies the criminal sanction to man and wife, the State has entered the innermost sanctum of the home. If it can make this law, it can enforce it. And proof of its violation necessarily involves an inquiry into the relations between man and wife.
>
> That is an invasion of the privacy that is implicit in a free society.

Justice Harlan continued with the theme of the relationship of privacy to the home, arguing that a woman's right to privacy in the use of birth control derives not from her status as woman, but as householder. His opinion outlines a right of privacy that not only protects the physical integrity of the home, as generally understood in Fourth Amendment litigation, but which must include:

> the life which characteristically has its place in the home.
>
> Certainly the safeguarding of the home does not follow merely from the sanctity of property rights. The home derives its pre-eminence as the seat of family life. And the integrity of that life is something so fundamental that it has been found to draw to its protection the principles of more than one explicitly granted Constitutional right.
>
> Of this whole "private realm of family life" it is difficult to imagine what is more private or more intimate than a husband and wife's marital relations. We would indeed be straining at a gnat and swallowing a camel were we to show concern for the niceties of property law under the Fourth Amendment . . . and yet fail at least to see any substantial claim here.

Four years later, this theme, the right to privacy inhering in the marital relationship, became the basis for the opinion of the Court in *Griswold*.

It is striking that in terms of *women*'s rights, neither Douglas's opinion for the Court nor the three concurring opinions vest the right to be free of state regulation in matters expressed as a "right to privacy," in the status of being a woman. Rather, this right is vested in the marital *relationship*. Seven years later, in another birth control case (involving distribution of birth control to a single woman), *Eisenstadt v. Baird* [405 U.S. 438 (1972)], the Supreme Court moved a step closer to giving constitutional support to the comprehensive right to reproductive autonomy by holding that "if the right to privacy means anything, it is the right of the *individual*, married or single, to be free from unwarranted governmental intrusion into matters so fundamentally affecting a person as the decision whether to bear or beget a child."

The now famous 1973 U.S. Supreme Court decision decriminalizing abortion, *Roe v. Wade* (410 U.S. 113), extends the doctrine outlined in the birth control cases that "the right to privacy grounded in the concept of personal liberty encompasses the woman's right to decide whether to terminate her pregnancy." The Court noted that laws criminalizing abortion are "not of ancient, or even of common-law origin, but rather gain momentum only in the latter half of the nineteenth century." Acknowledging the special relationship women have to childbirth, the Court said:

This right of privacy . . . is broad enough to encompass a woman's decision whether or not to terminate her pregnancy. The detriment that the State would impose upon the pregnant woman by denying this choice altogether is apparent. Specific and direct harm medically diagnosable even in early pregnancy may be involved. Maternity, or additional offspring, may force upon the woman a distressful life and future. Psychological harm may be imminent. Mental and physical health may be taxed by child care. There is also the distress, for all concerned, associated with the unwanted child, and there is the problem of bringing a child into a family already unable, psychologically and otherwise, to care for it. In other cases, as in this one, the additional difficulties and continuing stigma of unwed motherhood may be involved.

Reluctant to give the woman full autonomy, however, the Court specified that these factors should be considered "in consultation with her physician." Furthermore, in striking down state antiabortion statutes as unconstitutional, the Court held that this fundamental right of personal liberty was not unqualified. The right of women, it said, must be considered against "compelling" state interests including the state's right to protect maternal and prenatal life. The Court ruled that in the second and third trimesters of pregnancy, states could regulate, or even prohibit abortion:

With respect to the State's important and legitimate interest in the health of the mother, the "compelling" point . . . is at approximately the end of the first trimester . . . from and after this point, a State may regulate the abortion procedure to the extent that the regulation reasonably relates to the preservation and protection of maternal health. Examples of permissible state regulation in this area are requirements as to the qualifications of the person who is to perform the abortion . . . as to the facility in which the procedure is to be performed.

With respect to the State's . . . interest in potential life, the "compelling" point is at viability. . . . If the State is interested in protecting fetal life after viability, it may go so far as to proscribe abortion during that period, except when it is necessary to preserve the life or health of the mother.

Immediately following the *Roe* decision, right-to-life groups, unhappy with the outcome of the litigation, initiated a highly organized lobby effort addressed to Congress, state legislatures, and local city councils. Although their long-range aims were to reverse the Supreme Court decision through constitutional amendment, for the immediate future they concentrated on weakening the decision by urging legislatures to withhold public funding of abortions, and in other ways to create obstacles for women who wished to have abortions. An early antiabortion movement success came with respect to the issue of funding: In 1980, in the case of *Harris v. McRae* (448 U.S. 297) the Court upheld the so-called Hyde Amendment by which Congress had limited federal funding of abortions under the Medicaid program to those necessary to save the life of the mother. Subsequently, in *Webster v. Reproductive Health Services* [492 U.S. 490 (1989)], the Supreme Court challenged *Roe*'s trimester formulation by upholding the legality of viability tests on a fetus thought to be at least of 20 weeks' gestation, and ruled that states may further limit government involvement in the provision of abortion services by prohibiting the use of public facilities or public employees.

In the 1980s and 1990s the movement to overturn *Roe* became highly political and sometimes physically violent. Both Ronald Reagan and George Bush campaigned for the presidency on antiabortion platforms; Bill Clinton was elected to the presidency on a pro-choice platform. Each president influenced the direction of Justice Department policy in abortion litigation, the nominations made for federal judgeships—in particular, the Supreme Court—and the nature of encouragement given to pro-choice and antiabortion groups. During the Reagan and Bush administrations, Justice Department lawyers asked the Supreme Court to overturn *Roe* in six separate cases.

Increasingly in these years, antichoice demonstrations at the site of reproductive health clinics resulted in confrontation and physical injuries to clients and clinic staff. In 1994, Congress enacted, and President Clinton signed into law, legislation intended to provide safe access to reproductive health clinics. The Freedom of Access to Clinic Entrances Act (FACE), passing over the objections of antiabortion groups concerned about infringement upon First Amendment rights, makes it a federal crime to block access to clinics that provide reproductive services.

The appointment, in the Reagan–Bush years, of several Supreme Court justices thought to disagree with the *Roe* decision led to speculation that the Supreme Court's narrowing of *Roe*'s protections would ultimately result in the decision being overturned. A critical test of *Roe*'s future occurred in the 1992 case, *Planned Parenthood v. Casey* (112 S. Ct. 2791). In *Casey*, a divided court reaffirmed the constitutional right to abortion, opening its opinion with the words, "Liberty finds no refuge in a jurisprudence of doubt. . . . The essential holding of *Roe v. Wade* should be retained and once again reaffirmed." But, using Justice Sandra Day O'Connor's new judicial test—whether a state abortion regulation has the purpose or effect of imposing an "undue burden," the court upheld the right of states to try to persuade a woman not to have an abortion, to impose a 24-hour waiting period prior to an abortion, and to require teenagers to have the consent of one parent or a judge before the procedure. The "undue burden" test does not require strict judicial scrutiny and, applying it, the court will likely permit more state regulation of abortion in the future. In *Casey*, however, the majority did strike down one regulation, a rule requiring that a wife notify her husband before an abortion. The justices reasoned that "A state may not give to a man the kind of dominion over his wife that parents exercise over their children." The court also chose to bar the regulation on the grounds that such notification might result in physical or psychological abuse against the wife.

The assertion of women's right to control their bodies in matters of birth control has, in large measure, succeeded despite a growing role for government regulation of abortion. Political and legal battles will no doubt continue with respect to questions of clinic access, teenagers' rights to abortion, and sexuality education. But the course of women's struggle to control their reproductive life has also moved in new legal directions.

In *International Union, U.A.W. v. Johnson Controls, Inc.* [499 U.S. 187 (1991)] women's groups and the U.A.W. challenged a company policy based upon female fertility and sex-role stereotyping that limited the access of women employees to jobs. Johnson Controls, a manufacturer of batteries, excluded female employees capable of bearing children from jobs involving exposure to lead because of concern for the health of the fetus the woman *might* conceive. Fertile women who wished these jobs had to agree to be sterilized. Company policy did not withhold such jobs from male workers who intended to become fathers. Relying upon the 1978 Pregnancy Discrimination Act, the Supreme Court ruled against Johnson Controls specifying that "women as capable of doing their job as their male counterparts may not be forced to choose between having a child and having a job." In a different context, the women's movement and civil liberties groups have opposed the criminal prosecution of pregnant women charged with fetal endangerment because of cocaine or alcohol use. They argue that addiction in pregnant women should be treated as a health problem, not a criminal one.

The new world of biomedical technology has also prompted legal debate about a range of reproductive issues barely considered—outside the pages of science fiction—until this past decade. The capacity to store eggs, sperm, and embryos raises questions about an individual's right to have—or not to have—a child in an entirely new context. The use of a deceased relative's stored sperm for artificial insemination has been contested in courts and divorced husbands have sued former wives to bar the implantation of frozen embryos. The federal government has refused to acknowledge the survivorship rights of a child conceived with frozen sperm after the death of the father. This "brave new world" compels the law to address issues of reproduction that remain central to the human condition but with which society has little experience.

FEMALE SEXUALITY AND COMMERCE

While the mainstream of American women has until recently been linked to home and family, an underworld subculture of women employed in sexual commerce exposes the social contradictions of our society. On the one hand, society demands chastity and innocence of women; at the same time, it creates a ready and profitable market for their sexual services. Thus, prostitution and pornography—and more recently, surrogate motherhood—have permitted women to find opportunities to earn through the commercialization of those aspects of their nature and biology with which the dominant culture has insisted upon identifying them. That laws and law enforcement governing prostitution and pornography are not always consistent reflects both the ambivalence of the dominant culture and the very real division of the dominant culture around these issues.

Prostitution most clearly demonstrates how women have been able to use their bodies (often the only resource available to them) to earn a living because of the demands of men who are their customers; these same men have nevertheless and simultaneously moralized and legislated against prostitution. The motivation for criminalizing prostitution is at least partly the view that unchecked prostitution would undermine "that foundation of American society—the family."[14] Thus, for example, in an early-twentieth-century Supreme Court decision, *United States v. Bitty* [208 U.S. 393, 401 (1908)], the Court wrote:

The lives and example of such persons [prostitutes] are in hostility to the idea of the family as consisting in and springing from the union for life of one man and one woman in the holy estate of matrimony; the sure foundation of all that is stable and noble in our civilization.

In this statement the Court's opinion mirrors that double sexual standard that has always surrounded the criminalization of prostitution. This double standard is implicitly based on a religious notion—the contrast between the "good woman," chaste, compliant, and domestic, who is confirmed in her goodness, if also her dependency, in the law, and the "bad woman," Eve, the temptress, the fallen woman, the source of original sin. Thus, women are viewed as worse than men when they depart from the ideal sexual norms of chastity, and are so treated in law. Indeed, historically it has always been the "harlot [who] has been branded as an outcast and flung to the wolves; she alone, never the man, her equal in responsibility."[15]

The criminalization of prostitution (an occupation that is mainly carried on by women), the unequal enforcement of prostitution laws (where women are arrested more frequently than male prostitutes), and the prosecution of the prostitute (but not her customer), are all ways in which American law demonstrates the moral hypocrisy which underlies it. As a New York court wrote, as early as 1920, "the men create the market, and the women who supply the demand pay the penalty. It is time that this unfair discrimination and injustice should cease."[16]

With the impact of the women's movement and increased sensitivity on the part of courts to gender discrimination, by 1979 some courts did conclude that statutes defining illegal prostitution as commercial sex offered by females and not males violated equal protection guarantees. In 1979 the Alaska appeals court, in *Plas v. State* (598 P.2d 966), agreed that their "females-only" prostitution statute violated such guarantees. While sensitive to the sex discrimination issue in the language of the statute, however, the court continued to hold, along with the rest of the nation's courts, that "[T]here is a legitimate national, state, and community interest in maintaining a decent society," and that the criminalization of prostitution in and of itself did not violate any constitutional guarantees. In its opinion, the Alaska court cited an earlier case, *Paris Adult Theatre v. Slaton* [413 U.S. 49 1973], in which the Supreme Court held that the monogamous male/female relationship within marriage is "a sensitive, key relationship of human existence, central to family life, community welfare, and the development of human personality, [that] can be debased and distorted by crass commercial exploitation of sex." In this conclusion the Court chose to ignore an alternative sociological view that prostitution reinforces home and family by providing an emotional and sexual safety valve both for married partners who do not find satisfaction of their needs within marriage, and as a sexual initiation for unmarried men at a time in our culture when female virginity was still prized.

Another issue which raises legal and moral questions about the commercialization of women's bodies is that of surrogate motherhood. In 1987 the United States was directly confronted by these questions when the "case of Baby M" came before a court in New Jersey. The litigation stemmed from the refusal of surrogate mother, Mary Beth Whitehead, to honor a contract arranged by the Infertility Center of New York with William Stern by which she would surrender custody of the infant child she had borne after artificial insemination by Stern. In February of 1986, Mr. Stern and Mr. and Mrs. Whitehead signed a Surrogate Parenting Agreement. The contract obligated Mrs. Whitehead to attempt conception by artificial insemination, to carry any conceived child to term, and to surrender the child to Mr. Stern at birth, renouncing all her parental rights. Mr. Stern assumed all legal responsibility for the child, agreed to pay for medical services for Mrs. Whitehead and received the right to name the child. It was understood that after birth, Mrs. Stern would legally adopt the child and the contract provided that in the event of Mr. Stern's death, Mrs. Stern would be given custody. The surrogate mother, Mrs. Whitehead, was to be paid $10,000 for her services.

Immediately after the child was born, Mrs. Whitehead claimed that she had bonded with the child and had changed her mind about giving it up to its biological father, Mr. Stern. The Sterns went to court to gain exclusive custody of the child, as had been provided for in the contract. In hearing the case, Judge Harvey R. Sorkow made it clear that the main issue presented by the litigation was the determination of what was in the best interests of the child, although, in the absence of any law on surrogacy, the force and validity of the contract would also be a prime consideration.

Judge Sorkow held that "the surrogate parenting agreement is a valid and enforceable contract pursuant to the laws of New Jersey, [that] the rights of the parties to contract are constitutionally protected under the Fourteenth Amendment of the United States Constitution, [and that] Mrs. Whitehead has breached her contract."[17] Following the testimony of experts, he further concluded that it was in the best interests of Baby M for the Sterns to be given custody and that Mrs. Whitehead be prohibited from seeing the child. In elaborating criteria for the best family environment, Sorkow stressed dominant culture values and attributes such as high regard for educational achievement, domestic stability, and male assertiveness as head of household. On these criteria the Sterns clearly surpassed Whitehead.

Cognizant of the criticism of surrogacy as a commercial activity and specifically concerned with state adoption law that prohibits the exchange of money for obtaining a child, Sorkow joins those who argue that "to produce or deal with a child for money denigrates human dignity."[18] In an attempt to reconcile this view with the money payment called for in the surrogacy contract, Sorkow differentiated payments for adoptive children from payments to a woman willing to perform surrogacy services. He also held that payment of money by a biological father was distinct from that of nonbiological adoptive parents.[19]

Many critics of surrogate mothering view it as a new form of prostitution made possible by modern technology, and another form of the systematic exploitation of women, in particular poor women, by well-off men. The analogy to prostitution is based upon the payment of money for the use of the woman's body, the involvement of surrogacy agencies as procurers (pimps) bringing together the necessary parties, and the role of the surrogate mother in performing a sexual service for a man that his wife is unable to provide. Sensitive to the effects these criticisms might have on their profits, surrogacy agencies have attempted to create an image of the surrogate mother, in contrast to that of the prostitute, as "bright, altruistic, and feminine . . . a very special girl next door . . . a plucky pioneer in a new industry, a girl who loves being pregnant."[20] Some, though not all, of the feminist community has been critical of this commercialization of women's bodies; another viewpoint holds that in this activity, as in prostitution, there is no reason that women should not benefit commercially from their bodies as men do when they sell their sperm.

Another focus of controversial litigation involving the commercial use of women's bodies is pornography. Pornography and laws to stop it date back to the early nineteenth century in the United States. These early state and federal laws were assumed by the states under their police powers and by the federal government through its commerce clause powers. The traditional attacks on pornography focused on its sexual explicitness that appeals to prurient sexual interest in material without otherwise "serious" literary, artistic, political, or scientific value. The constitutional claim advanced by those who would protect sexually explicit materials (both those with and those without serious socially redeeming value) rests on the First Amendment.

As pornography has become more widespread, and perceived to be more intrusive, coarse, and violent, antipornography activists—including atypical alliances among feminists, fundamentalists, political conservatives, and activists fighting hate speech—have increased their political efforts. While the fundamentalists emphasize that pornography is unprotected First Amendment expression that undermines family values, the feminist antipornography movement, led by Andrea Dworkin and Catherine MacKinnon, emphasizes that "pornography is sex discrimination which degrades women, portrays them as appropriate and deserving targets for sexual violence, denies them equal opportunities, and contributes to restricting their full exercise of citizenship."[21]

These feminists have pressed for the passage of local ordinances prohibiting pornography. Some initial successes included the enactment of nearly identical ordinances in Minneapolis and Indianapolis. In Minneapolis, for example, the City Council concluded that the presence of pornography in the community created and maintained the civil inequality of the sexes, and promoted physical harm including harassment, denigration, battery, and rape. The Minneapolis ordinance ordered that anyone found trafficking in pornography, coercing others into pornographic performances, or forcing pornography on a person would be held in violation of the ordinance. Any person who was attacked or assaulted as a result of pornography would be able to make a claim of damages against the perpetrator and the creator, seller, and exhibitor of the pornographic material.

Proponents of the ordinance claim that pornography is not protected by First Amendment free speech guarantees. They argue, to the contrary, that pornography is not speech about the subordination of women, but that it *is* the subordination of women, and that it should therefore be regulated and prohibited like other discriminatory acts.[22] The Indianapolis ordinance was immediately challenged in litigation and both a federal trial and appeals court held that the ordinance violated First Amendment freedom of speech. The appeals court, in its opinion in *American Booksellers Association, Inc. v. Hudnut* [771 F.2nd 323 7th Cir. (1985)], expressly rejected the city's argument that pornography is an act, an injury, rather than an idea. The court nevertheless agreed that as speech, pornography did have the power to perpetuate women's subordination. It concluded, however, that, "If the fact that speech plays a role in a process of conditioning [leading to discrimination] were enough to permit governmental regulation, that would be the end of freedom of speech."

In 1986 the Supreme Court affirmed the decision of this federal appeals court without opinion. For feminists who oppose pornography, this leaves the First Amendment "as the cornerstone of constitutional misogyny—an obstruction to the realization of equality and autonomy for women."[23] But the campaign waged by MacKinnon and Dworkin, although severely criticized by many mainstream feminists on First Amendment grounds, may have contributed positively to public acceptance of violence against women as a major public policy issue. The whole of the women's movement has succeeded, since the early 1980s, in breaking the silence about violence against women and, specifically, establishing the groundwork of a jurisprudence defining sexual harassment,[24] educating and changing criminal justice system response to domestic violence, introducing the battered wife defense in criminal prosecutions, continuing the reform of rape laws that long made prosecution humiliating and unsuccessful, and, in 1994, achieving passage of the "Violence Against Women Act" as part of a major federal legislative initiative against crime.

This chapter's review of the changing status of women as considered in the laws affecting their political participation, economic opportunities, reproductive rights, and commercial use of their bodies shows a clear and reinforcing relation between the cultural stereotypes of women and their legal treatment. It is now a moment of transition: Law, having been built upon images of women as innocent, dependent, and belonging to the world of home and hearth, has changed and many of the barriers that circumscribed women's world have been dismantled. This dismantling of legal barriers, however, leaves in place many of the more subtle and informal barriers to full dignity and participation of women in our society. While the law has been used successfully to change aspects of women's economic and political status, it has yet to deal with the impact of a history that uses men as the legal norm. This suggests that the struggle to bring about true equality between men and women in our society, through courts, will continue for some time.

NOTES

1. *Taylor v. Louisiana*, 419 U.S. 522, 530-31 (1975).

2. American Association of University Women Educational Foundation, *How Schools Shortchange Women* (Washington, DC: AAUW, 1992).

3. Alice Kessler-Harris, *Out to Work* (New York: Oxford University Press, 1982), 184–85. For an overview of the stages of contemporary feminist thought, see Rosemarie Tong, *Feminist Thought* (Boulder, CO: Westview Press, 1989). For a discussion of this topic as it specifically relates to morality, justice, and law, see Carol Gilligan, *In a Different Voice: Psychological Theory and Women's Development* (Cambridge, MA: Harvard University Press, 1982).

4. Leo Kanowitz, *Women and the Law: The Unfinished Revolution* (Albuquerque, NM: University of New Mexico Press, 1969), 152.

5. In spite of significant economic gains in the 1980s, women at every education level earn less money than men with equal schooling. The inequity increases with age. For a summary of data, see Sylvia Nasar, "Women's Progress Stalled? Just Not So," *New York Times*, October 18, 1992, 10. On comparable pay, see *Washington v. American Federation of State, County, and Municipal Employees*, 770 F.2d 1401 (9th Cir. 1985).

6. The issue of withholding more responsible, better-paying positions from women with families arose in the much-discussed Sears case. This class action suit was brought by women employees who claimed that women at Sears were discriminated against and kept out of commission sales and managerial positions. These employees used statistical evidence to demonstrate their claims of discrimination. Sears contended that it did not discriminate against women but rather that women preferred not to take these jobs. A federal district and appeals

court found in favor of Sears, holding that statistical evidence was not by itself sufficient to prove discrimination and that intent to discriminate had to be found. These courts did not find that Sears had the intent to discriminate. *EEOC v. Sears*, 628 F. Supp. 1264 (N.D.Ill. 1986), aff'd 839 F.2d 302 (7th Cir. 1988). But several years later, in a settlement that many feminists saw as a "rebuke" to the Sears case, Lucky Stores Inc., a large grocery chain, agreed to pay $75 million in damages to women employees who were denied promotion opportunities and to invest $20 million in affirmative action programs for female employees. Lynn Hecht Schafran, an attorney with NOW Legal Defense and Education Fund, said the settlement was a landmark, in part, because it damaged the defense used in the Sears case—that women often do not aspire to the same positions or promotions as men.

7. *Frontiero* might be considered a cultural victory but a strategic legal defeat. Members of the women's movement had hoped, using this case, to win Supreme Court approval for the doctrine that sex-based classifications, like those based upon race, were suspect, triggering strict judicial scrutiny. Only four justices in *Frontiero* voted for treating sex as a suspect classification. Three years later, in *Craig v. Boren*, a consensus was established: The Court would apply a heightened, intermediate level of scrutiny to gender-based classifications.

8. Barbara Sinclair Deckard, *The Women's Movement: Political, Socioeconomic, and Psychological Issues* (New York: Harper and Row, 1983), 157–58.

9. Ibid., 420.

10. Leonore J. Weitzman, *The Divorce Revolution* (New York: The Free Press, 1985), 144.

11. Ibid., 283–84.

12. Ibid., 339.

13. Ibid., 213.

14. Lois J. Frankel, "Sex Discrimination in the Criminal Law: The Effect of the Equal Rights Amendment," *American Criminal Law Review* 2 (Winter 1973): 373.

15. Ibid., 387.

16. Ibid., 373.

17. *In the Matter of Baby "M," a pseudonym for an actual person*. Typed preprint of the Opinion of Superior Court of New Jersey Chancery Division/Family Part Bergen County, Docket No., FM 25314-86E, March 31, 1987, 95.

18. Ibid., 70.

19. Ibid., 70–71.

20. Susan Ince, "Test-Tube Women," in *Taking Sides: Clashing Views on Controversial Issues in Human Sexuality*, ed. Robert T. Francoeur (Guilford, CT: Dushkin Publishing Group, 1987), 172.

21. Joel B. Grossman, "The First Amendment and the New Anti-Pornography Statutes," *News for Teachers for Political Science* (Spring 1985), 1. See also, Catharine A. MacKinnon, *Only Words* (Cambridge, MA: Harvard University Press, 1993), and Nadine Strossen, *Defending Pornography: Free Speech, Sex, and the Fight for Women's Rights* (New York: Scribner, 1995).

22. Grossman, "The First Amendment and the New Anti-Pornography Statutes," 3.

23. Ibid., 1.

24. *Meritor Saving Bank FSB v. Vinson*, 477 U.S. 57 (1986) upheld the use of

Title VII against *quid pro quo* sexual demands and approved the extension of Title VII to redress hostile sexual environments. *Harris v. Forklift*, 114 S. Ct. 367, 370–71 (1993) reaffirmed "a middle path between making actionable any conduct that is merely offensive and requiring the conduct to cause a tangible psychological injury."

Part IV

Community

11

Language, Law, and Latinos

For ethnic groups, a common language has important functions: It affirms the group's ethnic identity and provides an important boundary between themselves and others. Indeed, the "imagined communities" of nation-states are often identified primarily in terms of language.[1] As a medium of communication in economic, political, and social life, language has obvious and important instrumental functions. Language functions as a political tool, not only in disseminating information critical to political rights and obligations, but also in fashioning group solidarity, and expressing relations of dominance and subordination within the civic culture.

The expressive uses of language are as important as its instrumental uses. A shared language is a central vehicle for conveying individual and cultural identity and for expressing the intimacy of social relations within an ethnic group and community. Moreover, language, unlike national costume, is not a relic in the United States for many ethnic groups. The ability to adapt language to new situations enables it to become part of the vitality of an ethnic culture. While this is true for many of America's ethnic groups, it is particularly relevant for Latinos, the largest minority group in the United States for which language is an ethnic marker.

LANGUAGE IDEOLOGY AND POLICY IN THE UNITED STATES

There is no *official* national language policy in the United States. National, state, and local language policies have been inconsistent, reflecting our territorial expansion, shifts in our immigration history, and perceived threats to our national security. There was no consensus by the framers of the Constitution over language, and the Constitution itself does not define English or any other language as the official language of the country. At the state level, the languages of European immigrants were sometimes permitted or even encouraged within an implied or explicit context of English as the official language, and sometimes, outlawed. Expansion westward, annexation of Mexican territory, and later Hawai'i, and the acquisition of Puerto Rico added other elements to U.S. language policy. Native Americans, viewed as a group that needed to overcome their "tribal barbarism," were forced to send their children to boarding schools, often hundreds of miles from their local communities, so that their children would be permanently wrenched away from their cultures and languages. In these schools there was an absolute prohibition on Native American children speaking their own languages, and those that did were humiliated, beaten, and had their mouths washed with lye soap.[2] While English was not a condition of citizenship in either the Mexican territories or Puerto Rico, in both places, as in Hawai'i and among Native Americans, the indigenous languages were viewed as significant barriers to assimilation. There were strenuous efforts, always resisted to be sure, to convert the populations to speaking English, particularly through education in the public schools.[3]

The controversies over acceptance and public recognition of second languages—in courts, voting, government, business, and education—were generally heavily weighted toward the dominant assimilationist view of the early settlers and those that shortly followed them from English-speaking countries. From the first, English was established as the lingua franca of the colonies. In 1814, De Witt Clinton, soon to become governor of New York, commented with undisguised pleasure: "The triumph and adoption of the English language have been the principal means of melting us down into one people, and of extinguishing those stubborn prejudices and violent animosities which formed a wall of partition between the inhabitants of the same land."[4] This view is still very widely shared today. Former Secretary of Education William Bennett said, "American citizens must share a common language in which to discuss our common affairs." The *New York Times* agrees, echoing Governor Clinton in 1814: "English is the pot in which the melting takes place."[5]

Some federal courts agree. In 1978, in *Guadalupe v. Tempe Elementary School District* (587 F.2d 1022), the Ninth Circuit denied the request of Spanish-speaking students for bilingual and bicultural education, stating emphatically, "[L]inguistic and cultural diversity within the nation-state, whatever may be its advantages from time to time, can restrict the scope of the fundamental compact. Diversity limits unity. . . . Effective action by the nation-state to its peak of strength only rises when it is in response to aspirations unreservedly shared by each constituent culture and language group . . . as the scope of sharing diminishes, the strength of the nation-state's government wanes."[6] Here the court determined that the state's legitimate interest in the preservation of a monolingual/monocultural society outweighed an ethnic community's interest in multicultural education.

Historically, various pressures to learn English were applied to immigrants. As part of the xenophobic nineteenth- and twentieth-century nativist movements, English literacy requirements were erected as conditions for public employment, naturalization, immigration, and voting, the latter an often blatant attempt to disenfranchise immigrants for political or economic purposes.[7] Changes in American language policy have occurred with waxing and waning fears about the national security threats posed by non-English-speaking immigrants perceived to be from the "lower classes," committed to nondemocratic political ideologies and "foreign customs," and who were "ignorant of our laws and language."

Conflicts over language policy were frequently fought out in the schools, which were the major institutions of assimilation through the use of the English language. World War I led to increased xenophobia, and teaching a foreign language was identified with disloyalty to the United States. Laws were passed in many states prohibiting the teaching of languages other than English in the public schools; their purposes were to separate young children from cultures considered both inferior and inimical to American ideals, and to prepare large numbers of people for participation in the American economy and civic culture through the use of English-language instruction. These laws fell particularly heavily on German immigrants, who were a large minority, and who had made strong efforts to preserve their own language through a system of private schools.[8] Nebraska was one of the states that had passed a statute prohibiting the teaching of a subject in any language other than English in public or private schools. Robert Meyer was convicted of violating this statute by teaching the Bible, in German, in an elementary school. Meyer claimed that the Nebraska statute violated his due process rights under the Fourteenth Amendment, and his case went to the Supreme Court.

Meyer v. Nebraska
262 U.S. 390 (1923)

The salutary purpose of the statute is clear. The legislature had seen the baneful effects of permitting foreigners who had taken residence in this country, to rear and educate their children in the language of their native land. The result of that condition was found to be inimical to our own safety. To allow the children of foreigners who had emigrated here, to be taught from early childhood the language of the country of their parents, was to rear them with that language as their mother tongue. It was to educate them so that they must always think in that language, and, as a consequence, naturally inculcate in them the ideas and sentiments foreign to the best interests of this country. The statute, therefore, was intended not only to require that the education of all children be conducted in the English language, but that, until they had grown into that language, and until it had become a part of them, they should not in the schools be taught any other language. The obvious purpose of this statute was that the English language should be and become the mother tongue of all children reared in this state. The enactment of such a statute comes reasonably within the police power of the state.

It is said the purpose of the legislation was to promote civic development by inhibiting training and education of the immature in foreign tongues and ideas before they could learn English and acquire American ideals; and "that the English language should be and become the mother tongue of all children reared in this state." It is also affirmed that the foreign-born population is very large, that certain communities commonly use foreign words, follow foreign leaders, move in a foreign atmosphere, and that children are thereby hindered from becoming citizens of the most useful type, and the public safety is imperiled.

That the state may do much, go very far, indeed, in order to improve the quality of its citizens, physically, mentally, and morally, is clear; but the individual has certain fundamental rights which must be respected. The protection of the Constitution extends to all,—to those who speak other languages as well as to those born with English on the tongue. Perhaps it would be highly advantageous if all had ready understanding of our ordinary speech, but this cannot be coerced by methods which conflict with the Constitution,—a desirable end cannot be promoted by prohibited means.

The desire of the legislature to foster a homogeneous people with American ideals, prepared readily to understand current discussions of civic matters, is easy to appreciate. Unfortunate experiences during the late war, and aversion toward every characteristic of truculent adversaries, were certainly enough to quicken that aspiration. But the means adopted, we think, exceed the limitations upon the power of the state, and conflict with rights assured to plaintiff in error. The interference is plain enough, and no adequate reason therefore in time of peace and domestic tranquility has been shown.

The power of the state to compel attendance at some school and to make reasonable regulations for all schools, including a requirement that they shall give instructions in English, is not questioned. . . . No emergency has arisen which renders knowledge by a child of some language other than English so clearly harmful as to justify its inhibition, with the consequent infringement of rights long freely enjoyed. We are constrained to conclude that the statute as applied is arbitrary, and without reasonable relation to any end within the competency of the state.

The Supreme Court decision in favor of Meyer is hailed as an important victory for cultural pluralism, not only because there are so few Supreme Court decisions affirming language rights, but also because the opinion established a notion of due process as not just a question of procedure, but also as encompassing *substantive* rights, values, and traditions.[9] On the other hand, the Court's opinion does not appear to us as an enthusiastic "celebration of cultural pluralism"; the Court expressed considerable empathy and approval of the intent of the Nebraska legislature to "prevent . . . the baneful effects of permitting foreigners . . . to rear and educate their children in the language of their native land . . . [and] to foster a homogeneous people with American ideals."[10]

The issue of language rights again became prominent in the mid-1960s, as part of the momentum of the civil rights movement. This was expressed first by congressionally mandated changes in English literacy requirements for voting, and later in legislation enabling bilingual education. In conjunction with the "war on poverty," Congress passed a number of acts designed to help educationally disadvantaged children. Because many of these children did not speak English as a first language, in 1965 the legislation was extended to include a provision for bilingual education, designed less to celebrate and preserve multiculturalism than to be transitional and compensatory, aimed at children with identifiable limitations with respect to school achievement.[11] The issue of the extent to which government had responsibility for providing bilingual education for non-English-speaking students was raised in the 1974 case, *Lau v. Nichols* (414 U.S. 563).

Unlike the controversy in *Meyer*, which centered upon the right to give general instruction in a foreign language, the conflict in *Lau* was whether or not the government ought to be required to provide general instruction in a foreign language for non-English-speaking students in public schools.

The plaintiffs in the case, non-English-speaking students of Chinese ancestry, charged the San Francisco school system with violating their civil rights by failing to provide them with adequate instruction in their native language and thus denying them a meaningful opportunity to participate in the public educational program. In its mandate to local schools, the California education code requires proficiency in English as well as other prescribed subjects. In its opinion, the court agreed with the lawyers representing the Chinese students, stating that

Basic English skills are at the very core of what these public schools teach. Imposition of a requirement that, before a child can effectively participate in the educational program, he must have already acquired those basic skills is to make a mockery of public education. We know that those who do not understand English are certain to find their classroom experiences wholly incomprehensible and in no way meaningful.

The justices recognized that the provision of equal facilities in a case where the children did not speak English could hardly be considered equal treatment under the law and ordered that

Where inability to speak and understand the English language excludes national origin-minority group children from effective participation in the educational program offered by a school district, the district must take affirmative steps to rectify the language deficiency in order to open its instructional program to these students.

The requirement of the Court in *Lau,* that public schools take "affirmative steps" to compensate for a child's lack of English skills is a significant "access right" for linguistic minorities, but in spite of the favorable decision in *Lau,* the courts have not created a constitutionally based federal entitlement to bilingual education. Indeed, claims of a right to bilingual/bicultural instruction on the ground of the equal protection clause of the Fourteenth Amendment have been specifically rejected in *Keyes v. Denver,* although courts have mandated implementation of bilingual and other remedial programs on the basis of violation of Title VI of the Civil Rights Act of 1964 and the Equal Educational Opportunities Act of 1974.[12]

The legal ambiguity regarding language rights in education is paralleled by the lack of a clear judicial pattern on language rights in general. Language rights have been manufactured piecemeal by judges and are inconsistent and even contradictory; the major effect of the courts has been to ensure constitutional rights otherwise guaranteed to non-English speakers, and to prohibit discrimination on the basis of national origin, and by extension, language.[13]

In the 1980s and 1990s, perhaps as a result of the perceived legislative and judicial support for minority language rights in voting, schools, and employment, combined with changes in immigration patterns, pressures to assure the predominance of English in the United States became more organized and more vocal, leading to the growth of the English-Only and Official English movements. Among other things, the ultimate aim of these groups is ratification of a constitutional amendment making English the official language of the United States. This would outlaw the mandating of bilingual programs and services provided by all levels of government, effect congressional repeal of the bilingual ballot requirements under the 1965 Voting Rights Act, and sharply reduce federal programs for bilingual education.[14] Some prominent Latinos support this movement because they feel that bilingual education programs particularly impede Latino assimilation by delaying or impeding the acquisition of English fluency. Their support therefore, is predicated more on the harm that multilingualism does to the Latino community than on the harm it does to the nation.[15]

Official English has had some success at the state and local levels. On November 4, 1986, a popular referendum passed in California requiring legislators and other state officials to "take all steps necessary to insure that the role of English as the common language of the State of California is preserved and enhanced." The resolution holds that legislators "shall make no law which diminishes or ignores the role of English as the common language" of California. Any person who lives or does business in California could sue the state to enforce the law. Similar laws, primarily directed against increasing numbers of Asian and Latino immigrants, and which could affect a wide range of bilingual services such as emergency services, bilingual voting information, and bilingual telephone operators, have been put into effect in 15 states and numerous local communities, where these populations have been particularly concentrated.[16]

Opponents of English-Only hold that Official English laws violate many state and federal constitutionally based freedoms, and are in conflict with judicial interpretations of our national Constitution which hold that basic rights cannot be limited by an inability to speak English. Indeed, the Official English movement already experienced its first legal setback when an Arizona judge found that the Arizona constitutional amendment mandating an English-Only policy violated federally protected free speech rights.[17] Although this ruling was binding only in Arizona, it is a signal that Official English statutes are legally on vulnerable ground.

English-Only supporters claim that their concerns are about the ability of new, and culturally and linguistically different immigrants to assimilate, and that bilingual programs and services are a disincentive for immigrants to learn English. For many of its critics, however, the Official English movement mirrors the thinly veiled racism and xenophobia of an earlier period. Thus, although the current English-Only movement's initiatives may seem irrelevant, extreme, and mainly symbolic, they encourage false and misleading stereotypes of immigrants as both unable and unwilling to assimilate into American society. The targets of these initiatives are most frequently Latinos and Asian Americans, and spokespeople for Latino groups have characterized Official English laws as "a cultural slap in the face of Hispanics . . . [a symbolic message] that we don't want you to bring your cultural baggage with you when you immigrate."[18] Because Latinos are a rapidly increasing population in the United States, and because of the high maintenance of the use of Spanish among Latinos, current discussions of language policy and language rights cases most significantly involve this group.

LATINOS AND LANGUAGE RIGHTS

Latinos in the United States are a large and diverse ethnic group. The approximately 21 million Latino immigrants and their descendants include about 13 million Mexican Americans; approximately three million

Puerto Ricans; one million Cuban Americans; and four million other Latin Americans, many of whom are from Central America. In recent decades, Latino immigration has sharply increased so that a larger proportion of Latinos, particularly Mexican Americans, are first generation immigrants.[19]

The immigration and settlement experiences of Latinos have varied over time, coinciding with particular historical events and economic trends. Mexican Americans originate in the populations of the Southwest and California, whose settlement predated the 1846–1848 Mexican American war. An originally settled rural population, their numbers were augmented by migrant workers, but since the 1950s, Mexican Americans have become about 90 percent urban, concentrated in California, Texas, New Mexico, and Arizona. Puerto Ricans and Cubans, in contrast, initially migrated to urban areas; the major Puerto Rican immigration began between the two world wars and centers on East Coast cities, while the Cubans, who began immigrating in large numbers after the 1959 Cuban revolution, have mainly concentrated in Miami, Florida. Upheavals in Central America led to increasing numbers of both documented and undocumented immigrants from Guatemala, Nicaragua, and El Salvador, and since the 1960s, there has been large-scale immigration from the Dominican Republic.

The different histories of each group have shaped their patterns of adaptation and assimilation, and their patterns of Spanish-language use. The motivations of the different immigrant groups and the extent to which a group considers itself permanently or only temporarily in the United States undoubtedly influence their willingness to acquire English and to assimilate within the dominant culture. Over and above this diversity, however, Latinos, more than any other ethnic group have retained their language, along with an increase in the acquisition of English.

As a result of immigration, population growth, and language maintenance, Spanish is the most widely used (non-English) language in the United States and the only one which has not lost, but actually gained adherents. Spanish has been, and remains today, a central identifying characteristic of Latinos, and is one of the clearest examples of the connection between a group's language and its national origins.[20] Thus, the ideology of English as the dominant, and for many, only acceptable language in the United States has been particularly burdensome for Latinos.

Anglos have largely viewed the persistence of Spanish language in the territory acquired through conquest of Mexico and in Puerto Rico as an insuperable barrier to Latino patriotism, and to the incorporation of Latinos into mainstream legal, economic, social, and educational institutions in the United States. Although in the early years after the treaty of Guadalupe Hidalgo, Spanish was officially used in the governments of

New Mexico and California, as the Anglo population increased in these areas pressure for anglicization was unrelenting, although not altogether unopposed.[21] In Puerto Rico, acquired by the United States from Spain in the Spanish American War of 1898, English was viewed as the major vehicle of assimilation of the island's population to American democratic ideals, and was the official language of education. Only in 1949 was this policy acknowledged as a failure by the U.S. government, and with increased political autonomy the Puerto Rican government reestablished Spanish instruction, although English is a required course of study. Most of the Puerto Ricans in the United States are bilingual; 91 percent speak Spanish at home, and 70 percent speak English very well.[22] In spite of the evidence that Spanish-speaking peoples in the United States are learning English, discriminatory policies—whether by intent or by impact—have burdened them in all important arenas of social life.

LANGUAGE RIGHTS IN COURT

Nowhere perhaps is the obligation of government to take into account the language concerns of non-English-speaking individuals as important as in criminal courtrooms where violations of an individual's rights based on linguistic misunderstandings can have the most devastating effects. It is only relatively recently that the right for a defendant to understand the charges against him, as guaranteed by the Sixth Amendment, has been guaranteed for non-English speakers.

In 1970, Rogelio Negron, a Puerto Rican farm laborer, killed a fellow worker during a drunken brawl. While an interpreter was hired by the prosecutor to translate Spanish testimony into English, no interpreter was available to translate the English part of the proceedings into Spanish for the defendant, who did not speak English. Negron's lawyer also did not speak Spanish. Although the court interpreter informally apprised Negron, during breaks, of what was going on, this was not sufficient to understand the testimony against him, or to confer with his lawyer. Negron was convicted of second-degree murder and sentenced to 20 years in prison. Although Negron had little formal education, acting as his own lawyer, he succeeded in winning a new trial. A federal appeals court ruled that Negron had been denied his Sixth Amendment right to confront his accusers. In his opinion, Judge Irving Kaufman stated that "The least we can require is that a court, put on notice of a defendant's severe language difficulty, make unmistakably clear to him that he has a right to a competent translator to assist him, at state expense, if need be, throughout his trial," and this principle has been adopted for federal criminal and immigration proceedings, and generally in state courts.[23]

Ensuring that Sixth Amendment rights—to understand the accusations, to meaningfully participate in one's trial with the effective assistance of counsel, and to confront the government's witnesses on cross-examination—are not violated for non-English speakers is severely hindered by the shortage of competent court interpreters. In an order issued in a criminal trial involving 18 Spanish-speaking defendants, Judge Jack Weinstein of the U.S. District Court for the Eastern District of New York, noted that while the financial burden on courts to provide translation services may be enormous, "costs alone do not override constitutional rights." Citing a balancing standard in the use of courtroom interpreters whereby the defendant's constitutional rights to confrontation and due process are balanced against the public's interest in the economical administration of criminal law, Judge Weinstein concluded that "If the government cannot afford to provide due process to those it prosecutes, it must forego prosecution," and that whatever problems the government has in providing qualified interpreters must not be permitted to "defeat a criminal defendant's Sixth Amendment interests," lest a criminal trial become "the Kafkaesque specter of an incomprehensible ritual which may terminate in punishment."[24]

Another case, *Dionisio Hernandez v. New York*, [111 S. Ct. 1859 (1991)], involved minority language rights in court as related to bilingualism. Dionisio Hernandez was convicted of murder. At the trial, the prosecutor peremptorily excused two bilingual Hispanic jurors on the basis that they hesitated and looked away from him when he asked them if they would only listen to the English translations of testimony and not the original testimony in Spanish. Hernandez' attorney appealed the conviction, claiming that the prosecution's peremptorily excusing bilingual jurors was impermissibly discriminatory and violated Hernandez' equal protection rights.

One of the defendant's arguments was that Spanish speakers in the United States are mainly bilingual, and that the prosecutor's exclusion of Spanish/English bilingual jurors was an unlawful bias against Spanish and Hispanics who understand Spanish.[25] Using anthropological and other linguistic evidence, the defendant's counsel argued that code switching by bilingual individuals is not a matter of voluntary, conscious choice but involves simultaneous attention to both languages. The defense claimed that the prosecutor's assumption that a delay in the response of the bilingual jurors to his question about their ability to rely on the English translation of testimony was evidence of their unsuitability as jurors demonstrated an impermissible bias against bilingual jurors. The defendant also claimed that this prosecutorial bias deprived him of a jury of his peers, that is, bilingual Hispanics. Indeed, he further argued that requiring bilingual Hispanics to affirm an ability which is in fact, an impossibility (that is, to ignore the original Spanish testimony) demonstrates that the prosecutor's question itself was unlawful.

The prosecutor defended his action by saying that it was not based on the jurors' group membership since he did not know if the jurors were Latino, and that he had no motive to exclude Latinos since the complainants and all the civilian witnesses were Latino. Hernandez' claim was rejected by the state appellate court, whose decision was affirmed in the U.S. Supreme Court. In its opinion the Supreme Court acknowledged that bilingualism was a complex phenomenon, and was careful to say that "[O]ur decision today does not imply that exclusion of bilinguals from jury service is wise, or even that it is constitutional in all cases. . . . It is a harsh paradox that one may become proficient enough in English to participate in trial, only to encounter disqualification because he knows a second language as well." The opinion further noted that in some cases, proficiency in a particular language "should be treated as a surrogate for race under an equal protection analysis," and "a policy of striking all who speak a given language . . . may be found by the trial judge to be a pretext for racial discrimination. But that case," said the Court, "is not before us [now]."[26]

While the Supreme Court opinion, written by Justice Kennedy, acknowledged that language can sometimes be treated as a surrogate for race and ethnicity based on national origin and thus constitute a basis for a claim of violation of equal protection, in this case, a majority of the justices agreed with the lower courts that the prosecutor's challenge to the jurors was race-neutral and thus constitutional even though it adversely impacted on Latinos. The Supreme Court reminded the defendants that claims that a prosecutor used peremptory challenges in a manner violating the equal protection clause must be proven by the defense to be *intentionally* discriminatory, because in official government actions a disparate impact on a particular protected group is not sufficient to show impermissible discrimination.

Justices Stevens, Marshall, and Blackmun dissented, giving more weight to the view that a discriminatory impact is "itself evidence" of discriminatory purpose. Justice Blackmun, writing the dissenting opinion for himself and Justice Marshall, pointed out that "even if a decision maker's honest belief is that his motive was entirely benign" the subsequent results are the best evidence of discriminatory intent. Because of its disparate impact on Spanish-speaking jurors, and because other, less discriminatory means could have been found to deal with the issue of competing language testimony, Justices Blackmun and Marshall found the prosecutor's explanation to be "merely a proxy for a discriminatory practice" and held that in this case, the prosecutor's explanation, rather than being accepted on its face, "should have been rejected as a matter of law."[27]

VOTING RIGHTS

The issue of a language barrier interfering with another fundamental right, that of voting, has not, surprisingly, frequently found its way into court. Where such litigation has occurred, the decisions have turned on the narrow interpretation of the unique relationship between the United States and the non-English-speaking Commonwealth of Puerto Rico. The United States government has appeared to foster the cultural autonomy of Puerto Rico, by encouraging Puerto Rico to teach its schoolchildren in Spanish; this policy has meant, however, that many Puerto Rican migrants, whose numbers have grown substantially since World War II, arrive on the mainland without the language skills necessary to participate in the civic culture. Therefore, with regard to this special population, that is, persons who have been educated in American flag schools, where the language of instruction is not English, courts have held that English-only election systems violate these citizens' rights under the Voting Rights Act of 1965 and its subsequent amendments. In the case of *Arroyo v. Tucker* (372 F. Supp 764, 1974), for example, the court decided that the right to vote included the "right to be informed," and that the city of Philadelphia, the defendant in this case, must provide all of the following in order to provide its Puerto Rican-born citizens with access to an "effective vote":

Defendants, their agents, employees, representatives and all those acting in concert with them are permanently enjoined from conducting elections and registration in English only and are required to (i) provide all written materials which are directly connected with the registration of and election by voters in both Spanish and English, including, but not limited to, sample ballots, voter's certificates, registration certificates and all instructions to voters; (ii) provide an unofficial Spanish translation of all propositions, questions, and amendments which will be affixed to the right inside of each voting booth; (iii) provide ballot labels which list office titles in both Spanish and English insofar as such bilingual listing is consistent with mechanical possibility and readability, provided that if the above criteria prevent such bilingual listing then sample ballots of a reduced size in Spanish will be provided to the voters for use in the polling booths; (iv) provide a sufficient number of individuals who speak, read, write, and understand both Spanish and English at Philadelphia City Hall where registration and voting occurs, and at all polling places and places of registration in the City of Philadelphia falling in whole or in part, in a census tract containing 5 percent or more persons of Puerto Rican birth or extraction pursuant to the most recent census report reflecting such information; (v) provide appropriate and conspicuous signs at all polling places and places of registration described in subparagraph 2(iv), indicating, in Spanish, that individuals are available to assist Spanish-speaking voters or registrants, and that bilingual written materials are available; (vi) publicize elections in all media proportionately in a way that reflects the language characteristics of plaintiffs, and (vii) communicate the contents of the Court's order to all agents, employees and representatives of the defendants involved in the registration and voting process.

EMPLOYMENT

Cases like *Lau* and *Arroyo* established at least a threshold commitment on the part of public institutions to bilingualism, even if only as a tool of cultural transition. In 1980, litigants in Texas petitioned the court with respect to the issue of whether employers in the private sector have the right to control completely when and where, and if at all, bilingual employees may use their native language while at work. The court ruled, that with the exception of coffee breaks, the employer can!

In this case, *Garcia v. Gloor*, the court ruled that the employer had the right to establish where at the workplace the language of home and community could be used by bilingual employees. In his opinion, Federal Circuit Judge Alvin Rubin dismissed the importance of language as a vehicle of personal and ethnic identity compared to the importance of the freedom of contract for employers.

Hector Garcia v. Alton V. W. Gloor
618 F.2d 264 (1980)

Hector Garcia, a native born American of Mexican descent, challenges as discriminatory his employer's rule that prohibits employees engaged in sales work from speaking Spanish on the job. We conclude that the "speak-only-English" rule, as it was applied to Mr. Garcia by his employer, does not discriminate on the basis of national origin. We therefore affirm the district court's judgment that Mr. Garcia's discharge for violating the rule was not unlawful.

Hector Garcia, who was twenty-four years of age at the time of trial, completed the first semester of the tenth grade in Texas public schools. He speaks both English and Spanish. His grandparents were immigrants from Mexico; he is native-born, but he has always spoken Spanish in his own household.

In 1975, he was employed as a salesman by Gloor Lumber and Supply, Inc., in Brownsville, Texas. His duties included stocking his department and keeping it in order, assisting other department salespersons and selling lumber, hardware and supplies. He had received compliments from management on his work and in May 1975 had received a bonus of $250. However, there also was evidence that Mr. Garcia was not a satisfactory employee, that management's compliments were bestowed as incentives to better performance when, on occasion, his work showed some improvement and that a bonus was awarded to all employees at year-end without regard to merit.

Gloor had a rule prohibiting employees from speaking Spanish on the job unless they were communicating with Spanish-speaking customers. Most of Gloor's employees were bilingual, but some who worked outside in the lumber yard did not speak English. The rule did not apply to those employees. It also did not apply to conversation during work breaks.

Mr. Garcia testified that, because Spanish is his primary language, he found the English-only rule difficult to follow. He testified that on June 10, 1975 he was asked a question by another Mexican-American employee about an item requested by a customer and he responded in Spanish that the article was not available. Alton Gloor, an officer and stockholder of Gloor, overheard the conversation. Thereafter Mr. Garcia was discharged.

The court . . . found that the English-only policy was not strictly enforced but that Mr. Garcia had violated it at every opportunity since the time of his hiring according to his own testimony . . . Mr. Gloor testified that there were business reasons for the language policy: English-speaking customers objected to communications between employees that they could not understand; pamphlets and trade literature were in English and were not available in Spanish, so it was important for employees to be fluent in English apart from conversations with English-speaking customers; if employees who normally spoke Spanish off the job were required to speak English on the job at all times and not only when waiting on English-speaking customers, they would improve their English; and the rule would permit supervisors, who did not speak Spanish, better to oversee the work of subordinates. The district court found that these were valid business reasons and that they, rather than discrimination, were the motive for the rule.

An expert witness called by the plaintiff testified that the Spanish language is the most important aspect of ethnic identification for Mexican-Americans, and it is to them what skin color is to others. Consequently, Mr. Garcia contends, with support from the Equal Employment Opportunity Commission [EEOC], that the rule violates the EEO Act and the Civil Rights Acts, 42 U.S.C. 1981 and 1985(c).

Of the eight salesman employed by Gloor in 1975, seven were Hispanic, a matter perhaps of business necessity, because 75% of the population in its business area is of Hispanic background and many of Gloor's customers wish to be waited on by a salesman who speaks Spanish. Of its 39 employees, 31 were Hispanic, and a Hispanic sat on the Board of Directors. There is no contention that Gloor discriminated against Hispanic-Americans in any other way.

The narrow issue is whether the English-only rule as applied to Mr. Garcia imposed a discriminatory condition of employment.

The EEO Act sought to assure equality of employment opportunity by making it unlawful for an employer "(1) to fail or refuse to hire or to discharge any individual, or otherwise to discriminate against any individual with respect to his compensation, terms, conditions, or privileges of employment, because of such individual's race, color, religion, sex, or national origin; and (2) to limit, segregate, or classify his employees or applicants for employment in any way which would deprive or tend to deprive any individual of employment opportunities or otherwise adversely affect his status as an employee, because of such individual's race, color, religion, sex, or national origin." 42 U.S.C. 2000e-2(a).

The statute forbids discrimination in employment on the basis of national origin. Neither the statute nor common understanding equates national origin with the language that one chooses to speak. Language may be used as a covert basis for national origin discrimination, but the English-only rule was not applied to Garcia by Gloor either to this end or with this result.

Mr. Garcia argues that it is discriminatory to prohibit employees from speaking a foreign language on the basis of a thesis that, if an employee whose most familiar language is not English is denied the right to converse in that language, he is denied a privilege of employment enjoyed by employees most comfortable in English; this, necessarily, discriminates against him on the basis of national origin because national origin influences or determines his language preference. Whether or not this argument might have a tenable basis if made on behalf of all employees who are bilingual or if invoked against a rule that forbade all use of any language but English, we need not consider. Mr. Garcia was fully bilingual. He chose deliberately to speak Spanish instead of English while actually at work. He was permitted to speak the language he preferred during work breaks.

No authority cited to us gives a person a right to speak any particular language while at work; unless imposed by statute, the rules of the workplace are made by collective bargaining or, in its absence, by the employer. An employer's failure to forbid employees to speak English does not grant them a privilege. The refusal to hire applicants who cannot speak English might be discriminatory if the jobs they seek can be performed without knowledge of that language, but the obverse is not correct: if the employer engages a bilingual person, that person is granted neither right nor privilege by the statute to use the language of his personal preference. Mr. Garcia was bilingual. Off the job, when he spoke one language or another, he exercised a preference. He was hired by Gloor precisely because he was bilingual, and, apart from the contested rule, his preference in language was restricted to some extent by the nature of his employment. On the job, in addressing English-speaking customers, he was obliged to use English; in serving Spanish-speaking patrons, he was required to speak Spanish. The English-only rule went a step further and restricted his preference while he was on the job and not serving a customer.

We do not denigrate the importance of a person's language of preference or other aspects of his national, ethnic or racial self-identification. Differences in language and other cultural attributes may not be used as a fulcrum for discrimination. However, the English-only rule, as applied by Gloor to Mr. Garcia, did not forbid cultural expression to persons for whom compliance with it might impose hardship. While Title VII forbids the imposition of burdensome terms and conditions of employment as well as those that produce an atmosphere of racial and ethnic oppression, the evidence does not support a finding that the English-only rule had this effect on Mr. Garcia.

The EEO Act does not support an interpretation that equates the language an employee prefers to use with his national origin. To a person who speaks only one tongue or to a person who has difficulty using another language than the one spoken in his home, language might well be an immutable characteristic like skin color, sex or place of birth. However, the language a person who is multilingual elects to speak at a particular time is by definition a matter of choice. No claim is made that Garcia and the other employees engaged in sales were unable to speak English. Indeed, it is conceded that all could do so and that this ability was an occupational qualification because of the requirement that they wait on customers who spoke only English or who used that language by choice. Nor are we confronted with a case where an employee inadvertently slipped into using a more familiar tongue.

The rule was confined to the work place and work hours. It did not apply to conversations during breaks or other employee free-time. There is no evidence that Gloor forbade speaking Spanish to discriminate in employment or that the effect of doing so was invidious to Hispanic Americans. We do not consider rules that turn on the language used in an employee's home, the one he chooses to speak when not at work or the tongue spoken by his parents or grandparents. In some circumstances, the ability to speak or the speaking of a language other than English might be equated with national origin, but this case concerns only a requirement that persons capable of speaking English do so while on duty.

That this rule prevents some employees, like Mr. Garcia, from exercising a preference to converse in Spanish does not convert it into discrimination based on national origin. Reduced to its simplest, the claim is "others like to speak English on the job and do so without penalty. Speaking Spanish is very important to me and is inherent in my ancestral national origin. Therefore, I should be permitted to speak it and the denial to me of that preference so important to my self-identity is statutorily forbidden." The argument thus reduces itself to a contention that the statute commands employers to permit employees to speak the tongue they prefer. We do not think the statute permits that interpretation, whether the preference be slight or strong or even one closely related to self-identity.

Mr. Garcia and the EEOC would have us adopt a standard that the employer's business needs must be accomplished in the manner that appears to us to be the least restrictive. The statute does not give the judiciary such latitude in the absence of discrimination. Judges, who have neither business experience nor the problem of meeting the employee's payroll, do not have the power to preempt an employer's business judgment by imposing a solution that appears less restrictive.

Our opinion does not impress a judicial imprimatur on all employment rules that require an employee to use or forbid him from using a language spoken by him at home or by his forebears. We hold only that an employer's rule forbidding a bilingual employee to speak anything but English in public areas while on the job is not discrimination based on national origin as applied to a person who is fully capable of speaking English and chooses not to do so in deliberate disregard of his employer's rule. Even if we assume that the violation of the rule was a substantial factor leading to Mr. Garcia's discharge, we, therefore, affirm the district court's judgment that Mr. Garcia was neither discharged because of his national origin nor denied equal conditions of employment based on that factor; instead, he was discharged because, having the ability to comply with his employer's rule, he did not do so.

The judgment is AFFIRMED.

When *Garcia v. Gloor* was decided there were few guidelines and a general dearth of judicial authority concerning English-only rules. In fact, *Garcia v. Gloor* was the only outstanding federal appellate court decision at that time. Subsequent to that decision, however, in December 1980, the United States Equal Employment Opportunity Commission (EEOC), the federal agency charged with administering employment discrimination law, established guidelines which were contrary to the position of the court in *Garcia*. The new EEOC guidelines held that a total prohibition on speaking languages other than English would be presumed invalid, and that a limited prohibition on speaking languages other than English would be permitted only when justified by a clear "business necessity" subsequently defined to include communications during emergencies and while conducting inherently dangerous work, but did not include customer preferences.[28]

In 1987, a federal court opinion in *Gutierrez v. Municipal Court* on English-only workplace rules was issued which contrasted with the opinion in *Garcia v. Gloor* in almost every respect.[29] Alva Gutierrez, a bilingual deputy court clerk in the Clerk's Office of the Southeast Judicial District of the Los Angeles Municipal Court (Municipal Court), translated for the court's non-English-speaking public as part of her official duties. In response to a complaint by a monolingual, English-speaking secretary that Spanish-speaking employees were using Spanish to gossip about her, the Municipal Court created an English-only rule prohibiting its employees from speaking any language at work except English, unless they were in their official capacity as translators, or on work breaks.

Ms. Gutierrez charged her employers with violating her equal protection rights and rights of free speech by imposing an English-only rule in the clerk's office, claiming that such a rule was both intentionally discriminatory against Hispanics and also had a disparate impact on them. The District Court found in her favor, granting an injunction against the rule. The Municipal Court appealed.

In his opinion for the three judge panel of the Ninth Circuit Court of Appeals in Los Angeles, Judge Stephen Reinhardt emphasized the stringent standards of the 1980 EEOC guidelines which forbid not only intentional discrimination, but also facially neutral rules, such as English-only personnel rules, which have a disparate impact on protected groups of workers. Judge Reinhardt noted that while EEOC guidelines are not binding on the courts, they are a "body of experience and informed judgment to which courts and litigants may properly resort for guidance," particularly because the contrary law (in *Garcia*) was established *before* the EEOC guidelines. Sympathetic to the importance of language in ethnic identity, Judge Reinhardt stated that "In the United States, persons of Asian and Hispanic origin constitute large minorities. Numerous members of these groups regularly communicate in a language other than English. For many of these individuals Spanish . . . or some other language is their primary tongue. Members of these minority groups have made great contributions to the development of our diverse multicultural society and its tradition of encouraging the free exchange of ideas. . . . The multicultural character of American society has a long and venerable history and is widely recognized as one of the United States' greatest strengths."[30]

Judge Reinhardt noted that workplace rules that have a negative effect on individuals with accents, or those who speak different languages, can "create an atmosphere of inferiority, isolation and intimidation," and "can readily mask an intent to discriminate on the basis of national origin."[31] He dismissed the Municipal Court's claim that its English-only rule was a business necessity, aimed at reducing the fears of non-Hispanic workers that Hispanics were speaking in Spanish to belittle them. Judge Reinhardt said that even if this were the case, the English-only rule could still not be justified because it has "an adverse impact on other persons based on *their* (emphasis in original) national origin. Existing racial fears or prejudices and their effects cannot justify a racial classification. Nor may such fears or prejudices constitute a business necessity for a rule that burdens a protected class."[32] Further, Judge Reinhardt pointed out, not only had the Municipal Court failed to demonstrate that the use of Spanish was creating ethnic conflict among its employees, but the evidence indicated the reverse: Non-Spanish-speaking employees had made racially discriminatory remarks directed atcs. Indeed, the English-only rule had increased racial hostility between Hispanics and non-Spanish-speaking employees because Hispanics felt belittled by it.[33]

Judge Reinhardt dismissed the Municipal Court's claim that because Ms. Gutierrez is bilingual and could easily comply with the English-only rule, the rule was not discriminatory. He found the bilingual ability of the employees irrelevant to the discriminatory impact of English-only workplace rules.[34] Judge Reinhardt also disagreed with the Municipal Court's view that English-only workplace rules were required by Section 6 of the California Constitution which declares that "English is the official language of the State of California," holding that declaration to be "primarily symbolic."[35] Furthermore, he noted that contrary to the Municipal Court's contention that the intention of Section 6 was to require that *all* communication at governmental offices be conducted in English, it was clear that Section 6 applied not to private conversations but *official* communications. Judge Reinhardt called attention to the irony that while the Municipal Court's English-only rule totally bars *private* speech in Spanish during on-duty periods, it not only permits, but mandates the use of Spanish for much *official* communication (emphasis in the original).[36] Judge Reinhardt concluded his opinion by emphasizing that an injunction against the English-only rule was necessary because money damages could not fully compensate for a practice that "contributed to a workplace atmosphere that derogates Hispanics, encourages discriminatory behavior by non-Hispanic [employees], and heightens racial animosity between Hispanics and non-Hispanics."[37]

The Municipal Court appealed but *Gutierrez* was vacated as moot by the U.S. Supreme Court because Ms. Gutierrez had left the Muncipal Court's employ. Thus, this case has no precedential value, though it is significant because it provides a thoughtful, alternative reasoning to *Garcia v. Gloor* that could serve as a guideline in subsequent cases. In fact, however, a more recent case on workplace English-only rules from the same judicial district as *Gutierrez* suggests that the lack of precedential authority in *Gutierrez* will give additional weight to the reasoning in *Garcia v. Gloor.*

Garcia v. Spun Steak Company [998 F.2d 1480 (1993)] was brought to the Ninth Circuit Court of Appeals in California after a district court found for Hispanic employees who brought suit claiming that Spun Steak's English-only rule violated EEOC's Title VII guidelines by adversely affecting Spanish-speaking employees in a significant way. Relying on the reasoning in *Gutierrez,* the Spanish-speaking employees claimed that the rule denied them the ability to express their cultural heritage on the job; denied them a privilege of employment enjoyed by monolingual speakers of English; and created an atmosphere of inferiority, isolation, and intimidation.

While Judge Diarmuid O'Scannlain, writing for the court, acknowledged that an individual's primary language can be an important link to ethnic culture and identity, he expressed his view that

Title VII does not protect the ability of workers to express their cultural heritage at the workplace; it is concerned only with disparities in treatment of workers and does not confer substantive privileges. . . . It is axiomatic that an employee must often sacrifice individual self-expression during working hours. Just as a private employer is not required to allow other types of self-expression, there is nothing in Title VII which requires an employer to allow employees to express their cultural identity.[38]

Regarding the right of employees to speak in a language with which they were most comfortable, Judge O'Scannlain stated that the ability to make small talk is a privilege of employment, indeed a significant privilege on an assembly-line job, and that as a privilege it is up to the employer to define it. He defended Spun Steak's right to define this privilege narrowly: While employees may speak on the job, they may not necessarily speak the language of their choice. Unlike Judge Reinhardt, Judge O'Scannlain's opinion held that Spun Steak's bilingual employees can "readily comply" with the English-only rule, and therefore the rule was not impermissibly discriminatory. In Judge O'Scannlain's opinion, Title VII was not meant to protect against rules that "merely inconvenience some employees, even if the inconvenience falls regularly on a protected class."[39]

Judge O'Scannlain dismissed the employees' charge that Spun Steak's English-only policy created a hostile environment; he noted that "discriminatory practices must be *pervasive*" before the employee has a Title VII claim under this justification. He also rejected as binding EEOC's Title VII guidelines that English-only rules are on their face discriminatory, and always infect the workplace to such a degree as to amount to a hostile or abusive work environment. Rather, he held, as a matter of law, each individual workplace will be differently affected by English-only policies. Judge O'Scannlain accepted Spun Steak's English-only rule as a legitimate solution aimed at preventing "employees from intentionally using their fluency in Spanish to isolate and to intimidate members of other ethnic groups," and he found no evidence that Hispanics were being treated in a way which isolated or intimidated them. He acknowledged that his conclusion opposed EEOC's long-standing position, and stated that although he did not take such a position lightly, he did not feel bound by it either.

The employees at Spun Steak, joined by several civil rights groups, asked the Supreme Court to review this decision. They asserted that English-only rules "even if well intended . . . are often based upon stereotyped assumptions or cater to bigoted attitudes," and that Judge O'Scannlain's ruling "all but removes English-only rules from scrutiny under Title VII."[40] The Supreme Court denied review, although generally it would want to take a case where circuit courts are split, in order to resolve an issue.

The relation of language to ethnicity, and by extension to cultural diversity, was eloquently stated by Judge Steven Reinhardt in a subsequent Spun Steak case, when he said,

Language is intimately tied to national origin and cultural identity. . . . Even when an individual learns English and becomes assimilated into American society, his native language remains an important . . . means of affirming links to his original culture. English-only rules not only symbolize a rejection of the excluded language and the culture it embodies, but also a denial of that side of an individual's personality. . . . Language is the lifeblood of every ethnic group. To economically and psychologically penalize a person for practicing his native tongue is to strike at the core of ethnicity.[41]

The bilingual cases discussed above, some of which support language rights in the relatively restricted context of the school, the voting booth, the courtroom, and the workplace, address the more fundamental and broader issue of the willingness of American institutions to accept or encourage linguistic and cultural diversity. This acceptance or encouragement is opposed by current efforts to make English the official language of the United States, a view based on the belief that government support of other languages divides the nation, and that the English language is the one thing, in the face of our racial and religious differences, that holds us together as a people. It remains to be seen how each of these views will fare in the courts, which both reflect and shape attitudes in the larger society.

NOTES

1. Benedict Anderson, *Imagined Communities: Reflections on the Origin and Spread of Nationalism* (New York: Routledge, 1991).

2. Robert Burnette and John Koster, *The Road to Wounded Knee* (New York: Bantam Books, 1974).

3. James Crawford, *Hold Your Tongue: Bilingualism and the Politics of "English Only"* (Reading, MA: Addison-Wesley, 1992), 51.

4. Steven Steinberg, *The Ethnic Myth* (New York: Atheneum, 1981).

5. "The Language Is the Melting Pot," *New York Times*, September 27, 1985, A30.

6. *Guadalupe v. Tempe Elementary School*, 587 F.2d 1022, 1027 (1978).

7. Crawford, *Hold Your Tongue*, 193.

8. Ibid., 57.

9. Ibid., 184.

10. *Meyer v. Nebraska*, 262 U.S. 390 (1923).

11. The Bilingual Education Act, also known as Title VII of the Elementary and Secondary Education Act, was passed in 1968. For an excellent history of the Act, and a discussion of the ambiguity of its purposes, see Crawford, *Hold Your Tongue*, 70–83; 84–89.

12. *Keyes v. School District No. 1, Denver, Colorado*, 521 F.2d 465 (1975)].

13. Crawford, *Hold Your Tongue*, 190–91.

14. Edward M. Chen and Wade Henderson, "New 'English Only' Movement Reflects Old Fear of Immigrants," *Civil Liberties* (Summer/Fall 1986): 8.

15. Linda Chavez, *Out of the Barrio: Toward a New Politics of Hispanic Assimilation* (New York: Basic Books, 1992).

16. Crawford, *Hold Your Tongue*, 19. For a discussion of the English-Only movement in the context of human rights, see Juan Cartagena, "The English-Only Movement: Violations of the International Covenant on Economic, Social and Cultural Rights," *International Review of Contemporary Law*, U.S. edition. *Human Rights Issues in the United States: Violations of International Law* (1990), 87–103.

17. "Judge Nullifies Law Mandating Use of English," *New York Times*, February 8, 1990, A1.

18. Ibid.

19. "Latinos," *Encyclopedia of World Cultures*, Vol. 1 (Boston, MA: G. K. Hall and Co., 1991), 202.

20. *Dionisio Hernandez v. New York*, 111 S. Ct. 1859 (1991). Brief for the Mexican American Legal Defense and Educational Fund and the Commonwealth of

Puerto Rico, Department of Puerto Rican Community Affairs in the United States, as Amici Curiae in Support of Petitioner, 2.

21. Crawford, *Hold Your Tongue*, 50–75.

22. *Hernandez v. New York*, Brief for Petitioners, 8.

23. *United States ex rel. Negron v. State of New York*, 434 F.2d 386 (1970).

24. *U.S.A v. Mosquera et al*, Memorandum and Order, C.R. 92-1228; CR 93-0036, U.S. District Court, Eastern District, March 16, 1993, Judge Jack Weinstein, 13.

25. *Hernandez v. New York*, Brief for Petitioner.

26. *Hernandez v. New York*, 111 S. Ct. 1859, 1877 (1991).

27. Ibid.

28. *Code of Federal Regulations, Labor*, 1993, "Speak-English-Only Rules," 29.

29. *Alva Gutierrez v. Municipal Court of Southeast Judicial District*, 838 F.2d 1031 (9th Cir. 1988), 1063.

30. Ibid., 1043.

31. Ibid., 1045.

32. Ibid., 1049.

33. Ibid., 1051.

34. Ibid., 1050.

35. Ibid., 1054.

36. Ibid.

37. Ibid., 1056–57.

38. *Garcia et al v. Spun Steak*, 13 F.3d 296 (1993), 8.

39. Ibid., 9.

40. "Supreme Court Asks Administration for Views on 'English-Only' Work Rules," *Daily Labor Report: Leading the News* 54 (March 22, 1994), AA, 1; "Supreme Court Roundup," *New York Times*, June 21, 1994, A1.

41. *Garcia et al v. Spun Steak*.

12

Folks Like Us, Lives Like Ours: The Homeless

Homelessness has become a major social issue in the United States. While the larger category of the homeless includes a diversity of people—single men and women, families, the mentally and physically ill, working and middle-class people down on their luck, and many others—we focus here upon single men, that part of the homeless subculture which is the most visible and has given rise to many legal cases.

The figure of the transient male has permeated our culture and our history from its beginnings. One of the liberties most associated with the United States is the right to free movement and travel. This right, derived from due process liberty expressed in the Fifth and Fourteenth Amendments, is closely tied to personal autonomy and economic freedom. And yet, stable residence was an essential part of the social order in colonial America, and the early immigrants were not eager to welcome transient strangers into their midst.[1] Outsiders were considered to pose a serious threat to society and were investigated by local authorities as to their reputations and ability to earn a living. Depending on the town's need for labor, the attitude toward the poor stranger varied, although residential stability remained the primary consideration for acceptance. Colonial assemblies enacted laws, like those of New York, for "preventing Vagabonds and Idle Persons" from both coming into the colony and from travelling within it.

Defining their responsibilities narrowly, American communities held that poor strangers were not their problem; however, despite the many settlement and workhouse laws attempting to drive the stranger from their midst and to insulate themselves, "undesirable" people did come into and remain—despite sanction—within these early American towns and villages. But many who heeded the order to leave made use of the vastness of North America, variously moving from community to community or to the frontier, which was beyond the reach of settled communities and their exclusionary laws. As a result, by the first decades of the nineteenth century, settlement laws were losing force even in the East, as it became apparent that they were not only parochial but unworkable, given the increase in immigration and migration.[2]

In addition, many in the new nation of the United States had a vision of a national economy. As new lands and opportunities opened up, the free movement of labor, mainly white but also including free blacks, was a prerequisite to economic growth. In light of the individual rights delineated in the U.S. Constitution, as well as the expanding economy, settlement laws became increasingly archaic. With the development of modern transportation, including railroads and improved river travel, America was literally on the move. Expanding transportation both facilitated itinerancy and made it nearly impossible to guard community boundaries. In addition, state and federal governmental interest in trade and commerce led to restrictions on local communities prohibiting intrastate and interstate movement.

In the North, particularly, with the expansion of industrialization, a stable, cheap, docile labor supply was an increasing concern. With the growth of railroads, the economic depressions of the late nineteenth century, and increasing worker consciousness, the movement of workers seeking employment for higher wages increased. Hundreds of thousands of workers took to the road both in search of work and in protest against unfair labor practices. Local governments viewed these "worker armies" as a suspect class. Unlike colonial authorities who distinguished between what they considered the "deserving poor" and tramps and vagrants, nineteenth-century state legislators passed Tramp Acts that were applied against all those living on the road. New York State's antitramp legislation, which was typical of other state laws, held, for example, that all persons who "rove about from place to place begging, and all vagrants living without labor or visible means of support, who stroll over the country without lawful occupation, shall be held to be tramps" and subject to imprisonment at hard labor.[3]

As new towns and cities grew along the routes of the railways, a subculture of "hoboes" arose that met the labor needs of the American West. The life of a hobo required him to move frequently, take up different kinds of work, and to adapt to new places and employers and to an ever-changing world of tools and machines. In contrast to the contemporary stereotype of the homeless leading a destitute and aimless existence, these nineteenth-century hoboes were usually literate, skilled, and sophisticated in their ability to utilize a variety of opportunities for making money and finding a group among whom they could socialize.

Many cities had "hobohemias" or "jungles" where hoboes would gather when they arrived in a new town to drink, to find out about work, and exchange information about the police.[4]

Hoboes faced opposition from both local public police and private railway police. In the many small Midwestern and Western communities of America, the residents viewed the hobo as a potential criminal and parasite; as someone who shared few values of settled family life. From the hoboes' point of view, the police were "the guardian angels of organized society." Whether vigilant, as in small towns, or more lenient, as in big cities, in enforcing vagrancy laws, the police and the courts presented a major obstacle to the hoboes' way of life.

While the immediate obstacle to the individual hobo was the vigilant policeman and the criminal justice system, the economic changes that were taking place were even more significant in transforming the subculture of transient life in America. Although the Great Depression of the 1930s is associated with migrant life, by this time the era of the hobo was already passing. Many of the ranches and farms on which hoboes had worked were broken up into smaller parcels with less need for migrant labor. In addition, mining towns now had developed their own permanent labor force. With the increasing affordability of the automobile, many men on the move brought their families with them. Other economic changes awaited. With automation, many of the unskilled jobs, such as dishwashing, that hoboes had depended upon, disappeared. To an increasing extent, the tramp, hobo, and cowboy of the nineteenth century became part of the stream of homeless men of the twentieth century.

CONTEMPORARY HOMELESSNESS: CONTINUITY AND CHANGE

American images of men on the move, expressed in music, art, and literature reflect our ambivalence about the dual values of freedom and responsibility: the romance of the hero-cowboy living in male company without family only marginally attached to the larger society, and the attributes of failure, dependency, lack of self-control, unpredictability, and excessive drinking that attach to those we label tramps and derelicts, and more recently, the homeless. As America has become more urban, these men have been subject to increasing control by law enforcement.

The desire of government to control those perceived as alienated from or in opposition to dominant cultural values of docile wage labor, home and property ownership, and social mobility and respectability may be seen in the many laws passed by local communities—against vagrancy, public drunkenness, and begging—that were, and are, employed to control these "dangerous classes." Because many hoboes and tramps drank, they were particularly vulnerable to laws against public drunkenness, which were a major way that government penalized a lifestyle so much in contradiction to mainstream American values.

Although jailing men for public drunkenness does not generally rehabilitate them and, in fact, may exacerbate their drinking, public policies and court decisions have relied upon and indeed asserted that jailing of chronic alcoholics is therapeutic. In the 1968 U.S. Supreme Court case, *Powell v. Texas* (392 U.S. 514), the Court upheld state laws making public drunkenness a crime. The Court agreed with the state of Texas that jail did provide "a not insubstantial" short-term therapeutic value for chronic alcoholics. The U.S. Supreme Court, however, showed some insight into the real purposes of public intoxication laws when it said that they "represent a criminal sanction for public behavior which . . . offends the moral and aesthetic sensibilities of a large segment of the community."[5] From a social perspective, laws against public intoxication stand as a public statement of the American belief that uncontrollable drinking symbolizes a moral defect and a threatening detachment from the American values which underlie our economic and political system: achievement orientation, consumerism, willingness to submit to the discipline of wage labor, and commitment to the nuclear family.

As Justice Fortas pointed out in his dissent in *Powell*, these laws fall most heavily and unequally upon the lower classes, which raises the question, also raised by America's drug laws, of how the behaviors of certain subcultures come to be defined as illegal. As James Spradley has written, "the lives of urban nomads are surrounded by institutions which . . . [rob] them of a sense of freedom . . . these are men who . . . will always be tramps . . . is American society large enough to tolerate and even welcome such diversity? . . . Can we allow men to drink from bottles in Skid Road alleys as well as from thermos jugs in football stadiums? Sleep in fields and under bridges as well as in camp grounds and public beaches? Beg from strangers as well as friends? Become intoxicated in full public view as well as behind the walls of expensive homes?"[6] The selective enforcement of laws against public drinking, as suggested by Spradley's questions above, suggest that indeed we cannot, and do not. It is not excessive drinking but the opposition to American values that is at the heart of legal actions denying these "urban nomads" the right to be different.

LIVING IN PUBLIC SPACES

Prior to the 1960s, many hoboes and urban transients either had intermittent housing or were homeless only because they were on the move. Beginning in the late 1960s, however, the number of people labelled as homeless increased rapidly and their character changed significantly. In many cities, urban redevelopment programs claimed many of the areas that had previously housed, in single-room occupancy hotels, mission lodgings, and shantytowns, Skid Row inhabitants. With the exception of the elderly, who were not perceived as threatening, most of the men and, now, increasingly women, who had found shelter in these areas were literally on the street. Because little new, low-income public housing was built after the 1960s, these people, like an increasing number of poor people, were displaced with nowhere to go. In addition, with the decriminalization of vagrancy and public drunkenness during these years, many of the homeless men who might have been jailed were now on the street.

Two other social phenomena during this time added to the homeless population. One was the deinstitutionalization of the mentally ill which was the result of some states' policies of closing their large psychiatric facilities, combined with the lack of community halfway houses. The other was the destruction of inexpensive Single Room Occupancy (SRO) housing as real estate developers were given tax incentives to gentrify urban neighborhoods. At the same time, the rapid expansion of drug use throughout the United States both brought many other dependent people to cities and increased the numbers of urban residents who, because of addiction, drifted down the ladder of poverty and joined other populations of homeless living in public spaces.

Given the importance of a home in American society, people who live in public spaces are often seen as alien and threatening. Further, in a nation whose dominant cultural myth is that "all people can make it if they really want to and work hard," anyone who lives on the street is easily stamped as a self-made failure deserving very little sympathy. In our culture, where social status and respectability are largely expressed by home and neighborhood, people who have achieved statuses of which they are proud resist sharing their space with the homeless. It is difficult for many Americans to be sympathetic to the homeless, who must create a life for themselves under the constraints of extreme poverty and often the liabilities of drug addiction, mental illness, physical disability, or alcoholism.

In addition, partly because the facilities for washing, changing clothes, and sleeping are not available to the homeless, they must perform many private acts of personal hygiene in public. And finally, not only are the homeless not usually considered part of the community despite their presence, but in addition, the presence of mental illness or drug addiction makes them appear unpredictable and therefore dangerous. For all these reasons the demand on the part of the homeless that they have unfettered access to public space goes beyond that which many Americans today are willing to accommodate. As a result, in the cities and suburbs of America laws and regulations are being both invoked and newly created in order to restrict the use of public places by the homeless.[7]

Many of the issues about the rights of the homeless to use public space emerged dramatically in a case involving the quiet suburban town of Morristown, New Jersey in the late 1980s.[8] Richard Kreimer was a longtime resident of the town who had become homeless ten years earlier. Since that time he, like many other homeless people around the country, had made it a habit to frequent the reading room of his town's public library. The clients of the library and the librarians objected to his presence because he had the habit of staring at other patrons and because the smell of his body and clothes was offensive.

Thus, in a specific effort to keep Mr. Kreimer out of the library, the library board of trustees adopted a set of written rules that permitted library staff broad latitude to eject patrons who were not engaged "in activities associated with use of a public library"; patrons who engaged in behaviors that harassed and annoyed other individuals in the library; and patrons "whose bodily hygiene is so offensive as to constitute a nuisance to other persons."[9]

On the basis of these regulations, Kreimer had been ejected from the library by six police officers, leading Kreimer to sue the police and officials of the library and the township in federal court, claiming a violation of his First Amendment rights. In a very sympathetic opinion, issued in May of 1991, federal district court Judge H. Lee Sarokin struck down the Morristown library regulations that had been used to eject Mr. Kreimer.

First, in holding that the library regulations violated Kreimer's First Amendment right to participate in free expressive activities, Judge Sarokin noted that "[T]he public library is one of our great symbols of democracy. It is a living embodiment of the First Amendment because it includes voices of dissent. It tolerates that which is offensive . . . [and] . . . provides access to books, newspapers and magazines."[10] Stating that the library was the "quintessential" traditional public forum for the communication of ideas, Judge Sarokin argued that any government attempt to restrict access to such forums must be justified by a significant government interest and be "narrowly tailored to serve that interest, and the government must leave open alternative channels of communication." He defined the permissible purposes of the library very broadly, including that of "quiet contemplation" as well as reading. While acknowledging that "[L]ibraries cannot and should not be transformed into hotels or kitchens, even for the needy," and that library governing boards had the right and obligation to assure that the library was used for its intended purposes, Judge Sarokin was also firm in stating that such regulations must be specific, neutral, and nondiscriminatory in their enforcement.

Finding the library regulations unconstitutionally broad and vague, Judge Sarokin was also sensitive to the social-class bias raised in this case. He characterized the bodily hygiene rule as a "smell test" that was also really a "wealth" test, with a disparate impact on the poor, and particularly on the homeless Mr. Kreimer who had no access to a shower. Noting that Mr. Kreimer could not afford newspapers and books, Judge Sarokin admonished society that "[I]f we wish to shield our eyes and noses from the homeless, we should revoke their condition, not their library cards."[11]

Continuing on the subject of personal hygiene, Judge Sarokin pointed out the dangers of regulations that give wide discretion to officials. He played on Justice William O. Douglas's famous observation that the evaluation of obscenity is difficult because one man's pornography is another man's pleasure; in this conflict, Sarokin noted that "one person's hay fever is another person's ambrosia." He then went on to say that the greatness of our country lies in its tolerance of a wide diversity of people, even those whom we may find repulsive, and particularly when the "cause of our revulsion may be of our own making."[12]

Nearly a year later, a federal appeals court reversed Judge Sarokin's decision.[13] The appeals court held that the Morristown library rules *were* consistent with the nature of a library; that a library was only a *limited* public forum; and that a person with offensive bodily hygiene illegitimately interfered with other patrons' rights and could be ejected.

THE RIGHT TO PRIVACY: IS A CAVE A HOME?

"The wind may enter, the rain may enter, the sun may enter, but the King may not enter." This quote from English common law lies at the basis of one of Americans' most cherished rights, that to be free from the intrusion of government in one's home. It is the basis of the Fourth Amendment's command that people hold the right against government "to be secure in their persons, houses, papers, and effects, against unreasonable searches and seizures" without probable cause. Among the questions raised by occupation of public spaces by the homeless—on a temporary or permanent basis—is the right of the homeless to enjoy that same protection.

In 1986, in Utah, state and federal authorities, seeking to arrest Frank Ruckman, against whom there were misdemeanor charges, went to the front of a natural cave, located on federally owned land, where Ruckman was reported to be living.

Ruckman had inhabited the cave for more than six months prior to the arrival of the police. He had attempted to "enclose" the cave by constructing an entrance wall surrounding a "door." When the police found that Ruckman was not inside, they entered and searched the cave, without a warrant, and found and seized firearms located there. At this moment, Ruckman returned and was arrested. Eight days later, authorities returned to the cave, continued their search, and found additional weapons, which they also seized.[14]

When the case went to trial, both sides agreed that a central issue was whether Ruckman had a *reasonable* expectation of privacy while living in a cave on land owned by the federal government and administered by the Bureau of Land Management. In ruling against Ruckman's claim that a cave fell within the Fourth Amendment's definition of a "house" and that therefore he had every expectation of privacy, the judge held that an expectation of privacy was not reasonable when the place an individual has been living in—even for several months—is located on land from which he can legally be ejected. The majority opinion never addressed the issue of whether a cave, furnished as a home, and used for several months, could constitute a "home" for purposes of the Fourth Amendment; it also attempted to avoid a body of legal opinion which held that the Fourth Amendment protects the privacy of people, and not places.[15]

The dissenting opinion looked more closely at the question of whether the cave was Ruckman's home at the time of his arrest, and also emphasized that privacy, for purposes of the Fourth Amendment, attaches to persons as well as places. Judge McKay, in his dissent, stated his belief that Ruckman's "expectation of privacy in his wilderness home [was] both reasonable and legitimate"; he pointed out that Ruckman had taken "normal precautions to maintain his privacy" in a place that had been "his sole living quarters in every sense, furnished with a bed and other crude furniture."[16]

In a similar case, which came before the Connecticut Supreme Court in 1991, the expectations of homeless people to privacy was an even more explicit issue. Early in August 1987, David Mooney was arrested for robbery and murder based on information provided by an acquaintance (who was an accomplice hoping to plea bargain). Seeking evidence, local police went to an area under a highway bridge abutment where Mooney had been living at the time of his arrest. There they found a closed duffel bag and a closed cardboard box containing personal belongings. Although they did not have a warrant, the police searched these containers and found evidence linking Mooney to the robbery and murder for which he was arrested, and subsequently convicted.[17]

On appeal, Mooney's court-appointed lawyer argued that the trial court should have suppressed evidence seized by the police from under his highway bridge abutment home. Mooney claimed that the police had violated his Fourth Amendment rights "by invading his home without a warrant" and that the police had further violated those rights when they seized and then searched his belongings, including the closed duffel bag and cardboard box. Mooney argued that the abutment was his home:

He had been living there for one month, he was the only person living in that place, he had no other residence during this period, and when he left the area during the day, he attempted to secure all of his belongings and to place them out of public view. When first seen by the police, Mooney's home included a blanket used as a mattress, a rolled up sleeping bag, a place for trash, and several closed containers, some of which were placed upon the beams of the highway support structure which were used as shelves.

Reversing the decision of the trial court, the Connecticut Appeals Court accepted that given the special circumstances of the manner in which Mooney had attempted to establish and protect the privacy of his belongings in this "home"—by placing them in closed containers out of public view—evidence seized from these containers could not be used by the prosecution.[18] A majority of the court argued that it would be contrary to American "values and notions of custom and civility" to deny Mooney his "last shred of privacy from the prying eyes of outsiders" to permit search of his belongings without a proper legal warrant. The majority of the court made clear, however, that it was not deciding whether the Fourth Amendment protects the belongings of all homeless people regardless of specific circumstances.

Sharply disagreeing with the majority, three dissenting judges argued that as Mooney's belongings were "knowingly exposed to the public," they could be legally considered abandoned, and thus Mooney could have no reasonable expectation of privacy. These judges insisted that homeless people should not have greater privacy rights in public places—even if they considered them their homes—than members of the general public. In a telling conclusion the dissenting judge's opinion criticized the majority, accusing them of "allow[ing] the current publicity and plight of the homeless to create an empathy that in turn has created bad Fourth Amendment law."[19]

ECONOMIC RIGHTS OF THE HOMELESS

In addition to court decisions on the use of public spaces, courts have also affected the ability of the homeless to survive through adjudicating issues involving their rights to make a living. One of the very important ways that the homeless today make money is by returning bottles and cans to retail food stores to claim deposits. In 1983, the New York State legislature enacted the Returnable Container Act that required retailers to redeem bottles and cans of products carried by that store, during business hours, with no proof of purchase. This law was intended to discourage litter and to protect the environment by contributing to the state's recycling program. Under this legislation, consumers were re-

quired to pay an additional five cents on each bottle or can to encourage
the return of containers rather than their casual disposal.

In urban communities such as New York City, the Returnable Container Act had the additional consequence of providing an important
source of income for the homeless as well as other economically marginal
people. The law permitted an individual to return up to 240 cans or
bottles at any one store per day. A problem for homeless pickers is that
they must dispose of their containers in the course of a day because of
the likelihood of theft while they sleep. Thus, the refusal of many food
stores to obey the state law by accepting only 10 to 20 bottles and cans
at a time severely affected the ability of the homeless to use picking as
a source of income. In 1988 staff members of the Legal Action Center for
the Homeless in New York City began to hear stories from the homeless
that store managers were refusing to accept the 240 cans and bottles
required by the state law. Lawyers at the Center, joined by attorneys
from the prestigious local law firm of Debevoise and Plimpton, decided
to initiate a legal action to protect the economic rights of the homeless.[20]

Overcoming technical issues of standing, these lawyers, in *Conway Farmer v. D'Agostino Supermarkets,* fashioned a class action suit charging that
"the homeless relied heavily on the refunds on cans for their daily bread
and board" and that the supermarkets' refusal to accept 240 cans "constituted a special injury against the homeless."[21] On behalf of their clients
these attorneys filed for damages, civil penalties, and injunctive relief.
Lawyers for the six supermarkets cited in the litigation responded that
the law imposed an unfair burden on their clients: The stores incurred
costs of labor and processing the refunds, they had to pay rent for the
storage of empties, they received more empties than they sold, and they
claimed that distributors often "balked" at picking up the empties. In
addition, the stores received complaints from customers, both about the
unpleasant appearance and smell of the homeless and that entranceways
were clogged by homeless waiting to redeem their cans and bottles. And
of course, supermarket management would prefer that containers not be
redeemed at all so that the store could keep the five-cent deposit. In fact,
since nowhere near all redeemable containers are returned, stores do
already get to keep much of the deposit which they could use to cover
their costs in redeeming containers.[22]

In July of 1989, *Conway Farmer v. D'Agostino* was heard in New York
County Supreme Court by Judge Beverly S. Cohen, who granted a preliminary injunction that ordered the supermarkets to accept 240 cans at
a time from any one individual, as required by state law. In her opinion,
Judge Cohen wrote that she understood the reluctance of the markets to
extend themselves to help the homeless. As she noted, "there is not much
incentive to the [supermarkets] to welcome numbers of the poor and
homeless onto their premises to engage in an activity which brings no

profit" and which brings problems to them. However, she also reminded the supermarkets that "[H]ardship resulting from obeying the law" cannot be taken into account.[23]

In finding for the homeless, Judge Cohen agreed that the homeless suffered irreparable economic harm from not being permitted to redeem their full quota of containers. She noted that the economic position of the homeless is precarious, and therefore rejected the claim made by the lawyers for the supermarkets that the homeless are no different from other people who receive money from returning cans and bottles. Quoting Anatole France, that "The Law in its majestic equality forbids all men, the rich as well as the poor, to sleep under bridges, to beg in the streets and to steal bread," Judge Cohen said that to treat the homeless as the same as others, would be, "acting blindly to ignore the huge disparity in economic position between the homeless and others in our city."[24]

That the homeless are indeed different from other people is most clearly seen in the case of those men and women who beg and panhandle in public spaces. Much of the public's hostility to panhandlers grows out of their perception that panhandlers could work if they wanted to; panhandlers themselves recognize this negative perception. In their pitches and speeches, they often attempt to persuade the public that they would prefer to work rather than beg, but are unable to.[25] The reasons homeless people cannot work include mental illness, physical disability, and drug and alcohol addiction. Not all these conditions preclude the homeless needy from doing irregular simple labor, but they do prevent them from holding regular jobs, even the few unskilled jobs that remain in our society. Lacking mental clarity, time discipline, and a general physical presentation of health and cleanliness, the homeless needy are unlikely candidates for most positions.

In urban areas with large pedestrian populations and heavily used mass transit, such as New York City, beggars and panhandlers are found in great numbers. While begging has always occurred in American cities, particularly around Skid Rows, with the growth of homelessness since the 1980s, begging has increased in frequency and also spread to more affluent areas of the city and into public transit.

In the fall of 1989, the New York City Transit Authority (TA), along with the managements of other public transit operations, commenced "Operation Enforcement," a program designed to enforce a long-standing prohibition on begging and panhandling which already existed in the city's subways. Claiming that passengers waiting for trains and buses, and subway riders felt "harassed and intimidated" by panhandlers whose demands for money included "unwanted touching, detaining, impeding and intimidating," the TA distributed a million and a half pamphlets summarizing their rules including "No panhandling or begging." These rules, which were also displayed on thousands of posters throughout the subway system, warned violators that they would be subject to arrest, fines, and removal.

Soon after this enforcement campaign began, the Legal Action Center for the Homeless brought a class action suit in federal district court, on behalf of all needy homeless persons who lived in the state of New York and "would be asking or soliciting others for charity for their own benefit" in train, bus, and other places of public transport.[26] In *Young v. NYTA,* the advocates for the homeless argued that the TA prohibitions on begging, which distinguished the homeless needy soliciting for themselves from organizations soliciting for charity, were in violation of the First Amendment right to free speech. They argued that begging in and of itself was a form of political and social communication protected by the free speech clause of the First Amendment. In their view, in the present economic and political situation in New York today, begging was a vital political speech because each destitute person who begs is communicating the uncomfortable, disturbing idea of extreme poverty in the midst of staggering wealth. Pushing beggars off the subways, the lawyers for the plaintiffs claimed, cuts off one of their most effective channels of communication.[27]

Federal district court Judge Leonard B. Sand agreed that begging is communicative conduct, deserving of First Amendment protection. He referred to the testimony of the two homeless plaintiffs, William Young, Jr., and Joseph Walley, who said that their begging often led to questions from passersby interested in knowing what it was like to be homeless, and their opinions on public programs for the homeless. Young and Walley described these conversations as opportunities for them to be advocates for the homeless. In addition, Judge Sand pointed out that the "simple request for money by a beggar . . . cannot but remind the passerby that people in the city live in poverty and often lack the essentials for survival."[28] For the judge, then, begging was a form of communication that was both "unmistakably informative and persuasive" about a major public policy issue.

Because the TA ban on soliciting money specifically exempted charitable organizations, an irony arose: TA regulations permitted others to solicit money for the homeless but prevented the homeless from soliciting money for themselves. Judge Sand saw the irony and held that there could be no meaningful distinction between soliciting money for others and soliciting money for oneself; indeed, he observed, persons giving directly to a beggar know that he will use the money for himself, while those giving to a solicitor for a charitable organization do not know where their money will go.[29]

Judge Sand drew on historical examples to show that there exists no clear legal precedent in American society totally to ban begging in the fashion implemented by the TA, although begging has often been regulated by law, sometimes distinguishing between able-bodied and non-able-bodied beggars, and at other times between "accosting" and other less intrusive forms of soliciting money. Holding that transportation terminals were public forums where people were entitled to practice free speech, Judge Sand suggested that the TA needed to try to regulate begging, using traditional "time, place and manner" restrictions, rather than imposing a total ban.

The Transit Authority appealed and the federal court of appeals overturned Sand's decision.[30] Contesting Judge Sand's position that "whenever a homeless and needy person is extending his hand [to beg], he is communicating," appeals court Judge Altimari expressed the court's "grave doubt as to whether begging and panhandling in the subway are sufficiently imbued with a communicative character to justify constitutional protection." The court held that begging was more in the nature of "expressive conduct" than "pure speech" and therefore entitled to less First Amendment protection. Central to the appeal court's argument was the view that "most individuals who beg are not doing so to convey any social or political message. Rather they beg to collect money."[31] In addition, the court stated that whatever possible social or political message was intended by begging and panhandling, most passengers were unlikely to discern the message and in any case were more likely to experience a sense of threat, harassment, or intimidation than a political message.

The appeals court, far more than Judge Sand, viewed the legal questions of the case through the eyes of the users of public transportation. In upholding the "substantial government interests" of the TA regulations, Judge Altimari pointed out that "[T]he subway is not a domain of the privileged and powerful . . . [but] the primary means of transportation for literally millions of people of modest means, including hardworking men and women, students and elderly pensioners." He further stated that begging and panhandling often involve "unwanted touching [and] detaining of passengers" and implied that panhandling is often very close to extortion. Altimari noted that begging is "inherently aggressive" to passengers who are "captive" in the subway. Indeed, the judge said that whether intended or not "begging in the subway often amounts to nothing less than assault, creating in the passengers the apprehension of imminent danger, [and thus] . . . raises legitimate concerns about public safety." Based upon this reasoning, the appeals court held that the decision of the district court reflected undue deference "to the alleged individual rights of beggars and panhandlers" and "amounts to nothing less than a menace to the common good."[32]

In summary, the appeals court rejected all of the conclusions of the district court by holding that begging per se was not even "expressive conduct," that terminals were not public forums for free speech, that there was a legitimate and important distinction between individual soliciting and organizational solicitation, and that historically government has always regulated begging. Thus the appeals court judges said that while they were sympathetic to the homeless, "it is not the role of this court to resolve all the problems of the homeless" and that, on balance, the TA prohibition on begging was reasonable.

Having lost this case, lawyers from the Legal Action Center for the Homeless, again representing homeless beggars, continued their challenge of the TA's prohibition on begging with another suit in the Supreme Court of the State of New York.[33] Here they argued that the free speech and equal protection clauses of the New York State Constitution provided broader protection for the activity of begging than the U.S. Constitution. Lawyers for the homeless also contended that a New York penal law that prohibited loitering for the purpose of begging violated the due process clause of the New York State Constitution on the grounds that it was too vague.

The New York State court rejected all of these arguments in an opinion even more sweeping and damaging to the claims of the homeless than that written by the federal appeals court. Drawing on the federal appeals court opinion, New York Judge Jules Spodek, in *Walley v. NYTA* reiterated the view that begging was not "expressive conduct" because it did not present a social and political message; that the TA restriction was reasonable, content neutral (i.e., "unrelated to the suppression of free expression"), and represented a substantial government interest; and that alternative methods of communication of their message were available to beggars; and, finally, that there was a legitimate distinction between soliciting money for one's self and organizational solicitation.[34]

The decisions of the federal appeals court and the New York Supreme Court against homeless needy beggars raise a number of questions. Both courts argued strongly that because beggars are not licensed and, therefore, presumptively screened by the state, they represent an "unknown element" insofar as their character, honesty, and intention. The Altimari opinion specifically stated that "government clearly has an interest in protecting the general public from being approached for money by *potentially* disruptive or intimidating sources," and both courts saw begging as a menace to the common good. The federal appeals court had also based much of its conclusion upon passenger surveys carried out by the TA which indicated that riders felt "high levels of fear" from begging and that this discouraged their use of the subways.

Advocates for the homeless, however, pointed out that the TA's own surveys showed that in a list of important problems of the subways, most passengers ranked the presence of the homeless last, citing other problems such as dirt, crowding, and unreliability of trains as more important.[35] Also, neither court addressed the point that while many forms of constitutionally protected solicitation, such as telephone solicitation or telemarketing, may not be experienced as physically intimidating, they may be experienced as inconvenient, harassing, or psychologically intimidating. Nor did the courts address door-to-door charitable solicitation, which presents the issue of "captive" audience in a potentially dangerous way because, unlike the subway, the home is not a public place.

More puzzling is these courts' rejection of begging as expressive conduct. At a time when so many responses to public begging in America provoke the question of how an affluent society such as our own can permit its citizens to be destitute and to live on the streets, it is difficult to understand the court's conclusion that since the *intent* of begging is to solicit money, it conveys no social and political message. While it may be true that in Western tradition "[the] virtue [of giving alms] is best served [through] ordered charity," as Judge Spodek argued, this is by no means a universal cultural tradition. In many religious traditions, giving alms directly to individual beggars soliciting on their own behalf is the higher value. One might also wish to contest Judge Altimari's conclusion that charitable organizations are entitled to a higher degree of constitutional protection because they are licensed or registered and thus subject to a screening procedure which enables the Transit Authority "to guarantee to the public the legitimacy of the solicitation, [including] where the money is going and what it is used for."[36] In light of financial scandals involving United Way and television evangelists it would seem more logical to conclude that the giver has at least an equal guarantee of where her/his money is going when one gives directly to a beggar.

A RIGHT TO BE HOMELESS?

The ambivalence of American culture toward the homeless is reflected in the varied legal positions taken by state and federal courts.[37] As noted in other cases involving litigation by subcultures, an important factor in explaining legal outcomes of cases involving the homeless is the degree to which the group in question is perceived as culturally distant from the larger American society. Judges sympathetic to the claims of the homeless explicitly reject cultural distance as a reason to deny rights. Judge H. Lee Sarokin stated this most clearly when he criticized the Morristown library officials who, he said, "suffer from the . . . discriminatory assumption that poverty is a proxy for 'moral pestilence.' "[38] In calling the library's "hygiene test" an "irrational and unreasonable wealth classification with a disparate impact on the poor," Judge Sarokin laid bare another aspect of the cultural distance that unsympathetic members of the larger society perceive between themselves and the homeless.

This lack of sympathy based on cultural distance is manifest in those court opinions rejecting the claims of the homeless. For example, in upholding New York City Transit Authority regulations which banned begging and panhandling, the federal appeals panel emphasized the cultural distance factor by citing the threat, fright, and intimidation that the ordinary subway rider experiences from the homeless panhandler. As the numbers of addicted and mentally ill homeless increase, and become more visible, the cultural distance factor may be expected to weigh heavily in legal outcomes.

While the homeless have always been among us, what is new is their willingness to challenge government action which curtails their most fundamental rights, those of privacy, access to public spaces, and the right to earn a living. The increased rights' consciousness of the 1960s and the emergence of public interest law groups (for example, the New York Coalition for the Homeless and the New York Legal Action Center for the Homeless) and private pro bono legal advocacy have been critical in the ability of the homeless to claim their rights. At the same time that some of these rights are being upheld, however, all over the nation the increasing hostility by local officials and some segments of the public toward the homeless is demonstrated by the growth of local ordinances directed against the homeless or which fall unequally on them. Many of these ordinances, characterized by advocates for the homeless as "attacks" and "persecution," rely on police enforcement, and give the police wide discretion in arresting the homeless, "moving them along," confiscating their personal property, and destroying their makeshift shelters.[39]

Advocates for the homeless charge that the "knee jerk response of criminalizing the symptoms of homelessness" are both inhumane and ineffective. While successful litigation reminds the public that homeless people have rights, it is costly and ultimately not the answer to the problem of homelessness. Law, then, may not be the solution to the problem of homelessness. Rather, the question may be one of tolerance and more humane treatment. James Spradley, in his study of "urban nomads" in Seattle, reminds us that there are men who will always be tramps and transients. He asks, "Is American society large enough to tolerate and even welcome such diversity?"[40] The public drunk, the homeless man, the tramp, the person who begs in public, is viewed by others as someone who has, by his lifestyle, rejected dominant cultural values. The willingness of the public to understand the problem of homelessness and to attack its root causes rather than attacking the homeless themselves is ultimately a choice of whether we are willing to reconstruct our society as one in which a conception of humanity could include people whose lives are very different from our own.

NOTES

1. David J. Rothman, *The Discovery of the Asylum: Social Order and Disorder in the New Republic* (Boston, MA: Little, Brown, 1971).

2. Ibid., 172.

3. Sidney L. Harring, "Class Conflict and the Suppression of Tramps in Buffalo, 1892-1884," *Law and Society Review* 11 (Summer 1977).

4. Nels Anderson, *The Hobo: The Sociology of the Homeless Man* (Chicago: University of Chicago Press, 1923; 1965).

5. *Powell v. Texas,* 392 U.S. 514, 538–39.

6. James P. Spradley, *You Owe Yourself a Drunk: An Ethnography of Urban Nomads* (Boston, MA: Little, Brown, 1970), 261–62.

7. *The Right to Remain Nowhere: A Report on Anti-Homeless Laws and Litigation in 16 United States Cities* (Washington, DC: National Law Center on Homelessness & Poverty, December 1993).

8. Robert Hanley, "Suing, A Homeless Man Refuses to Yield," *New York Times,* October 10, 1991, B1; Robert Hanley, "Homeless Man Has Deal in 2nd Suit in Morristown," *New York Times,* March 3, 1992, B7; Robert Hanley, "Library Wins in Homeless Man Case," *New York Times,* March 26, 1992, B8.

9. *Kreimer v. Bureau of Police for Town of Morristown,* 765 F. Supp. 181 (D.J.N. 1991), 184.

10. Ibid., 182.

11. Ibid., 183.

12. Ibid.

13. *Joint Free Public Library of Morristown and Morristown Township v. Kreimer,* 958 F.2d 1242 (1992).

14. "A Homeless Person's Cave Is His or Her Castle," *New York Times,* December 4, 1990, A30.

15. *United States v. Ruckman,* 806 F.2d 1471 (10th Cir. 1986).

16. Ibid., 1478.

17. Kirk Johnson, "Property of a Homeless Man Is Private, Hartford Court Says," *New York Times,* March 19, 1991, B1.

18. *State of Connecticut v. Mooney,* 218 Conn. 85 (1991).

19. Ibid., 143–44.

20. *Conway Farmer et al v. D'Agostino Supermarkets, Inc., et al,* Supreme Court: New York County, IAS Part 31, Index No. 11170/89, Opinion, Beverly S. Cohen, Judge, July 20, 1989.

21. Ibid., Opinion, 7.

22. Ibid., Opinion, 11.

23. Ibid., Opinion, 13, 14.

24. Ibid., Opinion, 7.

25. Brackette F. Williams, "Homework on Homelessness and Begging in Two U.S. Cities," *Current Anthropology* 36(1) (February 1995): 25–51.

26. *Young v. New York City Transit Authority,* 729 Supp. 341 (S.D.N.Y., 1990).

27. Douglas H. Lasdon, Patrick Horvath, and Geoffrey Potter, "What Homeless Beggars Must Keep Telling Us," *New York Times,* February 11, 1990.

28. *Young v. NYTA* (1990), 352.

29. Ibid.

30. *Young v. NYTA*, 903 F.2d 146 (2nd Cir. 1990).

31. *Young v. NYTA* (1990), 153.

32. Ibid., 149, 156, 158.

33. *Walley v. NYTA*, Sup. Ct. State of NY, Kings County, Decision, Index No. 177/91, June 3, 1991. Opinion, Judge Jules L. Spodek.

34. *Walley v. NYTA* (1991), 13.

35. Lasdon, Horvath, and Potter, "What Homeless Beggars Must Keep Telling Us."

36. *Young v. NYTA* (1990), 156.

37. *The Right to Remain Nowhere*, 18.

38. *Kreimer v. Morristown* (1991), 196.

39. *The Right to Remain Nowhere*, 5.

40. Spradley, *Urban Nomads*, 261.

13

Courts and Culture

Law, it has been said, is our national religion, lawyers the priesthood, and courtrooms the cathedral where our contemporary passion plays are enacted.[1] Although courts are not the only place where cultural performances take place, they are surely among the most important. Courts are also, as we have seen, a central arena for negotiating between dominant cultural values and those of subcultures. American law, however (and the English law on which it is largely based), does not formally take culture into account. Indeed, for the most part, American courts assume a cultural homogeneity for purposes of applying one standard of the law to everyone.[2] Since the 1970s, however, with increased immigration from nations culturally very different than our own, courts are paying more attention to cultural diversity. Focusing on the issue of the cultural defense, a national debate has emerged over the degree to which American law can and should be modified to take into account foreign cultural practices.

THE CULTURAL DEFENSE

A cultural defense holds that persons socialized in a minority or foreign culture, who regularly conduct themselves in accordance with their own culture's norms, should not be held fully accountable for conduct that violates official United States law, if those individuals' conduct conforms to the prescriptions of their own culture. The intention of a cultural defense in a criminal case is to negate or mitigate criminal responsibility where acts are committed under a reasonable, good-faith belief in their propriety, based upon the actor's cultural heritage or tradition.[3]

Because the American legal system is based on a view of the individual as having an ability to reason and to understand the law, a cultural defense is incompatible with our most basic legal values. American law does recognize mitigation, but addresses the gap between legal fault and moral fault in ways consistent with our own central cultural value of individual responsibility. American courts formally recognize different degrees of moral culpability in considering intention, knowledge, recklessness, and negligence. Consistent with the American value of individualized justice, various defenses involving diminished mental capacity, such as the insanity defense, and more recently the "battered wife" defense have been officially recognized by American courts.

Both English and American courts reject the official use of the cultural defense. In England, in the 1836 case of *Rex v. Esop*, in which a native of Baghdad was convicted of committing an "unnatural offense" which was not a crime in his native land, the judges ruled that "custom had to be subordinated to the law of the land." In 1851, in the United States, then Secretary of State Daniel Webster affirmed this position by stating that "Every foreigner born residing in a country owest to that country allegiance and obedience to its laws so long as he remains in it, as a duty upon him by the mere fact of his residence, and . . . is as much bound to obey its laws as native subjects or citizens. This is the universal understanding in all civilized States, and nowhere a more established doctrine than in this country."[4]

At the heart of the official rejection of the cultural defense by American courts is the degree to which American law can take into account the concept of culture. On this critical point, law and social science are in fundamental disagreement. The social science view embeds the individual in culture and assumes that culture and its institutions are powerful forces, not only shaping individuals and limiting their choices, but defining their rationality as well. Social science assumes that culture and the institutions of socialization—class, family, schools, religion—play a preeminent part in "determining" (or at the very least influencing, conditioning, shaping, or channelling) personality, values, and behavior. This position is the basis of the cultural defense: Even if an individual is aware of the conflict between their own, culturally appropriate behavior and American law, the power of their cultural background is so strong that it overcomes the knowledge that their act is a criminal offense in the United States.[5]

Depending, then, on a deterministic notion of culture, the cultural defense conflicts with the Western legal assumption that all persons are free to make and act upon decisions, limited only by physical coercion or extremes of mental duress. It is on this basis that Western law assigns criminal responsibility to the individual. For the law to recognize that culture and social structures may limit free will, or render individuals not fully responsible for their actions, as a cultural defense contends, would bring the law dangerously close to an admission that culture is always coercive, and that the free will upon which the legal system is based is illusory. By not (formally) acknowledging the coercive powers of social class, culture, and socialization, courts can preserve the legal fiction that individuals generally act by free choice.

Yet American courts, while generally having been hostile to the cultural defense mounted as an independent, substantive defense in criminal trials, do sometimes use cultural evidence as relevant in explaining the state of mind underlying the criminal actions taken by a person from a foreign culture in reducing charges, and thus in mitigating the severity of sentences. A cultural defense in a homicide case might, for example, claim that because of extreme provocation as experienced by a person from a particular foreign culture, a defendant was unable to form the degree of intent necessary to convict for murder. Cultural evidence would be presented here to reduce a murder charge to manslaughter. The cultural issue involved, as we will see in some of the cases below, is that both the nature of extreme provocation and sanctioned responses to extreme provocation differ among cultures. In other cases, however, a temporary insanity defense may be chosen over the cultural defense. Here, the cultural beliefs and practices of another society which compelled the accused to commit a crime would be considered delusional, such as, for example, a belief in witchcraft. This becomes problematical, however, as it is not only inaccurate, but ethnocentric. As the following cases indicate, cultural evidence has been used in a wide variety of ways, with variable results. As understanding of the role of culture in shaping behavior becomes more widespread, and as our nation becomes more culturally diverse, dispensing justice without taking culture explicitly into account may become more difficult for American courts.

Because the disciplining of children varies among cultures, cultural defenses have been raised in some cases involving charges of child abuse. In 1985, in Fairbanks, Alaska, an Inupiaq Inuit (Eskimo), Jack Jones, who had moved to Fairbanks several years previously from an isolated region in northwest Alaska, was arrested on charges that he had molested three young boys. The charges involved Mr. Jones's behavior at a birthday party, where he roughhoused with a twelve-year-old white child, coming at him "like a bear," according to the child's testimony. During the horseplay, Jones also swatted at the boy's crotch area and tried to pull down his pants. Feeling threatened, the boy told his father, who made a complaint to the Alaska state troopers.

The defense for Mr. Jones called several Inuit men from remote villages who testified that this kind of horseplay between an older man and a prepubescent boy was common in traditional Inuit culture, though the custom was now declining. Anthropologists testified that the conduct was part of traditional Inuit teasing behavior designed to teach young boys to "laugh off adversity, protect themselves from attack and respond quickly" and that this "ritual" could also be a mark of affection and attention for a favorite child, particularly one with the same name as an ancestor. The child's name, Paul, was also the name of Mr. Jones's father. The defense also noted that Mr. Jones's interrogation after his arrest was conducted through an interpreter and that Jones's attempt to explain what he was doing "lost something in translation." Mr. Jones was acquitted. The judge found, based on the cultural evidence, that his behavior was within the bounds of traditional Inuit culture and did not have an erotic intent.[6]

In another child abuse case, in New York, a Nigerian man was charged with administering excessive corporal punishment to his seven-year-old son, by striking the child repeatedly with his hands, a belt, and his feet, in the presence of the assistant principal of his child's school, after being summoned to discuss the child's poor performance and misbehavior in school. The principal reported the incident to the Bureau of Child Welfare and the case came to Family Court. The respondent denied kicking his child, but defended striking him on the basis that in Nigeria, if a child misbehaves in school and thus causes shame to the family, the parent has the duty to immediately punish him in any manner he sees fit. The father also claimed that his son, by looking the assistant principal directly in the eyes during the discussion, was showing disrespect and that this, too, required harsh discipline. In his opinion, the judge acknowledged cultural differences in solving problems, but stated that "the court has the obligation to apply the law equally to all men," and found the respondent guilty of excessive corporal punishment. Although expressing sympathy with the respondent's motives, and noting that "in a society as culturally amorphous as our[s], it is incumbent upon all members of society to be tolerant and understanding of customs that differ from their own," the judge found the respondent's discipline was so excessively harsh that motive could not mitigate his decision.[7]

In homicide cases, cultural factors may be introduced as evidence of diminished capacity as a result of extreme emotional disturbance, for example, the extreme rage experienced by men from some cultures who react violently to perceived threats or attacks on their honor. Some of these cases involve Latino men who have immigrated to the United States and who remain immersed in their ethnic communities where a cultural focus on male honor remains central.[8] In a homicide involving an immigrant from the Dominican Republic, cultural evidence was introduced by an anthropologist as a key to understanding the defendant's rage upon being repeatedly ejected from a bar by a bouncer hurling racial insults.

The anthropologist emphasized that Dominican society is relatively "color-blind" and social acceptability across the color line is the norm. Thus, most Dominican adults build up little emotional protection against racial insults. The defendant expressed strong resentment about racial discrimination in the United States, and attributed his being ejected from the bar, which had a largely white clientele, to his color. His rage at being so disrespectfully treated was exacerbated because he held a steady job, an important indicator of success among Dominican immigrants. In rural Dominican society there are few material resources, and *respeto*, or civil behavior among men is a core value. A *falta de respeto* (or uncivil behavior) strikes at the very core of the Dominican male's sense of self-worth and manliness and is perceived as an extreme, insulting provocation. The anthropologist testified that, contrary to popular American stereotypes which associate Latinos with violent behavior, Latino culture actually trains individuals to avoid violence by repressing insults and by using reason. When the bouncer ignored the defendant's attempts to reason with him, the cultural factors converged so that the defendant was overcome by rage and no longer in control of himself when he fired the fatal shot.

Another case of homicide in which cultural factors were central involved Fumito Kimura, a Japanese immigrant residing in the United States for about 16 years, charged with the murder of her two children. On January 29, 1985, Kimura took her six-month-old daughter, Yuri, and four-year-old son, Kazutaka, on a long bus ride from their suburban Los Angeles home to the Santa Monica beach. At the beach, Mrs. Kimura carried her daughter and walked her son into the ocean, where the water was soon over their heads. Passersby rescued Mrs. Kimura, but her two children drowned. She was charged with two counts of first degree murder and two counts of felony child endangerment and because the crime was a double homicide, she faced the death penalty.[9]

Mrs. Kimura explained her action by reference to the Japanese custom of *oyako-shinju* or "parent-child" suicide, an act that is criminal in Japan, but is a not uncommon way of dealing with some intolerable situations, specifically, the shame of a failed marriage. Mrs. Kimura said that she had recently discovered that her husband had been keeping a mistress, who had contacted Mrs. Kimura, giving her the details of her husband's infidelities. Mrs. Kimura was greatly distressed at this shame brought on the family and blamed herself as a bad wife and mother. In response, she attempted to commit oyako-shinju.

The cultural logic underlying oyako-shinju is that a "child is not an individual human being but a family member, that the child is the parent's possession, and that it is more merciful to kill children than to leave them in the cruel world without parental protection. The mother who commits suicide without taking her child with her is blamed as a demon-like person."[10] In Japan, because of the "inseparability between mother

and child" and in Mrs. Kimura's circumstances, oyako-shinju is a traditional and culturally acceptable response. Generally treated as involuntary manslaughter in Japan, oyako-shinju would probably be
punished by a suspended sentence with probation and supervised rehabilitation.[11]

The Japanese community in Los Angeles rallied to Mrs. Kimura's support; over 25,000 persons from the Los Angeles Japanese American community and other parts of the United States, Japan, and Europe signed
a petition to the Los Angeles district attorney requesting leniency for
Mrs. Kimura. The petition first noted the high respect Japanese culture
has for authority and for obedience to the law, as evidenced by the low
crime rate among Japanese Americans. It then asked that modern Japanese legal standards (a charge of involuntary manslaughter and its appropriate punishment) be applied to Mrs. Kimura because "the roots of
her Japanese culture" directed her actions, which were "totally without
malice and without intent to do harm to her children whom she deeply
loved."[12]

The district attorney refused this request, citing United States legal
precedent that a crime cannot be mitigated by legal or cultural standards
from another country. She indicated, however, that Mrs. Kimura's cultural background, as well as her isolation within the Japanese community, could be taken into account in determining her mental state at the
time of the incident. Indeed, Mrs. Kimura's attorney also rejected the
"cultural defense," because, if Mrs. Kimura were following Japanese custom, it would mean that she did indeed, intend to kill her children, a
view which would have supported a first degree murder conviction.
Rather, her defense pleaded temporary insanity, relying on psychiatric
testimony that Mrs. Kimura was "ill" and "mentally deranged" and
therefore lacked the intent necessary for first degree murder because the
element of malice was absent. In drawing upon the California legal code,
which refers to "mental condition and cultural background" as factors
which prevent a defendant from perceiving his or her actions as illegal,
the defense succeeded in reducing the charge against Mrs. Kimura to
voluntary manslaughter. She received a sentence of one year in the
county jail (with credit for time already served), five years' probation,
and intensive psychiatric treatment.

THE CULTURAL DEFENSE AND VIOLENCE AGAINST WOMEN

In the case of *People v. Moua* (1985), cultural evidence also played a
central role.[13] Kong Moua was a Hmong immigrant from the isolated
mountain areas of Laos; their traditional rural economy was based on
slash-and-burn horticulture, hunting and fishing, and opium production.

Hmong have patrilineal clans, and male elders adjudicate disputes, a cultural practice they continue in the United States.

Many Hmong worked for the Central Intelligence Agency during the American war in Vietnam, fighting Vietnamese and Laotian communists; after 1980, in fear of retribution against them when the Americans left Vietnam, approximately 30,000 Hmong found refuge in California, where they generally keep themselves within the immigrant community. Most of the Hmong immigrants were illiterate, did not speak English, were terrified of the police, lacked any knowledge of American law, and continued cultural practices such as polygamy, child-marriage, and opium production, that are illegal in the United States.

A traditional Hmong marriage practice is called *zij poj niam*, which is actually similar to elopement, though it is translated into English as "marriage by capture." Zij poj niam begins with a ritualized flirtation to which a woman acquiesces by giving the man some token item. The man then takes the woman to his family's home to consummate the union. To demonstrate her virtue, the woman must ritually protest this by saying, "No, no, I'm not ready," and by weeping and moaning. To demonstrate his masculinity, the man must ignore these protests and firmly lead the woman to the bedroom where they consummate the marriage. Thereafter, the woman is considered unmarriageable by other Hmong men. If the woman does not protest sufficiently she is considered unchaste, and if the man does not assert himself, he is considered weak.

In this case, Kong Moua followed Hmong custom, claiming that both he and his "wife," Xeng Xiong, who was an "Americanized" 19-year-old working in a local college, had observed the traditional ritual by flirting and exchanging tokens of affection.[14] Kong Moua claimed that he sincerely believed that Xeng Xiong wanted to marry him, but Xeng Xiong's parents called the police and filed rape and kidnapping charges against him. Because a conviction for rape requires intent, and a defendant who reasonably and honestly believes that the female's lack of resistance communicated her consent can be acquitted, the prosecutor and judge had to determine whether Moua was in fact sincere, and whether the woman's protests were authentic or merely ritualistic. Based on anthropological literature documenting Hmong marital customs as well as interviews with Moua and Xiong introduced in the pretrial negotiations, the judge and prosecutor decided that Moua was sincere, but also that Xiong had not consented. After conferring with Hmong clan elders, Moua was allowed to plead guilty to a lesser charge of false imprisonment, sentenced to 120 days in jail and fined $1,200, of which $900 went to Xiong's parents as reparations.[15]

Where the cultural defense has involved spousal homicide following accusations of infidelity, courts have acted inconsistently. In one case, occurring in 1982 in New York, a Laotian man murdered his wife, claiming that the "shame" brought on by her alleged relationship with another man drove him into "extreme emotional stress." The trial judge refused to permit cultural evidence regarding the stress and disorientation encountered by Laotian refugees in attempting to assimilate into American culture before the jury, and the defendant, who was convicted of second degree murder, was sentenced to 15 years to life at Attica.[16] The defendant appealed and the New York Court of Appeals ruled in his favor, stating that the cultural evidence regarding the shame brought on the defendant and his family by his wife's display of affection for another man was relevant in that it was sufficient to trigger the defendant's loss of control.[17]

Cultural evidence influenced the outcome of another Hmong case in 1985.[18] Tou Moua, a Hmong man, admitted killing his Hmong wife after reportedly learning from an acquaintance, in an all-day drinking bout, that this man had had sexual relations with Tou's wife. Tou stormed home and confronted his wife who reportedly admitted some of his allegations. Enraged, Tou shot his wife dead. During the trial, expert testimony was introduced maintaining that according to Hmong culture, a wife's adultery is punishable by death and the husband must be the executioner. The defense argued that since Tou had acted properly according to his own culture's norms, he should not receive more than a probationary sentence. The prosecution, however, in asking for a maximum sentence of 13 years for voluntary manslaughter, countered that Hmong culture does not require a man to kill his adulterous wife; he can also send her home to her parents in disgrace. In what appeared to all concerned as a compassionate compromise, the judge sentenced Tou to eight years. Indeed, had the couple not been Hmong, the prosecution would probably have brought a first degree murder charge.

A similar case, *New York v. Chen*, received wide national criticism, with particular censure of the Court's decision from the Chinese American community.[19] On the morning of September 7, 1987, Dong Lu Chen, a recent immigrant from Hong Kong, originally from the People's Republic of China, had an argument with his wife of 23 years, Jian Wan Chen, in their Brooklyn apartment. Mr. Chen suspected his wife of an affair and just prior to the murder, he said, Mrs. Chen refused to sleep with him, reportedly saying that "this need was being taken care of elsewhere." Chen took this to mean that his wife admitted having an affair. He became so enraged that he went from the bedroom, where they were arguing, into the living room, picked up a claw hammer lying in a corner, returned to the bedroom and struck his wife eight times on the head, which resulted in her death. The couple's son entered the apartment just after the killing and called the police. As Mr. Chen spoke only Toishan, a Cantonese dialect, a Chinese translator met Chen and the police officers at the station house. Chen had admitted the killing to his son, and did so again, speaking through the interpreter on a video tape at the police station.

Mr. Chen had been in the United States for a little more than a year prior to the killing, employed most recently as a dishwasher in Maryland where he lived much of the time while his wife and two teenaged children remained in New York City. Chen lived in a Chinese-speaking community and appeared to have known little beyond its cultural walls. There was also some suggestion in his records of a learning disability. As far as could be ascertained, Mr. Chen had no history of criminal behavior in China and had not previously been in any trouble in the United States. Because Chen had been unable to raise bail he had remained at Rikers Island for about one and one-half years after his arrest.

Mr. Chen's court-appointed lawyer mounted a cultural defense, drawing on the expertise of an anthropologist whose specialty was Taiwanese and Chinese culture. The anthropologist testified that Chen felt enormous humiliation and shame at the thought of his wife's (alleged) adultery, a condition that made him subject to, at minimum, extreme emotional distress. The anthropologist also testified that the shame and dishonor which falls upon a man if his wife's infidelity becomes known within the Chinese community is so great that he could not hope to marry again if he divorced his wife. This shame, combined with the absence of a community that in China would have offered intervention and prevented the killing, led to Chen's attack on his wife. Repeatedly, the anthropological expert sought to explain to the presiding judge the great extent to which Mr. Chen's actions were dictated by cultural factors so deeply ingrained in him that Chen could not—as an individual—resist them. Chen's lawyer argued that the overwhelming sense of shame and humiliation brought on by his wife's adultery had put Mr. Chen into a frame of mind where he was no longer in control of his actions. The defense stressed Chen's social isolation from the larger American community which resulted from his inability to speak or understand English and from his very short residence in the United States.

Judge Edward Pincus was persuaded by the cultural defense. He ruled that because Chen "took all his Chinese culture with him to the United States, he was not entirely responsible for his actions . . . he was the product of his culture." Although Pincus stated that "The culture was never an excuse," he went on to say that "it [was] something that made [Chen] crack more easily."[20] No relatives of the victim, other than the couple's children, testified in court. Judge Pincus found Chen guilty of second degree manslaughter (the prosecutor had originally planned a charge of second degree murder) and sentenced him to five years' probation, less time already served, and mandated psychiatric help. Judge Pincus defended his light sentence by noting that Chen's children and other relatives in New York offered Chen a home with them, and promised to

take care of him. In addition, Judge Pincus noted that during the one
and one-half years Chen had already served in jail he had been greatly
harassed because he did not speak English, and that his chances for
rehabilitation in prison seemed nonexistent.[21]

Chen's sentence was strongly protested by women's groups, Asian
American groups, the district attorney's office, legal scholars, and the
press.[22] On hearing the sentence, then Brooklyn District Attorney Elizabeth Holtzman was "enraged," arguing that "anyone who comes to this
country must be prepared to live by and obey the laws of this country.
There should be one standard of justice, not one that depends on the
cultural background of the defendant," Holtzman said. "There may be
barbaric customs in various parts of the world, but that cannot excuse
criminal conduct here."[23]

Women's groups viewed Chen's sentence as "declar[ing] open season
on women," and two Asian groups in New York, the Committee Against
Anti-Asian Violence and the Organization of Asian Women, joined the
National Organization for Women's New York City chapter in filing a
complaint with the state Commission on Judicial Conduct.[24] The Committee Against Anti-Asian Violence said that this case "sends a simple
and dangerous message: Asian women may not be protected under
American law from domestic violence, even unto death."[25] The over-
whelmingly negative reactions to Judge Pincus's decision in the Chen
case raised the question of whether, under the guise of cultural sensitivity, judges are only masking a willingness to undervalue the life of a
woman who has committed, or who was believed to have committed,
adultery.

Experts in Chinese law also criticized Pincus's decision for relying too
heavily on inaccurate anthropological data, claiming that Chinese law
today very specifically condemns domestic violence, and that the Chinese government is making great efforts to reverse the past cultural acceptance of wife abuse. Indeed, this group of scholars pointed out that
any number of equally expert witnesses in Chinese culture could have
been brought forth to contradict the defense witnesses and that, in spite
of her outrage with the decision, it was the weakness of the prosecutor's
office to challenge this cultural testimony that was significantly responsible for its outcome. Asian groups were also concerned that the acceptance of the cultural defense in this case, based on faulty evidence, cast
a shadow over Chinese culture.[26]

The connections between culturally rooted concepts of honor, shame,
patriarchy, the treatment of women as property, and gender violence
pose a dilemma for American courts, which find themselves having to
mediate the contradictions between serving justice in a culturally diverse
society and adhering to the requirements of a single standard of law.
Cultural sensitivity is reasonable, and even necessary, in a multicultural

society like our own, and yet these sensitivities are sometimes clearly at odds with other powerful necessities, for example, the need to protect women from violence.

The conflict experienced in American courts as they try to steer a course between respecting cultural differences and protecting women's rights has international legal dimensions. The United Nations Universal Declaration of Human Rights proclaims that all humans have equal and inalienable rights to liberty, dignity, and the security of their persons. It explicitly includes the protection of women against gender-specific violence, however contrary this may be to local cultural custom and even law. Can American courts, facing the same issue, do less?

In the conflict between respecting custom and protecting women against violence that emerges when the cultural defense is raised, courts are reexamining the relation between patriarchy and gender violence. In Brazil, for example, judges have recently criticized the "privileged homicide" defense, which claimed that a husband who killed an allegedly adulterous wife was legitimately protecting customary morality and social life. In such cases, where the male defendant claimed that his honor was so impugned by the alleged infidelity that he could not control himself, juries, particularly in the interior of the country, frequently acquitted. Only recently has the Brazilian Supreme Court reversed such a jury acquittal (upheld by an appeals court). The majority opinion, characterized as "outlawing" the "honor killing of wives," held that "Homicide cannot be seen as a normal and legitimate way of reacting to adultery. ... Because in this kind of crime what is defended is not honor, but vanity, exaggerated self-importance and the pride of the lord who sees a woman as his personal property."[27] This statement can well serve courts in the United States as they try to steer a course between respect for cultural differences and the protection of women's rights and lives.

The conflict between universal women's rights and cultural values is also at the center of a debate over the appropriate legal responses to the various African cultural practices of female circumcision, which as a result of increasing immigration from Africa, are now occurring in the United States and England.[28] In the United States, the wide publicity given to these practices, partly as the result of a deportation case, resulted in legislation being proposed (but not yet voted on) to outlaw all forms of genital mutilation; in England, these practices are illegal.

In February 1994, in Portland, Oregon, deportation proceedings were held in the case of a Nigerian citizen, Lydia Omowunmi Oluloro, who was an illegal resident in the United States. Ms. Oluloro, who had two daughters, sought asylum in the United States, because she claimed that if she were to return to Nigeria with her two daughters, they would be forcibly circumcised, as she had been as a child, and that her opposition and resistance to this cultural practice for her daughters would result in ostracism, abuse, or even jailing. Evidence on the issue of female genital mutilation was central in this case. In her first deportation hearing, the immigration judge recognized the potential dilemma raised by the conflict between universal human rights and specific cultural practices: "Initially, with all due respect to foreign cultures, the Court agrees [with the respondent] that the custom of Female Genital Mutilation is reprehensible, unfair, and disgusting, notwithstanding its long history and numerous faithful adherents. While uncritical multiculturalists might argue that it is improper to pass judgment on long-established mores and customs of other cultures, this Court will note that torture and other forms of barbarity, . . . are traditional in many cultures today, and cannot be condoned."[29] He nevertheless turned down her request for asylum. In a second hearing, where the same issue was central to her defense, the immigration judge found in her favor. He noted that "although this court attempts to respect the traditions and cultures of other societies, as to this practice [female genital mutilation], the court concludes that it is cruel and serves no known medical purpose. While it could possibly have had some purpose in ancient cultures, whatever the utility the practice might ever have had, it no longer exists." He concluded that the forcible circumcision of Ms. Oluloro's daughters was likely if she returned to Nigeria and that this constituted a sufficiently "extreme hardship" to permit her to remain in the United States.[30]

The cultural issues raised in these cases bring up important questions about the role of law in mediating the clash of values in a culturally heterogenous society such as our own, particularly where this involves immigrants who may be only partially acculturated. Treating a group more leniently under the law because they are immigrants has been, in principle, unacceptable in the United States, accounting for the rejection of the cultural defense by courts. Yet alternatives to the substantive cultural defense are also problematic. As in the Kimura case, an action that is comprehensible and unavoidable from a subjective (i.e., the defendant's) point of view, is transformed into "irrationality" in a defense of "temporary insanity." In choosing to use the insanity defense in the Kimura case, the Japanese cultural belief that children are not independent, autonomous beings, but an extension of the parent's self, was transformed into a pathological mental state of "introjection," which psychiatrists determined prevented Kimura from distinguishing between her own life and those of her children.[31]

The current debates over the cultural defense grow out of the increasingly multicultural nature of our society and ambivalence over the issue of local cultural autonomy in nation-states that were posed in the introduction to this study. Those favoring a cultural defense argue that one standard of justice is too rigid to accommodate the experiences of people socialized under different culturally based moralities than those embedded in American law. They argue further that one "monolithic" standard of justice not only betrays America's commitment to individualized justice (that is, tailoring the punishment to the degree of personal culpability) but is unworkable in a culturally pluralistic society like our own.[32]

Furthermore, while ignorance of the law is generally not an acceptable defense in the United States, it may be more valid in the case of new immigrants particularly, who are unlikely to have had the same opportunity to absorb the norms underlying our criminal laws as persons brought up in this country. Rejection of the cultural defense may also send an unacceptable message of cultural inferiority to ethnic groups, and purvey the view that "an ethnic group must trade in its cultural values for that of the mainstream if it is to be accepted as an equal by the majority." Indeed, proponents argue that acceptance of the cultural defense, in expressing respect for other cultures, will enhance the immigrant's view of the legitimacy of the American legal system, and thus promote conformity to it.

Those advocating that a cultural defense be given the same legitimacy as the insanity defense, or the more recently accepted "battered wife" defense, note that its discretionary acceptance could be based on a number of factors, including whether the crime is victimless, whether the victims voluntarily participated in the act, whether the crime is likely to be repeated, the seriousness of the crime; whether it affects society as a whole or only the immigrant, culturally relevant group; and the size of the affected group. Advocates for the cultural defense claim that exempting a small cultural minority from a monolithically imposed law would pose little threat to the social order.[33]

Those who reject the substantive cultural defense argue that a major function of the law is to lay down a common set of values necessary to maintaining social order, and a body of positive law that compels the obedience of all regardless of individual notions of morality.[34] Only a unitary cultural standard enacted in law can act as an effective deterrent against criminal behavior. Critics claim that even if many of the cultural defense cases involve extraordinary circumstances which are unlikely to be repeated, courts nevertheless send out messages in their treatment of such cases, as for example, in the Chen case. If courts hold an individual socialized in another culture responsible for a crime under American law, this may indeed have an educational value in bringing conflicts between immigrant cultural practices and American law to the attention of the immigrant community and diffusing knowledge of which the group was otherwise ignorant.

Rejection of the cultural defense has a history in the United States, in the century-old American legal distinction between belief and action, articulated in the Mormon cases.[35] There the courts held that while we can acknowledge the existence of culturally different value systems, this recognition does not force us to relinquish our own standards for judging action. Even where an action is accepted as an integral part of a culturally based belief system (and this cannot be assumed, but must be established), courts cannot be receptive to cultural defenses which undermine the legitimacy of the law.

Fundamental to the "glue" which holds all societies together is the control and sanctioning of the behavior of its citizens. Thus, the debate over the cultural defense is not only about a substantive issue, but also about how far the United States can go in testing the limits of its social institutions. Those who see increasing multiculturalism as a threat to our nationhood stand firm against the cultural defense. For others, the basic strength of our nation, and the Constitution, are sufficiently strong bulwarks against the slight threats to national disintegration that might be posed by opening up our criminal justice system to the acceptance, in some special cases, of the cultural defense.

COURTS, CULTURE, AND ALTERNATIVE CONFLICT RESOLUTION STRATEGIES

> Avenge not yourselves . . . for it is written, vengeance is mine, I will repay, sayeth the Lord.[36]

This book has explored the role of courts as they have functioned to negotiate between dominant cultural values and those of subcultures. It is impossible, however, to understand the relationship between subcultures and law, without also looking at processes outside formal law which are simultaneously at work in relating subcultures to the larger society. A too rigidly legal centralist perspective tends to dismiss both historical and contemporary evidence that alternatives to courts and law as means of dispute resolution have always been part of the "landscape of disputing" in the United States.

In colonial America, "[L]itigation was perceived as a form of self-aggrandizement contrary to the best interests of the community. It was . . . un-Christian . . . law . . . a heart without affection, a mind without passion."[37] Coming together as a religious community, inhabitants of the colonial villages were expected to meet face-to-face in front of the entire congregation, "a process designed to reassert harmony and consensus . . . the purpose of individual participation was to encourage a collective congregational judgment, which would isolate offenders, restore them to congregational fellowship, and thereby strengthen communal values."[38]

The changing nature of American society in the course of the eighteenth and the nineteenth centuries led to an expansion of formal mechanisms of social control and dispute resolution. Urbanism, secularism, industrialization, and later, in the twentieth century, dispersion of ethnic control over economic enterprise and labor, all were factors which played a role in diminishing the use and power of informal, community-based means of dispute resolution. Yet in spite of this, there persisted and persist today subcultures for which courts and formal law may be neither central, legitimate, nor functional. These include subcultures based on illegal activity, such as organized crime; religiously based law-averse subcultures such as the Amish; economic subcultures based on business interests or workplace association; ethnic subcultures; neighborhood and residential communities; subcultures of "self-reliance" which include vigilantism, violence, and "people's justice," and the myriad of other voluntary associations who depend on the power they have over their memberships to solve their problems without recourse to external disputing processes.

SANDER COUNTY: CULTURAL VALUES AND COURT USE

Sander County is a small farming community in Illinois, made up mainly of Norwegians, and until recently relatively homogeneous with few ethnic, religious, or social class differences.[39] Recently the county has experienced an influx of industry which has brought with it a needed economic boost, but also a working-class population—white, Hispanic, and Black—with different values and social needs, who are perceived as outsiders threatening to the traditional value system and social structure. In this farming community, where dangerous implements and machinery are commonly used, risk of physical injury is high. The usual response to such injuries, however, even when inflicted by someone else's carelessness, is to absorb the consequences of the injury without seeking help or restitution. Transforming a personal injury into a claim against someone else is viewed as an attempt to escape responsibility for one's own actions. An attempt to recover damages is seen as trying to "cash in" wrongfully and is related to the value that money is something one acquires through hard work, not by exhibiting one's misfortunes to a judge and jury. In most cases the injured party would neither sue nor demand compensation. Traditionally the claim might be negotiated through a third party, informally, or the injured party would engage in gossip, which not only adversely affects the person at fault, but enhances the dignity of the grievant by letting it be known that they remained impassive in the face of misconduct and injury. David Engel, an anthropologist who studied this community in which "the invocation of formal law is viewed as an *anti*-social act and as a contravention of established cultural norms," views individualism as the key cultural value which explains Sander County law-averseness in personal-injury cases.[40] This individualism is not, according to Engel, the aggressive rights-oriented individualism which underlies much of the civil suit action in the courts today. Rather, it is "an individualism emphasizing self-sufficiency and personal responsibility ... [the idea that] people should ordinarily provide their own protection against injuries and should personally absorb the consequences of harms they fail to ward off."[41]

Local juries and judges in Sander County agree, which discourages personal injury claims. As a local insurance adjuster told Engel:

[T]he jury will be people from right around here that are, a good share of them will be farmers, and they've been out there slaving away for every penny they've got and they aren't about to just give it away to make that free gift to anybody.[42]

A local trial lawyer summed up the situation by saying, "If I can figure out a way not to try a case in [this] county for injury, I try to."[43]

Injured persons in Sander County generally do not take any overt action when they experience personal injury because they either do not view the problem in terms of a claim against or conflict with another person, or because they hesitate to press such a claim in this close-knit community where they know it would be looked down upon. Even lawyers for potential plaintiffs who in other parts of the country are aggressive about pressing for personal-injury lawsuits, in Sander County hesitate to press such claims, first because knowing the attitudes of local residents who will serve on juries, they have little confidence of winning, and second because they themselves have internalized the local values that inhibit resort to courts for such claims.

While sometimes individuals, who have been injured simply swallow their grievance, view the injury as a result of their own insufficient attention, or settle injury claims without using courts by accepting the smaller sums offered by insurance companies, other residents of Sander County resort to gossip intended to ruin the personal reputations of those that they blame for the harm:

beauty parlors, barber shops, local taverns, coffeeshops, clubs, and bowling leagues were settings where residents often brought problems or complaints that they did not pursue elsewhere. Handling conflict in this manner permitted aggrieved persons to retaliate without exposing themselves to public disapproval. They were merely telling others "what had happened." They were not seeking compensation for their injuries, but by gossiping about the problem they might achieve other desired ends: they might damage their adversary's social status and reputation in the community; they might cause their adversary economic harm by encouraging others to engage in a boycott of goods or services; they might enhance their own prestige by letting it be known that they had remained dignified and impassive in the face of misconduct and injury.[44]

The few personal-injury cases brought to court by Sander County plaintiffs all have the common feature that the plaintiff and defendant are socially or geographically distant from one another, a type of social relationship generally related to formal dispute resolution mechanisms. Almost all Sander County plaintiffs in personal injury cases are outsiders: some are long-time but socially marginal residents of the county, others are newcomers to the county. In both cases, the nonlegal sanctions such as gossip and social disapproval have no utility for them as plaintiffs, and no force upon them where they are defendants. Thus, the court emerges as a mediator between outsiders and insiders; by virtue of this legal authority over all persons and groups, it can bridge procedurally the gaps between socially distant relationships. The courts do not resolve conflict between these groups, however. In fact they exacerbate it. For Sander County insiders, then, court use in personal-injury cases became symbolic of the challenges to the normative order by outsiders, and the denouncing of personal-injury litigation was engaged in as a "ceremony of regret" and a symbolic attempt to preserve a sense of meaning and coherence in the face of social change.

The cultural norms stressing self-reliance that inhibit personal-injury suits in Sander County do not extend to other kinds of claims. Suits for breach of contract, for example, are regarded as legitimate because the alleged loss has been caused by a failure of the defendant to conform to a standard which both parties have agreed upon. Most contract suits involve efforts to collect payment for sales, services, and loans. Sander County residents see these obligations as extremely important and associated with the cultural value of "the sanctity of the promise." They view reliance upon promises as essential to the maintenance of their community. Thus in Sander County the cultural value on individualism works itself out in two different ways: in personal-injury cases it emphasizes self-sufficiency while in contractual breaches it emphasizes rights and remedies.[45]

"PRAYING FOR JUSTICE"—LAW AVERSENESS IN A SOUTHERN TOWN

As in America's colonial period, there are still today a number of American subcultures whose law-averseness is based on religious principles. One such subculture studied by Carol Greenhouse is a town of about 4,000 residents, which is a suburb of Atlanta, Georgia.[46] The town's population is exceptionally homogeneous: virtually all white, educated, and middle-class homeowners. Of the town's long-term established residents, about 1,500 are devout Southern Baptists. The members of this congregation, the oldest in the town, *never* use courts. Their religious ideology proscribes litigation or any attempts at redress apart from forgiveness or prayer. Their law-averse culture is based on New Testament Scripture, Romans 13:18–19, which admonishes Christians to "avenge not yourselves, for it is written, vengeance is mine, I will repay saith the Lord." For these Baptists, then, "access to justice means access to God," not to secular courts of law.[47] Greenhouse describes the religious basis of the community's law averseness in the following manner:

[The Baptists] prohibit . . . remedial initiatives involving any third party but Jesus. To act otherwise is sacrilege, a failure of faith. Furthermore, the Bible preaches forgiveness, sacrifice, and a community built on love. By these things, Christians can distinguish themselves from non-Christians: " . . . Love one another: . . . by this shall all men know that ye are my disciples" (John 13:34–35). Finally, the Baptists' concern with spreading their faith ("witnessing") to non-Baptists inspires them to lead "lives of good witness," i.e., exemplary lives that will attract non-Baptists to the church. These three factors: proscription of secular justice, the ideal of Christian community, and evangelism, justify avoidance of the courts and all other agents of secular law, e.g., lawyers, for purposes of interpersonal disputing. Baptists view the court itself as a profane institution, needed only by non-believers and the unfaithful. Their rejection of the court applies equally to the roles of plaintiff and defendant. They explain that the Bible is quite explicit on the matter of threatened lawsuits (Matthew 6:40): "And if any man will sue thee at law, and take away thy coat, let him have thy cloak also." Thus in the local ideology, a devout Baptist settles out of court quickly and fully any demands made against him.[48]

These Baptists do suffer grievances, but allow themselves only the remedies of avoidance, prayer, apology, joking, gossip, counseling, and mediation. These categories of remedies apply to different social fields: avoidance applies only to outsiders, and is precluded within the community. The other remedies are for members of the church community and those who are prospects for joining. Within their church community the possibility of conflict is excluded. Disputes are interpreted as spiritual lapses. When disagreements and minor disputes occur within the community, they are handled by the verbal remedies described above, and referred to as speech. Conflict is not a question of rules or interests, but of an individual's spiritual state.

Law is based on certain "cultural prerequisites," including an extension of the cultural domain to all persons, both inside and outside one's own community, the legitimacy of conflict among competing interests, and a secular authority which provides a link between individuals and their wider social context. Law is a means of social participation. The Baptists have no interest in identifying with the wider society and thus reject law as a bridge in human relations.

ENDURANCE, AVOIDANCE, AND VIOLENCE: DISPUTE MANAGEMENT IN AN URBAN "COMMUNITY"

Dover Square is a low-income housing project in a major Northeastern city.[49] Eleven hundred people live in the project, of whom 55 percent are Chinese, 25 percent are Black, 10 percent are white, and 10 percent are Hispanic. No one group can be called dominant, however, as there are no ethnically controlled territories, and ethnic groups are dispersed all over the project. Disputes and conflict, as well as crime, appear ubiquitous in Dover Square, and because of the inter-ethnic nature of the project, there are no project-wide, informal dispute resolution mechanisms. Friendship and kinship are within ethnic groups, and these groups themselves have evolved different patterns of dispute management. While gossip is frequently used within all the ethnic communities, it is only influential as a means of social control among the Chinese. The most prevalent dispute management mechanisms in the project as a whole are endurance (lumping it), violence, avoidance, and exit. Courts are used by the weaker elements of the community, older people, and women. When anthropologist Sally Merry studied Dover Square, she found that although the use of violence varied across ethnic groups living in the project, young men from all the ethnic groups made effective use of violence as a mechanism of dispute resolution. She describes this in the "Case of the Revengeful Brother":

In this case the plaintiffs, young Chinese males, were able to fight and were wary of the court. A teenage white boy who lived in the project began to date a teenage Chinese girl, also a project resident. The boy tried to persuade this girl to work for him as a prostitute and introduced her to drugs such as Valium. The Chinese girl did spend at least one night out with a customer. . . . Late that night when she did not return home, her brothers came to look for her boyfriend, angry that he had turned their sister to drugs and prostitution. The boy was nowhere to be found. The next day the brothers did find him and beat him up. The white boy and Chinese girl were not seen together again.[50]

Appeals are made in Dover Square to official third parties—the housing project manager, the police, and courts. These are not effective in *resolving* disputes, however, though they may be effective as part of a mixed strategy of dispute resolution. In contrast to much of the dispute resolution literature, in Dover Square courts do have a function in ongoing relationships but one quite different from their role as dispute resolvers. There are about ten black women in the project who are known for taking offenders to court; in most cases these women have friends or relations who work in the criminal justice system, and their experience as "repeat players" tends to make them successful in using the courts as sanctions. These sanctions are especially effective against young men who have criminal records and/or are known to the police as trouble-makers. The courts are accessible and free, and if the case is a criminal allegation, can at the very least get the defendant to come into court. No one expects the courts to resolve disputes, nor are courts regarded in general as the source of authoritative norms of effective regulation. But for those who can't or who don't want to fight, they can be a source of harassment and a lever in evening out relationships where otherwise the weaker party would be continually subject to victimization.

While many conflicts in Dover Square are addressed by a single strat-egy or form of dispute management, it is more typical for disputes to be prolonged over time and to involve a complex dance of many partici-pants using several strategies. Merry's "Case of the Jilted Lover's Slap" illustrates this:

The case of the jilted lover's slap erupted between a young black man and his ex-lover, a young black woman, both about 20 years old. They had lived together for three years and had a baby, but two weeks before the incident, the young woman, Renee, packed up her belongings and the baby and moved back to her mother's apartment in another part of the project, where she had lived the pre-vious eight years. George, her boyfriend, was lounging in the project one morn-ing after her departure when she walked by. Surrounded by a group of their mutual friends, he complained that she had taken their daughter for a ride in the car of his bitter enemy and rival, and she responded that she was free to do as she pleased and didn't like him "jumping up in her face." He was angered and slapped her. Infuriated, she raced home to her mother.

A few minutes later, Renee's older brother Bill, age 21, and a close friend of his, Fred, who lived in the project and had a reputation as a tough person, appeared in the local hangout in the project looking for George. Bill had a pipe thinly concealed in his pants pocket. Renee's mother appeared brandishing a bent aluminum lawn chair leg, not an effective weapon but a symbolic one, followed by her boyfriend feebly waving a wooden chair leg. Bill told his mother to go home, that he would take care of George. George was nowhere to be seen, but no one made any effort to look for him, remaining in the same hangout for two hours waiting for him to return. When I asked why no one went to George's apartment, about 100 yards away, to look for him, Bill explained to me that it would be risky as well as inappropriate, since according to "people's law," if you break into someone's house, they have the right to do whatever they want to you since you have no right to be there.

An audience of other project residents, mostly black, quickly gathered to join the vigil waiting for George's return and his punishment. Renee's mother an-nounced that George was a homosexual, that "he does it with little boys, right here in the playground." Several said that George had no right to slap Renee. Yet no one mentioned that while George and Renee were together, he had hit her frequently. I suspect that the slap generated this response because once the relationship was terminated, he no longer had the same rights to hit her. Further, as one of his friends observed, his real offense was not simply that he hit her, but that he hit her in public.

Later that afternoon, Renee's mother, whose brother was a policeman, went to the courthouse and took out an application for a complaint against George. When the news traveled through Dover Square, listeners were impressed with the severity of her action. She charged George with assault against her daughter. I have only reports of what happened in court, since I did not attend. The first day the case was heard, both Bill and George were in the courtroom. Bill threatened to beat up George, so George filed an application for a complaint against Bill, charging him with assault. At the next hearing, both cases came up before the judge at the same time, and he dismissed them both.

Two weeks after this incident, George spotted his bitter enemy and rival for Renee's affection a few blocks away and attacked and injured him. He also gossiped that Renee was robbing him by clearing out the apartment that he had deserted and that her daughter was actually not his but belonged to his rival.

The incident of the slap and the surrounding events did drive George from the project. He did not return to his apartment but left all his clothes and belongings there and moved in with a friend a few blocks away. Five months after the incident, when I last observed the state of the conflict, he had still made only fleeting visits back to Dover Square and regularly "hung" in another park.[51]

Professionals close to the legal establishment and many legal scholars assume that American courts and formal law have an all-encompassing role in resolving conflict, providing the basis for social order and dispensing justice. The work of David Engel, Carol Greenhouse, and Sally Merry in three distinctly different American communities clearly demonstrates that this is not the case. American pluralism expresses itself not only in the different issues brought to courts for resolution, but also in decisions not to use courts at all. Even when courts are called upon in dispute resolution situations, it may not be for their traditional, and legitimate, dispute resolution functions. Courts do cast a shadow; but it is often distorted. We have seen that they may serve, as they do in Sander County, as negative symbols of community breakdown; or, as they do among Southern Baptists, as representatives of a non-moral order; or, as they do in Dover Square, as institutions to be manipulated in intracommunity and interpersonal struggles. Thus, in answering the question posed by legal historian Jerold Auerbach, "Is there Justice without Law?" America would answer in many voices—Yes!

NOTES

1. Jerold S. Auerbach, *Justice Without Law?: Resolving Disputes without Lawyers* (New York: Oxford University Press, 1983), 9.

2. An exception to this is obscenity law which takes into account the standards of the local community. See Kimberle Williams Crenshaw, "Beyond Racism and Misogyny: Black Feminism and 2 Live Crew," in Mari J. Matsuda,

Charles R. Lawrence III, Richard Delgado, and Kimberle Williams Crenshaw, *Words that Wound: Critical Race Theory, Assaultive Speech, and the First Amendment* (Boulder, CO: Westview Press, 1993).

3. Paul J. Mangarella, "Justice in a Culturally Pluralistic Society: The Cultural Defense on Trial," *The Journal of Ethnic Studies* 19(3) (1991): 67.

4. J. Lyman, "Cultural Defense: Viable Doctrine or Wishful Thinking?" *Criminal Justice Journal* 9(1) (Fall 1989): 89.

5. Jean G. Zorn, "Cults and the Ideology of Individualism in First Amendment Discourse," *The Journal of Law and Religion* 7 (1989): 483–530; Lyman, "Cultural Defense," 102–3.

6. Sheila Toomey, "Eskimo Erotica?" *National Law Journal* (February 4, 1985), 6.

7. *Dumpson v. Daniel M., New York Law Journal* (October 16, 1974), 17, col. 7.

8. Andrew Gordon, personal communication; Michael Winkelman, personal communication.

9. Several articles on the cultural defense discuss this case; see, for example, "The Cultural Defense in the Criminal Law," *Harvard Law Review*, 99(6) (April 1986): 1293–1311; Alison Dundes Renteln, "Culture and Culpability: A Study of Contrasts," in *Folk Law: Essays in the Theory and Practice of Lex Non Scripta*, ed. Alison Dundes Renteln and Alan Dundes. Vol. II (New York: Garland, 1994), 863–80. For an in-depth discussion of the cultural factors involved, see Deborah Woo, "The People v. Fumiko Kimura: But Which People," *International Journal of the Sociology of Law* 17 (1989): 403–28.

10. Woo, "The People v. Fumiko Kimura," 411.

11. Mangarella, "Justice in a Culturally Pluralistic Society," 71.

12. Woo, "The People v. Fumiko Kimura," 415.

13. *People v. Moua*, No. 315972-0, Fresno Superior Ct. (1985).

14. Renteln, "Culture and Culpability," 866.

15. Mangarella, "Justice in a Culturally Pluralistic Society," 70.

16. "Refugee to Get New Murder Trial," *New York Times*, April 16, 1986.

17. *People v. Aphaylath*, 510 N.Y.S.2d 83 (Ct. App. 1986).

18. *People v. Moua*, No. 328106-0, Fresno Superior Ct. (1985); Mangarella, "Justice in a Culturally Pluralistic Society."

19. *New York v. Chen*, Indictment No. 7774/87, Supreme Court of the State of New York, Kings County, December 2, 1988 (trial transcript), Judge Edward Pincus.

20. Celestine Bohlen, "Holtzman May Appeal Probation in the Killing of a Chinese Woman," *New York Times*, April 5, 1989, B3.

21. *New York v. Chen*, 352–63.

22. "Wife Killing Is Murder!" *The CAAAV Voice* (Newsletter of the Committee Against Anti-Asian Violence), Spring 1989, vol. 1, no. 2, 1.

23. Bohlen, "Holtzman May Appeal Probation."

24. Rorie Sherman, " 'Cultural' Defenses Draw Fire," *National Law Journal*, (April 17, 1989), 28.

25. "Wife Killing Is Murder!" *CAAAV Voice*, 2.

26. Ibid.

27. *Criminal Injustice: Violence Against Women in Brazil* (New York: Human Rights Watch, 1991), 20ff.

28. Judith S. Seddon, "Possible or Impossible: A Tale of Two Worlds in One Culture," *Yale Journal of Law and Feminism* 5(2) (Spring 1993): 265–88.

29. *In re Lydia Omowunmi Ohuloro,* Trial Memorandum, #A72147491, U.S. Department of Justice, Portland, Oregon, February 7, 1994.

30. *In re Lydia Omowunmi Ohuloro,* Oral Decision, U.S. Department of Justice, Executive Office for Immigration Review, Seattle, Washington, March 23, 1994.

31. Woo, "The People v. Fumiko Kimura," 418.

32. "The Cultural Defense in Criminal Law," *Harvard Law Review,* 1293.

33. Ibid., 1304.

34. Julia P. Sams, "The Availability of the 'Cultural Defense' as an Excuse for Criminal Behavior," *Georgia Journal of International & Comparative Law* 16 (Spring 1986): 335.

35. Renteln, "Culture and Culpability," 867.

36. Carol J. Greenhouse, "Nature Is to Culture as Praying Is to Suing," *Journal of Legal Pluralism* 20 (1982): 22.

37. Auerbach, *Resolving Disputes without Lawyers,* 22.

38. Ibid., 22–24.

39. David M. Engel, "The Oven Bird's Song: Insiders, Outsiders, and Personal Injuries in an American Community," *Law and Society Review* 18(4) (1984).

40. Ibid., 552.

41. Ibid., 558–59.

42. Ibid., 560.

43. Ibid.

44. David M. Engel, "The Oven Bird's Song: Insiders, Outsiders, and Personal Injuries in an American Community." Unpublished paper, 9.

45. Engel, "The Oven Bird's Song," 557.

46. Carol J. Greenhouse, *Praying for Justice: Faith, Order, and Community in an American Town* (Ithaca, NY: Cornell University Press, 1986).

47. Ibid., 22.

48. Ibid., 33.

49. Sally Engle Merry, *Urban Danger: Life in a Neighborhood of Strangers* (Philadelphia, PA: Temple University Press, 1981).

50. Sally Engle Merry, "Going to Court: Strategies of Dispute Management in an American Urban Neighborhood," *Law and Society Review* 13 (Summer 1979): 912.

51. Merry, "Going to Court," 908–10.

Selected Bibliography

INTRODUCTION

Anderson, Benedict. *Imagined Communities: Reflections on the Origin and Spread of Nationalism.* Rev. ed. New York: Verso, 1991.

Dees, Morris. *Hate on Trial: The Trial of America's Most Dangerous Neo-Nazi.* New York: Random House; Villard Books, 1993.

Hall, Kermit L., ed. *The Oxford Companion to the Supreme Court of the United States.* New York: Oxford University Press, 1992.

Horowitz, Donald. *Ethnic Groups in Conflict.* Berkeley: University of California Press, 1985.

Hunter, James Davison. *Culture Wars: The Struggle to Define America.* New York: Basic Books, 1991.

Merriam, Eve. "A Wasp Hymn." *The New Republic,* July 12, 1969.

Minow, Martha. *Making All the Difference: Inclusion, Exclusion, and American Law.* Ithaca, NY: Cornell University Press, 1991.

Rosenberg, Gerald. *The Hollow Hope: Can Courts Bring about Social Change?* Chicago: University of Chicago Press, 1991.

Schlesinger, Arthur M., Jr. *The Disuniting of America: Reflections on a Multicultural Society.* New York: W. W. Norton, 1991.

Steinberg, Stephen. *The Ethnic Myth: Race, Ethnicity, and Class in America.* 2d ed. New York: Atheneum, 1989.

Takaki, Ronald. *Different Mirror: The Making of Multicultural America.* Boston: Little, Brown, 1993.

Urofsky, Melvin I., ed. *The Supreme Court Justices: A Biographical Dictionary.* New York: Garland Publishing, 1994.

Winkelman, Michael. *Ethnic Relations in the U.S.* Eagan, MN: West, 1993.

CHAPTER 1

Brown, Dee. *Bury My Heart at Wounded Knee.* New York: Holt, Rinehart and Winston, 1971.

Campisi, Jack. *The Mashpee Indians: Tribe on Trial.* Syracuse, NY: Syracuse University Press, 1991.

Deloria, Vine, Jr., and Clifford M. Lytle. *American Indians, American Justice.* Austin: University of Texas Press, 1983.

Harring, Sidney. *Crow Dog's Case: American Indian Sovereignty, Tribal Law, and United States Law in the Nineteenth Century.* New York: Cambridge University Press, 1994.

Jaimes, M. Annette. *The State of Native America: Genocide, Colonization, and Resistance.* Boston: South End Press, 1992.

Nabokov, Peter, ed. *Native American Testimony.* New York: Viking, 1991.

Norgren, Jill. *The Cherokee Cases: The Confrontation of Law and Politics.* New York: McGraw-Hill, 1995.

O'Brien, Sharon. *American Indian Tribal Governments.* Norman: University of Oklahoma Press, 1993.

Prucha, Francis Paul, ed. *American Indian Treaties: The History of a Political Anomaly.* Berkeley: University of California Press, 1994.

———. *Documents of United States Indian Policy.* Lincoln: University of Nebraska Press, 1984.

Shattuck, Petra T., and Jill Norgren. *Partial Justice: Federal Indian Law in a Liberal Constitutional System.* New York/Oxford: Berg Publisher, 1991.

Wilkinson, Charles F. *American Indians, Time, and the Law: Native Societies in a Modern Constitutional Democracy.* New Haven: Yale University Press, 1987.

CHAPTER 2

Buck, Elizabeth. *Paradise Remade: The Politics of Culture and History in Hawaii.* Philadelphia: Temple University Press, 1993.

Trask, Haunani-Kay. *From a Native Daughter: Colonialism and Sovereignty in Hawai'i.* Monroe, ME: Common Courage Press, 1993.

Watanabe, Sylvia. *Talking to the Dead and Other Stories.* New York: Doubleday, 1993.

CHAPTER 3

Bell, Derrick. *Faces at the Bottom of the Well: The Permanence of Racism.* New York: Basic Books, 1992.

Branch, Taylor. *Parting the Waters: America in the King Years, 1954–1963.* New York: Simon and Schuster, 1988.

Garrow, David J. *Bearing the Cross.* New York: W. Morrow, 1986.

Hacker, Andrew. *Two Nations: Black, White, Separate, Hostile, Unequal.* New York: Charles Scribner's, 1992.

Higginbotham, A. Leon, Jr. *In the Matter of Color: Race and the American Legal Process: The Colonial Period*. New York: Oxford University Press, 1978.

Hopkins, Vincent C. *Dred Scott's Case*. New York: Atheneum, 1971.

Kluger, Richard. *Simple Justice: The History of Brown v. Board of Education and Black America's Struggle for Equality*. New York: Random House, 1975.

Lemann, Nicholas. *The Promised Land: The Great Black Migration and How It Changed America*. New York: Random House, 1992.

Lukas, J. Anthony. *Common Ground: A Turbulent Decade in the Lives of Three American Families*. New York: Knopf, 1985.

Matsuda, Mari J., Charles R. Lawrence III, Richard Delgado, and Kimberle Williams Crenshaw. *Words That Wound: Critical Race Theory, Assaultive Speech, and the First Amendment*. Boulder, CO: Westview Press, 1993.

McLaurin, Melton A. *Celia: A Slave*. New York: Avon, 1993.

Powerful Days: The Civil Rights Photography of Charles Moore. New York: Stewart, Tabori & Chang, 1995.

Williams, Patricia J. *The Alchemy of Race and Rights*. Cambridge, MA: Harvard University Press, 1992.

Woodward, C. Vann. *The Strange Career of Jim Crow*. New York: Oxford University Press, 1955.

CHAPTER 4

Adachi, Ken. *The Enemy That Never Was*. Toronto: McClelland and Stewart, 1976.

Aguilar-San Juan, Karin, ed. *The State of Asian America*. Boston: South End Press, 1993.

Daniels, Roger. *Prisoners without Trial: Japanese Americans in World War II*. New York: Hill and Wang, 1993.

Daniels, Roger, Sandra C. Taylor, and Harry H. L. Kitano, eds. *Japanese Americans: From Relocation to Redress*. Salt Lake City: University of Utah Press, 1986.

Drinnon, Richard. *Keeper of Concentration Camps*. Berkeley: University of California Press, 1987.

Houston, Jeanne Wakatsuki, and James D. Houston. *Arrival at Manzanar*. New York: Oxford University Press, 1983.

Irons, Peter. *Justice at War: The Story of the Japanese American Internment Cases*. New York: Oxford University Press, 1983.

Kim, Hyyung-chan. *A Legal History of Asian Americans*. Boston: Little, Brown, 1989.

Kwong, Peter. *The New Chinatown*. New York: Hill and Wang, 1988.

McClain, Charles J. *In Search of Equality: The Chinese Struggle against Discrimination in 19th-Century America*. Berkeley: University of California Press, 1994.

Takaki, Ronald. *Strangers from a Different Shore: A History of Asian Americans*. New York: Viking/Penguin, 1990.

Tateishi, J. *And Justice for All: An Oral History of Japanese American Detention Camps*. New York: Random House, 1984.

Wakatsuki, Jeanne. *Justice Delayed: The Record of the Japanese American Internment Cases*. Middletown, CT: Wesleyan University Press, 1988.

CHAPTER 5

Bradley, Martha Sonntag. *Kidnapped from That Land: The Government Raids on the Short Creek Polygamists.* Salt Lake City: University of Utah Press, 1993.

Ellsworth, Maria S. *Mormon Odyssey: The Story of Ida Hunt Udall, Plural Wife.* Chicago: University of Chicago Press, 1992.

Hansen, Klaus J. *Mormonism and the American Experience.* Chicago: University of Chicago Press, 1981.

Kilbride, Philip L. *Plural Marriage for Our Times: A Reinvented Option.* Westport, CT: Bergin & Garvey, 1994.

Wells, Merle W. *Anti-Mormonism in Idaho, 1872–92.* Provo, UT: Brigham Young University Press, 1978.

CHAPTER 6

Fisher, Sara E., and Rachel K. Stahl. *The Amish School.* Intercourse, PA: Good Books, 1986.

Hostetler, John A. *Amish Society.* 3d ed. Baltimore, MD: Johns Hopkins University Press, 1980.

Kraybill, Donald B., ed. *The Amish and the State.* Baltimore, MD: Johns Hopkins University Press, 1993.

———. *The Riddle of Amish Culture.* Baltimore, MD: Johns Hopkins University Press, 1989.

CHAPTER 7

Belcove-Shalin, ed. *New World Hasidism: Ethnographic Studies of Hasidic Jews in America.* Ithaca, NY: SUNY Press, 1995.

Erling, Jorstad. *The New Christian Right.* Lewiston, NY: Edwin Mellen Press, 1987.

Frankel, Marvin E. *Faith and Freedom: Religious Liberty in America.* New York: Hill and Wang, 1994.

Toumey, Christopher P. *God's Own Scientists: Creationists in a Secular World.* New Brunswick, NJ: Rutgers University Press, 1994.

CHAPTER 8

Grinspoon, Lester, and James B. Bakalar. *Marihuana, the Forbidden Medicine.* New Haven: Yale University Press, 1993.

Lewis, William F. *Soul Rebels: The Rastafari.* Prospect Heights, IL: Waveland Press, 1993.

Steinmetz, Paul B. *Pipe, Bible, and Peyote among the Oglala Lakota.* Knoxville: University of Tennessee Press, 1990.

Stewart, Omer C. *Peyote Religion: A History.* Norman: University of Oklahoma Press, 1987.

CHAPTER 9

Bawer, Bruce. *A Place at the Table: The Gay Individual in American Society.* New York: Touchstone/Simon and Schuster, 1993.

Boswell, John. *Christianity, Social Tolerance, and Homosexuality: Gay People in Western Europe from the Beginning of the Christian Era to the Fourteenth Century.* Chicago: University of Chicago Press, 1980.

———. *Same-Sex Unions in Premodern Europe.* New York: Random House; Villard Books, 1994.

Dyer, Kate, ed. *Gays in Uniform: The Pentagon's Secret Reports.* Boston: Alyson Publications, 1990.

Humphrey, Mary Ann. *My Country, My Right to Serve: Experiences of Gay Men and Women in the Military, World War II to the Present.* New York: HarperCollins, 1991.

Marcus, Eric. *Making History: The Struggle for Gay and Lesbian Equal Rights, 1945–1990: An Oral History.* New York: HarperCollins, 1995.

Mohr, Richard. *Gays/Justice: A Study of Ethics, Society, and Law.* Boulder: University of Colorado Press, 1989.

Shilts, Randy. *And the Band Played On: Politics and People, and the AIDS Epidemic.* New York: St. Martin's Press, 1987.

———. *Conduct Unbecoming: Gays and Lesbians in the U.S. Military.* New York: St. Martin's Press, 1993.

Wolinsky, Marc, and Kenneth Sherrill, eds. *Gays and the Military: Joseph Steffan versus the United States.* New York: St. Martin's Press, 1993.

CHAPTER 10

Bartels, Dianne, ed. *Beyond Baby M: Ethical Issues in New Reproductive Techniques.* Clifton, NJ: Humana Press, 1990. Includes a copy of the Baby M contract.

Chafe, William. *The Paradox of Change: American Women in the 20th Century.* New York: Oxford University Press, 1991.

Colker, Ruth. *Abortion and Dialogue: Pro-Choice, Pro-Life, and American Law.* Bloomington: Indiana University Press, 1993.

Evans, Sara. *Born for Liberty: A History of Women in America.* New York: The Free Press, 1989.

Forer, Lois. *Unequal Protection: Women, Children, and the Elderly in Court.* New York: W. W. Norton, 1991.

Garrow, David J. *Liberty and Sexuality: The Right to Privacy and the Making of Roe v. Wade.* New York: Macmillan Publishing, 1993.

Ginsburg, Faye D. *Contested Lives: The Abortion Debate in an American Community.* Berkeley: University of California Press, 1989.

Higginbotham, Evelyn. *Righteous Discontent: The Women's Movement in the Black Baptist Church, 1880–1920.* Cambridge, MA: Harvard University Press, 1993.

Hobson, Barbara Meil. *Uneasy Virtue: The Politics of Prostitution and the American Reform Tradition.* Chicago: University of Chicago Press, 1990.

Hoff, Joan. *Law, Gender, and Injustice: A Legal History of U.S. Women.* New York: New York University Press, 1994.

Hooks, Bell. *Yearning*. Boston: South End Press, 1990.

MacKinnon, Catherine. *Only Words*. Cambridge, MA: Harvard University Press, 1993.

Swisher, Karin L., Carol Wekesser, and William Barbour. *Violence Against Women*. San Diego: Greenhaven Press, 1994.

CHAPTER 11

Chavez, Linda. *Out of the Barrio: Toward a New Politics of Hispanic Assimilation*. New York: Basic Books, 1992.

Conover, Ted. *Coyotes: A Journey Through the Secret World of America's Illegal Aliens*. New York: Vintage, 1987.

Langum, David J. *Law and Community on the Mexican California Frontier: Anglo-American Expatriates and the Clash of Legal Traditions, 1821–1846*. Norman: University of Oklahoma Press, 1995.

Meier, Matt S., and Feliciano Ribera. *Mexican Americans/American Mexicans: From Conquistadors to Chicanos*. New York: Hill and Wang, 1993.

Rodriguez, Clara. *Puerto Ricans: Born in the U.S.A.* Boston: Unwin Hyman, 1989.

Rodriguez, Richard. *Hunger of Memory: The Education of Richard Rodriguez: An Autobiography*. Boston: D. R. Godine, 1982.

Nichols, John T. *The Milagro Beanfield War*. New York: Ballantine, 1987.

Shorris, Earl. *Latinos: A Biography of the People*. New York: Avon, 1944.

CHAPTER 12

Blau, Joel. *The Visible Poor: Homelessness in the United States*. New York: Oxford University Press, 1992.

Dear, Michael, and Jennifer Wolch. *Landscapes of Despair: From Deinstitutionalization to Homelessness*. Princeton: Princeton University Press, 1992.

Eighner, Lars. *Travels with Lizbeth*. New York: St. Martin's Press, 1993.

Glasser, Irene. *More Than Bread: Ethnography of a Soup Kitchen*. Tuscaloosa: University of Alabama Press, 1988.

Golden, Stephanie. *The Women Outside: Meanings and Myths of Homelessness*. Berkeley: University of California Press, 1992.

Green, George Dawes. *The Caveman's Valentine*. New York: Warner, 1995.

Jencks, Christopher. *The Homeless*. Cambridge, MA: Harvard University Press, 1994.

Kennedy, William. *Ironweed*. New York: Viking, 1983.

Liebow, Elliot. *Tell Them Who I Am: The Lives of Homeless Women*. New York: The Free Press, 1993.

Rossi, Peter H. *Down and Out in America: The Origins of Homelessness*. Chicago: University of Chicago Press, 1991.

Snow, David A., and Leon Anderson. *Down on Their Luck: A Study of Homeless Street People*. Berkeley: University of California Press, 1992.

Timmer, Doug A., D. Stanley Eitzen, and Kathryn D. Talley. *Paths to Homelessness: Extreme Poverty and the Urban Housing Crisis*. Boulder, CO: Westview Press, 1994.

CHAPTER 13

Auerbach, Jerold S. *Justice without Law? Resolving Disputes without Lawyers.* New York: Oxford University Press, 1983.

Greenhouse, Carol J., Barbara Yngvesson, and David M. Engel. *Law and Community in Three American Towns.* Ithaca, NY: Cornell University Press, 1994.

Merry, Sally Engle. *Getting Justice and Getting Even: Legal Consciousness among Working Class Americans.* Chicago: University of Chicago Press, 1990.

Montell, William Lynwood. *Killings: Folk Justice in the Upper South.* Lexington: University of Kentucky Press, 1986.

Index

About the Authors

JILL NORGREN, Ph.D. (University of Michigan), is Professor of Political Science at the John Jay College of Criminal Justice and the University Graduate Center, The City University of New York. She has done extensive research under various fellowships in the area of federal Indian law. She is the author of many articles in this area as well as two books, *Partial Justice: Federal Indian Law in a Liberal Constitutional System* (with P. T. Shattuck), and *The Cherokee Cases: The Confrontation of Law and Politics.* She is currently writing a biography of the nineteenth-century lawyer Belva Lockwood.

SERENA NANDA, Ph.D. (New York University), is Professor of Anthropology at the John Jay College of Criminal Justice. She is the author of *Cultural Anthropology,* a widely used undergraduate text now in its fifth edition; *Neither Man or Woman: The Hijras of India;* and articles on teaching cultural anthropology. In 1995, she received an NEH summer seminar grant at Yale University, where she will continue to develop her interests on the politics of cultural identity.

ISBN 0-275-94855-2

9 780275 948559

HARDCOVER BAR CODE